Empress San Francisco

*The Pacific Rim, the Great West, and California
at the Panama-Pacific International Exposition*

ABIGAIL M. MARKWYN

University of Nebraska Press † Lincoln

Part of chapters 1 and 7 originally appeared in *Gendering the Fair: Histories of Women and Gender at World's Fairs* edited by Tracey Jean Boisseau and Abigail Markwyn. Copyright 2010 by the Board of Trustees of the University of Illinois. Used with permission of the University of Illinois Press. Part of chapter 4 originally appeared in "Economic Partner and Exotic Other: China and Japan at San Francisco's Panama-Pacific International Exposition," *Western Historical Quarterly* 39 (Winter 2008): 439–65. Copyright by Western History Association. Reprinted by permission. All rights reserved. ∞

Publication of this volume was assisted by The Virginia Faulkner Fund, established in memory of Virginia Faulkner, editor in chief of the University of Nebraska Press.

LIBRARY OF CONGRESS CATALOGING-IN-PUBLICATION DATA

Markwyn, Abigail M.
Empress San Francisco: the Pacific Rim, the Great West, and California at the Panama-Pacific International Exposition / Abigail M. Markwyn.
pages   cm
Includes bibliographical references and index.
ISBN 978-0-8032-4384-2 (hardcover: alk. paper)
ISBN 978-1-4962-2490-3 (paperback)
ISBN 978-0-8032-6781-7 (pdf)
ISBN 978-0-8032-6782-4 (epub)
ISBN 978-0-8032-6783-1 (mobi) 1. Panama-Pacific International Exposition (1915 : San Francisco, Calif.) 2. Group identity—California—San Francisco—History—20th century. 3. San Francisco (Calif.)—Ethnic relations. 4. Chinese Americans—California—San Francisco—Ethnic identity. 5. Japanese Americans—California—San Francisco—Ethnic identity. 6. Women—California—San Francisco—Social conditions. 7. San Francisco (Calif.)—Moral conditions. 8. San Francisco Bay Area (Calif.)—Social life and customs. I. Title. II. Title: Pacific Rim, the Great West, and California at the Panama-Pacific International Exposition.
TC781.B1M37 2014   907.4'79461—dc23   2014008053

Set in Arno Pro by Renni Johnson. Designed by A. Shahan.

For my family

Contents

Illustrations

ORIGINAL PLATES

Following page 176

Acknowledgments

Like many first books, *Empress San Francisco* began many years ago as my dissertation. And like my children, it has grown and developed in sometimes unexpected ways. What has remained constant are the many debts I have accrued along the way. My training in history began at Carleton College, where Robert Bonner introduced me to the formal study of the history of the American West and Kirk Jeffrey guided me through the senior thesis project that convinced me that this could be my career. At the University of Wisconsin (UW)–Madison, I encountered a host of excellent scholars and teachers who taught me how to do the work I do today. The guidance of Bill Cronon, the late Jeanne Boydston, Susan Lee Johnson, and the ever-patient Nan Enstad helped bring my dissertation to fruition. I am particularly grateful to Nan for her support of my personal and professional choices throughout the dissertation process. Camille Guerin-Gonzales provided an important outside perspective. Many other excellent scholars and teachers at Madison, including Judith Walzer Leavitt, Florencia Mallon, Francisco Scarano, Steve Stern, and Steven Kantrowitz, helped me grow as a scholar.

Other scholars provided assistance throughout this project. The ever-generous Robert Rydell offered support and advice and even helped me find an editor. His generosity toward younger scholars is a model for all. T. J. Boisseau and I met at a conference and immediately found common ground in our interest in women and fairs. The result was our coedited volume and a friendship and mentorship that has sustained me through this project. Alan Bain, Judy Yung, Yong Chen, and Janet Davis all provided answers and helped me locate resources for the project. Sarah Moore, Andrea Radke-Moss, and many other fellow world's fair scholars have provided valuable feedback on conference papers. Thanks to Lauren Rabinovitz and my fellow junior faculty fellows at the 2008 University of Iowa Workshop on Women of Color in Popular Culture for offering excellent comments on my work in progress. Amanda Cannata, Robert Chase, and Jamaica Hutchins pointed me to essential primary sources at critical junctures. Ben Rosenberg and Winifred Chang provided translation assistance. Colleagues at Carroll University, including Lilly Goren, Scott Hendrix, Jim Grimshaw, Lori Kelly, and Charlie Byler, have listened to me discuss this project ad infinitum and offered helpful feedback and friendship. At the University of Nebraska Press, Matthew Bokovoy has proved himself an extraordinary editor. His practical assistance and close editing eye have made this project an immensely better book. The staff at the press have been terrific help as well, and I thank them for their efforts during the publication process. Thanks also to Gray Brechin, Bob Rydell, and two anonymous readers for the University of Nebraska Press for providing insightful feedback on my earlier draft. Nonetheless, all errors remain my own.

Archivists around the Bay Area helped me locate sources for this project about the Panama-Pacific International Exposition (PPIE), and to them I am extremely grateful. From the moment I began this research at the Bancroft Library David Kessler was friendly, helpful, and enthusiastic. The staff there was unfailingly helpful. I owe particular thanks to Susan Snyder for helping me locate and gain permissions for a number of the images in this book. The staff at the San Francisco Public Library (SFPL), the California Historical Society, the Mechanics Institute Library, and the California State Library provided assistance as well. Carrie Musick of the San Francisco Young Woman's Christian Association allowed me to paw through musty boxes of files, as did the staff at the African American Museum and Library of Oakland. Christina Moretta and Susan Goldstein at SFPL helped me acquire images and permissions. Tammy Lau and Adam Wallace at the California State University–Fresno Library supplied a last-minute windfall of images for which I am very thankful. Nathan Kerr and Suzanne Fischer helped me locate ephemera and images from the Oakland Museum of California. At the Smithsonian Institution, Maria Eipert provided generous assistance in gaining access to previously unpublished color photographs of the fair. Chuck Petterson, collector of PPIE memorabilia, graciously allowed me the use of some of his images as well. The interlibrary loan staff at UW-Madison and Carroll University made this research possible.

Over the years I have had financial support from UW-Madison and Carroll University. The William Appleman Williams Dissertator Fellowship allowed me time to write, and travel funds enabled me to do the research. Numerous faculty development and travel grants from Carroll University supported later research trips and conference presentations. Thanks to Sue Lewis for financial assistance from Carroll's Faculty Development Fund. Students Emily Claflin and Lucas Phelps assisted with the final manuscript's preparation.

My scholarly and personal debts remain intertwined. Many fellow graduate students provided support, particularly in my early years. Megan Balzer, Thea Browder, Flannery Burke, Kendra Smith-Howard, Katie Benton-Cohen, Maggie Hogan, and Stacey Smith all helped me traverse the early hurdles of graduate school. I thank Molly Todd for many things, but helping to found a dissertator writing group is certainly one of them. Along with Michelle Morgan, Libbie Freed, and Gary Marquardt, she provided excellent feedback on some early drafts. Without Michelle's friendship, support, and critical reading skills, this book would not be what it is today. I am grateful for having such a terrific fellow academic-parent-writer with whom to share this journey. Friends around the country offered me hospitality and company during research trips and conferences. Thanks to Michelle, Kira Blaisdell-Sloan, Stacey Pelika, Joanne Penko, Amanda Jamieson, Sharon and John Tapia, Tom Bernard, Molly Milano, and Cami Johnson for keeping me sane on those trips.

My final thanks go to my family. Without the examples of my historian parents, Daniel Markwyn and Jo Markwyn, I would never have set off on this path in the first place. And their support has never faltered. During this project they served as child care providers, long-distance research assistants, editors, and sources of financial and emotional support, and I thank them a thousand times over for all of it. Thanks go to Jon and Jody Kasparek and Margaret Hostetler for loving our children. Finally, I dedicate this book to my husband, Kevin Guilfoy, and our children: James, who arrived as I was beginning this research many years ago; William; Harry; and Molly, who joined us between submitting the manuscript and reviewing the copy edits. You remind me that although I love the past, the present matters more.

Empress San Francisco

Fig. 1. One segment of the Panama-Pacific International Exposition's opening day parade. (#1996.003—ALB, 3:131, Bancroft Library, University of California, Berkeley.)

Introduction

On a cool morning in late February 1915, 150,000 people massed in downtown San Francisco to participate in the parade celebrating the grand opening of the Panama-Pacific International Exposition (PPIE).[1] Local newspapers lauded the democratic nature of the event. The *San Francisco Chronicle* noted, "It was the people's day," since the people of San Francisco and California had built the exposition with their own funds, imbuing the event with true "San Francisco spirit."[2] Yet fair officials scripted this seemingly democratic display, carefully delineating meeting places and the order of march for participating groups. Once en route, however, the parade was out of the officials' control. This apparent contradiction reveals much about the PPIE. Although fair planners carefully planned the exposition, the fair could not exist without the millions of local residents and tourists who spilled onto the fairgrounds for sixteen hours a day during its nine-month run.[3] Nor could the fair succeed without the cooperation of foreign governments, federal officials, and national and international business interests. Together, these varied interests created the fair.

Outside the gates of the fair, social and political conflicts wracked the nation. The newly formed National Association for the Advancement of Colored People (NAACP) boycotted the immensely popular white supremacist film *Birth of a Nation*. Woman suffragists advocated for a federal suffrage amendment. Young women worked in ever-larger numbers outside the home, while their fearful parents worried about the rumored rings of white slavers sweeping the nation. Labor leaders clung to the gains they had made in the past decades. The growing anti-immigrant movement angered foreign leaders who resented American restrictions on immigration. American businessmen and missionaries in China worked to convince officials to cooperate with American interests. At home, newspapers published ever more serious reports about the war in Europe and the bloody revolution in nearby Mexico. In April, horrified Americans read about the sinking of RMS *Lusitania* and increasing German submarine warfare as the war raging in Europe reached closer to Americans.

Racial violence. Social unrest. Sex. Immigration. War. The 1910s were a time of great upheaval. Technological changes facilitated better communication and transportation, speeding the nation's move toward modernity. Progressive reformers tried to impose order on the nation's unruly social milieu and faced resistance at every turn. Anti-immigrant voices grew more powerful and targeted the excluded Chinese and Japanese, as well as supposed inferior "races" of southern and eastern Europe: Jews, Italians, Portuguese, Poles, and Czechs, among others. Others targeted Catholics, continuing to argue that they could never truly be loyal Americans while practicing their faith. And the United States continued to flex its diplomatic and military muscle in demonstrations of its imperial ambitions.

From February to December 1915 visitors could ostensibly escape this disorder by visiting the carefully planned avenues of the Panama-Pacific International Exposition. The 635-acre fairgrounds offered visitors a host of attractions. Nations ranging from Siam to Honduras to China showed off their history and culture in elaborate pavilions. A huge display of modern art greeted visitors to the Palace of Fine Arts. Films on topics including immigration and social hygiene played in the different buildings across the grounds. The varied entertainments of the Joy Zone, or amusement section, promised something for everyone. The fair brought millions of visitors to San Francisco and conveyed visions of California, the United States, and the Pacific world to all who entered its gates. Held just before the full impact of World War I was unleashed on the world, the fair has largely vanished from American historical memory. San Franciscans and world's fair enthusiasts remember it, but it has never held the same significance in the American historical narrative as the 1893 Columbian Exposition in Chicago or even the 1904 Louisiana Purchase Exposition in St. Louis.[4]

World's fairs and expositions emerged as some of the most significant international and national cultural events at home and abroad during the Victorian and Progressive Eras. They offered unparalleled opportunities for nations to present themselves to the world, for businesses to show off their latest products to consumers, and for entertainers to dazzle and shock audiences with ever more exciting amusements. The PPIE was the largest pre–World War I world's fair held on the Pacific coast and therefore deserves closer scholarly attention. Its reliance on local rather than federal funding, combined with its location in an urban western U.S. city and its attention to the Pacific world, renders it unique for the time. With these characteristics the PPIE offers us new insights into the Progressive Era's political and social dynamics in the urban West.

Scholars such as Robert Rydell have persuasively argued that fairs are best understood as hegemonic expressions of elite power, designed to accustom American citizens to the idea of modernization and empire.[5] Fairs expressed power relationships through pageantry, symbols, and official recognition.[6] These enormous events commemorated epic cultural achievements and showcased technological developments and cultural heritages in an attempt to "stave off political unrest at home and to build support for specific national imperial policies."[7] Visitors entered carefully landscaped imaginary cities whose palatial buildings held the thousands of exhibits sent by foreign nations and the U.S. government, manufacturers, states, and local, state, and national organizations. Fairs introduced visitors to new technologies, new foods, new peoples, and new amusements. They influenced city planners and architects, musicians, artists, and reformers.[8]

The PPIE succeeded in all of these aspects. It introduced visitors to new foods, technologies, and entertainment as Chinese, Japanese, and Mexican delicacies were all produced on the grounds; Model T Fords rolled off an assembly line every day; and Hawaiian entertainers launched a ukulele fad on the mainland after appearing at the fair. The fair celebrated naked evidence of U.S. imperial economic desires by commemorating both the completion of the Panama Canal and the four hundredth anniversary of Vasco Nuñez de Balboa's sighting of the Pacific Ocean. Underlying this celebration lay the ambitions of San Francisco's business elite, who hoped the fair would cement the city's claim as the gateway to the Pacific. Boosters wanted the event to bring both national and international business to the region. Some hoped the opening of the canal would bring European rather than Asian immigrants to the shores of

California. The fair seemed key to the region's prosperity. Fair organizers attempted to build an ideal city on the shores of San Francisco Bay that eliminated the myriad political and social debates of 1915. Their chosen focus on service, education, and progress reflected their attempt to orient the fair forward, into the future, rather than to reflect on past challenges. Even the fair's Pacific focus reoriented the nation away from war-torn Europe and west toward the economic possibilities of the Pacific Rim.

Fair organizers could never shield their 635-acre ideal city from the political and social realities of 1915. World conflicts over power and politics pervaded the grounds of the PPIE and suffused the site, its workforce, international participants, amusements, and celebrations of special days with an immediacy that belied its utopian visions. Woman suffragists launched a renewed political campaign for the vote at the fair, moral reformers criticized the attractions offered on the Zone, African Americans sought to claim rights as citizens on the grounds, and the Chinese and Japanese governments used the fair to negotiate better treatment for their citizens in California. These episodes confirm what many recent scholars, beginning with Stuart Hall, have argued: popular culture and cultural events, rather than being peripheral to political and social debates, are the canvases upon which such struggles unfold.[9]

The fair could not succeed without the cooperation of local, national, and international interests, whose goals did not always reflect those of the fair officials. Outside interests frequently foiled the best-laid plans of fair organizers.[10] Fairs became spaces where competing groups vied for social and political power. The conflicts that emerged over their representation, space, and use of the fair demonstrate the many meanings that individuals attached to the fair. As James Gilbert argues regarding the Louisiana Purchase Exposition, a world's fair could mean many things to many people. Restricting our exploration of the fair's significance to the motives of its organizers limits our ability to understand the complete event.[11] Recent works by European scholars, including Alexander Geppert and Pieter van Wesemael, call for placing fairs in larger sociohistorical context and recognizing the roles of expositions in displaying modernity for visitors. They call for scholarly recognition of the multilayered nature of expositions and for more rigorous interrogations of them, acknowledging, in Geppert's words, that "expositions can be seen as closely knit textures spread over time that reveal multiple perspectives for interpretation. They were intended to represent contingent versions of the global in local contexts and constituted, in the words of Georg Simmel, 'momentary centers of world civilization.'"[12] *Empress San Francisco* builds on these arguments to more deeply explore the intersections of the local, national, and international interests that met in San Francisco in 1915.

Conflicts over city development, religious and ethnic identity formation, foreign affairs, immigration policy, labor relations, race relations, moral reform, and women's political power plagued fair officials from the moment the city won the fair in 1911. The elite male businessmen who controlled San Francisco politics and composed the fair's Board of Directors responded in ways consistent with their ultimate goal of maintaining the fair and the city's image so as to make the event profitable. This effort often required compromising with groups that also had an interest in the fair. The resulting negotiations demonstrated the complexity of Progressive Era California political culture. California's unique history, population, and economic conditions shaped political and social debates of the Progressive Era in ways that set the West apart from the East and Midwest. Regional priorities affected not only the shape of national-level debates but also the messages about California, the United States, and the Pacific world conveyed to visitors at this world's fair. Rather than presenting to visitors an uncomplicated statement of U.S. masculinist imperialism, as others argue, the fair offered a stage for discussing a host of issues preoccupying the Progressive Era United States.[13]

San Francisco was no stranger to fairs. *San Francisco Chronicle* publisher Michael H. de Young brought the 1894 Midwinter International Exposition to the newly created Golden Gate Park with exhibits from the 1893 Columbian Exposition. The six-month-long Midwinter Expo was the first U.S. international exposition held west of Chicago. As with the later PPIE, it offered city boosters the opportunity to craft a new image of the city. As Barbara Berglund has eloquently argued, city leaders used the fair as one of many cultural projects to "make San Francisco American" by presenting San Francisco's unique history within a framework that downplayed its disorderly roots.[14] The PPIE continued this process, reshaping the city's frontier past into a cosmopolitan present.

Ten years after the success of the Midwinter Expo, Hale Brothers Department Store magnate Reuben Brooks Hale suggested that the city hold another fair. The construction of the Panama Canal and the publicity accorded the Louisiana Purchase Exposition no doubt inspired him. The event could "be advertised as the opening of San Francisco as the center of trade for the Pacific Ocean, or in commemoration of the completion of the Panama Canal," he told fellow businessmen, since San Francisco was "the beginning of the east, and the ending of the west."[15] Hale and other supporters rallied interest until the devastating earthquake and fire of 1906 forced them to rethink their plans. As the recovery effort progressed, these boosters decided that the fair could be used also to prove San Francisco's economic strength to the nation and the world. "People are more interested in California and San Francisco, its metropolis, than ever before," argued one early piece of propaganda, "and there will be a great interest evinced in the progress San Francisco will have made seven years after the catastrophe...insuring...a large attendance from outside."[16] Rather than dissuading boosters, the earthquake and fire convinced them that staging the fair was necessary to demonstrate San Francisco's strength to the world.

The campaign for the fair was intertwined with attempts to downplay the devastation wrought by the earthquake and fire. The 7.8-magnitude earthquake that struck San Francisco in the early hours of April 18, 1906, killed thousands of people and left hundreds of thousands homeless. Devastating fires in the central city left 98 percent of the city's most heavily populated 521 blocks in ruins.[17] Andrea Rees Davies argues that despite the destruction wrought by the earthquake, city leaders created a narrative of the disaster in which they downplayed the earthquake and instead blamed the fire for the city's destruction. Cities can recover from fires, but they cannot avoid earthquakes.[18] Boosters worked hard to rebuild the city and demonstrate its economic and social vitality in the face of disaster. The fair quickly emerged as a panacea for the city's ills as the city was wracked by a series of disputes over rebuilding and relief. Staging a successful fair would prove to the world that San Francisco was back on its feet.

Hale and fellow city leaders soon embarked on the lengthy project of generating the required local, and eventually national, support necessary to stage the fair. In December 1906, fourteen men, led by Bank of California president Homer S. King, created the Pacific Ocean Exposition Company, whose stated goal was "to inaugurate and hold an International or World's Exposition in San Francisco commemorative of the 400th anniversary of the discovery of the Pacific Ocean by Balboa, and in celebration of the completion of the Panama Canal."[19] The company quickly introduced a bill to the state legislature for an early bond act, but the national depression of 1907 threw a wrench in its plans and stalled preparations for the fair until 1909. That year, the city tested its ability to hold a fair by hosting the weeklong Gaspar de Portola Festival.

Gaspar de Portolà was the first Spanish governor of California and the supposed "discoverer" of San Francisco Bay. Although a figure of minor historical importance, he became a convenient figurehead for an event that organizers hoped would mark San Francisco's renewal and emphasize the Spanish heritage of the city and the state. Extensive local financial support for the festival proved to boosters that the city could finance a fair. Donations from "every financial grade of citizen," ranging from ten cents to a thousand dollars, poured in to the festival's offices.[20] Downtown businessmen and Chinese merchants bedecked their buildings with the colors of the event.[21] Local civic organizations staged fund-raisers and musical programs in honor of the festival.[22] The Portola Festival was no match for the later PPIE, but for boosters in 1909, it was enough to prove that the city could host such an event. Organizers negotiated with railroads to set reduced rates for the event, setting a precedent implemented during the PPIE.[23] Hotel men rushed to reassure the public that they would have plenty of available hotel rooms.[24] Almost half a million people poured into the city during the festival, demonstrating that the city could comfortably host an exposition.

The Portola Festival transformed San Francisco into an international cultural center and was a resounding success. Future PPIE president Charles C. Moore single-handedly convinced the nations of Italy, Japan, Holland, Germany, and Britain to send warships to San Francisco to join the celebration.[25] Publicity lauded the city's Spanish heritage, likening it to an old city of Europe, a place where "our own race, once here, soon yields to the spell of the Spanish carnival."[26] Chinatown, often of moral concern to reformers, became a key attraction for the Portola. Tours

were offered for visitors, and the Chinese community participated in the festival's parades en masse, with the largest dragon ever seen outside China.[27] The Portola demonstrated that San Francisco could host a half million people and not appear crowded. It could put on a good show and provide visitors with a taste of Old Europe and the Pacific Rim, an intriguing mixture for the new century.

Organizing for the Panama-Pacific International Exposition picked up steam after the Portola Festival. Chamber of Commerce president James McNab met with the heads of the city's leading commercial enterprises to solidify the city's claim to a fair celebrating the completion of the canal.[28] Only four days after the festival ended, Hale hosted thirteen "prominent citizens" at the Bohemian Club, one of the most exclusive clubs in the city, in another attempt to stimulate support.[29] The men present at that dinner included the nucleus of the exposition's future Board of Directors.

Shortly thereafter, Moore pushed his fellow organizers to hold a public meeting from which to officially launch the fair. His actions demonstrated a canny understanding of the need to build public support for what would become an expensive and complicated enterprise. He called

Fig. 2. Second meeting of the PPIE at the Merchants Exchange
Building, San Francisco. The April 1910 mass meeting demonstrated
the enormous public support for the fair. (Library of Congress.)

for a public declaration of the formal birth of the project, arguing that
"if the public doesn't want the Exposition . . . we shall make a mistake
if we try to hold it."[30] Boosters spearheaded a survey of the city's most
elite men at the exclusive Bohemian Club, where they canvassed 2,500
residents to determine their support for the fair. Responses, according
to fair historian Frank Morton Todd, were overwhelmingly positive.
"Greatest chance San Francisco has ever had to promote her growth,"
wrote one. Another simply stated: "Get busy."[31] Those responses convinced Moore and others to organize a public meeting, which was held
in December 1909 at the Merchants Exchange. The approximately 150
men who attended that meeting became the core of the Ways and Means
Committee, a group of eventually 300 local businessmen charged with
raising support and funds for the project.[32]

These meetings jump-started an extensive public campaign to convince all San Franciscans, Californians, and eventually Congress that

San Francisco must host the proposed exposition. April's mass meeting demonstrated the effort's success. Attendees filled the floor of the Merchants Exchange and raised more than $4 million in only an hour and fifty minutes. Governor James Gillett and a delegation of exposition supporters left two days later for Washington, where they lobbied on behalf of the fair.[33] Boosters forged ahead with a campaign that included mass mailings, buttons, a "Shoe Leather Day" (in which volunteers solicited pledges from every local business in the city), and the passage of city and state bond issues.[34] Outside challenges arose as approval for the project grew in San Francisco. Other cities vied for the right to hold an exposition celebrating the completion of the canal. Galveston, New Orleans, San Diego, and other cities began to lobby Congress for official recognition and backing. The San Diego challenge threatened to derail San Francisco's plans, for it would divide the state's congressmen when voting between the two sites. San Diego eventually gave up the fight after quite a bit of political maneuvering, which included a statewide meeting of the city leaders. Its boosters settled for hosting the Panama-California Exposition, a smaller-scale fair that also took place in 1915.[35]

The fight narrowed to a choice between San Francisco and New Orleans. Both cities claimed that their proximity to the canal made them the "logical point" for the location of the Panama Exposition.[36] They launched lobbying efforts and public relations campaigns to convince Congress to choose their city. The barrage of propaganda produced included "illustrated booklets . . . argumentative statements . . . trunk labels, letter-heads and stickers for letters and envelopes, slips for outgoing fruit boxes, [and] cards for hotel guests."[37] The campaign grew increasingly aggressive, as representatives of both cities plied congressmen with such delicacies as fruit, wine, and gin fizzes.[38] San Francisco's eventual victory depended both on the organizers' promise that they would require no federal financial funding for the exposition and on the city's closer proximity to Asia.[39] At long last, on January 31, 1911, the House of Representatives passed the resolution in favor of San Francisco, 189 to 159.[40] San Franciscans rejoiced. The fair was on!

Congressional debates over the fair reveal that the goals of San Francisco's businessmen resonated with national political leaders. Many congressmen agreed that holding the fair in San Francisco would be

Fig. 3. One of many pieces of propaganda that fair boosters for New Orleans issued in their attempt to win the fair. (Charles Petterson personal collection.)

an important step toward cementing stronger trade relationships with Asia and present a fitting tribute to the genius of American expansionism. Congressman George Foss of Illinois remarked: "Westward the star of empire takes its way. Let this country keep step with the march of progress. Let us have an exposition on the Pacific coast of such grandeur as the indomitable American spirit of the people there alone can make; that will cause not only the Occident, but the Orient, to wonder at the marvelous resources, the power, and the influence of the American nation."[41] The issue of Asian trade surfaced repeatedly in the debates, demonstrating the relationship between the Panama Canal, the fair, and American economic interests in Asia. "The great field for exploitation lies in the Orient," promised the report from the Congressional Committee on Industrial Expositions. Holding the exposition in San Francisco, the report continued, would allow America and Asia to stimulate "trade between the two countries [sic] and . . . cement . . . the ties of cordial friendship between America and the nations of the Far East."[42]

Congressmen may have paid tribute to the city's "true, indomitable spirit" and its proximity to Asia, but it was the economics of San Francisco's offer that won the city the contest.[43] Legislators proved wary of committing U.S. dollars to an exposition after a string of federally funded expositions had lost money. San Francisco asked only for official recognition of the event and for the president to issue official invitations to foreign nations. The event's organizers promised to fund the rest of the event with local dollars. Their pledge convinced Congress to vote in their favor and propelled fair officials into unknown territory. They would have to raise all the necessary money through state or city bond issues and through private investment. Practically, this promise profoundly affected the fair. The fair's board was forced to cultivate public support for what was essentially a private venture.[44] This reliance on local and state funding forced fair directors to balance the interests of local groups with both state interests and the desires of foreign nations, since ostracizing any of these bases of support risked the financial viability of the fair itself.

Fair officials assured city residents that the fair would be an economic stimulus, bringing new business, tourists, and potential settlers to the city. Rhetoric about civic unity echoed through many of the discussions in San Francisco concerning the fair. Boosters drew on desires to bring the city together after the upheavals of the previous decade. San Francisco attorney Gavin McNab promised the public during the first mass meeting that the exposition would showcase the city and cause "all differences among our people [to] . . . pass away. In its place will rise the genius of municipal unity. . . . We shall be only San Franciscans—one for all and all for one, and all for San Francisco."[45] Thousands of San Franciscans would go on to debate the location of the fair and admission prices and to participate in parades, exhibits, and other activities on the fairgrounds, demonstrating that they found his argument compelling.

McNab emphasized the need to unify San Francisco because political and social turmoil had beset the city over the past decade. The first years of the century had witnessed plague outbreaks that periodically terrified city residents and threatened the city's and state's economy.[46] Not long after that threat was finally contained, the 1906 earthquake and fire had ravaged the city. Soon after, allegations of widespread graft and corruption at City Hall had brought national attention to the resulting graft trials. City leaders hoped the fair would be a way to unify warring economic and political interests in the city and to repair the city's national reputation. Just as with the Midwinter Exposition, the PPIE seemed to offer city boosters a way to prove their city's "Americanness" and to demonstrate its total incorporation into the American body politic. But the lingering conflicts of the previous decades proved difficult to overcome and underlay a number of the debates that emerged before and during the fair.

San Franciscans prided themselves on their city's Gold Rush roots, but the city's frontier reputation made potential visitors wary. The area that would eventually become San Francisco began as the site of a native village, then developed as a Spanish presidio and mission. The 1848 discovery of gold transformed it almost overnight into a booming entrepôt.[47] The city's access to the Pacific Ocean and the Sacramento River made it a logical hub for mining activities. Merchants also struck gold while outfitting eager miners and laid the groundwork for the city's twentieth-century commercial activities. Saloon keepers, gamblers, and madams also set up shop, serving the thousands of single men who flowed through the city in search of wealth. The original "Barbary Coast" vice district remained a lively source of income and entertainment for San Franciscans into the twentieth century. Even in 1910, the city's still uneven sex ratio contributed to the sense that the city was still slightly raw and seemingly uncivilized.[48] The post–Gold Rush history of vigilante activities in the 1850s, a story that many San Franciscans valued as a part of their history, exacerbated visions of a lawless city.[49]

The Gold Rush created San Francisco's economic and social world. Thousands of immigrants from around the world poured into the city, seeking their fortune and forming the basis for the cosmopolitan society that eventually would shape the PPIE. Catholics and Jews shared political power with local Protestants. By 1915 the city had elected mayors of all three faiths and Jewish state representatives and congressmen. Irish and German Catholics dominated city politics; thus the anti-Catholicism prevalent in other parts of the country had little effect on San Francisco politics or culture. The meeting of so many different peoples resulted in a city full of active ethnic communities. French, Germans, Italians, Irish, Russians, Norwegians, and Swedes—all had benevolent and fraternal organizations in the city that they could mobilize in support of the PPIE. The fair's board contained Jews, Catholics, and Protestants, and they sponsored the creation of local PPIE auxiliaries for every immigrant community they could contact, helping to fashion an event with a particularly local feel.

The city's tolerance did not, however, extend to the Chinese residents within its bounds. Chinese immigrants had come to the state seeking the promise of gold or arrived as bound laborers. Many eventually settled in San Francisco, where they established the largest Chinatown on the West Coast. Despite building a strong immigrant community, they faced persistent discrimination and racism throughout California.[50] Chinese immigrants were the victims of racially motivated legislation and acts of violence in the city and across the West.[51] After the economic downturn of the 1870s, white labor leaders increasingly blamed the Chinese for their economic woes, spouting racially motivated anti-Asian rhetoric. San Francisco Irish immigrant Denis Kearney, for instance, cultivated support for his Workingmen's Party by demanding anti-Chinese legislation. This pressure, primarily from white, working-class organized labor, culminated in the 1882 Chinese Exclusion Act, which forbade the entry of Chinese laborers into the United States. Congress extended the act indefinitely in 1902.[52] Despite this act, Chinese immigration continued, as did legal prosecution of the Chinese, creating an often tense situation for the local Chinese community.

The Exclusion Act did not quell anti-immigrant sentiment in the West or in San Francisco. When Chinese immigration declined in the late nineteenth century, Japanese immigrants began to enter the state. They too soon faced resentment from white California residents.[53] Many Japanese settled in the state's farming districts, but others made San Francisco their home, attracting some of the state's wealthiest Japanese immigrants. They built a small Japantown community, where they formed religious and community organizations. Many whites continued to view Asians as unassimilable aliens and limited their employment opportunities in the city; therefore, Asians occupied the bottom rungs of the social and occupational ladders in San Francisco.

Racial tensions persisted throughout the early twentieth century. White San Franciscans seized upon both the plague outbreak and the earthquake and subsequent fire as a chance to lobby for the wholesale removal of Chinatown from its valuable downtown location. The powerful Chinese merchant community successfully resisted this campaign with the backing of the Chinese government. Their victory revealed the economic significance of the Chinese to the city, an issue that would shape the fair.[54] Japanese residents also faced a racially motivated boycott and acts of violence on the streets of San Francisco in the months following the earthquake.[55] The concerns over the presence of so many Japanese in the city eventually culminated in the school board's effort to segregate the city's Japanese students into an "Oriental" public school. The representatives of the deeply angry nation of Japan and President Theodore Roosevelt eventually negotiated the so-called Gentlemen's Agreement of 1907 in which Japan agreed to end the emigration of laborers to the United States while the city promised to desegregate the school, but bitterness remained.[56] The crisis brought national attention both to the city's, and the state's, anti-Asian attitudes, and to the presence of Asians in the city.

McNab's concerns about civic unity also reflected the business community's attempts to move past the 1907 graft trials. The conflict between labor and capital had long dominated San Francisco politics, and tensions increased after the election of musician and Union Labor Party leader Eugene Schmitz as mayor in 1902. Local political powerhouse Abe Ruef, a man often labeled as a "political boss" by both contemporaries and scholars, engineered Schmitz's election, and the two men's political strategies included a number of corrupt and unsavory practices.[57] Glenn Gendzel argues that after Schmitz's election in 1902, "word went out to owners of saloons, gambling halls, and brothels that a portion of their proceeds must now flow his [Ruef's] way or else the police would shut down their establishments."[58] Local reformers soon attacked the Union Labor Party for its underhanded dealings, reflecting the national Progressive Era trend toward ridding urban politics of corruption.

Local reformer and newspaper editor Fremont Older began exposing Ruef and Schmitz's corruption in editorials in the *San Francisco Bulletin*. Popular resentment grew, and soon former Democratic mayor James A. Phelan and businessman Rudolph Spreckels built on Older's muckraking campaign to expose a series of backroom payoffs by city businessmen to supervisors. The resulting series of high-profile trials and a graft investigation drew national attention to San Francisco's sordid political life and to its active vice district.[59] Schmitz and the offending supervisors resigned in disgrace, and the prosecution replaced Schmitz with "good government" nonpartisan candidate Dr. Edward R. Taylor. After the first burst of enthusiasm, however, city interest in the trials waned, and elite businessmen withdrew their support of the effort after they became targets. These men, many of whom would go on to join the PPIE's Board of Directors, turned the city's attention away from class conflict and toward city development.[60] The trial witnessed both the dramatic courtroom shooting of Assistant District Attorney Francis J. Heney, who was in charge of the graft prosecution, and the "kidnapping" (by Southern California sheriff deputies) of Older himself. The shooting and kidnapping only lent more credence to the city's image as a rough-and-ready town.[61] When McNab pointed out, then, that San Franciscans needed to unite behind the fair, he argued for putting the legacy of the graft trials in the past and working together to combat San Francisco's national reputation as a corrupt and lawless place.

The past decade of San Francisco's history motivated city leaders to make the fair into a resounding success and to demonstrate the city's recovery from disaster and political upheaval, while simultaneously reminding visitors of simmering urban social anxieties. Progressive Era politicians and social reformers frequently targeted cities for their corrupt governments, vice districts, and seemingly unassimilable immigrant populations. San Francisco's history of government graft, active vice district, skewed male–female population, and relatively sizable Asian population meant that the city encapsulated a number of key social issues for concerned Americans. PPIE boosters wanted to create an event that was uniquely San Franciscan but that somehow also mitigated the social and political conflicts that threatened the city's national reputation. They needed to find a way to reassure potential visitors that San Francisco was not controlled by corrupt labor bosses, that brothels did not lure unsuspecting young men into a life of vice, and that Asian immigrants and their children were tourist attractions rather than threats to the racial order. At the same time, fair officials had to keep local businesses, including saloon owners and prominent Chinese merchants, happy because their financial contributions were essential to the fair's success. To complicate matters further, they needed to convince Asian nations—China and Japan, most notably—to devote resources to a fair held in a state with a strong anti-Asian movement. Without the participation of China and Japan, fair officials feared that the fair would be neither "international" nor representative of the Pacific and that it might fail completely. This task would keep the fair directors busy in the years ahead.

Those exposition directors represented the most prominent businesses in the city. The life and career of Charles C. Moore, first the finance chairman of the PPIE and eventually its president, was fairly typical of these men. Moore's family moved to California when he was young, and he grew up in the Bay Area, attending high school in Benicia and later St. Augustine College. He entered the iron shops of the San Francisco Tool Company and eventually founded his own engineering firm. By 1915, his firm had installed steam and hydroelectric plants across the West and had branches throughout the West and in New York. Moore held positions on the boards of numerous other firms and served as president of the San Francisco Chamber of Commerce, during which time he organized the Association of the Chambers of Commerce of the Pacific Coast. In the pre-fair years he assumed responsibility of convincing assorted foreign nations to send their warships to San Francisco and participate in the celebration of the Portola Festival. He was a man deeply familiar with administration and apparently quite adept at management.[62]

The other members of the fair's thirty-man board were equally well connected and experienced. William H. Crocker, another director, was the son of Charles Crocker, one of the "Big Four" backers of the transcontinental railroad; a regent of the University of California; a vice president of Pacific Telephone and Telegraph; and the president of Crocker National Bank. Department store president Hale also served as director of both the Merchants' Association and the Association for the Improvement and Adornment of San Francisco. Isaias Hellman, originally from Southern California, was president of the Union Trust Company and director of numerous other banks. He and fellow director Leon Sloss, president of the Northern Commercial Company and trustee of Stanford University, were prominent members of the San Francisco Jewish community, demonstrating the religious diversity of the fair's board.[63] Other members of the Board of Directors included the publishers of three major San Francisco daily newspapers—the *Chronicle, Call,* and *Examiner*—the vice president of Pacific Gas and Electric Company, the president of the Spring Valley Water Company, the passenger traffic manager of the Southern Pacific Company, and the president of the Alaska

Fig. 4. Board of directors for the PPIE. (#1959.087—ALB, 1:3,
Bancroft Library, University of California, Berkeley.)

Packers' Association, one of the city's most significant sources of commerce.[64] James Rolph, Jr., president of the Merchants' Association and the city's mayor from 1912 until he became governor in 1931, was another key member of the board.

The board did not fully represent other political interests in the city or the state. Despite the power of local labor unions, the only labor representative on the board was former mayor Patrick H. McCarthy. McCarthy's service on the board represented his general pro-business sympathies and his relatively conservative leadership of the Building Trades Council. The men who backed the 1907 graft trials appear to have been deliberately excluded from membership on the board. Despite urging from leading progressive Chester Rowell, member of the State PPIE Commission, to include former mayor and Democrat James Phelan on the board, the officials were predominantly Republicans.[65] No members of Chinese or Japanese communities participated in the board. Nor did any women participate as directors, although they did have a place in the fair's administrative structure. The fair's board represented the elite business class of San Francisco—that is, wealthy, Republican males of European descent. Religion offered the only element of diversity on the board.

The board reflected a fairly conservative perspective in the broader context of San Francisco and California politics. Their rejection of the members of the graft prosecution suggested a desire to unite and move past the discord of the trials and to reject the allegations of corruption that had been levied at that time. But graft prosecutor Hiram Johnson was elected governor in 1910, and the statewide Progressive Party gained strength over the years leading up to the fair. Johnson's election meant that the State PPIE Commission, the body appointed to oversee distribution of the funds raised by the state's bond issue, was composed of Rowell and other Progressive Party leaders. As this book reveals, the ensuing political conflict between the fair's board and the California Progressive Party at times played out on the stage of the PPIE.

Local society women united to form their own board, which became an official part of the fair's administrative structure. A group of white club women met in April 1911 at the St. Francis Hotel and discussed forming a PPIE women's association. Three hundred local women soon chartered the Panama-Pacific International Association of Women, which later became the Woman's Board. Officially, the members of the Woman's Board acted as the fair hostesses. They ran the California State Building and hosted a variety of social events during and before the exposition. Their involvement in the fair was not atypical. Women had served on Boards of Lady Managers since the first U.S. world's fair, the Centennial Exposition of 1876 in Philadelphia. These women, like those at the 1893 Columbian Exposition in Chicago devoted themselves to creating separate women's buildings in which to house exhibits of women's work. Historian Mary Frances Cordato argued that the women of both Philadelphia and Chicago saw their mission as using the Woman's Building to further women's culture and place in society. The Board of Lady Managers at the 1904 St. Louis exposition, however, urged the integration of women's exhibits with those of their male counterparts. Their building was used only for hospitality and administrative purposes rather than for exhibiting women's work.[66] No official woman's building existed at the PPIE. In some ways the California Building served that function, since it housed the offices of the Woman's Board and was the site of their receptions and parties.

The composition of the PPIE's Woman's Board differed dramatically from those of earlier fairs. At earlier federally funded fairs, women from across the nation were appointed to honorary positions on the Woman's Board, leaving much of the work to a small number of local women. At the PPIE, members mostly came from the Bay Area, or at least from California, and met in person on a regular basis. Honorary president Phoebe Hearst—widow of mining magnate George Hearst, mother of William Randolph Hearst, and a significant philanthropist and powerful member of the University of California Board of Regents in her own right—lent considerable status to the body. A staunch supporter of female reform efforts and the suffrage movement, Hearst involved other women with similar viewpoints in the fair. Helen Sanborn, for instance, brought her long history of working with social relief organizations in San Francisco to her service as practical head of the board.

The class and race bias of the board, however, was clear. Its members were from the wealthiest families in the Bay Area and were women who had the leisure time and energy to devote to volunteer causes. Some of them were suffragists, who in the fall of 1911 celebrated their victory in winning the vote for California women. Like Hearst, others had long-standing connections to female reform organizations, such as the Young Women's Christian Association (YWCA), and at times were at odds with the male fair directors. During the fair the women hosted formal events to honor prominent visitors. They were thus officially placed in a customarily feminine role, a fact that has obscured the very real influence of women on the PPIE for previous historians. In reality, along with hundreds of other interested women, the board members engaged in political work as well, lobbying in favor of the exposition, drawing financial support from women across the state, and smoothing the way for women interested in the fair. Moreover, a number of women were appointed as assistants to various departments of the exposition's administration, providing them an additional role in the fair's bureaucracy and a voice in its planning and organization.[67] Their effect on the fair is a key part of this narrative.

Fig. 5. Mrs. Phoebe Hearst, member of the National Advisory
Council of Congressional Union for Woman Suffrage and honorary
president of the PPIE Woman's Board. (Library of Congress.)

Elite San Francisco men and women staged the fair to assert both the city's recovery and reunification after a decade of conflict and its place on the international stage. They promised to create a fair that would unify the city, profit all San Franciscans, and open Asian markets to U.S. businesses. To do so, they created a splendid 635-acre wonderland that entranced visitors and created a vision of California, and the Pacific, dominated by San Francisco. Fair directors created the texture of that world—its sights, sounds, and colors—in conjunction with a host of outside interests. Foreign nations, local organizations, and federal interests each had a hand in shaping the event. To understand the effect of those forces, we must begin with the fairgrounds themselves. Let us now turn to the world of the fair.

1 ☙ The Spectacle of the Fair

"One of the most spectacular and interesting special events of the expo-sition period," according to the *San Francisco Chronicle*, was the June cel-ebration of the "Night in Hawaii" that the fair's Hawaiian Commission staged on the Palace of Fine Arts' lagoon. Socialite Marion Dowsett Worthington ruled as queen for the evening. The event featured five prin-cesses representing the territory's five major islands, men in native cos-tume rowing outrigger canoes, fireworks, and musical accompaniment by the popular Philippine Constabulary Band.[1] The colonial implications of this performance could not be missed. A white American socialite queen ruled the islands, bringing them civilization and progress. The princesses and canoeists evoked nostalgia for the supposed traditional Hawaiian past while implying that the presence of American culture would doom that Hawaiʻi to fade away and remain simply as a tourist attraction.[2] Territo-rial governor Lucius Pinkham's speech earlier in the day spelled out the relationship between Hawaiʻi and the United States even more clearly when he focused on the military significance of Hawaiʻi to the safety of the Pacific coast. "It is not for Hawaii that this great military and naval outpost is being established," he stated, but rather for the protection of "your Pacific Coast, your cities, your commerce, and the mighty mate-rial and political progress of the United States of America."[3] It would be difficult to find a more naked statement of U.S. intentions in the Pacific.

This performance contained complicated messages about race, gen-der, and U.S. expansionism. Although Hawaiʻi's queen for the day was unequivocally white, the princesses who accompanied her were of mixed race, and they and other young mixed-race Hawaiian men and women featured prominently in performances at the Hawaiian Building. Some-times these young men and women appeared at celebrations and in news-paper reports dressed as modern American youth, and only their wearing leis identified their "Hawaiianness." Many scholars argue that the role of the nonwhite "other" at fairs was to appear as a foil to the supposed superior white American.[4] The Panama-Pacific International Exposition (PPIE) emphasized social Darwinist ideals and scientific approaches to society and marriage and glorified the white male.[5] The PPIE brought eugenics to the public's attention through the Race Betterment Booth and meetings and widely publicized these ideas through such events as Night in Hawaii. But the lived reality of the fair was much more complex, and the PPIE's official messages were more complicated than social Darwinism suggests.

Night in Hawaii juxtaposed a white socialite and the native princesses in a predictable way. But young Hawaiian women wearing shirtwaists and leis did not fit into this dichotomy of allegedly primitive versus civilized ideals. Instead, as children of both white and nonwhite parents, they suggested the possibility for peaceful racial integration and intermarriage. Hawai'i's status as a newly acquired U.S. territory highlighted the nation's expanded role as an imperial power, while the competing goals of haole (whites who lived in Hawai'i) organizers, native Hawaiian performers, and U.S. businessmen represented the tensions contained in U.S. expansionism. San Francisco businessmen staged the exposition to boost their city's economic prospects. Within the walls of the PPIE fair directors designed a world that conveyed a vision of California history, U.S. society, and the U.S. relationship to the Pacific and Latin America that posited a dichotomy between perceived primitive and civilized cultures and nations. Much of the artwork and exhibits reflected popular theories of social evolution and the dominance of white men while reinforcing eugenic ideas about social progress and racial purity. But the participation of the young Hawaiian women reveals that this official narrative contained contradictions and faced competition from the contributions of other fair exhibitors. These participants from around the United States and the world, from the PPIE Woman's Board to the government of Argentina, had their own agendas and goals for the fair that together conveyed a complicated and sometimes competing set of narratives about the world to visitors.

The elaborately landscaped and brilliantly colored grounds of the PPIE impressed upon visitors the accomplishments of California, the United States, and mankind. The lush gardens and colorful buildings emphasized the state's natural bounty and beauty and implied the success of American expansionism in bringing U.S. culture to this paradise of a state. Huge exhibit palaces awed visitors with the newest examples of technological, artistic, and social development. Etiquette maven Emily Post wrote one of the most evocative descriptions of the grounds, noting that "to visualize the . . . Exposition in a few sentences is impossible. . . . In the shade or fog, it was a city of baked earth color, oxidized with any quantity of terra cotta; in the sun it was deep cream glowing with light." The fair was perhaps most impressive, she noted, at a distance, after coming down from the hills of the city, when "you saw a biscuit-colored city with terra-cotta roofs, green domes and blue. Beyond it the wide waters of a glorious bay, rimmed with far gray-green mountains . . . or perhaps you looked down upon it at night when the scintillating central point, the Tower of Jewels, looked like a diamond and turquoise wedding cake and behind it an aurora of prismatic-colored searchlights."[6]

The exposition stretched across the southern shore of San Francisco Bay. Officials acquired the 635-acre site from the federal government and through lease and purchase from private owners.[7] Close study of previous fairs convinced fair directors of the necessity of designing a compact site, so they laid out the central section of the fair on a "block" plan. Designers arranged the main palaces in four blocks joined by covered corridors. Extensively decorated outdoor courts accompanied the palaces, making the PPIE a uniquely outdoor event that was quite distinct from previous American fairs. This central area contained the eleven main exhibit palaces and the Festival Hall. Farther west lay first the buildings of the states and foreign nations and, farther on, stood the livestock exhibit buildings, racetrack, aviation field, and drill grounds. The Joy Zone, or amusement section, covered 70 acres to the east of the central section.[8]

Rather than replicate the Beaux Arts "white city" of the 1893 Columbian Exposition, PPIE designers chose colors that reflected the California landscape and visually linked the fair to its western location. Directors appointed muralist Jules Guerin the first ever official "colorist" of an exposition, and he blended a palette of Mediterranean colors into the buildings across the fair, using "terra-cotta, ivory, cerulean blue, gold, green and rose."[9] Color even spilled onto the paths of the fair, where tinted red sand subtly accented the buildings' colors.[10] California writer

Fig. 6. Panoramic view of the exposition. (Donald G. Larson Collection, Special Collections Research Center, California State University, Fresno.)

Mary Austin noted Guerin's success in echoing the colors of a California summer: "[The West] has made this exposition the richest dyed, the patterned splendor of all their acres of poppies, of lupines, of amber wheat, of rosy orchard, and of jade-tinted lake."[11] The abundant use of electric lights, particularly at night, emphasized the warm colors of the grounds. The beloved Tower of Jewels, a 435-foot tower covered with 125,000 reflecting "novagem" jewels of every color that sparkled in the sunlight, further accentuated the fair's color scheme.

Extensive greenery and flowers added bursts of color to the grounds. A living wall of shrubbery enclosed the site in part to shield visitors from the unpredictable bay winds and weather. This wall extended 1,150 feet along the southern boundary of the fair and reinforced the link between the fair and the California landscape. Within the grounds, as Portia Lee notes, vast flower beds and fountains further emphasized the "integration of the natural and built environment" and the "inherent, yet elabo-

Fig. 7. South Gardens looking east and Tower of Jewels. (*The Blue Book.*)

rated beauty of California nature."[12] The Court of Flowers alone featured fifty thousand yellow pansies and fifty thousand red anemones (replaced by begonias later in the season), borders of topiary mimosa trees, large lawns bordered by beds of creeping juniper, and boxed orange trees lining the paths.[13]

The color scheme visually united the fairgrounds, but the architecture remained eclectic. Although dominated by classical styles, the courts and palaces defied easy classification. A visitor using the popular Scott Street entrance walked into the Court of Palms, a formal garden with lines of palm trees extending in both directions. To the left lay the Byzantine-inspired Palace of Horticulture, while on the right stood Festival Hall, which more closely resembled a Beaux Arts French theater. In front of the visitor stood the Tower of Jewels, which drew on Italian Renaissance themes.[14] Beyond the Tower of Jewels lay the impressive Court of the Universe, modeled on St. Peter's Basilica in Rome and further incorporating Italian Renaissance styles.[15] There East and West met, metaphorically represented in two statuary groups—*Nations of the East* and *Nations of the West*. Around the Court of the Universe stood four of the main exhibit palaces dedicated to agriculture, transportation, manufacturers, and liberal arts—each designed in its own unique combination of architectural styles. To the west of the Agricultural and Liberal Arts Palaces stood the Food Products Palace and the Education and Social Economy Palace. Across a small lagoon lay Bernard Maybeck's famed Palace of Fine Arts and to the east of the Transportation and Manufactures Palaces stood the Mines and Metallurgy, Machinery, and Varied Industries Palaces. The architecture of the palaces may have been eclectic, but the color scheme and the compact court plan meant that visitors experienced a seamless transition from one part of the central fair to the other, walking in and out of impressively decorated courts and palaces.

In the eleven huge exhibit palaces, fair visitors could peruse seventy thousand separate exhibits along fifty miles of aisles. Exhibitors hoped their eye-catching displays would advertise goods to willing consumers and impress visitors with the progress and technological innovation evinced by American business, all while drumming up national and international customers. From the school-related displays in the Palace of Education and Social Economy to the pure food laboratory, the displays

Fig. 8. The Court of Palms, facade of the Palace of Liberal Arts (*left*)
and the facade of the Palace of Education and Social Economy (*right*),
PPIE, San Francisco. (Library of Congress.)

Fig. 9. The Court of
the Universe. (Donald
G. Larson Collection,
Special Collections
Research Center,
California State
University, Fresno.)

Fig. 10. One of many service and reform-minded exhibits that greeted visitors at the PPIE. (Library of Congress.)

inundated visitors with information about new products, technologies, and processes. The Model T Fords that rolled off the assembly line in the Palace of Transportation signified for many the fair's emphasis on technological progress. Visitors eagerly lined up at the Sperry Flour Company display in the Palace of Varied Industries to taste its famously delicious scones. A huge tower of Heinz 57 products impressed upon visitors the wonders of packaged foods and the variety of Heinz products as well.

Fair visitors thronged to the palaces to try out new gadgets and to learn about new inventions. Photographer Ansel Adams noted in his autobiography, "The intent of the Exposition was to encourage interest in and purchase of the items displayed. It was much more sensible than ordinary advertising: everything was there to see and handle and try out if you wished."[16] The new devices and electronics on display at the fair particularly appealed to young visitors. About the Eastman Kodak exhibit in the same building, thirteen-year old Doris Barr remarked, "They have some of the most beautiful Kodaks exhibited. . . . I wouldn't mind having one at all!"[17] Many visitors noted the fascinating new commodities they viewed at the fair. Numerous visitors praised the "House Electrical," a full-size bungalow built right inside the Palace of Manufacturers. The small, California-style house featured all of the latest electrical appliances, from an electric dishwasher to a bottle warmer to an electric heater for a shaving mug.[18] For visitors still amazed by the idea of an electrified house, the wonders contained therein must have been astonishing. Schoolteacher Annie Fader Haskell remarked that it "made one want to go housekeeping at once."[19]

Moving west past the Horticulture Palace brought a visitor to the foreign buildings. Although some foreign nations failed to erect their planned buildings owing to the financial exigencies of war, many others put hundreds of thousands of dollars into staging impressive presences at the fair. Here, Japan, France, Siam, Panama, Persia, Honduras, Guatemala, Switzerland, Cuba, New Zealand, Denmark, Italy, Turkey, China, Argentina, the Netherlands, Bolivia, Sweden, Canada, and the Philippines all erected buildings. Inside, their commissions displayed historical relics and examples of traditional arts and crafts and showcased current agricultural and industrial products. North of the foreign pavilions stood the state buildings, where state commissions likewise featured examples of their own history and products. Still farther west lay the model marine camp, the livestock exhibits, the athletic stadium, and the polo fields.

Turning east out of the Scott Street entrance brought a visitor through the South Gardens and eventually to the Joy Zone, the amusement section named in honor of the Panama Canal Zone that featured the usual assortment of concessions. Visitors could tempt fate on roller coasters and thrill rides (one of which, the Bowls of Joy, resulted in multiple fatalities during the fair). Or they could watch dancing girls performing what contemporaries called "muscle dances." Even more popular attractions included reenactments of key events in world history such as the biblical story of creation and the Dayton flood of 1913. Other displays, such as the enormously popular scale model of the Panama Canal and a display of premature infants in newly invented incubators, combined education and entertainment. Like all fairs of the era, the Zone also included the so-called ethnic villages, where groups of people envisioned as "others" by mainstream American society performed the tasks of their daily lives for observers.

Fair visitors faced myriad choices once they entered the PPIE's gates. They could admire modern art either in the Palace of Fine Arts or along the avenues of the grounds, watch a theater performance, learn about educational reform in China or the Philippines, catch a glimpse of the salacious *Stella* (a painting of a nude woman that visitors swore breathed on its own) on the Zone, ride the Aeroscope for a stunning Bay Area view from high above the Zone, or learn more about the states and nations of the world in the buildings they designed and built. Many exhibitors featured "moving pictures" in their displays, and they became enough of a draw that after a few months, the official program issued each day of the fair included a lengthy list of times and locations where visitors could view the films.[20] The fair offered visitors new experiences of all kinds—from art to food to amusement rides.

The outdoor nature of the fair offered an extensive canvas for works of art of all sorts. This art reinforced the fair's larger messages about race, progress, and expansionism. PPIE head sculptor Alexander Stirling Calder noted, "It is the sculpture that interprets the meaning of the exposition, that symbolizes the spirit of conquest and adventure, and lends imagery to all the elements that have resulted in the union of the Eastern and Western seas."[21] Sculpture adorned every nook and cranny of the large palaces, courts, and towers. The *San Francisco Chronicle* proudly reported after opening day that the exposition "embodies completely the ultimate achievement of the race."[22] To PPIE officials, these achievements included U.S. domination of the American West, expansion in the Pacific, and the completion of the Panama Canal, which signaled the nation's destiny "to dominate the politics and commerce of the Pacific."[23] They hoped that the exposition would provide the city with "world-wide power and fame and prominence" and assert San Francisco's position as the preeminent city of the Pacific.[24] Underlying those assertions was a belief in the inevitability of progress and of American expansionism, in the fact of both social and scientific evolution, and in the superiority of U.S. values and culture, all of which found expression in the public art of the fair.

Any visitor who somehow missed the fair's rhetorical celebration of progress could find it visually inscribed in the fair's courts and statuary, most prominently in the *Column of Progress*, and in the Court of the Ages (also called the Court of Abundance). The 185-foot-high *Column of Progress* dominated the fair's South Gardens and caught the attention of all who entered. According to Calder, the statue celebrated "the unconquerable impulse that forever impels man to strive onward."[25] Atop the statue stood the *Adventurous Bowman,* a partially nude man shooting an arrow into the sky while surrounded by a "circle of toilers" and a patiently attentive woman. A series of relief sculptures symbolizing the "labors and aspirations of men" circled the base of the column.[26] While the column encapsulated the entire narrative of the fair in its story of man's social advancement and achievement, the Court of Ages depicted the process of biological evolution and progress. Designed by architect Louis C. Mullgardt, the court featured the 219-foot-high Tower of Ages, whose successive altars depicted the ascent of man from "primitive savage to the regnant modern spirit."[27] The arcades housed the oft-praised murals of Frank Brangwyn that depicted in bold color men's engagement with the elements: air, earth, fire, and water. Figures of primitive men and women engaged in the toil of everyday life appeared around the base of the tower. Images of less evolved life forms, such as crabs and fish, along the tower's lower edge further emphasized the ideas of evolution. Four statuary groups of human figures stood within the central fountain. Their titles included *Natural Selection* and *Survival of the Fittest,* further encapsulating the theme of life as men's struggle with each other for success and dominance.[28] Both scientific and social Darwinism claimed a prominent place in the art of the fair.

Artwork depicting U.S. territorial expansion appeared at the fair to prove the inevitability of human progress. Murals and sculptures across the grounds glorified the energetic, virile western spirit. Across from the *Column of Progress* stood the *Fountain of Energy,* which featured a young, athletic man riding a "fiery horse, tearing across the globe."[29] The fountain was, in Calder's words, "a joyous aquatic triumph celebrating the completion of the Panama Canal."[30] Another critic described it as "a symbol of the vigor and daring of our mighty nation, which carried to a successful ending a gigantic task abandoned by another great republic."[31] While this fountain and the *Column of Progress* immortalized American achievements, other pieces offered a western inflection of the national narrative, with statues commemorating the Spanish conquest of the Americas and California. Statues of both Francisco Pizarro

Fig. 11. Palace of Agriculture and *Column of Progress*. (Donald G. Larson Collection, Special Collections Research Center, California State University, Fresno.)

and Hernán Cortés stood in front of the Tower of Jewels, while figures of a padre and a pioneer appeared in its niches. Two fountains designed by female artists—*El Dorado* (Gertrude Vanderbilt Whitney), which celebrated the discovery of gold in California, and *Youth* (Edith Woodman Burroughs)—reminded viewers of the restless California spirit. Beneath the Tower of Jewels, visitors could admire murals depicting the history of the Panama Canal in visual form, from Balboa's encounter with the Pacific to the canal's triumphant completion by Americans. The richly colored grounds, abundant flowering bushes and trees, and eclectic architecture further accentuated the active, vibrant western nature of the fair. It represented a West and a California settled by white men who triumphed over nature and savagery and who remained full of energy for the challenges to come.[32]

Two of the fair's most popular statues accentuated this celebration of expansionism. *The End of the Trail* and *The American Pioneer* each provided important visual symbols to Californians intent on writing their own history. *The End of the Trail* went on to become an icon, but its pair-

Fig. 12. *The End of the Trail* by James Earle Fraser. (Donald G. Larson Collection, Special Collections Research Center, California State University, Fresno.)

ing at the PPIE with *The American Pioneer* emphasized the racial over-tones of the statue.[33] James Earle Fraser's *The End of the Trail* depicted an Indian man slumped forward on the back of an exhausted pony. According to the exposition's *Blue Book*, "The drooping storm-beaten figure of the Indian on the spent pony symbolizes the end of the race which was once a mighty people."[34] Solon Borglum's *The American Pioneer* showed an old frontiersman wielding an ax and rifle on the back of a prancing horse. The *Blue Book* informed readers that the man "muse[d] on past

Fig. 13. *The American Pioneer* by Solon Borglum. (San Francisco
History Center, San Francisco Public Library.)

days of hardship, when these implements and the log hut and stockade
dimly indicated on the buffalo robe which forms his saddle housing,
were his aids in subjugation of the wilderness."[35]

Together these statues celebrated the ascendance of Anglo men in
California and evoked the power of the pioneer myth in San Francisco.
While Fraser's Indian leaned over his pony, defeated, utterly fatigued,

and held his spear pointed down toward the earth, the pioneer, although past his glory days, was still able to look back at his weapons and wield them with youthful vigor. These two statues fit logically into a historical narrative of the West that was influenced by social Darwinism and contemporary rhetoric about the "vanishing Indian." The frontier was closed—both the census of 1890 and historian Frederick Jackson Turner had made that clear—so the days of both the Indian and the pioneer were finished. Yet as the pioneer had succeeded in his mission, he was able to reminisce in peace while the Indian fought to stay astride his tired steed.

A children's book published in 1915 chronicling one family's visit to the fair reveals the power of the two statues to convey their message about race and progress: "We saw just how tired both man and horse were and felt sorry for them. We asked Father why they had come so far to get themselves exhausted like that, and he again told us something of symbolism. The statue is intended to represent the redman, and denotes that the race is vanishing, and is supposed to be studied in connection with the 'Pioneer.' . . . That is meant to say that the white race will take up the work of progress and carry it on."[36]

It is no surprise that fair directors welcomed *The American Pioneer* to the fairgrounds since San Franciscans still clung to the image of the pioneer as their link to their Gold Rush past and the city's founding.[37] The Gold Rush played the primary role in the narrative of the city's development. City residents embraced memories of the rough and tumble Gold Rush days, when prospectors set out for the gold fields from the city and clever merchants set up shop to outfit miners and made large fortunes in the business. These statues reemphasized the deep connections between the city of San Francisco and the racialized mythology of the exposition.

Nowhere were the mythic pioneer and his companions more heartily celebrated than in the Court of the Universe. There, two huge sculptural groups, *Nations of the East* and *Nations of the West*, visually represented the fair's joining of the East and West. Both groups contained stereotypical representations of their subjects, particularly of women, but closer examination reveals they were more nuanced than they first appeared. The *Nations of the East* depicted an "Indian prince on the ornamented seat and the Spirit of the East in the howdah, of his elephant, an Arab sheik on his Arabian horse, a negro slave bearing fruit on his head, an Egyptian on a camel carrying a Mohammedan standard, an Arab falconer with a bird, a Buddhist priest, or Lama, from Thibet, bearing his symbol of authority, a Mohammedan with his crescent, a second negro slave and a Mongolian on horseback."[38] As one art critic noted, this composition "breathed the spirit of Oriental life wherever found."[39] The *Nations of the West* comprised a French-Canadian trapper, an Alaskan woman, a Latin American, a German and an Italian on either side of a pair of oxen, an Anglo on horseback, an "American squaw" with a papoose, and an Indian man on horseback. *Mother of Tomorrow*, depicting a pioneer woman leading a prairie schooner, appeared at the center of the group. The *Heroes of Tomorrow*, featuring two young boys, one white and one black, stood above her and beneath the crowning depiction of the spirit of *Enterprise*. Given that the two groups literally towered above the heads of exposition goers, it is difficult to know what fairgoers made of them or how closely they were able to examine the finely detailed figures. Did they perceive the *Nations of the East* as examples of "exotic but primitive peoples," as Elizabeth Armstrong has claimed, or did they simply admire them as one more Asian element of this Pacific exposition?[40]

The *Nations of the West* offered a more complicated picture of westward expansion than did *The End of the Trail* or *The American Pioneer*. One official guidebook told visitors that the group was designed to depict the "types of those colonizing nations that have at one time or place or other left their stamp on our country."[41] The three native figures—one Alaskan and two Indians—were portrayed as weighed down with labor and care, but their very presence in the composition wrote them into the story of the West and acknowledged their contributions to American life. The *Mother of Tomorrow* limited women to a reproductive role, but it acknowledged women's place in the move west and expanded the story beyond the solitary male pioneer. The most interesting figures, however, were the *Heroes of Tomorrow*. Here, Calder chose to depict a white child and a black child holding hands and to label them both "heroes," suggesting they represented hope for the future. Was this piece an interracial vision of harmony? At least one African American contemporary writer chose to interpret them this way. Freeman Henry Murray Mor-

Fig. 14. *Nations of the East.* (*Souvenir Views of the Panama-Pacific International Exposition.* San Francisco, 1915.)

Fig. 15. *Nations of the West.* (*Souvenir Views of the Panama-Pacific International Exposition.* San Francisco, 1915.)

ris argued that the *Heroes of Tomorrow*, which was also called *Hopes of the Future*, represented a hopeful vision of racial harmony. He went on to argue that the two "Negro servitors" in the *Nations of the East* were no more servants than were the German and Italian figures "attendants" to the oxen. Whether viewers shared this view is unknown, but Morris's argument makes clear both the malleability of the interpretation of these artworks and the progressive nature of Calder's artistic vision.[42]

The *Mother of Tomorrow* found a compatriot on the grounds thanks to the PPIE Woman's Board, whose widely praised *Pioneer Mother* statue commemorated the female role in westward expansion. The debates surrounding this statue reveal the presence of a gendered agenda on the fairgrounds and offer a glimpse into the polarizing nature of the fair. The statue also demonstrates the ways in which the fair offered multiple official messages about U.S. society and the world. The Woman's Board deliberately inserted itself into the fair's official narrative by erecting a statue that filled a perceived void in the fair's official historical narrative.

In 1913 Ella Sterling Mighels suggested the idea for a tribute to the pioneer mother, and to mothers in general, to John E. D. Trask, director of the PPIE Department of Fine Arts. Mighels, a conservative proponent of what scholars have termed "maternalism," had long worked for an appropriate memorial to the work of pioneer mothers. Brenda Frink argues that Mighels was motivated by a desire to "promote white women's traditional moral influence over middle-class men, to argue against both labor unrest and Asian immigration, and to inculcate old-fashioned pioneer morality among urban children."[43] Mighels's goals were soon subsumed by those of the PPIE Woman's Board, to whom Trask brought the idea. The board found the idea "irresistible," despite worries about raising funds in a state already beset with pleas from the PPIE for support. The board quickly organized the Pioneer Mother Monument Association to solicit donations from women across the state.[44]

The association promised that the monument would commemorate "the Pioneer Mothers of the West—the self-sacrificing women, with their little ones at their side, who braved the dangers and underwent the hardships and privations ... [of] pioneer life."[45] Supporter Anna Morrison Reed, a newspaper editor in Ukiah, California, reminded readers that these women "gave, during the hardships of the early days, the comfort and the refining touch to their rough surroundings, and turned the camps of men into the homes of the early Pioneers. . . . Many died along the way, . . . martyrs to their duty to their families."[46] This emphasis on the noble sacrifice of pioneer mothers permeated the campaign.

The goal of the Woman's Board of constructing its own vision of California history struck a chord with fellow Californians. Pioneer heritage groups and individual donors contributed extensively.[47] Governor Hiram Johnson even declared October 24, 1914, "Mother Monument Day" in an effort to raise funds. Striking support came from schoolchildren. Because "there was a sincere desire [on the part of organizers] that the monument should represent the little given by many so that its significance should not be lost," President of the Woman's Board Helen Sanborn arranged with the state schools' superintendent to involve children in the fundraising effort. Children contributed their pennies to a total of $1,362.02, an amount estimated to represent 136,000 children.[48]

A conflict soon arose between the board and sculptor Charles Grafly that revealed the class and race assumptions underlying the monument effort. Grafly's original design featured a woman wearing buckskins, sheltering two nude children. Mighels hated the statue, as did the editor of the *San Francisco Call*, who noted the pioneer mother must be "a figure of strength, of dignity, but worn by hardship and courage, and with that fine beauty which comes with self-sacrifice, devotion, maternity and love."[49] A primitive mother who wore skins evoked the ideal of primitive womanhood against which these white women were actively constructing themselves and not the vision of "American womanhood" that they wished to convey. Mighels rallied the women of the Native Daughters of the Golden West to protest Grafly's design, and the Woman's Board summoned him to San Francisco. The conflict continued after he refused to clothe the children. The Woman's Board and Grafly volleyed back and forth over the issue until they reached a solution that left the children unclad but slightly less visible in the composition.[50] Woman's Board historian Anna Pratt Simpson noted that the solution was solved once Grafly realized "the original idea of the universal mother."[51] Apparently, the women of the board were able to tolerate nude children as long as their mother appeared to be a white, middle-class American rather than a skin-clad primitive woman of indeterminate race and class status.

Fig. 16. *Pioneer Mother.* (*Souvenir Views of the Panama-Pacific International Exposition.* San Francisco, 1915.)

The finished statue depicts a mother with two small children in front of her. The mother wears a small sunbonnet, a homespun dress, and a short cape around her shoulders. Arms outstretched, she holds the hand of her small daughter. The son echoes his mother's gesture, wrapping his other arm around his sister. Both children are nude and appear to be walking forward with their mother, whose rough boot peeks out from beneath her skirt. The woman memorialized in this statue is clearly marked as white rather than as native or Californio. By defining her as the *Pioneer Mother* the Woman's Board erased the experiences of the many other women who lived in California at the same time. By calling for a monument of a white pioneer mother to stand for "Motherhood, the Womanhood of the nation," the Woman's Board asserted in strong terms the link between white women, civilization, and nation building. The pioneer mother was the mother of the nation, according to this formulation, a position that vested in white, middle-class women the power to turn a rough men's camp into a home and a state, ready for inclusion in the national polity. White, middle-class mothers became absolutely essential to the creation of civilization.

The *Pioneer Mother* stood in a prominent location near the Palace of Fine Arts. It stimulated a great deal of local interest and debate, suggesting the power of the image for many Californians. Some, like Mighels, continued to oppose the final version, preferring instead a romanticized, sentimentalized portrait of a refined, middle-class matron rather than the more realistic image of a woman in homespun and half-soled shoes. Such an image suggested the primitive rather than the civilized, and boosters of the statue did not want to imagine their mothers or grandmothers as primitive. Frink also suggests that the statue's secularism and nudity fell far short of Mighels's vision of women as a moralizing and Christianizing force.[52]

Other fairgoers commented positively on *Pioneer Mother*, confirming that the Woman's Board's efforts to centralize motherhood within their vision of womanhood and California history had struck a nerve. Laura Ingalls Wilder, later the famed children's author of the *Little House on the Prairie* books, spent the summer with her daughter, Rose Wilder Lane, in San Francisco and wrote home to her husband about *Pioneer Mother*, noting, "It is wonderful and so true in detail."[53] Through the campaign for *Pioneer Mother*, the members of the Woman's Board staked out a space— one that was visual, three-dimensional, and rhetorical—for a vision of white womanhood in which women were absolutely essential to westward expansion. In a fair that celebrated the conquest of California and America's position as an imperial power, this claim was a powerful one.

Visitors to the fair encountered another visual link between whiteness, womanhood, and California history in the official California State

Building, which the PPIE Woman's Board ran. Architects designed it in the style of the California missions, complete with a reproduction of the Santa Barbara Mission's "Forbidden Garden."[54] There, the group of elite Bay Area women held *dansants* (afternoon dances) for invited guests and hosted dinners and receptions for visiting dignitaries from around the nation and the world. Their position in the California Building complemented the message of the *Pioneer Mother*. The design's visual link to the white (in this case Spanish) conquest of California affirmed the board members' relative position to the nonwhite peoples of the fair. As the official protectors and hostesses of women on the grounds, the members of the Woman's Board appeared at the fair as models of propriety and decorum, with their staid portraits often reproduced in fair publicity.[55]

The PPIE Woman's Board officially worked to improve the reputation of both California and San Francisco rather than address issues of women's status or rights. These actions somewhat aligned their mission with that of the exposition board. Simpson's history of the Woman's Board noted that the "Board . . . saw that, unlike other expositions, the one to be held in San Francisco vivified a great issue and was not commemorative of century-old happenings, and that it would mean responsibilities in the years to come that should be borne in part by the women, if the State received the greatest possible benefit." These responsibilities included readying the state for the "tide of immigration" expected after the opening of the canal and addressing "the serious problems [that] could arise with greatly increased travel"—that is, undertaking extensive protective measures for young people and those traveling alone.[56] The board perceived helping immigrants and protecting young people as integrally connected. If the fair and the city appeared to be morally suspect and dangerous to travelers, then settlers would be wary of making the long journey to California. Where the women of the board differed from their male counterparts was in their belief that moral protective work was essential to furthering the reputation of their city and state. They worked to bring attention to specific issues that threatened the success of the exposition.

The board involved women throughout the state in their efforts by creating a State Auxiliary, which raised funds for the fair and advertised the bounty and beauty of California to visitors. County groups, which

Fig. 17. Mrs. Phoebe Hearst speaking at the ground-breaking for the California Building, May 7, 1914. (San Francisco History Center, San Francisco Public Library.)

swelled to a membership of more than fifteen thousand by 1915, publicized the fair in their home counties and kept the California Building running smoothly throughout the fair. Their role, however, was far more than simply that of raising funds. According to an early outline of the plan for county auxiliaries, the local groups would be responsible not only for supporting efforts surrounding the fair but also in preparing their home counties for the "visitors and prospective settlers who will be looking over the state with a view to securing congenial homes and profitable locations." Women serving as county chairmen were also charged with finding capable women who could serve on juries for determining fair awards and with cooperating with local county exposition commissioners, chambers of commerce, and county supervisors in order to "exploit [sic] . . . their county resources and to further the work of adequate display at the exposition."[57]

Celebrating the success of the white pioneer and his helpmate, the pioneer mother, and emphasizing the bounty and fertility of California's countryside fit into boosters' plans for the PPIE. Publicists created idealized visions of both California and San Francisco to draw businesses, tourists, and settlers to the state. The opening of the Panama Canal would make it easier for European immigrants to reach California, so publicists emphasized the state's ties to Europe. Despite the fair's Pacific theme, fair publicists were careful not to imply that California was a part of this non-white Pacific world. San Francisco offered businessmen both a taste of the goods of Asia and an entrée to Asian markets, but the city and state itself, the PPIE proclaimed, were safely "white." Publicity linked California to Europe, not Asia, and envisioned a state populated with Europeans rather than Asians, Latin Americans, or native peoples. As one pamphlet described "California the Hostess": "Take the sunniest parts of sunny Italy and Spain and the South of France with their wealth of vineyards and orchards; . . . place here and there the more beautiful bits of the French and Italian Rivieras with their wooded slopes and silvery beaches, joyous crowds, and gay life; bound this collection on one side by the earth's longest mountain range and on the other by the largest ocean, and cover with a canopy of turquoise blue sky and brilliant sunshine and you have a picture that yet falls short of—CALIFORNIA THE GOLDEN."[58] Comparing California to the nations of western Europe continued the fair's privileging of European culture and defined a host of other peoples as outside the bounds of the white race.[59] Emphasizing California's similarity to Europe reassured potential visitors who feared the state was simply too far away—or too full of Asians and other nonwhites—to be "civilized."[60]

Celebrations of California communities held during the fair visually and rhetorically linked whiteness, gender, and California society for visitors. During each county's "special day" at the fair, representatives showed off their home counties' unique products and features in an extended advertisement for the bounty and beauty of the state. Most, if not all, of these celebrations (as well as the celebrations of other states and cities) included the participation of young, attractive white women who showed off the produce of the county in question. Local newspapers prominently displayed pictures of these women alongside reports on the events. The *San Francisco Chronicle*'s report on Orange County Day described the "orange girls wearing orange ribbons in their hair and tossing oranges by the armful to the crowd." Alongside the story appeared the picture of "Miss Freda Sander, one of the pretty orange girls distributing oranges from Orange County yesterday at the exposition." Her face and upper body appeared superimposed on a gigantic orange, as if to emphasize the link between oranges and youthful beauty.[61] These women represented California's fecundity, and their beauty advertised the state's natural bounty and plenty. Using young white women to represent the state's fertility served as one way to reassure potential settlers that the future of the state lay with its white inhabitants.

The PPIE's narrative of the American conquest of the West led seamlessly into a celebration of the opportunities the Panama Canal would bring to California and the nation. Late nineteenth-century and early twentieth-century advocates of American imperialism believed that American westward expansion laid the groundwork for U.S. expansion abroad. The fair highlighted California's connections to both Latin America and the Pacific, reflecting the nation's growing role on the world stage and its political and economic interests abroad. The 1904 Roosevelt Corollary justified U.S. involvement in Latin America, and in 1915, U.S. troops occupied the nation of Haiti in one of the many resulting military interventions. Meanwhile, makers of foreign policy closely watched the ongoing Mexican Revolution, where the United States had intervened the year before by occupying the port of Veracruz. In the Pacific, the question of Philippine independence continued to fester, as Filipinos demanded it and U.S. lawmakers discussed its possibility in Congress. The 1911–12 Chinese Revolution had offered American missionaries and businessmen new opportunities to push for American influence in Asia. The PPIE explicitly highlighted U.S. involvement in the Pacific and Caribbean by emphasizing the economic possibilities that the completion of the Panama Canal offered and by glorifying the virility of the pioneer male who had conquered California and the West.

To make these claims real, fair directors introduced visitors to a Pacific and Latin American world intertwined with U.S. interests. First, they solicited the involvement of foreign nations. The federal government appointed official commissions to travel to Europe, Asia, and Latin America and to make official diplomatic overtures to the governments of as many nations as possible. PPIE officials used informal forms of diplomacy as well, drawing on information and support from U.S. businessmen and foreign residents of the Bay Area. When visiting commissioners came to San Francisco, the PPIE spared no expense on wining and dining them in an attempt to convince them to commit to participating in the fair. Although the war in Europe prevented the participation of many European nations, a substantial number of nations and colonies from the rest of the world showed up in San Francisco. From the Pacific Rim, Japan, China, Siam, Australia, the Philippines, Hawai'i, and New Zealand sent official commissions, and amusement attractions featuring Hawaiians, Maoris, and Samoans greeted fair visitors. Latin American nations, including Argentina, Cuba, Honduras, Guatemala, and Bolivia, also participated.

Boosters believed that the opening of the Panama Canal would stimulate trade with both Asia and the Americas. Pre-fair discussions and publicity emphasized the opening of Asian markets. Boosters also sang the praises of increased hemispheric cooperation. When the California Development Board and the PPIE directors feted U.S. secretary of state Philander Knox at a 1912 dinner, he told San Franciscans of the benefits of "opening the Isthmian golden gate for the material and profitable interchange of all the communities of the three Americas."[62] Moreover, he assured them, "the function of the canal in promoting the good mutual relations of different communities is hardly to be exaggerated."[63] Such rhetoric permeated internal exposition reports about the nations of the Americas. The official South American PPIE Commission noted upon its return, "The opportunities for investors and colonists [in Latin America] are numerous . . . the colonist or investor who has a knowledge of his requirements can be suited in the various countries of South America."[64] Canal and fair boosters promised that huge swaths of Latin America would now be more easily accessible for both Americans and Europeans and that San Franciscans and Californians need only seize the moment to profit.[65] Local residents similarly hoped for an increase in economic and social exchanges between Latin America and San Francisco. In 1914, Oscar Galeno and J. J. Martin launched a new biweekly newspaper, *Las Americas*, in San Francisco with the goal of reporting on the "commercial and social relations" within the Americas and with the Philippines, which they perceived as essential to the economic future of the United States.[66]

Scholars have largely ignored the Pan-American nature of the PPIE since San Diego's Panama-California Exposition more strongly emphasized the state's ties to Latin America. Nonetheless, other American nations staged impressive presences at the fair, and ideas of Pan-Americanism and hemispheric unity lurked beneath the surface of the fair. Robert Gonzalez details the elements of Pan-Americanism, or "hemispherism," as it emerged at earlier fairs: "Hemisphericism was denoted in three ways: through the selective participation of nations; through the careful selection of the contents displayed at each fair; and with the invocation of hemispheric themes of a common Pan-American heritage explored in the fairs' architecture, propaganda, and events."[67] Although the hemispherism of the PPIE was more limited than that of the 1901 Pan-American Exposition held in Buffalo, New York, for instance, the active interest and participation of Latin American nations in the PPIE and the emphasis on a shared Spanish past made the fair a Pan-American event.

For those already interested in Pan-American affairs, the PPIE offered a significant opportunity to strengthen ties among the nations of the Western Hemisphere. The visits of Latin American dignitaries to San Francisco allowed for informal strengthening of diplomatic relations between the United States and various nations. When Brazilian foreign minister Lauro Müller toured the United States in 1913, John Barrett, the head of the Pan American Union, reminded fair officials that his stop in San Francisco would be "one of the most important events in the history of Pan American relations."[68] Brazil failed to erect a building at the fair because of financial exigencies after the outbreak of war, but in the pre-fair years its representatives received much attention from fair officials. When Latin American officials spoke publicly on these visits, they usually emphasized their desire for progress, in keeping with the fair's themes of progress and civilization. A Dominican representative noted at his nation's site dedication that he and his nation hoped "we may not be left behind in that westward race by which Civilization, arrayed with Steam and Electricity, and with Law and Justice, goes on and on, opening seas, laying out rails, immersing cables, . . . cleaving continents, in order that all shadows shall disappear."[69]

The PPIE occurred at a time when the relationship between the United States and Latin America was in flux. Barrett and many Latin Americans were pushing for a multilateral relationship between the United States and Latin America that would downplay the Monroe Doctrine and create an equal political relationship among all of the nations of the region.[70] The official rhetoric of the PPIE, however, reiterated the relationship first set out in 1823 in the Monroe Doctrine and more recently reaffirmed in the Roosevelt Corollary. Upon the dedication of the Honduras Building, for instance, Michael H. de Young presented an honorary bronze plaque to the Honduras Commission, noting, "We, as the big brother—the great republic—look on every republic on this hemisphere as part of us, and we congratulate ourselves that the power and strength of the people has risen in every section of our hemisphere until all are republics."[71] Some canny Latin American representatives echoed these sentiments, praising the U.S. role in the region. On Cuba's dedication day Gen. Enrico Loynaz del Castillo, a hero of the Cuban war for independence, praised the role the United States had played on the island, noting that "a government, powerful like this of yours . . . must be forever the guardian of Cuban emancipation."[72] Such sentiments are hardly surprising given the context. The exposition was held in the United States, and it was pro forma for visiting dignitaries to praise the host nation. Moreover, the celebration of the Panama Canal necessitated recognition of the U.S. role in the region, and any respectable diplomat would make the correct statements about his nation's gratitude for this momentous achievement.

These public statements by both U.S. and Latin American officials suggest that the fair presented a portrait of U.S.–Latin American relations that echoed the U.S. government's official diplomatic position on Latin America. The United States was the protector of the region and would act as a policeman when necessary. The fair's focus on the economic possibilities that the canal offered added further nuance to this vision, as both Latin American and U.S. representatives stressed the enormous economic opportunities that Latin American nations presented. Other commentators emphasized the opportunity that the Panama Canal would afford for immigration, not only to the U.S. Pacific coast, but also to the nations of Latin America. Barrett noted in a 1915 publication promoting the fair that the canal would allow much easier access to the Pacific coast of Latin America, where he hoped both Europeans and Americans would settle after the war.[73]

But the nations of Latin America had their own goals for the fair, and they did not always mesh with those of the United States. Every nation

Fig. 18. The Argentine exhibit in the Palace of Education and Social Economy was among many foreign exhibits designed to show off the progress of the exhibiting nations. (San Francisco History Center, San Francisco Public Library.)

emphasized their economic possibilities. Honduras and Guatemala, for instance, each displayed their many natural resources—coffee, sugar, bananas, tobacco, coffee, and so on—as well as their recent history of "ordered, progressive government."[74] Political and economic instability in many nineteenth-century Latin American nations had made it difficult for them to gain foreign investors. As the region entered the twentieth century and political conflicts between Liberals and Conservatives lessened and presidents held office for somewhat longer terms, they began to look north and east for investors. Participation in the PPIE was a part of their strategy to attract foreign investment and to stimulate their economies, and painting a picture of their nations as politically stable and rich with natural resources helped them achieve that goal.

Although these nations presented themselves within a framework that envisioned them as junior partners to the United States, chinks in that picture emerged. Argentina built one of the most impressive palaces at the fair and spent hundreds of thousands of dollars presenting itself as a progressive, modern nation. Frank Morton Todd, official fair historian, noted, "The lesson was borne in upon the beholder that he would have to throw away the old teachings . . . and instead of thinking of Argentina as a land of vast undeveloped natural resources, begin to think of it as a country with her feet set upon the highway of the world's best progress; her capital . . . the abode of wealth and culture . . . her government scientifically administrated."[75] Another visitor noted that the building had a "fine library . . . and much information regarding commerce of the country, showing it to be most progressive."[76]

Fair visitors who picked up the official souvenir books available at the Argentina Building received concrete examples of Argentina's modernity and progress. The pamphlet began by likening Argentina to the United States, with similar histories of conquest and warfare leading to a liberal and just state. But the author soon offered substantive critiques of U.S. policy.[77] In Argentina, for instance, no immigrant faced limitations on property ownership or employment opportunities. Overall, Argentina had "fewer limitations" on foreign residents than the United States did, the author noted, suggesting a clear comparison to the latter's discriminatory policy toward Asian immigrants.[78] Since Argentina's neighbor Brazil began actively recruiting Japanese immigrants in 1908, after the United States had banned the entry of Japanese laborers, Argentina may also have been attempting to recruit Asian immigrants. An exhibit in the building about the "Immigrant Hotel" in which immigrants were housed while waiting processing also emphasized the nation's welcoming attitude toward all immigrants, one that stood in direct contrast to the increasing anti-immigrant agitation brewing in the United States.[79]

The pamphlet also emphasized Argentina's growing international political power. One of the nation's recent achievements, the author related, was the adoption of a new international agreement regarding the collection of national debts owed to foreigners. Long an issue between Latin American governments and the European powers, the 1902 doctrine adopted at The Hague in 1907 stated that foreign powers could no longer use armed forces (usually warships) to gain repayment of debts. The choice to discuss this issue in the souvenir publication indicates Argentina's desire to be seen as a world power able to make its own diplomatic decisions and policy.[80] The publication's author offered even stronger criticism of U.S. economic policies in its discussion of Argentina's enormous economic potential. High tariffs and insufficient steamship lines badly hindered U.S. trade with Argentina, suggested the author. Now, however, the time had come to make Argentina's commercial relations with the United States "more reciprocal."[81]

In the foreign pavilions, visitors encountered visions of nations carefully crafted by their commissions and not by fair officials. From Cuba to Honduras to Argentina, visitors saw both examples of the rich and varied natural resources of the Americas and concrete evidence of each nation's moves toward modernity and progress as defined by the Western powers. Cuba's building emphasized, not surprisingly, links between the United States and Cuba and the favorable influence of the U.S. occupation on the island's progress, particularly in terms of education. As one visitor remembered, the building "made much of public schools showing increase in attendance."[82] Guatemala and Honduras emphasized their political stability and developing education systems, as well as the many opportunities awaiting investors and immigrants.

The displays of territories tied to the United States wholeheartedly celebrated U.S. expansionism and asserted San Francisco as an entrée to that world. The Philippines Building featured examples of the U.S.-implemented education system on the islands and of the progress made under U.S. rule. One guide noted, "The progress of the inhabitants since their [Philippines] acquisition by our government is one of the most interesting studies in this building."[83] Young Doris Barr pasted into her diary an excerpt from a guidebook that described the Philippine portion of the U.S. government's exhibit in the Palace of Liberal Arts. The display showed a group of people, presumably a family, inside a hut and wearing loincloths and skins. One young boy holds a parrot in his hand while his father wields what appears to be a spear. The overall impression was one of stereotypical "primitiveness." The caption reads: "Here are shown, in excellently made lifelike figures, some of our wards in the Philippine Islands. These are some of the people for whom self-government is proposed."[84]

Some exhibits juxtaposed the "primitive" with the "civilized" in an effort to demonstrate progress to viewers. Laura Foote Bruml's record of her visit to the Philippines Building noted the many improvements made to the islands since the Americans took possession of them. Juxtaposed with these "improvements in roadways, bridges, buildings, and locomotion" were "horrid knives, swords, cleavers, etc., which had seen use by wild tribes." Finally, she praised the "intelligent Phillipino [sic] exhibitors who say the new generation will make it a wonderful country."[85] About the Philippine school exhibit in the Palace of Education and Social Economy, she noted, "Phillipines [sic] are temperate people and have made wonderful advancements in civilization."[86] Laura Ingalls Wilder observed that in the New Zealand display, she and Rose saw "the ugly native islanders that used to be the cannibal tribes in Australia and New Zealand."[87] Both Bruml's and Wilder's perceptions of the exhibits reveal a contrast of "primitive" and "modern," of "horrid knives" and "ugly native islanders" with "improvements" and "wonderful advancements," that provide the subtext of a clear imperialist project.

Zone concessions featuring peoples of the Pacific also contributed to this juxtaposition of primitive and civilized cultures. Thirty-odd villagers from American Samoa lived from February to September 1915 in the Samoan Village, and a group of Maori lived in the Australasian Village until August. These men and women lived their lives in full public view. A young Samoan man and woman married in an event used to advertise the concession, and a prominent member of the group died, forcing the attraction to close for three days. These Samoan men and women wore clothes, performed work, and lived in homes that accentuated their difference from modern life. Although Chinese, Japanese, Filipinos, and Hawaiians all at times appeared on the grounds and in the papers dressed in Western-style clothes, working and performing activities that were part and parcel of Western culture, the Samoan and Maori performers of the Joy Zone appeared perpetually different, demonstrating their supposed uncivilized status. Local papers printed photos of the Samoan women wearing skimpy clothing or even bare breasted. During their days on the Zone they paddled canoes on a man-made lake, manufactured traditional crafts and handiwork, and danced for visitors. Samoa had no official presence at the fair beyond this concession. As had the displays of Filipinos at previous fairs, no voice offered any variation on this display of Samoan life that was seemingly designed to accentuate the "primitive" nature of native Samoans.

Likewise, the Maori residents of the Australasian Village were presented to visitors as embodiments of exotic others who were still in need of the guiding hand of a civilizing nation. Advertising for the Zone noted the presence of "Maori belles and native warriors," emphasizing their supposed warlike culture.[88] In the first few months of the fair the Daily Program included an ad for the village that suggested its nature: "Australasian Village. New Zealand Maori Carved Village. British Government's Collection of Maori Carved Houses. A Real World's Fair Attraction. Native Dancing. War Haka. Poi Dances. Native Games."[89] As with so many of the ethnic villages of other fairs, the Australasian Village offered little nuance; instead, it portrayed the Maori as exotic, primitive others whose lives were reduced, according to the ad, to war dances and games. The concession lasted until August, when it finally proved unprofitable and the attraction folded.

Visitors' responses to these and other native villages on the Zone demonstrated not only an appreciation of the unfamiliar but also an even stronger sense of the ultimate foreignness of the people therein. After watching a performance of the Samoan Island dancers, Wilder wrote to her husband: "The girls danced by themselves, the girls and men danced together, and the men alone danced the dance of the headhunters with long, ugly knives." Although she praised the dance, noting that "they were very graceful and I did enjoy every bit of it," her final remark about their being "covered with tattooing from the waist to the knees" demonstrated her overall impression that they were an exotic people.[90] Both Wilder and Bruml remarked on the bodies of those on display, revealing the importance of the body in creating this viewing experience. As Jane Desmond has noted in her work on cultural and animal tourism in Hawai'i, this sort of tourism "rests on the physical display of bodies perceived as fundamentally, radically different from those of the majority of the audience who pays to see them."[91]

Bodies and physical appearance played a key role in conveying these messages about primitive and civilized to fair visitors. Fair publicity and newspaper reporting continually commented on the physical appearance of Zone performers, particularly of the women. Articles and publicity often stereotyped Chinese and Japanese women, describing them as "dainty" or "exotic" or "doll-like." Stories reported on their dresses, their hair, and their appearance, reducing them to their physical attributes. Samoan and Maori women were depicted as primitive and backward, with descriptions commenting on their lack of clothing and "odd" habits. Pages on the "South Seas Villages" and on Japan from the magazine section of the *San Francisco Examiner* each prominently featured women dressed in native costume. According to the report on the Hawaiian Village on the Zone, the "native Hawaiian girls are famous for their dusky beauty and grace."[92] Although the smaller report on the Samoan village featured photographs of both men and women in native costume, the description focused on the traditional crafts performed by Samoan women, implying that the women were the true culture bearers. A similar piece on Japan at the exposition included "pretty native women" as key attractions of the Japan Beautiful concession, alongside "landscape, trees, plants and flowers."[93]

Such reporting was typical of publicity that highlighted the physical appearance of the women of color who worked on the Zone. Sometimes its tone was in praise and sometimes in disdain, but it always made an effort to distinguish between these women and the perceived normative white audience. When local feature columnist Helen Dare dedicated a column to the question of "feminine fashion on the Zone," she began by juxtaposing the "Occident" and the "Orient," followed by the words "the civilized and the—er—otherwise." Her description of the clothing of the women of the Zone—Hawaiian, Samoan, Maori, and others—highlighted the visible differences between them and those she perceived as her audience.[94] An article on the competition for the queen of the "nine years after [the 1906 earthquake] ball," in which the women of the Zone competed for the aforesaid honor pointed to the difference and otherness of the contestants. The judge "cannot decide whether the queen . . . should wear a ring in her nose or display a tattooed back."[95] The racialization of these Zone performers reinforced the fair's emphasis on racial hierarchy and social Darwinism. These women existed, in this formulation, to represent the supposedly authentic traditions of their homelands to fair visitors and to delineate the differences between the exotic or primitive and civilized culture.

Other exhibits across the grounds asserted the progress and superiority of mainstream white American culture. The Race Betterment Booth

Fig. 19. *The Blue Book* promised visitors they would see many
"types of lovely women on the Zone." (*The Blue Book.*)

drew visitors into the Palace of Education and Social Economy, promising visitors that the movement would "create a new and superior race through personal and public hygiene."[96] The booth showcased examples of successful attempts at selective breeding of plants and animals with the suggestion that such strategies be implemented with humans as well.[97] The Race Betterment Congress, held during the month of August, focused on the problem of eugenics and drew extensive attention from the press. Another exhibit in the Palace of Education included newly developed IQ tests, informing visitors that scientists could now accurately measure intelligence.[98] Films featuring the "flood" of recent immigrants to Ellis Island also implied the need to restrict immigration. Together, these exhibits bolstered support for policies designed to weed out those deemed undesirable—usually nonwhites—and to restrict economic and social opportunities to those deemed fit, usually white northern Europeans. They also reified popular attitudes that American society must exemplify a kind of progress that included the uplifting of supposed lower societies.[99]

The narrative of the PPIE conveyed by publicity, rhetoric, statuary, artwork, and Zone attractions emphasized the dominance of white Americans over nonwhites and that of the United States over the Pacific Rim and Latin America. Yet, the multiplicity of official voices—from the Woman's Board to the governments of foreign nations to territorial officials—meant that this narrative contained considerably more nuance than previous examinations of the fair have revealed. The appearance and performance of young Hawaiian women in the celebration of the Night in Hawaii both validated and subverted the racial messages of the fair. A closer look at the participation of Hawai'i at the fair reveals that the fair's official messages about race, gender, and colonialism proved difficult to maintain.

The fair made explicit U.S. claims over its Pacific territories. Haole officials seized the opportunity during the fair to advertise the islands. Historically, white Americans stereotyped native Hawaiians as docile and exotic rather than threatening and savage, allowing tourist promoters to create the trappings of Hawaiian tourism that we know today: pineapples, hula dances, leis, and beach scenes. At the PPIE, the Hawaiian territorial government erected a Hawaiian Building located directly across from the California Building on the northern edge of the grounds. A consortium of Hawaiian pineapple-packing companies funded a large Hawaiian garden and teahouse in the Palace of Horticulture, where visitors sipped pineapple juice and listened to ukulele music. Native Hawaiians had appeared solely on the midway at earlier fairs; however, at the PPIE, Native Hawaiians performed as part of the state's official representatives.[100] Young Hawaiian women served juice and sang to delighted visitors in the Hawaiian gardens, and young Hawaiian men played the ukulele (which became a national fad after the PPIE) in both venues. Meanwhile, on the Zone, entrepreneurs staged a large Hawaiian Village that featured alleged authentic hula dancing.

This dual depiction of Hawai'i, in both the civilized Hawaiian Building and in an attraction in the primitive Zone, suggests the liminal place of Hawai'i in the U.S. mind and soon erupted in controversy. A. P. Taylor, the enraged director of the Hawaii Promotion Committee, accused the concessionaire of the Zone's Hawaiian Village of charging visitors to watch a "vulgar" and "rotten" version of the controversial hula dance.[101]

American missionaries had long attacked the hula as immoral. By 1915, however, the hula had become accepted as a visible marker of Hawaiian culture that tourism promoters used to promote tourism to the islands. But the vestige of the debate over the hula remained. Taylor and other haole officials wanted to appropriate the hula as an advertising tactic, as they had with the pineapple and the ukulele. But female sexuality was not so easy to contain on the grounds of the fair.

Territorial officials wanted to prove that Hawai'i was a modern place, where the hula and native Hawaiians were safely tamed. The Zone attraction threatened that goal. Taylor told Moore, "Hawaii is not in the category of the remote South Seas, but it is as up to date and modern almost as San Francisco."[102] His subsequent offhand comment that the few Native Hawaiians involved with the show had quit suggests that they too found the hula performance offensive, although probably for different reasons. Clearly, haoles hoped to use the fair to advertise a modern yet safely exotic tourist destination, unsullied by accusations of immorality, but the desire of mainland Americans to consume the supposedly exotic, morally questionable image of Hawai'i challenged this goal. PPIE officials agreed to close the attraction, at least temporarily, recognizing the right of haoles to determine the way their home was represented at the fair.

Hawaiian women appeared at the fair as embodiments of the territory's sanitized and romanticized history and as the key to the haole boosters' campaign to bring tourism to the islands. Like many women at the fair, they acted as culture bearers both on the Zone and in the official Hawaiian displays. Yet the presence of these young mixed-race women challenged the fair's racial hierarchy and its larger emphasis on eugenics and race betterment. Whether or not haole organizers intended it, the vision they created of a modern, racially mixed Hawai'i unsettled the fair's race and gender hierarchy. These young women were neither pioneer mothers nor eugenic mothers of tomorrow. When young, racially mixed Hawaiian women appeared in Hawaiian celebrations in a stylish shirtwaist and skirt rather than in attire typically associated with the hula, they implicitly challenged the ideals of "scientific marriage" espoused by the supporters of racial betterment. Their identities were not disguised. On the contrary, newspapers chose to publish their full names—often a European first and last name with a Hawaiian middle name—drawing attention to their mixed heritage. A photograph of the dedication of the Hawaiian Building shows more than two dozen young Hawaiian men and women, all dressed in Western clothing and wearing leis while the men carried ukuleles.[103] Newspaper readers and fair visitors could encounter young Hawaiian women either dancing the hula or dressed in a typical shirtwaist and skirt. The latter reinforced the image of Hawai'i as the "up to date and modern" territory that haole organizers sought to depict instead of the remote South Seas image from which they sought to distance themselves.[104] A photograph of Elizabeth Victor and Mary Lash, two young women described as "typical Hawaiian beauties," exemplified this effort. Photographed not in hula outfits but in shirtwaists and skirts and while holding a pineapple, they look very similar to the many photographs that appeared of California women advertising the agricultural bounty of their state. The only distinction was that Victor and Lash were visibly of mixed racial ancestry. Such images inverted the fair's racial hierarchy in complicated ways and provided a surprising contrast to Adria Imada's description of how Hawaiian women in the popular culture of the 1920s and 1930s were represented almost solely as "aloha girls" in hula costume.[105]

One young Hawaiian woman's actions demonstrate precisely how mixed-race Hawaiians challenged California's racial politics. Only one week into the fair's run, local papers announced on February 28, 1915, the impending nuptials of two young people who were in San Francisco for the fair—Amoy Tai, a young Hawaiian woman employed as a singer in the Hawaiian gardens, and her fiancé, Edward Hall, an engineer on a steamship that sailed between San Francisco and Hawai'i. They were hoping to wed in the Hawaiian gardens before a crowd of well-wishers and fairgoers. Multiple articles in local papers advertised the event. Presumably, Hawaiian organizers and fair officials agreed that the ceremony would lend the blush of romance to the newly opened fair and further advertise the Hawaiian gardens to the fair's visitors. Their plans were rudely interrupted however, when Tai and Hall attempted to obtain a marriage license at the San Francisco County Courthouse. There, after learning Tai's father was Chinese and her mother native Hawaiian and seeing that Hall was white, the county clerk informed them that their hoped-for marriage was illegal. California's antimiscegenation law forbade any

Fig. 20. Dedication of Hawaiian Building. (San Francisco
History Center, San Francisco Public Library.)

marriage between a white person and one of Asian descent. With their
license refused, Hall was forced to sail back to Hawai'i an unwed man.[106]

Exactly why no one mentioned to Hall and Tai that their marriage
would be illegal under California law remains a mystery. Presumably fair
officials were consulted regarding permission to hold the wedding in the
Palace of Horticulture. Newspapers reported on the impending event
with no mention of legal hurdles despite including Tai's name and picture,
both of which clearly indicated that she was Asian. Were the would-be-
weds, fair officials, and journalists all ignorant of the laws? Or did they
assume that the county clerk would ignore the laws in order to please
fair officials? We do not know. But this nonevent reveals the contradictions that the fair's welcoming of the Pacific world and its peoples had
produced. Had this wedding occurred, it would have undermined the
Palace of Education and Social Economy's exhibits promoting eugenics
and scientifically planned marriages and called into question the fair's

racial hierarchy. That it did not demonstrates the extent to which California's political culture extended to the fairgrounds.

The PPIE celebrated the dominance of San Francisco and the United States over the Pacific and reflected the goals of local and national fair boosters, foreign nations, and international businesses. Despite the dominant images of California's having been successfully conquered by white pioneers and Catholic padres, of a Pacific under peaceful U.S. control, and of women dominated by men, alternative visions appeared, as Argentina's exhibit and the example of the Hawaiian attractions suggest. Voices, both foreign and domestic, created the vision of California and the Pacific that appeared at the fair. On the local level, from the moment San Francisco won the fair in 1911, many voices also weighed in on how the event could best serve the city. Where should the fair be located? How much should it cost? Should it favor tourists or residents? Just as multiple official voices created the fair, so too did multiple community voices challenge fair officials about the fair's relationship to the city. These debates reflected current concerns about public good versus private profit and demonstrated that the fair became a lightning rod for local political issues and global economic interests. To their dismay, local residents frequently discovered that the economic interests of fair officials would be paramount in resolving these debates.

2 ❧ Uniting San Francisco

San Francisco's "joy bells rang, her streets and her bright cafes swarmed with revelers all night, and her street-sweeping squad took wagon-loads of confetti off the pavements the next day" after President William Howard Taft signed the resolution granting San Francisco the right to hold the Panama-Pacific International Exposition.[1] This united joy in winning the battle with New Orleans for the fair faded, and soon San Franciscans "plunged into a good old family row as to the best place to put the fruits of victory."[2] Although most fair boosters and city residents assumed that Golden Gate Park, the site of the 1894 Midwinter International Exposition, would host the event, fair officials had not decided on a site. Serious questions remained about whether the park could, or should, support a large-scale exposition and whether other sites in the city might be more appropriate and affordable. The city's momentary unity at winning the fair dissolved as it became clear that some San Franciscans and fair officials disagreed about how the site of the fair could best serve the city.

The debate over the site of the fair raged in newspapers, in neighborhood and city council meetings, and on the streets of San Francisco for most of 1911. Debates about the availability of transportation, the location of saloons, and the regulation of hotels also emerged. Once the fair opened, citizens criticized the price of the fair and, ultimately, the relationship of the fair to the city. Was it a true public celebration to be shared by all residents, or was it simply a huge show staged by elite boosters that privileged the wealthy? The resulting discussions about public good and private profit in the city encapsulated the tensions facing Progressive Era political leaders who sought to expand public services while also meeting their own desire for financial gain. City residents and interest groups repeatedly seized upon the fair as a way to reshape the physical and social geography of the city. They all eventually discovered that their success depended on whether their plans fit the larger economic goals of the fair management.

Residents inundated exposition officials with proposals for possible fair sites. The suggestions varied from the unworkable—Goat Island, Alameda Flats, and Tanforan—to the elaborate, such as a dual-level waterfront site suggested by Senator Francis Newlands of Nevada.[3] By mid-summer, the debate narrowed to three possibilities: Harbor View, Golden Gate Park, and Lake Merced. The prolonged debate occupied the front pages of city papers and the agendas of local clubs for months. Residents sought to convince fair officials to locate the event in a place that would meet the long-term needs of city residents rather than the temporary needs of tourists or the financial exigencies of the fair. Officials claimed to weigh such issues as the cost of securing the necessary lands, the time before the land could be appropriated for grading and construction, the climate, the long-term results of occupying the site, the view, and the convenience of the site for both residents and visitors.[4]

Many believed that Golden Gate Park offered the only appropriate location because the event would leave the park with concrete improvements that would benefit city residents for years to come. Since the propaganda issued during the campaign for the fair and the local bond issue passed to fund the fair all mentioned Golden Gate Park as the site, this assumption was not unwarranted. As the focal point of the city's outdoor activities, and the pride of city residents, the park seemed the logical location. Many previous expositions, including the recent 1904 Louisiana Purchase Exposition in St. Louis, had been held in city parks.[5]

Golden Gate Park contained a few permanent buildings, athletic fields, playgrounds, and some landscaped areas in 1911. The buildings included relics of the Midwinter Expo, such as the Japanese Tea Garden and Art Museum, while the western end of the park remained undeveloped. Some local residents, such as the exposition vice president and *San Francisco Chronicle* publisher (and the mind behind the Midwinter Expo) Michael de Young, assumed that the PPIE offered another opportunity to further develop the park. "Golden Gate Park was intended for a people's pleasure ground," argued one *Chronicle* editorial, "and not for a wildwood. It was meant to be used in a manner calculated to give enjoyment to the greatest number." The *Chronicle*, and presumably many residents of the city, favored this developed model of the park, with "flower beds, lawns and playgrounds," rather than the wild forest that then existed in the western, undeveloped section under question.[6]

Not everyone agreed with de Young's vision. In early May, William Hammond Hall, a local civil engineer and first superintendent of the park, provided exposition officials with the drawbacks of using the park. He argued it would permanently wipe out part of the grounds and cost the city (and thus citizens) a great deal to rebuild and relandscape the park after the fair ended.[7] The debate over whether to locate the fair in the park was part of a larger debate about what kind of good the park should bring the city. Should it be a carefully landscaped site of museums and playgrounds, or should it be a forest park, with significant portions left undeveloped? The discussion reflected larger Progressive debates between those who favored romantic versus rationalistic parks.[8] In keeping with Progressive Era concerns about social disorder, backers of the rationalistic model urged that these well-ordered spaces were necessary counterpoints to the dangers of urban life and composed a key part of "their formula for encouraging a good society."[9] Reformers believed that such parks offered city residential activities a needed focus for recreation. Many San Franciscans agreed that the concrete benefits the fair might bring—stadiums, museums, paths, and landscaped areas—would be more useful to city society than the wild dunes at the western edge of the park would be.

The PPIE Board of Directors surprised many city residents in May 1911 when it published a report that favored not Golden Gate Park but Harbor View as the fair's site. The Harbor View area was on the northern edge of the city, bounded by Lyon Street, Lewis Street, Laguna Street, Bay Street, Van Ness Avenue, and Lombard Street and with the bay on the north. The region served as a recreation area for the city in the 1880s, hosting the popular Harbor View Baths, but the lack of accessible transportation caused a decline in its popularity. The baths closed in 1909 when the city decided to extend Lyon Street to the bay so it could begin to incorporate the area into a tax assessment district, a move that suggested the city's desire to further develop the neighborhood.[10] Some described the neighborhood as an "eyesore" for those wealthy San Franciscans in Pacific Heights who dwelled above it. Harbor View housed a mixed neighborhood of industry, boardinghouses, saloons, earthquake cottages, and other structures built as emergency housing after the 1906 disaster.[11] One former resident described the area as "a place we, as kids, liked to go to collect old scraps of metal such as window weights and other discarded articles to sell for pennies in the years we lived in Cow Hollow as refugees from the Earthquake and Fire of 1906."[12] Acres of what would be the exposition site were still underwater and would need to be filled in with soil to expand the available land for the fair.

The earthquake and fire reshaped Harbor View. Tons of refuse and rubble were dumped in the sparsely populated area during the rebuilding process and would eventually become the fill necessary to making the site buildable for the fair. Since the neighborhood and the adjacent Presidio had extensive open space, they had housed multiple refugee camps. The last camp closed in 1908, but earthquake cottages and shacks remained sprinkled throughout the southern part of the site. The city's Health Commission forced one owner of hundreds of refugee shacks in the neighborhood to move the buildings and evict his indigent tenants in the fall of 1911, again indicating the city's desire to spruce up the area.[13] Many of the northern blocks remained underwater, awaiting the dredging and filling that would make them usable. No fire insurance company maps were produced between the earthquake and 1912, when the PPIE began to raze the buildings on the site. But 1905 maps from the Sanborn Map Company reveal the neighborhood comprised primarily two-flat residences, suggesting it included a large number of rental properties. Significant large-property owners included the Fulton Iron Works and the Pacific Gas and Electric Company.

Although it was the only proposed site with significant buildings, the board's report dismissed their importance, because those buildings were of negligible value. Of the 540 buildings on the site, 263 were "the poorer and cheaper type of buildings." Half of the remaining 277 structures were located on the site's southern edge and might easily be excluded from the grounds. The total buildings cited, however, did not include the area's "refugee shacks and sheds." Given that the owner approached by the Health Commission had 144 such buildings on the site, it is likely that far more buildings were eventually razed or moved to make way for the fair.[14] Nor did the figure include the buildings of the Fulton Iron Works, the United Railroads, or the San Francisco Gas and Electric Company.[15] The report's writer evidently expected that the exposition would be able to secure the cooperation of local industries without a problem.

The report offered clear arguments against other possible sites. Islais Creek, an area of about 400 acres that lay west of Kentucky Street and south of Army Street, was completely inappropriate. Not only would the marshland require a huge amount of fill to turn it into solid ground, but also it was too close to "Butchertown" and would therefore expose visitors to "unattractive portions of the city." Sutro Forest posed the opposite problem. Although currently undeveloped, the report concluded that it would "probably be a future high class residence section," whose owners might require significant restoration work after the fair, adding an indeterminate cost to the endeavor. The preservation of a potentially wealthy neighborhood trumped any desire to develop the location for the fair. Harbor View soon emerged as the cheapest site despite its large number of existing structures.[16]

Neither the report on the sites nor the fair directors appear to have ever considered the fate of those city residents who lived in Harbor View. The public debate over the site never mentioned the San Franciscans who lived in Harbor View or their opinions on having their neighborhood turned into the exposition site. This working-class neighborhood, though, may have been one that its neighbors in Pacific Heights were all too pleased to eradicate.

City residents and interested parties continued to vigorously debate the issue for the next two months. The active engagement of the city's many neighborhood associations indicates the passion with which many San Franciscans approached the issue. Residents spent a great deal of time explaining why the site nearest to their particular neighborhood was the only suitable place for the fair. These claims often contradicted each other. The North Beach Promotion Association (located near the Harbor View site), for instance, told fair officials in April that Harbor View was the best choice because it had the best climate, was easily accessible for night-time revelers, and was located close enough to downtown to benefit merchants, whose interests were "paramount."[17] The Park Richmond Improvement Club boosted Golden Gate Park, asserting that "the park is the most accessible, the space is ample, it is the people's choice, will get the greatest gate receipts, and is where we can best exhibit the lord of oceans, the mighty Pacific."[18] A site's suitability depended on one's location in the city.

Financial gain remained at the root of these arguments. Many asserted that the most important long-lasting effect of the fair would be to raise property values in the city. Newspaper reports on the stagnating real estate market in early 1911 attributed the problem to an uncertainty about the fair site. This condition persisted throughout the spring, particularly in the currently underdeveloped outlying areas of the city that might suddenly be located near the exposition site. City real estate agents were probably quite eager to have the question decided.[19]

Many residents believed the fair would profoundly affect the city's residential development. One San Francisco real estate agent informed department store president Reuben Hale that the city would provide the much-needed housing for the "great middle class" only if the fair occurred in the park. The fair would prompt the development of the areas lying to the north and south of the park, drawing back some of the residents who had fled the city for the East Bay after the earthquake. Harbor View offered no nearby desirable neighborhood ripe for development; instead, he worried, it might boost the cities across the bay.[20] Others feared that Harbor View's easy accessibility to the East and North Bay areas via ferries would hurt owners hoping to lease their city properties during the fair's run in 1915.[21] Those who boosted the Lake Merced or Sutro-Merced site also stressed that residential development would be a permanent legacy of locating the fair in the southern part of the city.[22]

Opponents to Harbor View latched onto the concern that the site might benefit cities outside San Francisco more than the city itself. One park booster wondered, "What is the use of our hottells [sic] and all our apartments, when the people can live in Oakland and all the cheap towns and you want to make it so they do not have to come to the city at all and you want to make it so all our . . . horses and teams lay idle we want the fair at the park and that's what will benefit San Francisco."[23] Memories of the recent Oakland campaign to depict the city as the region's transportation hub likely heightened those anxieties. When Oakland portrayed itself as "as the potential supplier of goods to the Orient . . . a transfer point for transcontinental freight destined for Pacific ports . . . a strategically situated port . . . as a market for the great producing areas of the Pacific Slope, and . . . as the gateway to the fertile interior valleys of California," it directly challenged San Francisco's claim to regional and Pacific dominance.[24] Locating the fair on the city's northern edge and in an area not yet effectively connected to the rest of the city through public transportation seemed a risky proposition to those city residents who wanted the event to bring prosperity to their own neighborhoods. East Bay residents, however, eagerly boosted the site, suggesting that the ease of transport across the bay would bring more visitors and workmen to the fair.[25]

Harbor View had plenty of supporters. Many downtown business owners favored the site because it was located close to downtown. They assumed that new rail lines would make it easy for tourists to travel back and forth between downtown and the fair. A group of property owners from the downtown "burned district," the Hotel Men's Association, and the Chinese Chamber of Commerce each passed resolutions favoring Harbor View, demonstrating that a variety of powerful business interests united behind this plan.[26] They boosted the Harbor View site because of its proximity to downtown and because of its lovely views and bayfront location. A fair fronting the city's gorgeous Golden Gate seemed the only appropriate location for a fair celebrating maritime commerce and the Panama Canal.[27]

Arguments soon grew ugly as allegations of bribery and graft surfaced, echoing the civic upheaval of the city's 1907 graft trials and stirring up debates about the difference between public good and private profit. Some residents objected because the property at Harbor View was privately owned unlike the publicly owned park site. Using public money subscribed to the fair to improve private property struck many as unfair. One angry citizen argued that having the fair at Harbor View would "benifit [sic] a few million heirs [sic] and fix up there [sic] property."[28] Such charges were not necessarily unwarranted since only three wealthy owners held title to a large chunk of the site still underwater.[29] Another writer accused then-acting exposition president Hale that "you can now afford to associate with people who own large interests and want those interests served by using the money of the people to fill up mudholes and take away an eye-sore that has bothered some of the people who live on Broadway and Pacific Heights."[30]

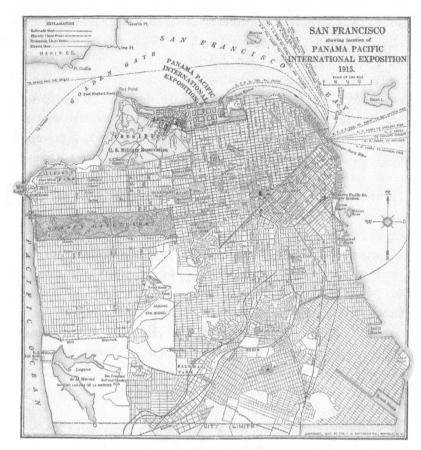

Fig. 21. Map of San Francisco showing exposition grounds. (Courtesy of the
Earth Sciences and Map Library, University of California, Berkeley.)

Meanwhile, de Young and the *San Francisco Chronicle* continued to
back the park site. The paper published a number of articles insinuating
that the campaign for Harbor View was led by unidentified "real estate
interests" that sought to profit at the cost of the public good. After the
city engineer's office prepared a secret report comparing the Harbor
View and Golden Gate Park sites, the *Chronicle* charged, "It is a well-
known fact that two or three real estate concerns are interested in pushing before the people the site designated as Harbor View, one-third of
which is under water."[31] Shortly thereafter, attendees at a meeting of the
Federated Improvement Clubs alleged that the plan to locate the fair
at Harbor View was the result of a real estate scheme. They called for

Governor Hiram Johnson to interfere in favor of Golden Gate Park.[32] The group again agitated against Harbor View advocates a week later, accusing them of deliberately misrepresenting the costs associated with the Harbor View site.[33] The *Chronicle* took its allegations a step further in mid-May. An article published in the real estate section argued, "It is generally understood in real estate circles, too, that certain operators have, to use a term of the business, 'loaded up,' with propositions in the vicinity of Harbor View.... Real estate agents have said that practically everything available in the way of real estate in the north end . . . has been secured under options for some time."[34] These articles stirred up resentment against supporters of Harbor View and created the sense that only those with some personal interest in the property preferred the site.

Exposition directors and city residents continued this rancorous public and private debate until a new option finally emerged in late June. This new plan proposed holding the fair in both Golden Gate and Lincoln Parks. The solution appealed to those who feared that Golden Gate Park would not have enough acreage to meet the needs of the event, for this option offered roughly a thousand acres.[35] De Young presented the idea before the Board of Directors, and the members responded with interest.[36] A call went out for the owners of those intermediary blocks to come forward and agree to lease their land to the exposition, and the *San Francisco Chronicle* began to boost this new plan with great vigor.[37]

On July 15, 1911, a unanimous vote of the directors approved a composite site that included Golden Gate and Lincoln Parks and Harbor View. The plan integrated ideas inspired by the pre-earthquake work of city planner Daniel Burnham into an elaborate call for a re-imagination of much of San Francisco.[38] Harbor View would be the site of the amusement district of the fair since it was located close to downtown. Lincoln Park would host a "giant commemorative statue" and be linked to Golden Gate Park by purchasing the block that divided them. The bulk of exhibit buildings, such as city, county, and national buildings and "especially . . . the Oriental exhibits," would be erected in Golden Gate Park. A permanent art gallery and athletic stadium would be built in the western edge of the park. Buildings in the park would be used "so far as possible for permanent improvements and such other exhibits as would be least destructive, and add most to its beauty." A lavish civic center downtown would be erected near Van Ness Avenue. Finally, the plan recommended that from the Ferry Building on Market Street to the Van Ness entrance to the fair, "such decorations be featured . . . that a visitor . . . would feel that he was entering an Exposition City."[39]

This site seemed to please everyone. The *San Francisco Chronicle* triumphantly stated, "Location Assures Permanent Improvements in Both Parks; Magnificent Marine Boulevard: Scope of Exposition Plan Surpasses Expectation."[40] Members of the Board of Directors issued glowing public statements that lauded the site. M. J. Brandenstein stated, "We have adopted the plan that makes San Francisco the greatest exposition city in the world. . . . The plan is unique and embraces the best features and advantages of San Francisco."[41] In October 1911, President Taft broke ground for the PPIE in Golden Gate Park, in keeping with the assumption that the fair would be located there; yet the exposition took place completely at the Harbor View site.

Little of the elaborate plan envisioned in the summer of 1911 ever developed because fair directors continued to explore the relative cost of various options. Finally, in December, the Executive Architectural Council of the PPIE submitted a report comparing the costs of three options: Golden Gate Park only, Harbor View and the Presidio, and the combined plan. According to their estimates, building the fair in Harbor View and adjoining government lands would cost over $1.2 million less than building it in the park and $1.9 million less than the combined plan. Significantly more money could then be spent on the buildings themselves. Moreover, the report continued, the experiences of other recent fairs suggested the value of a compact site for retaining visitors' attention.[42] The council recommended holding the fair only at Harbor View, and on December 15, 1911, the exposition directors approved a plan to erect all exposition buildings at the Harbor View–Presidio location, demonstrating the triumph of financial imperative over the will of city residents.[43] Popular discontent continued in some quarters. In January a meeting of neighborhood improvement groups approved a resolution calling for the fair to be held in the park rather than at Harbor View, since the buildings could be retained for the public's future use.[44] Yet when local papers published the drawings of the proposed grounds in May, they were accompanied by celebratory comments and descriptions of

Fig. 22. President Taft breaking ground in Golden Gate Park, reflecting the dominant assumption that the fair would occur there. (San Francisco History Center, San Francisco Public Library.)

the proposed features of the grounds with nary a comment on their location. The public debate was over.

Clearly many San Franciscans felt deeply invested in the fair, and they believed their voices should be heard in the debate over the site. Although they might agree the fair should benefit the city, they could not agree on how the fair should do that. The outpouring of support for Golden Gate Park versus Harbor View reveals that many San Franciscans believed the fair should bring concrete benefits to all city residents, not just to wealthy investors. Those imbued with the progressive spirit favored a rationalistic type of park and believed that locating it there would leave a legacy beneficial to park enthusiasts. The Harbor View site conveyed benefits solely to private landowners. Yet the fair was ultimately a private venture—run by a private corporation but funded by public subscription—and as their ultimate decision reflected, the fair directors had no responsibility to city residents to design the fair to serve their needs.

The rationale that Harbor View would be cheaper and more scenic did not appease those who believed that locating it on private land was a betrayal of the public trust. In the proposal for the composite site the Board of Directors had delineated its definition of the relationship between the fair and the city. They stated that the fair must be located somewhere that was easily accessible to all parts of San Francisco and not simply to the surrounding area. It should leave "the greatest possible number of real permanent improvements" and should help to build up the city generally rather than focusing on boosting one particular location. But the location of the fair at Harbor View did little to advance these goals. The site did not yet have a streetcar connection to the rest of the city. The private ownership of the land meant any improvements to the neighborhood might not be accessible to city residents in the long term. Nor did the board clearly explain how this site would build up the city. This contradiction called into question the fair directors' dedication to the city's public good. The lingering history of the graft trials and the allegations of corruption and bribery they unearthed only four years before exacerbated this debate, raising unsettling questions about the goals of fair directors. Rather than bringing the city together, the debate over the site reinvigorated existing debates about public good and private gain.

Once the site was set, fair officials had to acquire legal rights to the property. Fortunately, local neighborhood improvement groups already had solicited lease agreements from many property owners during their lobbying efforts. The groups' work eased the way for fair officials, who then had to convince only a few recalcitrant owners to make their property available to the fair.[45] This process occurred fairly easily. Most property owners likely believed, as one group of owners told officials, that the fair would bring a clear "increase in value" to their property.[46] For the more reluctant owners, the land department adopted a policy of "delaying settlements of leases for the time being" in the hope that those demanding higher prices could be convinced otherwise as the fair removed houses and as they witnessed the "gradual depopulation of the neighborhood."[47] Eventually, the legal department filed condemnation suits against a few owners that ironically resulted in smaller judgments than the fair officials originally offered. Whatever their tactics, fair officials eventually obtained title to all the necessary lands, gaining 330 acres from 175 different owners. The entire operation cost the fair almost $1.2 million.[48] Most of the land was procured by paying a monthly rental fee and property taxes.

Fig. 23. A Marina home purchased by the Panama-Pacific International Exposition. (San Francisco History Center, San Francisco Public Library.)

Other owners settled only for tax payments, and in a few other cases the PPIE bought the properties outright. Once the land was acquired, any existing improvements had to be removed. The fair disposed of more than 400 structures, "ranging from a 50 room apartment house to a fisherman's shack," through both auctions and private sales.[49]

This process forced hundreds of people living in the site's southern portion to relocate during 1912. Some went willingly, but others resisted and resented the fair's appropriation of their homes. Since many buildings were rentals, those actually living on the property did not make the decision to lease or sell the land. This situation resulted in a confusing relationship between tenants, owners, and the fair. A PPIE land department report indicated that one resident, a Mrs. Castiglione, was "unable to speak English and does not appear to understand about moving," while A. Penazzio's residence also included "parties [who] do not seem to understand that they must move."[50] Four tenants of rentals on Van Ness refused to pay their last rent payments since they knew they would be evicted shortly.[51] Other renters resented the difficulties caused by moving. Mrs. Ida West Hale wrote to Mayor James Rolph in February 1912, asking if he could provide financial assistance to her and her husband, who were both in their seventies and faced a move from their residence on Van Ness.[52] Mrs. Mary Suters likewise wrote an eloquent letter to the PPIE Board in which she cited the difficulties she had endured since the earthquake had left her penniless. She supported her two sons by taking in boarders, but she would have to double her rent and lose half her boarders upon moving. Could she therefore, she asked, be released from her last month's rent? Alas, replied Director of Works Harris Connick, this request was impossible.[53]

Fair officials dealt with property owners far more generously than they did with renters like Suters. A number of letters remain from other residents who faced serious financial difficulties, but in no case did fair officials offer any financial assistance to renters affected by these circumstances. Harbor View grocer Frank Fassio worried about how to restart his business in a new location and received early promises of assistance from fair officials. Fair officials told him in March 1912, however, that despite their regret about his hardship, they had "no authority to use any of the Exposition money for anything except for the regular Exposition business."[54] Yet when Harbor View saloon owner Mr. Driscoll resisted the fair's attempt to obtain the land on which his saloon was located, the fair went to great lengths to gain the property. They not only paid him for the land but also moved his saloon, home, and personal property for no charge.[55] They justified this expense by the need to acquire his land, while relieving working-class San Franciscans of their rent (often $20 to $50 a month) was not a priority.

No records detail what these displaced San Franciscans thought of the PPIE after it opened, but their stories remind us that these events occurred at a human cost. Property owners likely benefited from the improvements made to their property and having their taxes paid for four years. Low-wage renters faced a much more challenging situation, losing their homes and sometimes their businesses at short notice. According to an official of the PPIE land department, no residents were "forcibly ejected in the true meaning of such an expression. Three of the people were a little stubborn about giving up their premises even after the buildings had been sold to wreckers. We did not turn the people out forcibly but the wreckers removed the houses while the owners were still occupying

Fig. 24. Construction site of PPIE. (San Francisco History
Center, San Francisco Public Library.)

them."[56] Whether these three resisters were owners or renters is unclear,
but plainly not all Harbor View residents welcomed the fair.

The fair transformed the neighborhood surrounding Harbor View.
Thousands of people came to the area each day, offering enterprising
San Franciscans a host of business opportunities. As local columnist Ben
Macomber reminded readers after the fair opened, inside the grounds
was "an orderly exhibition of all the best and latest that modern civilization and progress have produced. Outside is a jumble of hucksters,
purveyors, merchants, fortune tellers, jitneys, bootblacks, steerers for
automobile parks, hot dog men, peanut venders, newsboys, souvenir
sellers, chafferers of every description."[57] The fair's prohibition on auto-
mobiles on the fairgrounds meant that auto-owning visitors had to park
their cars elsewhere. The solution? To turn vacant lots into parking lots
and gas stations, which offered huge profits to those who held out long
enough on renting their lots to eager businessmen. Other aspiring entrepreneurs opened lunch counters in "every little hole in the wall," first

serving the five thousand men who built the fair and eventually serving the thousands of daily visitors who decided the food on the grounds was too expensive. According to Macomber, the "outside fair" was as cosmopolitan as the inside fair, with immigrants of every description flocking to the neighborhood to set up shop.[58] The PPIE revamped this neighborhood, a process that reveals the unintentional economic and social consequences of the fair, as well as the ingenious ways local residents took advantage of the event.

Just how to get those thousands of people to Harbor View posed a major challenge for fair and city officials. No major streetcar lines ran near the proposed fair site. The closest stop to any fair entrance was located a thousand feet away, a distance judged inconvenient for most tourists. Existing lines could accommodate only 13,500 passengers an hour. How would the tens of thousands of people expected to journey to the fair each day reach the site?[59] The question of transportation and the possibility of expanding existing street railway lines in the city occupied city officials, fair directors, and city residents during the spring and summer of 1913, and it offers another window into the relationship between the fair, urban development, and conceptions of public good in San Francisco in the 1910s.

San Francisco's streetcar system had been a thorny political issue since the turn of the century. City officials debated the merits of municipal ownership amid allegations of corruption and bribery levied at United Railroads, the corporation that controlled most of the lines in the city. The city's reform charter of 1900 declared that it was "the purpose and intention of the people of the City and County of San Francisco" to acquire ownership of its public utilities.[60] The 1913 Board of Supervisors had been elected on a platform of municipal ownership, a position that responded to the city's frustration with the influence of United Railroads. In 1902 the company had acquired control of 226 miles of track and roughly a thousand cars, or nearly all of the lines located in San Francisco. Three years later, company president Patrick Calhoun sought to convert all of its lines to electricity. After the 1905 victory of the Labor Party, local political boss Abe Ruef informed Calhoun that a $200,000 payment would ensure the Board of Supervisor's approval of the electrification plan. Witnesses revealed this bribe during the graft trials, enraging city residents and triggering a Carmen's Union strike against the Union Railroads. Calhoun's vicious strike-breaking tactics then angered the local labor community. His antilabor stance and corrupt business practices helped boosters of municipal ownership to make their case. Voters finally approved two bond issues in December 1910 to acquire the Geary Street line, which Union Railroads did not own; to convert it to electric cars; and to extend it down Market Street. Thus was San Francisco's Municipal Railway, one of the first in the nation, born.[61]

Exposition officials stepped into this heated political context as they sought to convince the San Francisco Board of Supervisors to approve the construction of new streetcar lines to the exposition grounds. Fair directors argued this project was essential for the public good of the exposition and, by extension, the city. A February meeting between PPIE officials and the Board of Supervisors hinted at the political battle ahead. "I certainly believed," President Charles Moore stated, "that our activities would be confined within the fence surrounding the grounds. And [I] had no idea that the city would not look after the transportation . . . problems that confront us." Supervisor George Gallagher rejoined, "The fair directors did not ask this board where to put their fair. . . . And I do not want any stigma left with this board on account of any action they may have taken."[62] Fair directors did not ask for municipal ownership; rather, they simply demanded that the city devise a way to transport the anticipated crowds to the Harbor View site. This meeting jump-started an active citywide debate about to how to solve the city's transportation problem.

Fair officials remained neutral about the question of municipal ownership. Boosters of public ownership quickly seized the opportunity to campaign for the expansion of municipal lines. A few days after the meeting between supervisors and fair officials, the *San Francisco Examiner* published an elaborate plan to solve the exposition's and the city's transportation problems. It called for four new publicly funded streetcar lines to bring visitors to the fairgrounds and to reach residential districts underserved by the rail system.[63] This solution, the paper promised, would solve the immediate transportation problem, bring profit to the city, and "free the city from the very obvious peril of being forced into undesirable franchise grants," such as those with the United Railroads.[64] Public reaction to the plans was immediate and positive. Mayor Rolph and many members of the Board of Supervisors and local improvement organizations all supported the plan.[65] The Harbor Commission announced it would seek state funds to construct a double-track railroad along the Embarcadero, with a tunnel under Fort Mason, to reach the exposition grounds.[66] Exposition directors responded to the plan cautiously. Board members publicly refused to endorse municipal ownership. They simply reiterated the necessity of finding "any solution that will give us the service."[67]

City politicians and residents debated the question of the streetcar lines and of municipal ownership throughout 1913. Conservatives, who regarded the idea of municipal ownership as a small step from socialism, found the idea repugnant. Many others in the city, however, eagerly embraced the plan. The *Examiner's* proposal soon gained momentum and evolved into a plan calling for nine new streetcar lines, which would be funded by a bond issue of $3.5 million.[68] The Board of Supervisors, local improvement groups, and other proponents of municipal ownership joined forces and called for passage of the bond issue. In disagreement stood the San Francisco Chamber of Commerce and a number of conservative businessmen—the peers of the fair directors—who opposed the idea of municipal ownership on principle. Other opponents argued that the plan was too expensive and insufficient to meet the needs of the anticipated exposition crowds. The plan's supporters brought together diverse interests in the city, from the Labor Council to those businessmen who saw the profitable municipally owned Geary Street line as proof that public ownership could bring real benefits to the city.

Despite widespread support for the measure, the exposition directors continued to refuse to take an official stand in support of public ownership. Their stance infuriated both the mayor and the Board of Supervisors. In late May as the bond issue heated up, the exposition directors formally resolved that "the Exposition Company shall remain neutral in the matter of said proposal and that it refrain from participating in any attempt to influence public opinion for or against said proposal."[69] Some directors outright opposed municipal ownership and resented that they were being forced to support it to gain the desperately needed transportation for the exposition. Others did not wish to support such a widespread expansion of the rail system. Still others argued that the funding offered by the bond issue would not be sufficient to provide enough transportation to the grounds.[70] Although President Moore and other directors repeatedly asserted that the debate was not about municipal ownership, the subtext of the debate over the neutrality resolution was clear. Many of the directors perceived a chasm between their political beliefs and those of the Board of Supervisors. They resented the supervisors' attempt to use the exposition to gain a political goal, an expanded municipal railway. Despite Rolph's fervent plea to support the bonds, the neutrality resolution passed by a vote of twelve to six.[71]

Public resentment against the fair directors' unwillingness to take a stand increased. The Board of Supervisors responded angrily to the neutrality resolution, resolving that since the Board of Directors' statement was "tantamount to a declaration that it has no interest in securing adequate passenger facilities for the exposition, and has no interest in relieving San Francisco . . . from the intolerable street-railway conditions now existing . . . be it resolved . . . that . . . the Board of Supervisors, deprecates the act . . . [of] taking a neutral stand on a question of such vital importance to the exposition and the city and county of San Francisco."[72] One supervisor argued that the directors' sympathy for the United Railroads clouded their ability to put the good of the city before that of their private interests.[73] The majority of the directors were conservative businessmen, and one of them was an assistant to the president of United Railroads.[74] Many probably had personal, if not also business, ties to the United Railroad Corporation that likely affected their opposition to municipal ownership. Fair officials thus found themselves in a double bind. Should they publicly oppose a measure that might threaten their personal financial interests and contradict their personal beliefs, even if it would bring success to the exposition? A neutrality vote thus offered them a way to remove themselves from a situation to which they saw no easy answer.

The citywide August bond measure passed by a strong majority, 51,569 to 13,700, despite the exposition officials' lack of enthusiasm. It carried equally in neighborhoods around the city, suggesting that most San Franciscans were united behind municipal ownership. Rolph heralded the vote as a sign that his vision of a "united San Francisco" and a "real live

Exposition" was being realized.[75] But the campaign against the bonds revealed the bitter divisions in the city between progressives and conservatives and the extent to which the fair became a flashpoint for political conflict as it reinvigorated old debates about municipal ownership and corrupt business practices. It demonstrated again that the economic success of the exposition was the fair officials' bottom line. They refused to oppose municipal ownership openly, even though it contradicted many of their political beliefs, because they knew that the project would help ensure the success of the fair. In this case, then, the fair directors' desire to make the fair profitable forced them to make concessions to boosters of municipal ownership. In so doing, they dramatically changed the shape of San Francisco, bringing public transportation to many new neighborhoods and enabling the eventual development of the exposition site as a residential neighborhood in the 1920s.

In their effort to make San Francisco into an "Exposition City," the fair directors intervened more directly in the practices of two local businesses—saloons and hotels. The exposition purchased a number of saloons as they acquired the land at Harbor View both because they needed access to the land and because they saw a benefit in removing businesses associated with vice and immoral practices from proximity to the fair. Some boosters worried that San Francisco's reputation as a stronghold of the liquor trade, along with its active vice district, threatened the success of the exposition. The city remained a solidly "wet" city throughout the Progressive Era even as agitation for temperance increased across the state and nation in the early 1910s.[76] Fair directors saw no reason to ban alcohol from the grounds, but they realized that having saloons—and their working-class patrons—nearby might concern reform-minded middle-class visitors. These establishments might draw other visitors and their money away from the grounds, so exposition officials were eager to move saloons as far away from the fair's entrances as possible.

Despite not being truly dedicated to the tenets of moral reform, fair officials appropriated the movement's rhetoric to oppose saloons near the grounds.[77] Officials feared that working-class saloons would be a bad influence "upon those whose business or pleasure calls them to the Exposition grounds." Further, according to one official, "it cannot but hurt the fair name of the City of San Francisco if the precedent is established of permitting the operation of saloons near the entrances to the grounds."[78] Such statements echoed concerns that working-class saloon culture threatened the moral order of the city and the fair. Local residents also weighed in. One man told Moore that he and others feared that "extraordinary efforts will be made to establish liquor saloons WITH THE USUAL ACCESSORIES" in the neighborhood near the grounds, so they wanted the exposition to take action against these potential threats to the "character and reputation and incidentally the value of their property."[79] For some residents the fair offered an ally in the fight against saloons and their clientele. San Francisco had a long history of establishments that provided free-flowing alcohol to all comers. Fair officials believed in this case that it was more important to cater to the sensibilities of elite and middle-class tourists than to the needs of working-class city residents who patronized these saloons.

That fair officials were motivated by any devotion to the principles of temperance is unlikely. Fair officials opposed making the fair itself "dry" and, reflecting the city's widespread use and tolerance of alcohol, opposed a statewide temperance bill in 1913. Although progressive good government measures found support in San Francisco, moral reformers faced a much tougher battle in the city. No evidence exists to suggest that this particular opposition to saloons was motivated by anything other than a desire to remove potential competition for tourist dollars from the neighborhood of the fair.

Moore argued during the fight over transportation that the board sought only to address issues contained within the fairgrounds, but the saloon issue revealed that claim to be patently untrue. As the PPIE acquired land at Harbor View, the fair board wielded its political muscle to demand that the Police Commission inform it when anyone petitioned for a liquor license on the land designated for the exposition.[80] Officials feared that the establishment of a new saloon on desired land would make it prohibitively expensive for them to acquire the relevant parcel.[81] The Police Commission cooperated and periodically sent lists of potentially objectionable saloon applicants to the Board of Directors for review.[82] Fair officials shaped the development of the neighborhood outside the gates of the fair, all in an attempt to make the PPIE profitable.

Frustrated saloon owners, and presumably their clients, resented the fair's interference. Some displaced saloon keepers petitioned the police commissioners for new space located as close to the fairgrounds as possible. Adolph E. Schwartz repeatedly asked for a space directly opposite the Fillmore Street entrance to the fair. Upon receiving confirmation from exposition officials that they absolutely opposed any such licenses, "regardless of the character of the saloon," the Police Commission vetoed his petition.[83] The commission finally informed the exposition in March 1914 that it would not grant any more saloon licenses near the fairgrounds to those owners displaced by the exposition. The police refused to meet the demands of those saloon keepers who had been bought out by the fair and who repeatedly appeared before the Police Commission to demand a new license for a site near a fair gate. In so doing, the police and exposition board denied these business owners any opportunity to present their claims that they too deserved to make a profit from fair visitors.[84]

When fair officials closed the saloons, they remade the city into a place that catered to middle- and upper-class tourists and city residents rather than to the working class. Fair officials sought a city that would welcome middle- and upper-class tourists, for they were the consumers and potential settlers whom officials hoped to draw to the fair. When the desires of city residents—such as the saloon owners and their patrons—seemed to interfere with those plans, they found their goals thwarted by fair officials. Like other saloon owners, Schwartz believed that the clearest benefit the fair could bring to him was more business, and what better place was there to locate his business than across the street from the fairgrounds? He and other saloon keepers relocated by the exposition deeply resented fair officials' beliefs that their institutions had no place in the "Exposition City" that the officials sought to create.

Fair officials put themselves at odds with another set of small businessmen when they attempted to regulate the city's hotels and rooming houses. Pre-fair publicity promised visitors that "San Francisco is prepared today to take care of 100,000 visitors daily."[85] Such promises relied on the willingness of hotel owners and managers to clarify both their rates and policies for the exposition period. Other cities hosting large fairs and celebrations experienced outrageous hotel rates during the events, scaring away visitors. Such episodes "left bitter memories with many," according to fair director Frank L. Brown, and he and other directors were determined that San Francisco not suffer the same fate.[86]

Exposition officials first worked with hotel owners on an informal basis by sponsoring the San Francisco Hotel Bureau. Members of this voluntary organization, founded in early 1914, agreed to publish their rates well in advance of the exposition and participated in a coordinated system for advertising and booking hotel rooms for visitors. Local hotel owners ran this group without exposition interference. Fair management supported the organization as long as it maintained a membership of the majority of the city's hotels.[87] The relationship between hotel owners and the exposition soon deteriorated, as a 1914 letter from Moore to the organization reveals. "That you should consider that you have a grievance against the exposition is surprising to me," he charged, "because from our point of view we consider that we are the aggrieved party." Moore maintained that hotel owners had never fully supported the fair. They failed to pledge an adequate amount of money to the original subscription drive and remained unwilling to cooperate with PPIE officials. Many hotels failed to publish their rates for 1915, creating bad press for the city, as "letters, reports, and newspaper clippings from various parts of the country" poured into the fair offices, "indicating the belief that visitors would be held up by the hotel interests here." Now, Moore complained, the fair suffered from bad publicity about the hotel situation and the problem of having secured hundreds of conventions for 1915 with no assurance of reasonably priced hotels to house these visitors.[88]

Hotel owners already resented the exposition for having chosen to erect its own hotel, the Inside Inn, on the fairgrounds. They perceived this decision as a direct attack on their business and worried that PPIE publicity would direct visitors solely to the Inside Inn at the expense of their establishments. Would visitors be more likely to stay at the Inside Inn rather than at a hotel located in the heart of the city? These concerns troubled local hotel owners so they began to agitate publicly against the Inside Inn. They petitioned the city's Board of Supervisors to disallow the construction of the inn and attempted to stop approval of the project.[89] At one meeting of the San Francisco Hotel Association, members decided to monitor the construction of the Inside Inn carefully and see to it that "every section of the fire ordinances is enforced." In addition,

Fig. 25. The Inside Inn advertised widely, frustrating
local hotel owners. (*Official Guide.*)

once construction began, "time will then be ripe for a protest from the hotel and retail store keepers against this totally unnecessary competition."[90] Hotel owners believed that the Inside Inn threatened their ability to profit from the increased business that the exposition would bring.

Moore, however, maintained that hotel owners had brought the situation on themselves. Only when "it became apparent that the hotels here, large and small, would not agree to make adequate arrangements for caring for the people coming to the numerous conventions and congresses to be held here," he reminded hotel owners, was the concession approved. According to him, the Inside Inn was not a direct attack on local hotels but a last resort in the fair's attempt to fulfill its "responsibility . . . to guarantee right treatment to visitors during their sojourn here" and, no doubt, to meet fair officials' goals for its financial success.[91] Moore saw no way to guarantee such treatment if hotels would not agree to publish their rates and to promise to abide by them during the fair. Moore and other officials were far more concerned about the prospect of bad publicity keeping visitors away from the fair than about the desires of hotel owners to profit from artificially higher rates.

Fair officials decided by late 1914 that the San Francisco Hotel Bureau was no longer adequate to the task. The PPIE created its own hotel bureau after determining that the old organization represented too few establishments and was "dominated by certain political influences." The Official Exposition Hotel Bureau absorbed the original San Francisco Hotel Bureau in early January 1915. By early February, 133 local hotels belonged, and officials hoped that by opening day they would have a list of between 250 and 300 participating hotels, representing between 20,000 and 30,000 available rooms in the city. Although the bureau was part of the PPIE Division of Exploitation, a board of leading hotel men supervised it.[92]

The creation of the hotel bureau demonstrated PPIE officials' willingness to borrow the progressive reform technique of using regulatory power to benefit the fair. In order to belong to the Official Exposition Hotel Bureau, a hotel owner had to submit the hotel's rates to the board for the organization's approval. Excessively high rates would not be accepted. Moreover, the bureau promised to distribute business evenly throughout member hotels, with only the patron's preference affecting hotel choice. The exposition sold this plan to hotel owners by promising to advertise all hotels equally throughout the world, thus taking the burden of advertisement off of them, a particular boon for small hotels. The exposition did not provide this service free of charge, however; a hotel owner paid a dollar for each room in his or her establishment in order to join the bureau.[93]

The exposition's takeover of the San Francisco Hotel Bureau apparently succeeded. It published an extensive list of available hotels, clearly showing their rates and the numbers of rooms available. Uniformed Official Exposition Hotel Bureau guides met every train and boat that approached the city and provided room information to visitors. The bureau offered free hotel reservations in advance. Or a visitor could locate a room simply by stopping by an Official Information Booth, which could be found at every terminal railway station, in downtown San Francisco, in downtown Oakland, and on the exposition grounds. The Universal Bus System would chauffeur anyone from any terminal station to any hotel for only twenty-five cents.[94] A report from the summer of 1915 noted that "adverse newspaper criticisms regarding expected high hotel rates has almost ceased," indicating that the fair's advertising strategy was successful.[95] And according to the bureau's final report, it had not received a single "reasonable" complaint of overcharging or mistreatment.[96] Moreover, San Francisco hotel owners had scored a victory in November 1914 when fair officials agreed to stop sending out pamphlets advertising the Inside Inn with all exposition correspondence and to circulate instead advertisements that included information about all hotels in the city.[97]

These conflicts between hotel owners and the exposition concerned both how much regulatory control the exposition should wield in the city and who should benefit from the event. Rather than the municipal government, a private corporation ran the fair, yet fair officials freely interfered in local business practices. This intrusion frustrated both saloon and hotel owners. On the one hand, local hotel owners joined the hotel bureau because they perceived the advantages of pooling resources to advertise nationwide, but they resented the exposition's heavy-handed treatment of their business. They believed that the Inside Inn was an absolute betrayal of the fair's promises to bring profits to the city. They had pledged to support the exposition because it would bring business to the city, and then the exposition erected a hotel that would directly compete with their business. What more evidence did they need that exposition officials were simply out for a profit? Exposition directors, on the other hand, believed hotel owners were deliberately obstructing their plans for a successful (profitable) fair, and they sought to institute regulations that would ensure fair rates for all visitors. Again, fair directors put their desires to make the fair financially successful above the desires of some city residents, unleashing the antagonism of those local residents.

Just who should benefit from the fair remained a thorny issue after the fair began. Fair officials, acutely aware of the need to make the fair profitable, repeatedly denied requests to lower ticket prices. This position frustrated many local residents. In March 1915, Mrs. C. H. McKenney of San Francisco wrote Mayor Rolph concerning her objection to the high admission prices to the exposition grounds. "I am writing this protest," she told him, "as I think you are a just man, and would like the poor as well as the rich to enjoy the Exposition."[98] Rolph's reply has been lost to history, but McKenney's letter raised a persistent issue during the period leading up to and during exposition. To whom did the exposition belong? Should all San Franciscans enjoy the fair? Would its benefits (whether financial, educational, or cultural) be reserved for wealthy San Franciscans, visiting tourists, and fair officials?

Canny residents repeatedly attempted to "beat the gate" by climbing into the fair and directly challenging fair officials' efforts to regulate access to the event. *San Francisco Chronicle* feature columnist Helen Dare revealed that fence climbers had become a problem when she devoted an entire Sunday column to "Beating—and NOT Beating—the Gate at the Exposition." Her rather entertaining explanation of the many ways that visitors attempted to enter without paying failed to mention that this tactic reflected a very real class conflict. Some attempts to beat the gate came not out of an attempt to cheat the system but out of an inability to pay for entrance to the fair. She focused on society women who haughtily entered the gates and professed to have "left their pass at home," only to have it revealed that they had no pass. Her mention of "a small army of men, women and children [who] broke through the Presidio gate to see the Vanderbilt Cup race" suggests that many people were frustrated enough by their lack of access to the grounds to resort to illegal means.[99] The desires of these residents to see the fair overtook any concerns about breaking the law. While some wealthy women may have brazened their way through the gates simply to prove that they could, far more people likely fought to enter the fairgrounds because they thought that as city residents they should be able to enjoy the same entertainment as their wealthier neighbors.

These episodes remind us that despite assurances that the fair would bring the city together, working people of all races and both genders had a hard time coming up with the money to visit the fair more than a few times during its nine-month run. A working family with two children faced an admission cost of $1.50 simply to enter the grounds, without even purchasing a view of the "breathing" painting *Stella* or of the Panama Canal in the Joy Zone.[100] Further, with the government exhibit palaces closed on Sundays, those who worked a six-day week might never have been able to visit those displays. Despite repeated pleas by visitors of all classes to reduce the children's cost of admission to the fair, exposition officials refused to do so unilaterally. Instead they occasionally did

Fig. 26. PPIEA stockholder season ticket book, 1915. (Collection of the Oakland Museum of California.)

Fig. 27. Turnstiles at the Fillmore Street entrance. Exposition
guards manned each entrance to the grounds. (#1959.087—ALB,
2:19, Bancroft Library, University of California, Berkeley.)

so for school groups or other "deserving" groups of children. Although
a limited number of discount passes costing $10 were available for sale
before the fair, the demand far outpaced the supply. Even that pass's
one-time payment still was out of reach for many working-class people.

It could be quite difficult for working and middle-class families to find
the money to fully enjoy the fair even after they entered the grounds.

Annie Fader Haskell, a widowed schoolteacher whose diary revealed her enthusiasm for the PPIE, noted, "I guess I will not be able to see the side shows if it costs over a hundred dollars to see them."[101] When she was finally able to visit the fair in early May, she "had a nice, well served, reasonably priced dinner" on the Zone.[102] Later that month she and her family "had to walk a long way back to get lunch. That is a mistake. We shall have to manage better next time. Maybe take a lunch or something."[103] Haskell thought very carefully about where she was going to eat on the grounds and what to purchase with her limited spending money.

Wealthier visitors, however, had no such dilemmas about how to spend their funds at the exposition. Mary Eugenia Pierce, a single Berkeley woman, enjoyed far more of the fair's luxuries than did Haskell. Pierce's first lengthy diary entry about the fair noted that she met her friend Mr. Poole at the ferry building, and they proceeded to the fair, where they ate dinner at the Inside Inn and took electric chairs for three hours in the evening to see the grounds.[104] The chairs, or "electriquettes," were wicker basket chairs on wheels propelled by a lead storage battery. At $1.00 per hour, they were a luxury for visitors. Pierce and Poole's use of the chairs for three hours—at a total cost of $6.00—reveals her ability to take advantage of the more expensive attractions on the grounds.[105] Four days later, the two friends met again and spent the day at the fair together, dining at the Old Faithful Inn for both lunch and dinner. Pierce, unlike Haskell, also ate out regularly while visiting the grounds.[106]

Pierce's use of the fairgrounds reveals that wealthy local residents integrated the PPIE into their already active social world. Social clubs hosted dinners at the Inside Inn and the Old Faithful Inn while the Woman's Board held regular dansants and teas in the California Building that were especially popular with the younger members of San Francisco's high society.[107] Upper-class San Franciscans visited the fair regularly. Clemens Max Richter, who lived quite near the grounds on Clay Street, noted in his autobiography, "Of course we visited the Exposition almost every day and we took the greatest delight in using the little auto-like vehicles for locomotion, or the miniature trains."[108]

The fair was a quite different experience for working-class San Franciscans. Exposition directors did little to make the fair more accessible to lower-income San Franciscans. Although Moore avowed before the fair

Fig. 28. Electric roller chairs rented by the hour and used at the exposition.
(San Francisco History Center, San Francisco Public Library.)

that "the Management feels it would be lacking in its duty if it did not do everything in its power to provide facilities whereby the people of San Francisco and the vicinity would derive the maximum benefit that can only be obtained by many visits to the Grounds," he and the other directors consistently refused to consider additional plans to admit those who could not afford the fair.[109] In October, the Executive Committee of the Board of Directors finally approved the issuance of twenty-five hundred passes for children and another twenty-five hundred passes for adults that would be dispensed by the Associated Charities, Catholic Humane Bureau, and Hebrew Board of Relief. The use of the reduced-rate passes, which cost a nickel for children and a quarter for adults, was closely regulated and restricted to the first and third Mondays and Fridays in October. Moreover, fair officials required that a member of the participating charities be present at the gate to identify each person who attempted to enter on a reduced-rate pass.[110] This process, which certainly allowed some needy people to view the fair, failed to reach those working people who had no contact with such charities. Thousands of San Franciscans were not recipients of these charities, and they could not easily afford admission to the fair. The restrictions placed on the passes also complicated their use by those whose work lives made it difficult for them to find time, as well as money, to visit the fair.

When working people voiced their concerns about the steep admission prices, they demonstrated their belief that the benefits of the exposition should extend to them. McKenney's letter to Rolph provides insight into the situation. Her husband was a mechanic who earned $4.00 a day, and, she told Rolph, the price of admission meant that at the most they could only hope to visit the exposition once a month, or not nearly enough time to see "half of it." They had gone on opening day and been "delighted with it all," but they could not afford to visit as often as they would like. She hoped that the mayor could mention her concerns to the exposition management, for she assumed that he would understand.[111] She, and many others, believed the fair boosters' claims that it was truly a public event; thus she felt that they should, as citizens of San Francisco, be able to enjoy it just as the wealthy did.

Working-class San Franciscans and fair directors often had differing conceptions of the benefits that the PPIE should bring the city. Since fair directors put financial success as their top priority, the concerns of those residents who could not afford the fair were of little interest. To the frustration of some residents, then, despite avowals that the fair would belong to all San Franciscans, it very clearly did not. The cost of the fair proved an insurmountable barrier for some would-be visitors, while for others, like Haskell, who could afford the entry fee, it meant that the experience inside was less convenient than it could have been. Haskell never hired an electriquette, rested at the Inside Inn, or ate at the Old Faithful Inn, activities that Pierce took completely for granted in her fair experience. Working-class citizens attempted to lay claim to the fair by beating the gate, by protesting admission prices, and by skimping and saving to pay for the few visits they could afford, but the experience of visiting the fair fundamentally belonged to tourists and those San Franciscans who easily could afford the entry fee. Working-class San Franciscans more often experienced the fair as a worker rather than as a regular visitor. Despite Moore's promise to make the benefits of the fair available to all San Franciscans, clearly neither the grounds nor the activities therein were ever available to all. It is thus difficult to conclude that the fair brought civic unity to all San Franciscans, since the fair directors' emphasis on economic success meant that only the most privileged were able to enjoy its benefits fully.

San Franciscans of all stripes were involved in debates over the fair. They weighed in on the location of the site, the extension of municipal rail lines, the placement of saloons, and the regulation of hotels. Many believed the fair should truly serve all San Franciscans. Once the fair opened, they sought access to the fair in whatever ways they could. They wanted to see the wonders of the Joy Zone, the artwork of the Palace of Fine Arts, the gorgeous gardens and palaces, and the splendid celebrations hosted by foreign governments. Individual residents might have failed to affect fair directors' decisions when it came to the fair's site or the regulation of local businesses—profit was still at the root of the fair officials' decisions—but residents were far more successful when they collectively claimed space for their communities on the grounds. Local and ethnic communities staged parades and pageants and hosted special days in honor of their ethnicity or homeland. Keeping powerful local ethnic and religious constituencies happy seemed essential at a fair funded primarily through local funds.

3 &/ Claiming Their Place

Thousands of Bay Area residents swarmed onto the fairgrounds on June 10 to celebrate Alameda County Day. County citizens staged a lengthy parade to crown the day's events, and it included two floats designed by members of the Oakland African American community.[1] One held fifty black schoolchildren dressed in their Sunday best and excitedly waving to onlookers. These local African Americans participated in the parade because they wanted to demonstrate their pride in their community and their claims to equal citizenship. Two months later, fair visitors likely noticed the large number of young Chinese men and women milling about the fairgrounds, all attendees at Chinese Students' Day, an event that drew hundreds of ethnically Chinese students. As a part of their celebration they sat together for a photograph commemorating the occasion; the impressive mass of young men and women were dressed mostly in contemporary Western attire: suits, ties, and long skirts.[2] This photo stood in stark contrast to popular images of Chinese in the United States that depicted them as exotic (and often morally corrupt) others. These two episodes demonstrate one way in which the Panama Pacific International Exposition offered local ethnic communities a place to construct their group identities.

San Francisco's ethnic, racial, and religious communities provided a broad base of support for the fair and took full advantage of the opportunities it presented to celebrate their heritage. Despite scholarly arguments that emphasize the exclusivity of the vision of the world presented at world's fairs, these and other events demonstrate that the PPIE offered space for visions of a far more inclusive society.[3] Many officially sanctioned exhibits at the fair celebrated American expansionism and the dominance of white Americans both at home and abroad, but that narrative never went unchallenged. From the young white and black boys holding hands as *The Heroes of Tomorrow* in the *Nations of the West* to the events described in the previous paragraph, the PPIE presented a contested vision of race and ethnicity.

Exposition directors maintained some control over exhibits, but they did not control all events on the grounds. Local residents celebrated their ethnic heritage, hometown, or county. Fraternal, political, and religious groups not only created parades, pageants, and speeches to assert their particular place in local society but also used the fair as a stage on which to declare and debate their place in American society. Members of local communities negotiated with fair directors and within their own communities about how they would participate in the event and about how they would be portrayed on the grounds. After the fair began, they actively inserted themselves into the vision of California created at the exposition. These attempts at times produced conflicts. The resolution of these conflicts and the resulting images of these sometimes-marginalized groups at the PPIE depended on their relationship with the city's power structure and the exposition's management, as well as on their relationship to the fair's larger narrative about California's history and society.

Local residents eagerly anticipated the coming of the PPIE. Real estate agents and business owners hoped the fair would work economic miracles, and local residents perceived possibilities for their own participation. The Bay Area's cosmopolitan population provided a rich source of support for the PPIE. Fair officials eventually formed sixteen official auxiliary groups representing local ethnic communities. Prominent professional men formed the nucleus of these organizations. The most active factions included German Americans, British Americans, Finnish Americans, Swedish Americans, Italian Americans, and Dutch Americans.[4] Fair officials called on these men to publicize the fair in diverse ways. They hosted events for visiting officials from their homelands, sent letters and telegrams to friends and relatives to convince them to support their nations' participation in the fair, and raised money to stage events at the fair. Some members were asked to travel with official PPIE delegations abroad to visit their homelands. Such delegations went to Finland, Greece, Norway, Portugal, Spain, Switzerland, and Serbia. Not all were successful. Of those nations only Greece, Norway, Portugal, and Switzerland agreed to participate. But these activities demonstrate these men's deep commitment to the success of the fair and the

Fig. 29. Dedication of the Swedish Building at the PPIE. (San Francisco History Center, San Francisco Public Library.)

importance they attached to seeing their ancestral homelands represented therein.[5]

Local members of these auxiliaries sometimes played a significant role in convincing foreign nations to participate. It was only the forceful persuasion of prominent local Norwegians that convinced Norway to send exhibits, and likewise enthusiastic Swedish San Franciscans convinced a reluctant Swedish government to erect a building at yet another exposition.[6] As James Kaplan argues, the early twentieth century was a time of great rivalry between ethnic groups in cities, with events such as tug-of-war and drill team competitions providing venues for friendly contests between local groups. Therefore, local ethnic leaders perceived the PPIE as an opportunity to increase their prestige and to show off elements of their distinct culture and history. For Swedes, he argues, it was a way for the urban professionals of the Bay Area to differentiate themselves from popular stereotypes that depicted Swedes as taciturn midwestern farmers.[7]

Fair officials may have seen the involvement of local ethnic groups as a way to drum up support and funds for the exposition at home and abroad, but local groups perceived their work in other ways. Local Welsh residents organized a huge eisteddfod—a traditional celebration of Welsh music and poetry dating to medieval times—for the fair, because they believed it would be in the "best interest of the Welsh people" to preserve and perpetuate its "traditions, literature, music, customs and language."[8] Given that letters poured into the exposition office from the idea's supporters in both the United States and Wales, exposition officials no doubt perceived the value of linking the eisteddfod to the fair as another means of drawing visitors rather than as a way of affirming Welsh heritage. In another example, upon the dedication of the fair's Swedish Pavilion, the local Swedish paper reported that there was no one in the crowd who "did not feel the indescribable joy of having the privilege of being Swedish."[9] The PPIE offered a remarkable opportunity for ethnic communities to affirm their own ethnic identity and to proclaim it to others.

The German community's efforts to bring Germany to the fair illustrated the effort that ethnic groups put into organizing a presence at the exposition, even when faced with their homeland's failure to participate. Their activities became deeply entwined with national political debates. German Americans organized early to try to urge the participation of their ancestral homeland. The head of the German-American Auxiliary, Edward Delger, even traveled across the United States, stopping at cities with large German populations as he attempted to drum up support for the PPIE.[10] Despite the enthusiasm of local Germans, the German government resisted the fair officials' overtures and declined their invitation to participate. Sources cited frustration with the large number of previous expositions recently held in Europe, as well as a sense that the expense associated with staging an "appropriate" exhibit for Germany was simply not justified.[11] After Germany chose not to participate, the German-American Auxiliary mounted a campaign to build a Palace of German-American History and Culture, soliciting funds from Germans around the United States. The beginning of World War I frustrated that plan. In July 1914 the auxiliary formally gave up its site on the grounds, admitting it would be unable to stage a German exhibit at the PPIE.[12] The official report explained that the war caused German Americans to divert their "pecuniary sacrifices" to the "relief of the wounded, widows and orphans of the Fatherland."[13] Nonetheless, the group managed to stage a weeklong celebration during German Week at the fair and arranged for a New York Beethoven choir to donate a Ludwig van Beethoven monument in Golden Gate Park as a permanent tribute to the members' German heritage.[14]

The *San Francisco Chronicle* reported that the celebration of German Day on August 5 would include "no floats and no military display, the idea being to represent merely the numbers and loyalty of the Germans in this country." Subsequent reports about the day's events reveal a more complicated story.[15] The parade included thirty-five thousand participants, including a group of "Irish Volunteers" bearing the Irish flag and a group of German military veterans marching in goose step. One headline informed readers that the "Exposition is captured by German-Americans," and the accompanying story contained multiple references to war and military strategy, making it hard to believe that the writer was not intending to link this celebration of German Americanness to the ongoing war in Europe.[16] Reports in other newspapers across the country, including the *Los Angeles Times*, the *New York Times*, and the *Decatur (Illinois) Review*, added a detail that was missing from the *Chronicle*'s account. Upon being informed that Warsaw had fallen to the Germans, the assembled crowd "went wild" cheering Germany's victory.[17]

Keynote speaker, Dr. C. J. Hexamer, president of the German-American Alliance, gave a public speech in which he focused primarily on German contributions to American culture, but he also insisted on the importance of preserving their "Germanness" and decried the move toward "hyphenated" Americans.[18] Such rhetoric avoided the war, but the concurrent meetings of the German-American Alliance squarely addressed the grievances of German Americans. Newspapers reported in great detail about the debate that ensued over a proposed "hot" letter to President Woodrow Wilson that heavily criticized his administration's policy toward Germany and the war. The membership failed to approve the letter after members of the elected leadership threatened to resign; instead, it adopted a milder but still critical resolution that focused mainly on decrying the U.S. policy of selling arms to the Allies,

Fig. 30. German Day at the PPIE. (#1996.003—ALB, 3:131,
Bancroft Library, University of California, Berkeley.)

a practice that the group perceived as a violation of neutrality.[19] Other
resolutions adopted during the sessions criticized eastern newspapers
for their allegedly pro-British bias and opposed increasingly strict immigration laws and the curtailing of civil liberties at home.[20]

German Week at the fair brought the national discussion about the
relationship of German Americans to the United States and Germany to
the fore. Although the United States would not enter the war for another
twenty months, tensions between supporters of Britain and Germany
were already building, and after the United States entered the war, they
would flare up into explicit anti-German discrimination and violence. At
the PPIE, German Americans attempted to negotiate these frictions. They
asserted themselves both as U.S. citizens with the right to criticize their
government's actions and as loyal children of the German fatherland.

The majority of local communities involved in the exposition seem to
have experienced little or no conflict with the fair. Although some officials might have quibbled about budgets or appointments, no records
remain of strains with most of these organizations. Some local groups,

however, did experience major debates regarding their participation in the fair. It is to those issues that we now turn, for they demonstrate the significance that local communities placed on the fair and the ways that the Bay Area's local political and social cultures shaped the vision of society that greeted fair visitors.

San Francisco's social structure affected the ability of ethnic groups to determine their representation on the fairgrounds. The popularity of *The American Pioneer* and *The End of the Trail* sculptures and the '49 Camp attraction in the Joy Zone remind us that the Panama-Pacific International Exposition celebrated American expansionism and the conquest of the West. This story, reproduced in postcards, souvenirs, and in the statuary of the fair, mirrored the fair's larger messages about the superiority of mainstream white American culture. Scholars debate precisely who qualified as "white" in the early twentieth century, however, recognizing the ways in which southern and eastern Europeans and Jews were often racialized as nonwhite others. Debates over immigration restriction in the 1910s focused on eliminating the presence of these supposedly inferior peoples. In the nineteenth century, Irish immigrants had faced similar prejudices, and a long history of anti-Catholicism plagued U.S. society. Irish, Roman Catholics, Chinese, and African Americans each faced discrimination in other parts of the country, but their status in San Francisco did not always reflect their marginalization in other parts of the nation. Their ability to make change on the fairgrounds was intimately connected to their status within the city.

San Francisco's Gold Rush history created a religiously and ethnically diverse social and cultural establishment. Jews, Catholics, and Protestants lived relatively harmoniously in the city, with all three groups wielding significant cultural, political, and economic power. As historian James P. Walsh notes, "In San Francisco during the 1850s, everyone was uprooted, Americans and foreigners alike. The Irish, however, enjoyed the distinct advantage of having had experiences in that condition. . . . San Francisco lacked an entrenched establishment. . . . The Irish were not easily shouldered aside in the competitive scramble for the good things this new society offered."[21] This assessment also applied to the opportunities available to other ethnic and religious groups and accurately reflects the social structure of the city's early history.

The most powerful Catholics in San Francisco were Irish and vice versa, but the city also had a large number of German Catholics and increasing numbers of Italians. The Latino population of the city was quite small in the early twentieth century and did not represent a power bloc within the church or the city.[22] Similarly, most Italian immigrants were more recent arrivals in the city and, as a group, did not yet wield the same kind of power as the more established Irish and German Catholics. Irish immigrants began to gain power in the city during the Gold Rush. By the time of the PPIE, the Irish composed a majority of the Catholic population in the city, and the Catholic Church claimed a majority of churchgoers. Of the six archbishops who held the office between 1853 and 1985, five were Irish.[23] Irish Catholic union men ran the powerful Building Trades Council (BTC) and sat on the San Francisco Labor Council (SFLC). Recent San Francisco mayors had been both Irish and Catholic. The dominance of the Irish in the Catholic Church was so extensive that new immigrant groups were shunted off into new "national" parishes rather than being integrated into existing Irish ones. The Irish and Italians had a particularly troubled relationship in the city, although it had improved by the time of the fair.[24] Prominent Irish Catholics actively assisted in planning the exposition and used the exposition to represent both their ethnic heritage and their faith to fairgoers.

Racial intolerance in San Francisco primarily targeted Asians, who were marked as permanent aliens in San Francisco society. As with thousands of others in the 1850s, the Chinese were drawn to the California gold fields but later moved from mining to the wage labor force, and they were often willing to work for lower wages than their counterparts were. By the 1870s, labor unions and those who feared the invasion of an alien workforce willing to work for low wages stoked anti-Chinese sentiment, which gained strength in the West. Racist propaganda depicted the Chinese as opium addicts and gamblers and their settlements as dens of vice.[25] Violent attacks against the Chinese occurred across the West, culminating in the federal 1882 Chinese Exclusion Act, which barred the entry of Chinese laborers to the United States. Despite this racist opposition, Chinese immigrants created a community for themselves in the city of San Francisco, and Chinatown remained home to the largest concentration of Chinese Americans in the nation.[26] Since the turn of the century anti-Asian sentiment had primarily targeted the Japanese, but the Chinese remained racialized as permanently outside the American body politic. Economically, however, the Chinese were a key part of San Francisco life. The decision to add traditional Chinese architectural details to the neighborhood during the post-earthquake rebuilding helped to make Chinatown a popular tourist attraction and a key part of the city's skyline.[27] As wealthy Chinese merchants wielded economic power in the city and white businessmen sought good relations with Chinese merchants both at home and in China, the coming of the exposition offered the local Chinese an opportunity to assert themselves in multiple ways. In the eyes of some non-Asian spectators, however, the Chinese remained racially and morally suspect.

Few African Americans lived in San Francisco, making their social position more tenuous than that of the Chinese.[28] Black San Franciscans experienced a difficult labor market. The vast majority of black women worked as domestics, and black men also worked menial jobs.[29] This occupational segregation suggests that many white San Franciscans felt an antipathy toward blacks, as well as a reluctance to work alongside them. When labor leader C. L. Dellums migrated to the Bay Area in the early 1920s, for instance, the train porter told him, "Let me give you some advice, young man. Get off in Oakland. There are not enough Negroes in San Francisco for you to find in order to make some connections over there."[30] African American activist W. E. B. Du Bois blamed this phenomenon partly on the strength of the city's labor unions, some of which deliberately excluded blacks.[31] Overt discrimination existed in the Bay Area as well, even if it was not legally sanctioned. Cheap restaurants sometimes carried "whites only" signs.[32] The same negative images of blacks that appeared in other parts of the country certainly also appeared in San Francisco. The film *Birth of a Nation* opened in early 1915 to great success in the city and was welcomed back for a second run in April.[33] African Americans, like the Chinese but unlike the Irish or Catholics, faced significant negative stereotypes both on and off the fairgrounds.[34]

As the Welsh and Swedish enthusiasm for the fair reveals, many San Franciscans seized the opportunity to celebrate their ethnic heritage at the PPIE. Local communities took the chance to stake a claim in U.S. society and to present themselves to the public in the way that they, rather than publicists or the media, chose. The fair's dependence on local monies meant that fair directors tread carefully with many of these groups, wanting to preserve relations with powerful local interest groups and valuable foreign partners. Pre-fair negotiations, both in and outside the Chinese, African American, and Irish communities, demonstrated their relative power in the city and the opportunities that the fair opened up for them.

Local Chinese hoped the fair could improve the status of Chinese Americans in California and boost China's worldwide reputation. The founding of the Republic of China in 1912 stimulated nationalist sentiment among Chinese overseas, and they were eager to support China's efforts to prove itself a strong nation. The editor of the San Francisco paper *Young China* urged, "At the Panama Exposition, we must devote all our energy to it so that Americans will know the reality of our national power."[35] The local *Chinese Western Daily* emphasized how important the fair could be to the development of China, since Chinese overseas could learn much to "push forward Chinese culture and civilization."[36] Others urged that city residents seize the chance to improve Chinatown's image and status both by cleaning up Chinatown so as to impress visitors with "Chinatown's fame" and by raising funds for electric lighting in the neighborhood to make it on par with "Western" neighborhoods.[37]

Members of the local Chinese community remained unsure about the exposition and of their role in it. Many Chinese merchants pledged generously to support the exposition in the early fund-raising drives, but that enthusiasm waned as the fair approached. The proposal of a harsh immigration bill, the debates over California's 1913 Alien Land Law, and a series of issues about the importation of Chinese exposition laborers complicated relations between Chinese residents and the fair's organizers. By early 1914, local attorney John McNab reported to Charles Moore, "The Chinese people feel that they are being called upon to assist a Government Exposition, while at the same time, they are as they see it, being unduly harassed by a Government with which they are friendly." This harassment included crackdowns on activities in Chinatown and changes in immigration procedures that made it more difficult for resident merchants to return to the state from abroad. These activities soured members of the Chinese community on financially supporting a fair sponsored by a state that persisted in discriminating against them and challenged exposition officials' attempts to solicit local Chinese support of the event.[38]

Fair officials responded to this skepticism by courting prominent local members of the Chinese community. The exposition established an official "Chinese Committee" to hold a series of meetings with representatives of the Chinese community and to iron out their concerns.[39] Fair officials organized outings and tours of the fairgrounds to impress prominent local Chinese merchants and bankers. PPIE lawyers attempted to convince them that the fair management "should not be held responsible for governmental immigration laws."[40] They hoped these efforts would both convince Chinese community members of the splendor of the fair and help to distance the fair from federal immigration laws.

Like the Chinese, Irish San Franciscans feared what images of their homeland might appear at the exposition. Earlier expositions had included Irish villages on their midways that presented negative stereotypes of the Irish. Although less anti-Irish sentiment existed in San Francisco than in other parts of the country, the San Francisco Irish remained concerned that the fair might include exhibits that would portray them as outsiders to American society rather than as valuable citizens. Those who supported Irish independence from Great Britain, meanwhile, hoped the fair might offer a space in which to assert that goal to an international audience.

Prominent local Irish residents formed the Celtic Society of the Panama-Pacific International Exposition to meet with fair directors and discuss Irish participation in the fair.[41] They wanted the fair to solicit an independent Irish exhibit, even though Ireland was still a part of Great Britain.[42] This full exhibit would highlight Ireland's commercial and manufacturing interests and "show the world that in every department of human endeavor Ireland . . . can stand with the best."[43] These men hoped that highlighting Ireland's economic success would dispel the visions of a preindustrial, backward nation that still circulated in parts of the United States. To their disappointment, the plan failed. Irish representatives declined to send an official exhibit to the fair, probably because participating in an international exposition during wartime became impossible.

In stark contrast to their active courting of local Chinese and Irish leaders, fair officials more often rebuffed and ignored African Americans when they attempted to contact fair officials. Prominent black leaders tried to approach exposition officials in the planning stages of the fair, but no evidence exists to suggest that they had any success.[44] As early as 1911, black Californians petitioned PPIE officials to organize a display featuring African American achievements but to no avail.[45] The only corroboration of a discussion between the fair organizers and black leaders is a letter from W. E. B. Du Bois, in which he refers to discussions held in 1913 with fair officials who decided that "a special Negro department was unwise." In 1914, he proposed the staging of an impressive pageant and celebration of black culture and history to music director George W. Stewart, but no evidence exists as to whether Du Bois pursued it after Stewart told him it was out of his purview.[46]

Nor did the fair bring many jobs to the black community. S. L. Mash, the president of the Colored Non-Partisan League of California, wrote to Moore in 1915 to complain that his investigation into the job situation for blacks had solicited a response by fair officials that "no Colored Man or Colored Help would be employed in certain positions and departments in the Panama Exposition." Mash argued that this policy would certainly bring the wrath of eastern blacks upon the exposition. Many black churches and organizations nationwide had staunchly backed San Francisco as the choice for the site over segregated New Orleans in the belief that discrimination would not be practiced in California. He pointed out that such exclusionary practices would betray this trust.[47]

Secretary Rudolph Taussig reassured Mash three weeks later that the fair would not do anything "so un-American." In fact, "there are quite a number of colored men employed in the buildings and on the Grounds," he informed him. He did admit that the fair had not hired any black guards since the force had "been made up mostly of veterans of the Spanish war, and were our force large enough, no doubt we would consider forming a colored company." Including blacks at that time remained out of the question. Taussig did not directly answer Mash's charge about the discrimination in "certain" departments.[48]

A private memo from James S. Tobin, exposition director and lawyer, to Moore about the situation revealed much about the fair officials' attitude toward the conflict. "I think a few tactful words will quiet the fears of these 'wards of the nation,'" he wrote.[49] This patronizing attitude suggests that neither Tobin nor Moore intended to take any actions to alter the fair's racial policies. His phrase "wards of the nation" shows that he perceived African Americans as less than full citizens of the United States. The term reflected decades of post–Civil War debate on the readiness of blacks to assume the economic and political rights of full citizenship. It was one used by those who sought to infantilize and patronize African Americans rather than include them in the body politic. The *Oakland Sunshine*, a local black paper, reported at the end of the fair, "The Negro ... derived but very little benefit [from the fair] outside of a few minor jobs as maids and helpers."[50] Many black employees on the grounds worked as restroom attendants or janitors, positions that did little to further their economic or social status in the city.

Some in the black community continued to support the event despite their exclusion from the planning process. They saw the fair as a space from which to voice their civic pride and to assert their citizenship. To this end, they worked to accommodate African American visitors. The *Western Outlook* voiced concern in January 1915 about whether the community was ready to "recognize our full responsibility towards those of our race who come here and who expect to find accommodations that will prove satisfactory and who will not be victims of discrimination." The writer argued, "If there is any mistake in the beginning, and the officials of the exposition are not able to fulfill promises ... it will be a big loss to them," keeping many visitors away from California.[51] Such discrimination would hurt not only the exposition but also the black community in the Bay Area.

A group of prominent Oakland blacks met soon after to discuss establishing a hotel bureau to meet the needs of visiting African Americans. They resolved to cooperate with local civic and fraternal organizations to create such a bureau.[52] A few weeks later, a group of black women in San Francisco sponsored the creation of a downtown Central Bureau of Information for Colored People to facilitate "the comfort and well-being of strangers who may chance to come among us and who care for the good name and reputation of our city."[53] In a similar, and perhaps competing, vein W. A. Butler of San Francisco established a "general information and room-renting agency" specifically designed to meet the needs of fairgoers.[54] No evidence exists to explain the relationship between these agencies or how long they functioned. Their establishment does demonstrate that many blacks perceived a pressing need to better accommodate visiting African Americans. Some local blacks hoped the exposition would draw a significant number of visiting African Americans to the city and distrusted the dedication of exposition officials to provide for them.

The three distinct ethnic communities—Chinese, Irish, and African American—each perceived the fair as a significant place from which to claim space to assert their political and social goals. So, too, did Catholic San Franciscans. Once the fair began, conflicts emerged over the representation of each of these groups on the fairgrounds, and their resolution demonstrated the local power of each group. The groups sought to use the fair to claim space within the city, and their ability to do so rested on their place in the city's social hierarchy.

Although fair officials attempted to maintain good relations with the local Chinese community, many Chinese residents remained skeptical. Yong Chen argues that the Chinese San Franciscans were embarrassed rather than proud of China's attempts to present a modern face to the world. As we will see, debates in the years before the fair about the status of those Chinese workers who had been brought to build the nation's pavilion highlighted the second-class legal status of Chinese immigrants in California. Moreover, Chen argues, when the Chinese government provided these workers with dirty quarters and ragged clothes, the immigrant community's embarrassment only increased. The Chinese government seemed insensitive to the need to present a dignified appearance to curious white Americans. To add insult to injury, on the fair's opening day, the main Chinese palaces remained closed. The only open teahouses served Japanese tea cakes, a situation that reemphasized China's inability to present itself effectively to the world.[55] The *Chinese Western Daily* angrily stated that the only Chinese features in the teahouses were "the clothes that the waitresses wear and the yellowish faces of the manager and cashiers."[56] It also published numerous articles over the next few months detailing the ineptitudes of the Chinese Commission and those charged with organizing the Chinese exhibits.

Unfortunately for Bay Area Chinese residents, the vision of China that greeted visitors at the fair included not only the half-finished Chi-

Fig. 31. View of the Zone at the PPIE showing Underground Chinatown at the Chinese Village. (San Francisco History Center, San Francisco Public Library.)

nese national exhibit but also the far more disturbing Underground Chinatown. Many attractions on the Zone displayed nonwhite peoples in their so-called traditional villages. Underground Chinatown ostensibly represented Chinese life in the United States by plunging visitors into a re-creation of the supposed underground warrens of San Francisco's Chinatown, where prostitutes and opium dealers and addicts plied their trade. Although such a place existed only in the white imagination, stories of an underground Chinatown circulated widely in nineteenth- and twentieth-century San Francisco. A contemporary report described one portion of the attraction: "A maudlin and degrading scene is enacted by a white man who knocks upon a door in company with a white woman and seeks admission to an opium smoking den within which is secreted an imaginary Chinese who demands to know if policemen are present.... When Chinese are not present among the visitors the slave-girl drama is enacted and a revolting scene in which women are inducted into slavery is made clear to the crowd."[57] The concessionaires included every possible nightmare about the Chinese and every contemporary social concern in the attraction. It played upon the history of the forced prostitution of Chinese immigrant women that had convinced many white Americans that all Chinese women were prostitutes.[58] It also drew on Progressive Era fears of white slavery that associated California's white slavers with Asian immigrants.[59]

Members of the Chinese community immediately voiced their displeasure with the demeaning attraction. Their language revealed their hopes for the fair. The Chinese Six Companies appealed to Moore "to end this outrageous travesty of the Chinese people."[60] They voiced their frustration about this concession, which drew the racial line between whites and the Chinese more strongly rather than easing it. Only a well-organized letter-writing campaign, however, forced the exposition into action.[61] In mid-March, Chinese merchants, ministers, and student leaders, as well as white missionaries who worked in Chinatown, all wrote to Moore deploring the Underground Chinatown. They argued that the attraction portrayed a false image of the Chinese and did a serious injustice to a valuable segment of the San Francisco community. The Chinese Chamber of Commerce argued that "the law abiding, peace loving Chinese who in every manner have endeavored to assist the Panama Pacific International Exposition and whose untiring effort . . . brought to you a Chinese Republic exhibit, are disregarded, disgraced, and should this exhibition continue our people will feel they have misplaced their confidence in you gentlemen and in the people of this country."[62] A group of white Protestant mission workers objected to "the gratuitous affront to the best classes of the Chinese community, many of whom are among the most upright and law-abiding of any residents who have come to us from other lands."[63]

The tenor of these complaints reveal that local Chinese residents recognized the power of the fair and of the Underground Chinatown concession to mark them as racial others who threatened white Americans' moral standards. It confirmed their fears that the exposition would strengthen anti-Chinese sentiment. They resented the perpetuation of old stereotypes of San Francisco's Chinatown in an event that was supposed to showcase the city. A group of Chinese ministers and elders noted, "The exhibitions [sic] . . . are deliberate falsehood, libel and slander and a disgrace to the Chinese race, for they are sheer fabrication from the imagination of the promoters . . . in order to make some dirty profit."[64] They pointed out that the conception of an Underground Chinatown originated years earlier when white guides led visitors interested in slumming into a fabricated vision of an Underground Chinatown that lay beneath the city. "We fought hard against this libelous concoction defaming our good name before the Police Department," noted representatives of the Chinese press. "At that time the police stood by these guides, evidently sharing with them the evil gains."[65] The Chinese community resented that old falsehoods continued to be propagated to an international audience, when they had hoped instead to use the fair to improve China's and Chinatown's reputations.

Moore and the fair board responded only after Chen Chi, the official Chinese PPIE commissioner, stated in stark terms his government's displeasure with the attraction and with the exposition's failure to address the complaint he had lodged after the concession opened three weeks before. "Is it fair," he asked Moore, "to our many law-abiding and moral Chinese residents that these unwise deeds and acts of perchance some immoral Chinese resident should be flaunted before the world?" China came to the exposition with the expectation that it would be welcomed as a friend, he argued, and "every country has a right to be judged not by the lowest elements of degeneracy in its past civilization but by its nobler attempts to develop the best that is in its peoples' ambitions."[66] Despite Chen's forceful objections and the censure of the Chinese government, the PPIE Committee on Concessions and Admissions closed the concession only under direct orders from Moore, who apparently realized the damage the attraction could do to the exposition's (and the state's) relationship with China.[67]

The concession reopened as Underground Slumming in June. Fair officials reassured the concerned Chinese community that it had dispensed with all offensive features. Although a San Francisco Chronicle article reported that the new attraction was "completely changed," refocused on the evils of the drug habit and with "nearly a mile of underground passages, wherein are over 100 figures, showing the destroying effects of various prohibited drugs," it remained closely associated with Chinatown.[68] An ad placed in the San Francisco Call revealed this connection.

It read: "On the Zone Underground Slumming Formerly Underground Chinatown More Impressive than any Play Book or Sermon."[69] The ad used a number of cues to inform readers that the attraction was still really about the Chinese. Changing "Chinatown" to "Slumming" did not remove the association with the Chinese, since slumming was the term for the popular practice of white men and women visiting Chinatown in search of a salacious view of the lifestyle they believed existed there.[70] The reference to "any Play Book or Sermon" on the surface reassured potential visitors that it was an educational exhibit, but it also attracted those eager to see rather than simply hear about the evils of slumming and, by insinuation, Chinatown. Viewing the effects of the drug habit had an appeal that no play, book, or sermon could ever provide.

Both Underground Slumming and Underground Chinatown reinforced the racialization of the Chinese as exotic, corrupt others. In California, where Asians, rather than African Americans, were often most actively discriminated against, these images of corrupt, violent, and overly sexual Chinese held great power. In reopening the attraction, the concessionaire (and exposition officials) reinforced the association with Underground Chinatown by including both names in the advertising. The concessionaire hoped that visitors who might have missed the original incarnation might be induced to try the new version, despite the change in its name.

Underground Chinatown revealed that the local Chinese community was correct to be wary of the exposition. Rather than affirming Chinese immigrants as valued members of the San Francisco community and sons and daughters of modernized China, the Zone construed the Chinese as deviant, exotic others. Although Chinese San Franciscans succeeded in closing the original attraction, as long as Underground Slumming existed on the Zone it provided a powerful foil to the official Chinese exhibit on the grounds. To visitors familiar with visions of opium-addicted Chinese prostitutes and gamblers, the new attraction offered affirmation that the official Chinese Pavilion and Chinese-sponsored events would be hard pressed to counteract.

Local Irish Americans became involved in a discussion over representation of their homeland at the fair as well, but the matter was resolved rather differently. Although the Celtic Committee campaigned to bring an official Irish exhibit to San Francisco, the only Irish exhibit at the

Fig. 32. Irish Village in the Zone at the PPIE. (San Francisco
History Center, San Francisco Public Library.)

PPIE was the Irish Village on the Zone, the Shamrock Isle. The concessionaires who funded Shamrock Isle solicited support both in Ireland
and in San Francisco. The exposition directors made an effort to gain
approval from prominent Irishmen in San Francisco before accepting
the application for the Shamrock Isle. In June 1913, the Committee on
Concessions and Admissions unanimously passed a resolution requir-

ing that "satisfactory reports in the form of letters be obtained from Mr. Mullally, Mr. Joseph B. Tobin, Father Jos. McQuaid, and Arch-Bishop Riordan"—all prominent San Francisco Irish Catholics—about the quality of the exhibit.[71] The committee feared the disapproval of the Irish community enough to ensure that the display would be unobjectionable before issuing a contract.

The proposed attraction remained controversial despite this gesture toward the Irish community. Radical labor leader Father Peter Yorke, the editor of the *Leader*, the weekly Irish Catholic paper in San Francisco, warned that those behind the concession were planning something "on the same level as the concession for the Hairy Hottentots or the Blubbery Esquimaux" and on par with "the miserable exhibitions made at Chicago and St.Louis."[72] Yet the *Monitor*, the pro-Irish paper of the Catholic archdiocese of San Francisco, published an extensive interview with Michael O'Sullivan, the manager of the proposed concession, in which the exhibit was described in only positive terms. The village he described featured "an array of enormous old castles, round towers and ivy-covered ruins . . . a row of characteristic cottages of various sizes and colors, each on a picture itself, . . . a sturdy Irish boy with his immortalized low-back car of song and story. . . . And behind him, two rosy-cheeked, colleens come riding merrily along in a donkey cart."[73] This concession replaced one caricature of Ireland with another. It drew on a heavily romanticized vision of the Ireland that reduced Irish citizens to inhabitants of magnificent castles or charming cottages and obscured the reality of Irish struggles with industrialization and poverty. For those who hoped to have an official Irish exhibit that would highlight Ireland's modernity and economic success, these plans for the Shamrock Isle must certainly have been a disappointment.

Yorke continued to criticize plans for the Shamrock Isle in 1914, but by 1915, discussions ended. Only periodic ads for the concession and general descriptions of fair attractions mentioned Shamrock Isle, suggesting that its depiction of Irish life may have been less damaging than was first feared.[74] Since Yorke loudly voiced his original complaints, it seems unlikely he would have avoided criticizing the exhibit had it been as objectionable as he first assumed. The Shamrock Isle closed a few months after opening, suggesting that the image of Ireland it presented did not appeal to visitors in the same way that Underground Chinatown or Underground

Slumming did. Fair historian Frank Morton Todd remarked that "the public did not seem especially interested in Irish singing and clog dancing—at least not enough of the public to make it pay."[75] Todd's offhand note suggests why the Shamrock Isle never generated the same sort of attention—positive or negative—as Underground Chinatown did. The image it presented of Ireland did not carry the salacious interest, or the racial power, of the Underground attractions. Todd also reported that Underground Slumming drew many visitors, suggesting that viewers chose to spend their money on that attraction rather than on the Shamrock Isle or other Zone concessions. Visitors to San Francisco were more eager to see contemporary concerns about drugs and sex acted out in a racialized context rather than watching charming Irish lasses milk cows.

The local Irish remained vigilant about the depiction of their homeland at the fair. The editor of the *Monitor* complained in July that Alexander Stirling Calder had excluded the Irish from *Nations of the West*. As noted previously, this prominent statuary group stood atop one of the arches in the Court of the Universe and depicted the peoples who had shaped the United States. The editor charged that the piece ignored the Irish, who had been instrumental in building the nation.[76] In response, Calder himself informed the paper that the Anglo-Saxon figure was intended to be "one collective representative of the whole British idea," which included the Irish. Moreover, he claimed that Celtic ideals inspired his composition of the *Mother of Tomorrow*. Calder's reply did not appease the *Monitor*, which termed it "alas, very lame."[77] The matter ended there, but the point was made. The San Francisco Irish, backed by the Catholic Church (as publishers of the paper), demanded representation on the grounds.

The complaint about *Nations of the West* seems trivial, but it demonstrates the power of Irish Catholics in San Francisco. Exposition officials worried enough about offending the archdiocese and the Irish community that it forwarded a complaint about a prominent piece of art on the grounds to the chief sculptor himself, presumably with a request that he address it. Their attempt to ensure that the Shamrock Isle proved inoffensive indicated a desire not to antagonize powerful members of San Francisco society. Exposition officials needed the financial support of the local Irish community. They would not risk affronting either the archdiocese, led by Irishman archbishop Edward Hanna, or the BTC, which was controlled by the Irish former mayor and exposition director Patrick H. McCarthy.[78]

Pleasing local Catholics, however, put the fair directors at risk of attack by the increasingly vocal anti-Catholic bloc in other parts of the nation. Nationwide, in the 1910s anti-Catholic papers focused on denouncing the "Catholics' perceived inability to embrace American civic virtues— insisting that their adherence to priestly hierarchies make Catholics unable to accept American values of egalitarianism, individualism, and tolerance."[79] In the summer of 1913, rumors circulated among Protestant groups that a model of the Vatican would appear at the exposition. National protest erupted, as Protestants across the country voiced their concerns to Moore. One Missourian promised Moore: "Protestants in these parts are going to boycott the Expo.... You Catholic fellows think you are smart but you can't fool us any longer. Every member of the Panama Exposition is a Jesuit."[80] Despite assurances that no such plan existed, religious issues continued to plague fair directors.

These tensions came to a head in the spring of 1914, when the Italian government announced the appointment of Ernesto Nathan, the mayor of Rome, as Italian commissioner to the Panama-Pacific International Exposition. Catholics, first in San Francisco and then across the nation, loudly protested his appointment. Nathan, an Italian Jew born in Great Britain, was a central figure in perpetuating the ideals of "Liberal Italy," the term used for the secular Italian state founded in 1860. He condemned the Vatican as a backward remnant of a dying civilization and dismissed papal infallibility while he served as mayor of Rome. He maintained that modern Rome was "the champion of liberty of thought" while papal Rome was "the fortress of dogma where the last despairing effort is being made to keep up the reign of ignorance."[81] International protest against Nathan continued throughout his tenure as mayor, with many American papers and clergy weighing in.[82] American Catholics who recognized the supreme authority of the pope and who viewed liberal Italy as an illegal state saw Nathan's official presence at the exposition as an unspeakable affront to their faith.[83]

Catholics in San Francisco drew on their brethren nationwide to mount a loud and vigorous campaign to keep Nathan away from the exposition. The *Monitor* sounded the call in February by stating:

Against such an appointment not only every Catholic in the United States, but every decent citizen of our country . . . must and will protest. . . . He is not only the avowed enemy of Christianity, but the world's arch-insulter of the Catholic Church. . . . Nathan is an English-born Jew and a violent Freemason of the most malignant European type. . . . All decent men of the Hebrew race repudiate him. . . . Let the Catholics of this city unite in one voice to protest against the coming of Nathan to San Francisco. Let them call upon their fair-minded non-Catholic brethren to join them in that protest.[84]

Letters from Catholics across the country poured into the exposition's offices. The State Federation of German Catholic Societies of the State of New Jersey wrote in a March letter that its members "feel that a grievous insult has been offered the Catholics of the United States . . . by the Italian government" by appointing Nathan.[85] The *Monitor* and the *Leader* continued to attack Nathan, blasting his reputation and reminding readers of the support the campaign was drawing from Catholics across the nation and world.

The debate over Nathan represented a constellation of social concerns about Catholicism, Freemasonry, anti-Semitism, the Italian state, and modernity in general. Anti-Catholic rhetoric came from devout Protestants and from anarchists and socialists who remained skeptical of any religion. Nathan's Jewish heritage only complicated the issue, with some of the attacks drawing on traditional anti-Semitic rhetorical tropes. Although the *Leader* featured a headline that screamed, "Specific Bigoted Acts of Nathan, Cockney Jew," the text did not dwell on his heritage other than to call him a "low type of Cockney." Other editors were not so generous. The *Western Catholic* of Springfield, Illinois, "castigated Nathan, 'the little Jew Mayor of Rome,' whose ancestors, 'hounded Jesus Christ to the darksome and bloody heights of Calvary.'"[86] San Francisco papers tended to shy away from this virulent rhetoric, but most objections noted his Jewish heritage. Anti-Semitism remained just beneath the surface of the Catholic press' editorials on the subject as well. The respect accorded to San Francisco's powerful Jewish community likely mediated the issue.[87] San Francisco witnessed little public anti-Semitism in the early twentieth century, demonstrating the city's religiously tolerant culture.[88]

Fig. 33. Luncheon tendered to Italian commissioner Ernesto Nathan by
the president and Board of Directors of the Panama-Pacific International
Exposition Company, Palace Hotel, June 2, 1914. (#1959.087—ALB,
1:138, Bancroft Library, University of California, Berkeley.)

Protestant Americans who feared a Catholic takeover took the opportunity to air their skepticism of the Catholic Church and their fears about
the threats that Catholics posed to the body politic. W. P. Oliver of La
Crosse, Wisconsin, noted, "As an American citizen . . . who hopes to visit
the Exposition I want to protest against these trouble makers being recognized. . . . If this is to be distinctly a Roman Catholic Exposition I and
thousands of others want to know it so that we may . . . arrange to spend
our time and money in other directions."[89] From the opposite perspective, a Chicago chapter of the Guardians of Liberty—a Chicago-based
anti-Catholic Masonic group—passed a resolution in favor of Nathan
and supporting the exposition's stand because Catholic protests were
"UnAmerican."[90]

Throughout this turmoil, the exposition directorate remained unmoved
and refused to protest Nathan's appointment. They welcomed Nathan
and local supporters of liberal Italy with an elaborate ceremony in June
when he came to dedicate the site of the Italian Building.[91] The local
Jewish community also celebrated his arrival. He remained the commissioner general of Italy to the exposition, although renewed protests

occurred in 1915 over allegations that Nathan had defrauded the Italian government in his capacity as the representative to the PPIE. Despite the failure to remove Nathan, the Catholic press congratulated itself in raising awareness of Nathan's faults. After Nathan's humiliating loss in Rome's June 1914 mayoral election to a Catholic monarchist, the *Monitor* had reported, "This tells its own story—the coming at last to the 'turn in the lane,' for Mr. Nathan, the world's most notorious libeler of things Catholic. . . . There is not the least question that the world-wide Catholic protest made against Nathan, on his appointment . . . helped to bring about his defeat in the Roman elections Tuesday. That protest, begun by THE MONITOR. . . riveted the attention of the world on the infamous character of Nathan."[92] Two months later the paper again had noted, "In Rome, Nathan the unspeakable has dwindled down to a mere nonentity, it seems."[93] Later in the year, when Nathan returned to San Francisco for the fair, exposition officials and supporters of the liberal Italian government again wined and dined him.

Nathan's successful tour at the fair, over the vociferous complaints of local Catholics, raises a question: if San Francisco Catholics held so much power, why did they fail to keep Nathan away from the exposition? Although the board included at least one local Catholic, it included even more members of the local Jewish community, suggesting the PPIE board had little personal or religious motivation to interfere in the Nathan controversy. Second, Nathan represented a foreign nation, and there was little the exposition could do to keep him from coming to San Francisco. Fair officials spent hundreds of thousands of dollars courting foreign governments. It was unlikely they would do anything to jeopardize those relationships, particularly as the war in Europe threatened the attendance of all European nations. Possibly offending the Italian government by asking it to recall the commissioner was likely not a step Moore or other officials wanted to take, even if they had seriously considered the Catholics' objections.

Although Catholics failed in their campaign to keep Nathan away from San Francisco, they certainly succeeded in attacking his reputation and in convincing many Catholics, and perhaps non-Catholics, that he was a danger to their faith. The threatened boycott of the exposition, however, did not take place. After an initial hesitation and despite Nathan's presence, Archbishop Hanna gave a benediction after the opening ceremonies.[94] Although the protests failed to remove Nathan, they unified both San Francisco and American Catholics of all ethnicities and strengthened their sense of themselves as Catholic.[95] They also highlighted differences within the city's Italian community. Many older Italian immigrants were fervent nationalists and anticlericals who supported the very liberal Italian state that Nathan represented, and their stance explains the support that some San Francisco Italians expressed for Nathan.[96] They may have resented the Catholic attacks on a representative of the government they supported. Moreover, Irish San Franciscans—who backed both the *Monitor* and the *Leader*—had historically voiced animosity toward their Italian compatriots. Although that tension was fading by the 1910s, this debate over Nathan may have rekindled old feelings. Both newspapers' opposition toward Nathan may have been a disguise for anti-Italian sentiments. The PPIE, an event designed to increase international cooperation, here became a stage for ethnic and religious debates on a local, national, and international level. Local immigrant communities such as the Italians, Irish, Germans, and Chinese each latched upon the fair as a way to define both their status as Americans and their relationship to their homelands.

Not long after the debate about Nathan emerged, local Catholics found themselves involved in another dispute with the fair. The editor of the *Monitor* learned in August 1914 that PPIE officials had invited the American Federation of Patriotic Voters, a national anti-Catholic organization, to hold its annual convention at the fair. Although the Board of Directors' first response to the editor's objection was to assert that the "Exposition extended invitations to all organizations without distinction as to their religious, political or other beliefs," their position quickly changed.[97] By October, Moore admitted to the board's Executive Committee that the group had been invited without knowledge of its members' beliefs. Further, "he had learned later that this was an anti-Catholic organization, and that . . . the Exposition's action in sending out the invitation to this organization might cause the Exposition unwillingly to offend an element in our population that there was certainly no desire to displease."[98] At an Executive Committee meeting the next week, Director Tobin, the only Catholic on the board, protested against the plan and informed his fellow directors that the invitation would surely cause ill feeling among all Catholics.[99]

Fortunately for fair officials, a tactless comment by a leader of the federation provided the exposition an easy way out of the situation, and in early 1915 the PPIE withdrew the invitation. A letter from the federation to the fair had stated that its members believed "that we need relief from a certain crooked grafting political machine posing as a religion." Director of Congresses and Conventions James Barr informed the group in reply, "[This] is a direct attack upon a religious faith held by many. The exposition authorities are of the opinion that a universal exposition should be in the largest sense constructive and they neither desire nor can they tolerate the participation of any organization or exhibitor having a contrary object."[100] This anti-Catholic rhetoric gave exposition officials an excuse to retract the invitation and to acquiesce to the Catholics' requests. The *Monitor* rejoiced in its victory and praised the exposition for respecting the rights of Catholics.[101]

The church's power in San Francisco allowed Catholics to approach the fair from a position of strength. PPIE officials needed the backing of the *Monitor* and the church, or they risked very bad local and national publicity. Such publicity could threaten the fair economically. A local Catholic boycott of the PPIE could even prove disastrous. Although the objections to Nathan and the Patriotic Voters appear quite different from the protests mounted by the Chinese or Irish, they stem from similar concerns about the effects of "othering" on the distribution of social and political power. Nathan's attacks on the pope and the Patriotic Voters' accusations against American Catholics placed Catholics in the position of being the other. Honoring Nathan and the federation with invitations to the fair seemed to Catholics to validate anti-Catholicism and to threaten their standing in the Bay Area, and they believed that they should be able to counter it. They used their power in the city to keep the federation from the fair, even if they could not successfully fight Nathan's appointment.

Local Irish, Catholics, and even Chinese Americans successfully wielded some influence with fair officials. Such was not the case for African Americans, who experienced outward discrimination on the fairgrounds and had no demonstrable influence with fair officials. In the

local black community in the spring of 1915 a debate about the useful-
ness of an official day dedicated to African Americans erupted between
those who hoped it might help showcase black achievements and those
who worried it would simply perpetuate discrimination. As the correspondence with Du Bois suggested, fair officials did not arrange any
celebration of a Negro Day when planning the PPIE. Shortly after opening day, a group of local blacks began to push for it, unleashing a heated
debate in the local and state African American community.[102] Backed by
a number of local ministers and the publisher of the *Oakland Sunshine*,
the San Francisco and Oakland Bureau of Information and Rooming
House Association hoped to raise $1,250 to fund a celebration of Negro
Day.[103] The event would include a choir of black schoolchildren, athletic
races of all kinds, and, organizers hoped, an appearance by none other
than Booker T. Washington.[104]

Others in the community vehemently opposed the plan for Negro
Day, regarding it as an offensive and patronizing offer.[105] After receiving
a letter outlining the plan, the editor of the *Western Outlook* responded:
"We have no exhibit as a race, no representation on any of the boards,
and nothing to point to with pride; and now comes forward a body of
men to be used as a side show, to draw lines that they fight against, and
for what? It smells bad to us, and we are against it. . . . As American citizens we can enjoy any day, county, State or national, but let us taboo
Negro Day. We don't want it, don't need it, and should not allow ourselves to be used like a set of dummies."[106] The Negro Business League
similarly opposed the idea, because with "nothing within the confines of
the fair over which to make merry," any attempt at a celebration would
be a "miserable failure." Finally, the league argued, the fair directors' sys-
tematic rejection of every attempt by African Americans to contribute
to the fair made it hypocritical to consider celebrating a Negro Day.[107]

African Americans throughout California used the debate about Negro
Day as a way to critique the fair's attitude toward their community and,
indirectly, the position of blacks in the Bay Area. Mabel Wilson has demonstrated that blacks throughout the nation used such fairs as the PPIE
to critique and assert their status in U.S. society.[108] Bay Area blacks were
no different. Attorney James C. Waters, Jr., argued in the *Western Outlook*
that since African Americans had absolutely no role in organizing the

exposition, the proposed Negro Day could be nothing more than "Jim Crow Day." Moreover, he reported that his attempt to pin down the official exposition stand on race relations came to naught. Executive Secretary Taussig answered his request for clarification about equal treatment of blacks on the grounds by curtly stating that "no distinction is made on account of race, color, or religion."[109]

Groups across the state voted to oppose Negro Day. The Interdenominational Ministerial Union of Los Angeles resolved that "Negroes cannot do now in four weeks what it has taken the white people four years to do."[110] The newly established Northern California branch of the National Association for the Advancement of Colored People (NAACP) passed a similar resolution. It noted that since the celebration was without popular support, it would "have a tendency to point to our lack of civic pride, and humble us as American citizens."[111] Reverend Allen Newman stated the case even more clearly in a letter to the *Western Outlook*: "Knowing as I do that Mr. Moore . . . has emphatically refused to lend any influence in helping the promoters of this movement to secure the representative men and women of our race for such a celebration . . . my judgment leads me to oppose . . . Negro Day."[112] Newman's explicit attack on Moore is the only such existing accusation, but the tenor of the other objections suggest that neither Moore nor other fair officials had done much to solicit opinions from local African Americans. Although little evidence remains about the extent to which the debate reached beyond California, at least one other black newspaper, the *Cleveland Gazette*, published a statement opposing the plan.[113] If those outside California ignored the debate, it may have been because they were busy planning for the national emancipation exposition in Chicago that summer.[114]

The debate over Negro Day suggests that local blacks understood the power of the spectacle created at the fair to racialize them as being outside of white American civic culture. Their many objections referred to the need to maintain their status as "American citizens" and suggested that they feared the effects of Negro Day on perceptions of that citizenship. As Lynn Hudson has pointed out, this debate over Negro Day took place in the larger context of Progressive Era race relations.[115] The release of D. W. Griffith's film *Birth of a Nation* in January 1915 drew the nation's attention to the relationship between blacks and whites in the South. The

Fig. 34. The "African Dip" in the Zone was only one of a number of attractions at the PPIE that displayed demeaning images of African Americans. (San Francisco History Center, San Francisco Public Library.)

film depicted blacks in harshly racist terms, focusing on the sexual threat black men posed to white women. The Bay Area's black community mobilized against the film, a situation that certainly provided a backdrop to the debate over Negro Day. Concessions that depicted blacks in stereotyped, primitive, and negative ways—the Dixie Plantation, Somaliland, and the African Dip—certainly existed on the grounds, but no records reveal any organized protest by African Americans against these concessions, perhaps because they realized fighting them was a losing battle.[116] Rather, they focused their energy on the question of Negro Day, which offered them an opportunity to take a proactive rather than a reactive response to white racialization of blacks. Debating Negro Day demonstrated the black community's attempt to wield some control over how its members would participate in any racial formation on the fairgrounds.

The African American debate over Negro Day outwardly differed from the protests of the Irish, Catholic, or Chinese communities, which all received significant recognition from fair officials. Yet those differences should not obscure the basic issues, which remained the same. Some African Americans felt that a poorly organized Negro Day would do the same kind of damage to their community that Underground Chinatown did to the Chinese. Because African Americans had no real relationship with the exposition and little power in the city, their debate remained focused internally rather than on pursuing negotiations with fair directors, who had already demonstrated a lack of interest in dealing with them.

Despite their conflicts with fair officials about their participation in the fair, these communities each found ways to use the spectacle of the fair to their advantage. Catholics, in particular, found affirmation of their history at the fair. As soon as the fair opened, the *Monitor* praised the event's depiction of Catholicism. From the statue of Father Junipero Serra above the California Building's entrance to the "cowled figure of the priest" on the portal of the Tower of Jewels, the writer noted, "[o]n every hand in the length and breadth of the great exposition, the Catholic spirit that blazed the trail for civilization in California is in evidence."[117]

Local Catholic residents had no trouble gaining permission to use the fair to pay tribute to the state's Catholic roots. In July, members of the Junipero Serra Club of Monterey performed "The Landing of Serra" on the shores of the lagoon located in front of the Palace of Fine Arts. In a tribute to the Catholic tradition of honoring holy relics, Father Serra's own vestments held a place of respect on an altar on the stage. According to the *Monitor*, "The land expedition of Don Gaspar de Portola with his Catalonian dragoons and muleteers and a few docile Indians... were shown awaiting Padre Junipero Serra ... who sailed over the tranquil waters of the lagoon." Written in blank verse, the pageant was "beautiful," reported the writer, even though few viewers could hear the actors' words because of the play's outdoor setting.[118] Local residents requested a repeat performance, and a month later the group staged the pageant in a larger and more visible venue, the Court of the Universe. A celebration of High Mass followed, truly imbuing the grounds with the "Catholic Spirit."[119]

This display of the Catholic contributions to the "founding" of California affirmed the Catholics' role at the expense of the conquest's toll on native peoples. The coming of Father Serra brought disease, death, and virtual enslavement to thousands of natives, as well as the imposition of a foreign religious and social system. Anglos hastened the damage when they engulfed the state during the Gold Rush and shot and killed natives for sport or forced them to labor. For native peoples the Catholic presence in the state was nothing to celebrate, but the Catholics' claim on California history fit neatly into the fair's dominant narrative. The landing of Serra signified the beginning of the conquest of California that the white male pioneer finished eighty years later. According to this narrative, Catholic priests brought civilization and Christianity to the natives just as surely as the pioneers did. The absence of significant anti-Catholic sentiment in San Francisco made it easy to collapse the two narratives together and to forget the differences between missionary priests and gold-seeking forty-niners.[120] The pioneer dominated the vision of California presented at the fair, but room remained for the padre, since his presence did not threaten the fair's larger racial message. This story of California history placed Catholics as an integral part of conquest and as valued members of the state and the nation. In the social Darwinist framework of the fair, Spanish conquest was simply evidence of one superior race supplanting another. It was natural selection in action.

Although anti-Catholic rhetoric during the Progressive Era focused on the Catholic threat to the American body politic, at the PPIE, Catholics were envisioned as important members of California's past and present. Catholics found their faith itself reaffirmed at the exposition. Fair officials welcomed Catholic priests to the grounds and allowed them to perform mass more than once. In 1914 the fair firmly had denied a request from a Protestant group to hold services on the grounds, rendering the welcome that Catholic priests received even more notable. In mid-July 1915, for example, exposition officials discussed having a special day in order to welcome Cardinal James Gibbons to the fair only a month after they tried unsuccessfully to cancel Protestant preacher Billy Sunday's appearance on the grounds.[121] The anti-Catholicism that emerged before the fair did not affect the PPIE. The Catholic Church's ability to participate actively in the fair may be seen as an affirmation of its entrenchment in the power structure of San Francisco.

One of the most compelling reasons for understanding the PPIE as a site for the construction of racial, ethnic, and religious identities is that the event offered local and national groups ways to construct their own spectacles that they could display to fairgoers. As the celebration of German Day revealed, these special days usually involved parades, speeches, or pageants, presumably organized by the group itself. These large celebrations offered local residents the chance to assert specific visions of their relation to the U.S. body politic to both fairgoers and newspaper readers. Every day, local papers contained headlines, pictures, and articles about the various goings-on at the fair. In an era in which many residents read one or more papers each day, this publicity proved a powerful way for the fair's visual and rhetorical messages to filter out beyond the grounds.

When Chinese American fraternal and political organizations met at the fair, they claimed the space of the exposition and included themselves in the public discourse surrounding the fair. The Chinese Nationalist League of America, the Chinese Students' Alliance in the United States, the International Buddhist Congress, the Chinese Students' Christian Association of North America, and the Asiatic Students' Alliance— all met on the grounds during the late summer of 1915.[122] In October, the United Parlor of the Native Sons of the Golden State, composed of second-generation Chinese San Franciscans, assembled on the grounds. This use of the grounds as a meeting place for local (and national) Chinese residents and immigrants presented a dramatically different vision of the Chinese in California society than did Underground Chinatown. As described in this chapter's opening anecdote, the photograph of Chinese Students' Day, with its rows and rows of young Asian men and women dressed in suits and ties and American-style dresses, presented a startling comparison to the robed, queued men of Underground Chinatown.[123] By using the grounds in the same way that other fraternal and political organizations did, Chinese Americans challenged the racialized vision of their lives offered by Underground Chinatown and the popular press.

When ethnic Chinese visitors celebrated China Day and Chinese Students' Day at the exposition, they downplayed traditional aspects of Chinese culture and instead focused on both China's relationship to the United States and its recent technological advancements. In the Chinese context, the pageantry that other nations displayed evoked anti-Asian sentiment and old stereotypes, so the Chinese avoided drawing attention to their history in these events. Instead, they inserted themselves into the spectacle of the fair as Westernized, modern citizens of China or of the United States rather than as symbols of an alien "yellow peril."[124]

Fig. 35. PPIE souvenir ribbon, 1915. (Collection of the Oakland Museum, gift of Ernest Isaacs.)

On St. Patrick's Day, local Irish citizens staged an elaborate celebration claiming their dual position as Americans and proud children of Ireland. Their celebration differed, however, from the Chinese celebration of China Day because they shouted their Irish pride to the rooftops. They turned lights green and held an enormous parade, High Mass, and a concert of favorite Irish songs. More than sixty local Irish societies participated in the planning and were represented on the grounds, a number that suggests the breadth of preparation and the importance many local Irish attached to the celebration.[125] More than seventy-five thousand people flooded the grounds that day, sporting green accessories of all sorts and their pride in their homeland.

Patrick McCarthy, former mayor, exposition director, and labor leader, served as honorary chairman of the celebration. His address to the crowd reflected the tenor of the event: "We are gathered here today to celebrate not only our national holiday, but to perpetuate the glory of our race ... a race which has produced ... men of great deeds in all times and in all kinds of human activities."[126] By choosing the word "race," McCarthy indicated that the Irish organizers felt confident in unabashedly celebrating their Irish identity. Unlike the Chinese, who perceived the dangers of playing into white Americans' visions of Asians, the San Francisco Irish had no difficulties claiming both Irish and American identities. An Irish identity did not, in this context, threaten their Americanness. Local Irish could proudly wave green flags and celebrate being both loyal citizens of the United States and proud sons of daughters of a romanticized Erin.

The event's speakers declared their loyalty to state and nation. These declarations were particularly important in 1915, since the Irish hostility to Great Britain had led many Irish to sympathize with the Germans in the European conflict. Although the United States remained neutral, much popular sympathy lay with the British; thus Irish support of Germany only called more attention to their outsider status in parts of the United States. Attorney John J. Barrett, the keynote speaker of the day, gave a lengthy speech that began with a clear affirmation of the Irish community's loyalty to the United States: "I know that I but give a tongue to every drop of Irish blood that stirs in this vast audience when I declare that, though the emerald emblem of the new-born nation across the sea is unfurled by us today in uncompromising homage, the Flag that now as ever is next to our heart and flutters in the breezes of its palpitating loyalty is the Stars and Stripes."[127] Despite the failure to depict an independent Ireland at the fair, the local Irish community drew on their position in San Francisco society to construct themselves as loyal sons and daughters of Ireland and the United States.

The Irish use of the grounds offered an explicitly anticolonial statement that called into question the fair's larger imperialist goals. When
the San Francisco Irish used the fair to call for an independent Ireland,
they directly criticized the imperial system that placed the Irish as colonial others in relation to the English. That fair directors facilitated this
display—because of the strength of the San Francisco Irish community—
demonstrates the effects of local politics on the fair's larger narrative.

Meanwhile, African Americans never celebrated Negro Day at the
PPIE. Instead, community leaders—particularly women—turned to urging participation in San Francisco Day and Alameda County Day. The
organizers of these efforts drew again on conceptions of citizenship and
civic pride as they drummed up support, suggesting the importance
they placed on the fair. The Civic Center, an organization of Oakland
black women, held repeated meetings to organize the community's participation in the event.[128] The *Oakland Sunshine* urged the community
to attend and show visitors "that this is our Fair and our State and that
we appreciate it."[129] And on June 10, as the opening vignette noted, the
Alameda County Day parade included two floats of African Americans.
The Colored Women's Club designed one float, and the other held fifty
schoolchildren and featured the appearance of Virginia Stephens, the
young girl who had coined the term "Jewel City" for the fair, winning
a *San Francisco Call and Post* contest. The *Oakland Sunshine* noted, "It
was indeed a great day for our county and especially our people."[130] In
November, the editors of the *Western Outlook* called for the participation of all African Americans in San Francisco Day as a symbol of solidarity and pride in the state. The week after the event, the paper proudly
reported, "We helped swell the throng by members of the race from all
parts of the state and were in evidence all over."[131] Although fair directors failed to respond to African Americans' desires to help plan the fair,
local blacks still wanted to lay claim to the event. They took what opportunity they could to hold the space as their own and to assert their status
as equal citizens of the Bay Area. Yet even as the African American press
praised the community's showing, the white San Francisco newspapers
completely ignored their presence. Their reports on both days ignored
the role of African Americans in the celebrations.

African Americans, meanwhile, inserted themselves into the spectacle of the fair as residents and citizens, proudly participating in these two days. Moreover, black women took the lead in organizing these events, demonstrating a gendered component to this activism. Lynn Hudson argues that their choice to feature children in the parade suggested "their desire to merge the politics of family and respectability with the tropes of nationalism and patriotism."[132] As with the Chinese, the fair offered African Americans a space in which to hold conventions and congresses. Some black groups, including the General Baptist Association and the California Federation of Colored Women's Clubs, chose to hold their annual meetings during the fair, presenting themselves to visitors as equal participants in civic society.[133]

The challenges African Americans faced at integrating themselves into the fair demonstrates the extent to which their presence as anything other than a sideshow fundamentally challenged the racial hierarchy that the PPIE had established. Neither victorious white pioneers nor vanishing Indians, blacks did not quite fit anywhere in the historical narrative of the fair, as the rapid failure of both the Somaliland and Dixie Plantation attractions on the Zone indicated. Unlike the Chinese, who provided an active foil for the construction of white identity in the city, blacks were often ignored in both the city and fair. Since pre-fair attempts at cooperation had failed, black leaders were left with few options for staging a presence on the grounds or claiming a place in the vision of society that the fair offered. Negro Day appeared as an option simply too late for it to be anything other than an embarrassment. For such an event to be successful, blacks argued, it needed to showcase black accomplishments in a deep and meaningful way, and they had felt it would have been impossible at a fair that did its best to ignore the existence of African Americans as anything beyond Zone attractions or examples of successful white "civilization" projects. They decided, then, to participate in the fair as citizens of their communities rather than as "Negroes." By participating in Alameda County Day and San Francisco Day and by holding meetings on the grounds, blacks used the fair to establish themselves as active citizens of Bay Area communities.

Local Chinese, Irish, Catholic, and African American residents visited, worked, and performed at the fair. If they were social elites, they joined with the official delegations from their homelands to host dinners, receptions, and other events for fair dignitaries and socially prominent San Franciscans. These events and encounters provide another way to understand the fair's visual and rhetorical power.

The relatively large local Chinese community brought local Chinese residents frequently to the fair, and as with all visitors, they made their own meanings from the event.[134] As Marvin Nathan has pointed out, fair visitors might have interpreted these grand spectacles in "intensely personal and libertarian ways" based both on gender and myriad other personal factors.[135] In 1915, sixteen-year-old Alice Sue Fun worked as a stock girl in the millinery department of I. Magnin, a department store in downtown San Francisco, and spent as much leisure time as she could at the PPIE.[136] She remembered, "We saved to go see the fair. . . . I was quite a young lady then and I enjoyed the entertainment." Her traditional Chinese mother rarely went out socially—usually only to Golden Gate Park or to the Chinese opera—but Fun recalled that "my mother also went many times" to the PPIE. "You don't just see it once because there were so many things to see." Although Fun visited many foreign pavilions, her favorite building was the official Chinese Pavilion. As she told historian Judy Yung, "You know why? Because they had Chinese art, ceramics, furniture, carvings, ivory, and fine embroidery." She concluded, "It was the highlight of my life."[137]

Fun's recollections demonstrate again the importance that local ethnic communities attached to their homeland's presence at the fair. Although Fun's mother rarely left home, as was expected of a traditional Chinese woman, the fair offered something to draw her out, whether the elaborate Chinese displays or the chance to experience whole new worlds in the exhibits of other nations. This scanty evidence provides no definitive conclusions, but we do know that Fun found affirmation of her Chinese heritage at the fair alongside good entertainment on the Zone.

Twenty-nine-year-old Tye Leung Schulze, another local Chinese American woman, spent 1915 working in the fair's Chinese Tea Garden.[138] She was one of the "dainty Chinese maids" so often described in advertising and newspaper reports, a description that hid her identity and obscured the political and social reality of her experience. The job provided necessary income for her family since her white husband had trouble keeping a job after employers discovered he was married to an

Asian woman. They had both been working civil service jobs on Angel Island when they met in 1913 but lost their jobs after they married in Vancouver, Washington, to avoid California's antimiscegenation laws. Schulze's short autobiography does not document her reaction to the fair, but it is safe to extrapolate from her status as an employee on the grounds that her experience was surely quite different from that of the carefree sixteen-year-old Fun. Schulze might have appreciated the fine Chinese embroidery and the attractions of the Zone, but for her the fair was ultimately a workplace.

No matter how much Fun and other Chinese Americans who could afford to attend the fair might have enjoyed their visits, they did so in a larger context of intense anti-Asian racism that threatened to disrupt their visits. The long history of anti-Chinese and anti-Japanese racism in California resulted in discriminatory legislation, rhetoric, and violence. Both Japanese and Chinese officials voiced concerns about participating in the fair because their citizens reported mistreatment on the streets of San Francisco, and the city had a troubled historical relationship with its Asian residents. Schulze's experience exemplifies the ways in which California's legalized racism shaped Chinese women's work and home lives.

Reports of both anti-Japanese and anti-black discrimination suggest that people of color likely experienced discrimination and harassment at the fair. T. Tatsumi, the proprietor of the Japan Beautiful concession on the Zone, reported that the guards repeatedly refused to honor his employees' entry passes at the gates. In late February he complained to PPIE president Charles Moore about the situation, who agreed that "your people are entitled to the same consideration as Americans and others."[139] The problem persisted. In July again Tatsumi complained that his employees were sometimes "held up at the gate for an hour or even two and sometimes have to pay their way in. . . . No later than last Saturday six girls were held up at the gate until after 6 o'clock."[140] No evidence exists as to whether paying visitors also experienced harassment, but the repeated nature of this behavior suggests that Asian visitors may also have experienced possible discrimination on the grounds.

Multiple patrons complained about the Dixie Land Restaurant on the Zone refusing to serve African Americans. In one instance, the *Western Outlook* reported, a black woman and her two children bought tickets for a meal from a cooperative white cashier, but they still were refused service by the black cook, demonstrating the power of racial practices to affect a fairgoer's experience on the grounds.[141] The problems persisted. Five months later, T. P. Mahummit, a "colored" visitor, reported to the Exposition Guards a similar case of discrimination at the restaurant. Such practices seemed endemic to the Zone, for another black man reported that he had paid his way into the '49 Camp only to be told to leave.[142]

Within this context of racism, however, men and women of color visited and appropriated the grounds of the fair. They created an event in which representations of Asians, for instance, were not restricted to official exhibits or the Zone. Instead, Fun and other local Chinese and Japanese residents mingled with fairgoers on a daily basis, offering a counter to the static exhibits of Asian culture displayed at the fair. An article published in the *San Francisco Call and Post* about the celebration of China Day at the fair demonstrates one way these actions could disrupt U.S. racial hierarchies. Under the caption "Fair's Latest Love" appeared a photograph of a young Chinese American teenage girl. Described as "Hettie Lum of Oakland, one of a group of dainty celestials who are celebrating China Day at the Exposition," she smiled for the camera, posing next to an example of Chinese decorative work. Although she was garbed in what appeared to be traditional Chinese dress, she sported a bobbed hairdo, and the image focused on her smiling face.[143]

This image stands out from the many articles featuring young women at the fair because it offered an alternative to the common depictions of Chinese women as exotic others. Unlike the countless pictures of young California white women showing off fruit or vegetables, this feature photograph spotlighted a Chinese American girl and described her as a local resident. The caption drew on traditional stereotypes of Chinese women with its use of the phrase "dainty celestials," but including her Chinese American name and her home in Oakland identified her both as an individual and a local resident rather than as simply a visual embodiment of the Asian other.[144] Perhaps, like Alice Sue Fun, she was a local teenager who loved the fair and appreciated the thrills of the Zone and the Chinese exhibits. Whatever her relationship to the fair, her picture in the paper reminded readers both of the participation of the local Chinese community in the fair and of the individuality of Chinese residents and

Chinese women. Such images contrasted with the visions of anonymous "Chinese maids" or "Orientals" that the fair often used to advertise the Zone and demonstrated the subtle challenge that the participation of local Asian residents posed to the stereotyped visions of Asian men and women prevalent in U.S. culture.

Fair directors invited the participation of local communities in the exposition because they knew that local support was necessary to ensure the event's financial success. Most groups easily staged events at the fair, while others, such as the Chinese, Catholics, Irish, and African Americans, found the process more challenging. All shared the belief that the fair had the potential to deeply influence the millions of visitors who entered the grounds. So, too, did participating foreign nations. Latin American nations used the fair to advertise the economic opportunities that the construction of the Panama Canal offered. The nations of China and Japan also saw the PPIE as an opportunity to display their cultures and achievements to the world. But how could they do it in a state so heavily dominated by anti-Asian political influences? As the debate over Underground Chinatown suggests, Asian nations faced particular challenges as they sought to participate in the PPIE. Fortunately for them, fair officials saw their involvement as essential to the fair's economic success.

4 &/ Economic Partner, Exotic Other

After fourteen-year-old Doris Barr viewed a Japanese exhibit in the Liberal Arts Building of the Panama-Pacific International Exposition, she recorded her disappointment that the display featured Western objects such as tennis rackets, bats, and clocks. She preferred the portion of the exhibit that featured old Japan with cherry tree blossom–lined streets and kimono-clad women to the image of new Japan, in which men wore Western-style suits.[1] Japanese officials wanted the fair to demonstrate their nation's emergence as a world power and its moves toward Western definitions of progress. They designed exhibits that featured examples of industrial and technical innovations alongside examples of traditional culture. The conflict between Barr's expectations and the exhibit itself reveal one of many tensions that persisted on the PPIE fairgrounds between the agendas of the exhibiting nations and the expectations of visitors.

PPIE officials dedicated enormous amounts of time and money to convincing foreign governments to commit to participating in the fair. These campaigns took a range of forms, from world tours of Asian and European nations to the publication of newspapers and journals designed to advertise the fair across the nation and the world. Officials focused much of their attention on recruiting the participation of Asian nations— particularly China and Japan—because they believed that Chinese and Japanese involvement was essential to making the fair the kind of international event they intended. They wanted the fair to confirm San Francisco's place as the dominant economic city of the Pacific and believed it would only happen if they could bring both Asian consumers and American and European manufacturers to the fair. One fair official argued, "The 'Audience' at this Exposition is the Pacific Area and the Orient is the proscenium boxes. Without a significant market as represented by participation here the interest of many foreign, and for that matter, domestic important commercial and financial institutions would diminish."[2] The national exhibits of China and Japan would also draw curious tourists. One piece of fair publicity promised: "Down Market Street will pass such Oriental pageants as the world has never seen."[3] Fair officials also knew that both nations were wary of committing resources to an event occurring in a state dominated by anti-Asian sentiment and political rhetoric.

California's political culture undermined fair organizers' determination to bring China and Japan to the event and fostered seemingly contradictory images of both countries for curious visitors. Japan and China were involved in a serious diplomatic dispute during 1915 and would not have perceived themselves as allies at the fair. But PPIE officials believed their fates were linked, so they dealt with the two nations in similar ways. Examining how fair officials interacted with these nations and with local Chinese and Japanese residents reveals first that local politics and priorities directly shaped the vision of China and Japan that was created for visitors to the fair. Second, it demonstrates that exposition officials intervened in California's social and political life in ways that inadvertently subverted debates over the place of Chinese and Japanese immigrants in the state. Finally, it builds on the discussion of local Chinese participation in the fair to elaborate on the Chinese government's role in attempting to use the fair to mediate anti-Chinese sentiment in California. On a national level, supporters of an "open door" with China had long worked for cordial relations with the Chinese and had been concerned about the impact of immigration restrictions and anti-Asian sentiment on their expanding business relations with China.[4] The debates surrounding the PPIE, and the contrasting images of China created therein, reveal that this national political discussion played itself out in the cultural arena as well. Rather than providing clear-cut representations of China and Japan, the exposition became the site of competing visions of both nations, reflecting the larger discourse in the state and the nation.

Boosters pointed to the city's proximity to Asia as a major reason that San Francisco should win the right to hold the PPIE. The Congressional Committee on Industrial Expositions cited this factor as a major reason for favoring San Francisco over New Orleans.[5] Yet even at that moment the state's anti-Asian sentiment threatened San Francisco's bid. The *New York Times* reported in the fall of 1910 that President Taft had informed then governor-elect Hiram Johnson that if he truly wanted the fair for

San Francisco, then he needed to rein in the state's anti-Asian political activities until a treaty pending with Japan had been ratified. Only two days before the January 1911 congressional vote on the fair's location, members of the state's congressional delegation affirmed that state legislators had resolved to put off any anti-Japanese bills until after the location was decided.[6] The relationship between the exposition, local and national politics, and the nations of Asia was fraught with conflict from the beginning.

U.S. fair organizers had long sought Asian participation in their events. Shelley S. Lee argues that at Seattle's 1909 Alaska-Yukon-Pacific (A-Y-P) Exposition city boosters' economic goals for the event "mitigated nativist forces" in the region. This effort opened a space for more positive representations of Japan and Japanese Americans, even if it did not allow for concrete changes in the conditions of Japanese Americans in Seattle.[7] China, however, refused to send an official exhibit to Seattle and remained in the eyes of most Americans a weak nation, so no such positive images existed of China at the A-Y-P Expo. By 1915, China had become a republic intent on asserting its position on the world stage, so PPIE officials eagerly sought the participation of both Japan and China. Since the PPIE was a much larger and longer event than the A-Y-P Expo was, it offered far more visitors a greater and more impressive array of events and exhibits featuring both Japan and China. California's active anti-Japanese movement, however, threatened the project. The resulting political conflict reveals the extent to which fair boosters were willing to actively construct positive images of Japan, demonstrating that in San Francisco the "cosmopolitanism" that Lee identified at the A-Y-P Expo was translated into political and social action.

Many white Californians had long viewed Asians as threats to the state's economic prosperity and to its moral and racial purity, and an active anti-Japanese movement thrived in the Progressive Era.[8] Fair directors therefore faced a challenge in convincing these two nations to dedicate their resources to a fair held in such an apparently hostile environment. San Francisco itself had been the center of both anti-Chinese and anti-Japanese agitation, which eventually had resulted in national legislation excluding Asian immigrants. San Francisco contributed some leaders of the anti-Chinese movement, including Denis Kearney of the Workingmen's Party and Congressman Thomas Geary, who in 1892 introduced the bill to extend the Chinese Exclusion Act for another ten years. The Exclusion Act stopped significant Chinese immigration to the United States, but a small stream still entered the country illegally. Meanwhile San Francisco's Chinatown remained a vibrant center of Chinese culture.

Anti-Asian sentiment persisted in the city in the early twentieth century. When the city experienced an outbreak of the bubonic plague in 1900, panicked citizens blamed the Chinese and Japanese, and a local policy was instituted of "injecting Asiatics, both men and women, against the disease in public."[9] That same year labor leaders and politicians led a mass meeting in the city and called for the extension of the Chinese Exclusion Act and for a new law to exclude the Japanese.[10] The 1906 earthquake and fire further inflamed racial tensions as some local politicians actively pursued a plan to permanently relocate Chinatown from its downtown location.[11] Japanese residents also experienced racial attacks and an economic boycott after the earthquake.[12] When the city attempted to consolidate all of its Asian students into the "Oriental School," its Japanese residents protested. The resulting dispute reached both the Japanese and U.S. federal governments, threatening the two nations' burgeoning treaty relationship. President Theodore Roosevelt brokered the Gentleman's Agreement of 1907 that resulted in the city's backing off its attempt to segregate the Japanese students in exchange for Japan's limiting further emigration of Japanese laborers to the United States. The city's and state's anti-Asian sentiment therefore already affected not only local but also national and international politics.

This history of anti-Asian racism made the governments of China and Japan understandably hesitant about committing their resources to an exposition held in California. Nonetheless, both nations saw an opportunity to display their recent economic and technological achievements to a world audience.[13] Chinese consul general S. C. Shu noted, "China at the Exposition expects to take the place to which she is entitled as a commercial nation. Never before has our nation had an opportunity such as the present to show to the world that China is an up to date and progressive nation."[14]

Japanese officials similarly recognized the possibilities that the Panama Canal offered for the Japanese economy. They hoped that participating in the fair would stimulate economic growth and "strengthen the link of mutual sympathy which exists between the United States and Japan."[15] As Angus Lockyer argues, Japan had long sought to use international expositions as a platform from which to "mak[e] the modern Japanese nation," although officials also recognized the challenge of countering Western imaginings and appropriation of Japanese culture.[16] Officials of both nations hoped that a display of their national accomplishments might counteract the anti-Asian prejudice rampant in the United States during the Progressive Era. The political and social climate of California, however, continued to challenge these hopes.

Government officials in both Japan and China responded with cautious enthusiasm to the invitation to participate in the fair. Exposition officials eagerly courted government officials and merchants in both nations. As early as 1911, Matsuzo Nagai, the acting consul general of Japan in San Francisco, informed exposition president Charles C. Moore that he expected his nation to "take a deep interest in this Exposition." He said, "National pride will find expression in these efforts and the sentiment of the Japanese people will demand that the showing made be dignified and typical of the best in Japanese life." Thus, he warned Moore if other, offensive depictions of Japan should appear on the grounds, "the Japanese people would feel aggrieved and perhaps humiliated."[17] In the spring of 1912, Michael H. de Young, fair director, *San Francisco Chronicle* publisher, and prominent San Franciscan, traveled around the world publicizing the fair and spent extensive time in both China and Japan. He reported that the Japanese were particularly enthusiastic since they recognized the economic benefits of the Panama Canal.[18] Japanese leaders demonstrated their enthusiasm when their nation became the first to choose a site for its national building in 1912, although later incidents delayed its official commitment until early 1914.[19] Chinese officials voiced similar sentiments. In 1912, only months after the founding of the Republic of China, one Chinese minister told Moore, "China has just become a republic and will do her best in the development of her natural resources and in the promotion of her industry."[20] Attending the fair would offer China the chance to study modern agricultural methods. He and other Chinese officials also hoped the fair would help foster trade between his nation and the United States. Yet, at the same time, American expo-

sition boosters in China reported among many Chinese a "feeling of resentment toward San Francisco" that complicated efforts to convince the Chinese government to participate.[21] Clearly, citizens and officials of both nations were aware of the potential risks of attending an event in California, where anti-Asian sentiments ran high.

As indicated earlier, local Chinese residents urged others to support the fair, and Japanese residents did as well. A 1912 editorial in San Francisco's *Japanese American News* argued, "It would not be trifling to say this exposition would be an ideal opportunity and a rare chance for us" to combat anti-Japanese sentiment.[22] As did the governments of China and Japan, then, local residents thought that their ancestral nations could use the fair to help improve the status of the Chinese and Japanese Americans in California. This situation points to a distinction between these residents' goals and the activities of other ethnic groups at the fair. Local Chinese and Japanese were acutely aware of their marginalized status and, unlike African Americans, had valued foreign powers on their side. They therefore used multiple strategies to assert their status at the PPIE.

California's political climate continually challenged these goals. Moore, his fellow fair directors, and a host of other fair boosters in California, Washington DC, and Asia worked to ameliorate the effects of anti-Asian actions and legislation on relations with China and Japan. Sometimes this effort meant addressing issues in the city of San Francisco itself, as an episode in the fall of 1912 revealed. Just before the Imperial Japanese commissioners arrived in San Francisco to select a site for the Japanese exhibit, there appeared "on prominent billboards of the city certain post-

Fig. 36. Ground-breaking for the Japanese concession at the PPIE. Hundreds of local Japanese residents attended this event, showing their support for the fair. (Library of Congress.)

ers which contained sentiments of an offensive nature to the Japanese." Moore, realizing the gravity of the situation, quickly appointed a committee to investigate. The posters were immediately removed and did not reappear.[23] Moore met with the consul general of Japan to discuss the presence of discrimination in the city. Nagai subsequently told Moore that the city's popular bathhouses—the Hammam, Lurline, and Sutro—all banned Japanese from entry and that bars discriminated more "sporadically."[24] Nagai suggested, however, that rather than launch a campaign to eradicate such discrimination, it was better to wait and see "how the attitude of bartenders would be changed under the new improving circumstances." Nagai seemed to believe that Japanese participation in the fair might ease race relations in the city.[25] Developments outside the city, however, suggested that the problem was far from solved.

Exposition officials carefully monitored the situation on the national and local level. The first crisis arose when Senator William Paul Dillingham introduced a 1912 immigration bill that included a provision to deny entry to all aliens "ineligible for citizenship." The subsequent flurry of contacts between Moore and his Washington correspondents, as well as local interests, demonstrated a real concern about the response to such legislation in Japan. George Shima, the famed "Potato King" and Japanese millionaire president of the Japanese Association of America, told Moore that the clause would be such an affront to the Japanese government and people that it very well might cause them to withdraw from the exposition.[26] Moore assured Shima that although he did not believe that the bill would be voted upon in that session, "we shall oppose all such legislation with our utmost strength," both publicly and privately.[27] Other fair supporters also weighed in. David Starr Jordan sent Moore a copy of the letter of objection he wrote to President Taft in which he approved all parts of the bill except the clause that the Japanese found offensive, the one banning "aliens ineligible for citizenship." Jordan noted that Japan had abided by the Gentleman's Agreement and, he implied, was a better partner in exclusion than China had been. So he asked why the United States should embarrass Japan now and create unnecessary tensions between the two nations. His defense of the Japanese government echoed that of others who saw the Japanese as the "white race" of Asia and as being closer to Europe than to China or the rest of Asia.[28] The Dillingham bill did not make it out of Congress, but its introduction prepared fair officials for the fight they took on the next year against the Alien Land Law.

In early 1913 the California State legislature began considering a bill to forbid Asian immigrants from owning land in California. Legislators had introduced similar measures in 1907, 1909, and 1911, but it was not until 1913 that anti-Japanese agitators succeeded in promoting a law that limited the length of leases and explicitly forbade "aliens ineligible for citizenship" from owning land in the state.[29] Although the Gentleman's Agreement prohibited the entry of Japanese laborers, many Japanese already lived in the state and worked hard to make the state's farmland productive. Wealthy Japanese began to hire cheap Japanese labor away from white farmers, becoming "active competitors for farm labor, farm land, and agricultural markets."[30] Frustrated white farmers watched their success with resentment while spouting increasingly racialized rhetoric. In both the 1909 and 1911 legislative sessions, federal pressure on the governor kept anti-Asian bills from passage. The situation became acute by 1913 when Republicans and Democrats introduced anti-Asian measures in both houses.[31] Anti-Japanese legislation had become a powerful force in California politics, and supporters were increasingly aggrieved at what they saw as unjust federal intervention in state legislation. Governor Johnson faced tremendous pressure in 1913 to favor the Alien Land Law, and the newly inaugurated president was unwilling to directly interfere with the debate.[32] The stage was therefore set for the passage of the law, despite the best efforts of PPIE officials.

Moore attempted to head off the legislation in January by sending President Pro Tempore A. E. Boynton a strongly worded letter in which he told him, in no uncertain terms, that if China and Japan chose not to participate in the fair, it would have a "disastrous effect" on the participation of other nations and make the international component of the PPIE a "failure." Therefore, Moore urged Boynton, as a "Patriotic Californian," not to introduce any anti-Asian legislation that could jeopardize this important event.[33] Exposition officials, meanwhile, maintained supporters in Sacramento who lobbied against the anti-Asian legislation. Local businessmen telegraphed state politicians, urging them to oppose anti-Japanese legislation because it would affect "participation in the World's Fair."[34]

The PPIE directors sprang into action as soon as the bills were introduced. Moore called an emergency meeting at which he passed out lists of those legislators in danger of proposing anti-Asian legislation. He told directors to inform him if they had any "knowledge as to how any of these Legislators could be influenced." Later that same day, nine fair officials visited Johnson to map out a strategy to keep such bills off the table. Johnson assured them of his support, yet he refused to commit to opposing the bills if they were introduced.[35] Moore and others mobilized quickly because they feared if word leaked out about the legislation that Japan might not participate in the fair. Furthermore, they worried "this influence would be transmitted to China and the other countries of the Orient and to Europe, and that the Exposition . . . [would] lose much of its international character. . . . [These nations] would probably take it that this was to be a local or provincial exposition and act accordingly."[36]

Exposition representatives repeatedly testified about the dangers that the proposed law posed to the fair. Progressive newspaper correspondent Franklin Hichborn reported on the last committee hearing on the bill: "The Directorate of the Exposition had made elaborate preparations to impress the farmers who were present, as well as members of the committee, that the Exposition is the most important thing in California, before which all other considerations must give way. . . . A complete moving picture outfit had been set up in the Senate Chamber. Scattered throughout the room were well-gowned women and carefully groomed men, wearing conspicuous badges—'Do it for San Francisco.'"[37] Hichborn was a Progressive Party supporter who voiced repeated skepticism of both the fair and San Francisco, but his report nonetheless reveals the impressive political and financial resources of the exposition.

Fair officials, boosters, and the local Japanese community worked hard in the spring of 1913 to defeat the law, but they faced entrenched opposition. During those final hearings on the bill, the well-groomed and elite pro-exposition spokesmen opposed a group of "very plain, rugged, untutored and uncultured men from the fields," whom the audience supported with roars of approval.[38] The bill's rural supporters did not appreciate the attempts of wealthy San Franciscans to try to affect the debate, highlighting the class—and regional—conflict of the issue. One of those farmers was a former Congregational minister, whose oft-quoted statement reflected contemporary fears of miscegenation: "Near my home is an eighty-acre tract of as fine land as there is in California. On that tract lives a Japanese. With that Japanese lives a white woman. In that woman's arms is a baby. What is that baby? It isn't a Japanese. It isn't white. It is a germ of the mightiest problem that ever faced this state; a problem that will make the black problem of the South look white."[39] Anti-Japanese propaganda regularly featured these accusations. Claims that the Japanese unfairly took good land from whites, that Japanese men threatened white women, and that miscegenation jeopardized American culture all struck a chord with fearful white Californians. Marriage between Asians and whites was already illegal in California, making the emphasis on the sexual danger and miscegenation so much hyperbole. Nonetheless, white Californians quite successfully portrayed Japanese residents as perils to the economic success of whites and to the purity of the white race and white womanhood.

Some San Franciscans failed to buy the exposition's argument. Matt Sullivan, San Francisco attorney and president of the State Exposition Commission, testified against passing the land law with the caveat that "he would rather not have an Exposition at all, than to have the Japanese gain a foothold in California as they have in Hawaii."[40] Such testimony in favor of the fair was lukewarm at best and failed to challenge the racial assumptions that underlay the bills. Former San Francisco mayor and longtime proponent of Asian exclusion James Phelan argued passionately that maintaining the racial purity of the state was more important than the needs of the exposition. Phelan insisted: "The future of California ... is of far greater importance than the success of this Exposition. And in saying this I do not believe for a moment that in enacting this land legislation you will jeopardize the success of the Exposition."[41] He raised the specter of a state in which "the whites submit to the reduced wages, reduced standards of living, and sink to the level of the Japanese."[42] The San Francisco Irish Catholic paper, the *Leader*, noted of the debate that "the interests of California must be made subsidiary to the interests of a private corporation, which, after all, is but a Barnum and Bailey on a large scale."[43] Although organized labor traditionally formed a key element of the fight against both Chinese and Japanese immigrants, the San Francisco Labor Council respected its agreement with fair officials to support the exposition and kept silent on the issue.[44]

Virulent opposition to the fair's claims circulated outside San Francisco. A January editorial published in the *Sacramento Union* represented the anti-exposition and anti-Japanese feeling generated by the controversy over the bill: "Never was an argument made of frailer fabric than that advanced by the exposition officials, and thus indorsed by the Governor. ... That is, to insure a Japanese tea-garden at the fair, we are requested to postpone, at least until after that event, those laws which are urgently demanded by American labor and the American land holder. Rome was burned to make Nero's holiday; we are to sacrifice our welfare to make a Japanese tea-garden!"[45] By reducing Japanese participation in the fair to "a Japanese tea-garden," the author suggested that a Japanese exhibit would be an amusing racial display rather than the showcase of strong nation-state. He dismissed outright the claim that Japan must be treated as a respected foreign nation and source of potential new markets. The *Union*, the *Sacramento Bee*, and other interior papers continued to publish pieces with similar sentiments throughout the debate. Some concerned Californians voiced their opinions about the bill to President Moore himself, revealing the challenge fair officials faced in selling their point of view. B. P. Schmidt, a Sonoma farmer, told him, "All you rich men are fighting this land bill in favor of the Japanese, ignoring us altogether."[46]

His accusation reflected many white California farmers' intense hatred toward the Japanese and resentment of the perceived elitist attitude of fair officials.

Throughout the debate, Japanese people in Japan and in California found the Alien Land Law offensive, objectionable, and clearly discriminatory. Local Japanese seized upon the exposition as a way to fight the Alien Land Law. In late December and early January, even before the bills were introduced in the legislature, the Japanese Association of America wrote to Moore, asking for help in fighting the law.[47] Moore assured Shima, as he had a year before, that exposition authorities would do what they could to oppose such legislation.[48]

Many in Japan doubted that they would be welcome in California if they attended the exposition.[49] Japanese merchants, officials, and ordinary citizens all protested the affront. Many seized on the fair as a bargaining chip in their objections to the law. In February, the Japanese ambassador called on Secretary of State William Jennings Bryan to tell him that Japan's participation in the fair was at risk if the bill passed. Japan's participation was aimed more toward showing "cordial relations between the two countries" rather than pursuing commercial motives, he told Bryan. Since Japan had not yet officially committed funds to the event, it was still possible the Japanese might back out of the exposition.[50] In early March, exposition officials received notification from Japan that if the bill passed, "Japan will withdraw her support from the Panama-Pacific International Exposition, refusing to exhibit and prohibiting Japanese citizens from having any connection with the Fair."[51] In April, the presidents of the chambers of commerce of Tokyo, Osaka, Kyoto, Yokohama, Kobe, and Nagoya notified President Moore of their "deep concern" that the bill's passage would hinder the growth of commercial relations between the two nations.[52] Newspaper articles that same week reported on unrest in Japan over the pending legislation and on threats that Japanese manufacturers would not attend the fair.[53] The actions of the California legislature triggered a significant international response.

The bill passed by a huge margin in both houses despite this opposition. Although President Woodrow Wilson asked Johnson to delay signing the bill until the federal government could ensure it did not abrogate treaty rights, Johnson went ahead and signed the bill on May 19 without any further objections from Wilson. Scholars debate the reasons why the bill passed, when federal pressure and previous state governors (including Johnson two years earlier) had managed to oppose legislation in the past. Johnson biographer Spencer Olin argues that Johnson reneged on his earlier assurances to exposition leaders that the damaging bills would not pass because he was intent on revealing the Democrats' "state's rights" doctrine to be, in his own words, a "sham and pretense." After President Wilson sent Secretary of State Bryan to meet with California legislators and attempt to defeat the bill, Johnson rebelled against this interference in what he believed was a state's right to legislate. Olin also argues that Johnson believed that passage of the Alien Land Law was necessary for his political survival, for it redeemed him in the eyes of skeptical Californians for passing other "excessively radical" legislation. Finally, legislators found the California farmers' sentiments against the Japanese simply more persuasive than were the pleas of wealthy San Francisco businessmen. Johnson himself explained to Theodore Roosevelt that the testimony of California farmers, insisting that "an alien land bill was absolutely essential for their protection," convinced many legislators to support the bills.[54]

Moore and other directors quickly turned to pacifying the outraged Japanese and downplaying anti-Japanese sentiment in California. Japanese government officials made it clear to Moore that they were wary of committing themselves and their assets to participating in the exposition if anti-Japanese agitation continued to proliferate in California. Numano Yasutoro, acting Japanese consulate general in San Francisco, laid out his concerns to Moore in the fall of 1913. "There is a feeling in Japan," he stated, "that the Japanese cannot get a square deal in California." The rash of proposed anti-Japanese legislation and passage of the Alien Land Law forced potential Japanese exhibitors to confront the fear that "the Legislature of California—even during the Exposition year— . . . [would] introduce some legislation hostile to Japanese interests and calculated to shame us before the assembled world." Stories of unfair treatment of individual Japanese on the streets of San Francisco, "at bars, in barber shops and other public places," made visitors wary of traveling across the Pacific only to "be exposed to similar insults and humiliating discrimination." Only the exposition director's specific assurances and guarantees that Japan and its citizens could come to the fair "without fear of national or individual humiliation" would allay these fears.[55]

Fair officials also worried about the effects of the Alien Land Law on other regions of the United States, where citizens did not share the anti-Japanese sentiment of so many Californians. Right after the bill passed, President Moore reported on the "dangerous situation for [the] Exposition in Massachusetts," where prominent Bostonian members of the American Peace Society were opposing their state's appropriation for the exposition. He also asserted that "many Eastern newspapers have informed us they do not care to print Exposition matter in view of California Legislature's attitude." Perhaps even more damaging, he acknowledged in a confidential postscript, was the possibility that "many big Eastern manufacturers who have applied for exhibit space have expressed deep resentment and manifested possibility of withdrawing."[56] Despite these fears, the PPIE's Washington DC correspondent reassured Moore that he had spoken with other leading progressives who were "inclined to support Johnson's position" and that leading progressive eastern papers praised the bills, indicating more support outside the state than Moore imagined.[57]

Moore and other fair officials continued to smooth over relations with the local Japanese community and with representatives of the Japanese government. "We are glad to know that you are aware of the Exposition's actions" regarding the legislation, he told the Japanese Association of America. The PPIE board took care to send copies of its resolutions opposing the legislation "throughout the country" to make its position clear.[58] Some Japanese officials had come to believe by late 1913 that despite the Alien Land Law, the fair still offered a valuable opportunity to show off their nation's achievements to curious Americans. The Japanese vice minister of commerce issued an official statement in which he noted that although officials understood the merchants' anger at the Alien Land Law, "such participation [in the fair] would ease the situation, and the Japanese Government hopes that the Nation will send as many exhibits as possible."[59] In December, the U.S. ambassador to Japan informed Secretary of State Bryan that despite hesitation in some quarters, "many business men [sic], especially in Yokohama . . . feel that such representation will probably be very beneficial to Japanese trade

and commerce." He warned, however, that any further offensive legislation could prove disastrous to relations between the two countries.[60]

Fair officials continued meeting with Shima, K. S. Inui, another leader
of the local Japanese American community, and representatives of the
Japanese government throughout 1914 and discussed Japanese participation in the fair and good treatment for visiting Japanese.[61] Some also
credited a visit from U.S. ambassador George Guthrie to Japan for easing
relations.[62] Fair officials honored visiting Japanese officials with elaborate
dinners and receptions. Numano thanked exposition officials in mid-1914
for "the kindly attentions showered upon Admiral Kuroi and his com-
mand during the past week . . . the luncheons, receptions, auto rides . . .
were most heartily enjoyed, but best of all was the kindly spirit in which
these evidences of good will found expression."[63] By showering the visiting Japanese with public praise and attention, exposition officials hoped
to reassure them that they would be received with equal respect in 1915.
Such events, which were often covered in local papers, contributed to
creating an image of Japan as a nation deserving such respect and countered negative reports of the Japanese as threats to the United States.[64]

The fight over the Alien Land Law revealed the lengths to which
PPIE officials would go to further the fair's financial interests. They truly
believed that if the law passed, Japan very well might boycott the exposition. If Japan did not come to the fair, then China would probably withdraw as well, and then the fair's claim to be an event that would open
the Pacific market for the United States and Europe would evaporate.
Officials actively intervened in a statewide political battle to guarantee
the success of the fair, and in so doing, they inadvertently complicated
racial constructions that placed Japanese and white Americans in conflict with one another. By emphasizing the necessity of Japan's participation in the fair, their public statements—reprinted in newspapers and
propaganda—suggested that Californians viewed Japan and the Japanese
as economic partners rather than as exotic others. As the advocates of
the Open Door Policy with China attempted to intervene in exclusion
debates, those who had an economic interest in developing a relationship with Japan also attempted to intervene here, depicting both China
and Japan as valued international partners to the United States. Fair officials suggested that Californians shared common ground with the Chi-

nese and Japanese at the exposition. These efforts reveal that those forces of economically motivated cosmopolitanism that Lee identified in the Seattle case as primarily rhetorical were transformed in the San Francisco context into concrete political action.[65]

China was less involved in the debate over the Alien Land Law, although the law applied to Chinese and Korean immigrants as well as to the Japanese. As did the Japanese government, the Chinese government continued to voice hesitations about investing in an exposition in a state that actively discriminated against citizens of its nation. Officials worried about the treatment their citizens would receive upon visiting California for the event. Would zealous immigration officials attempt to keep all visiting Chinese out of the state, even though the Exclusion Act applied only to laborers? Many of these fears stemmed from experiences at earlier expositions, particularly the 1904 Louisiana Purchase Exposition in St. Louis, where visitors were harassed and "subjected to continuous restraint and supervision which amounted practically to imprisonment."[66] Some Chinese merchants were detained for weeks in San Francisco en route to St. Louis while their papers were being processed, and the end of the exposition witnessed an immigration raid on the fair's Chinese Village.[67] If that treatment occurred in a state without an active anti-Asian movement, what could happen at a fair in California? Yet, if they were assured of fair treatment, one fair booster reported, "a great many Chinese merchants and educated men would visit the United States" during the exposition, "thus strengthening materially the friendly relations between those two countries."[68]

Exposition officials dispelled some of the concerns that both Chinese and Japanese officials raised by urging the Bureau of Immigration to issue clear rules governing the entry of Asian laborers for the fair. A 1902 act allowed any foreign exhibitor at a congressionally authorized exposition to bring in workers deemed necessary for preparing or erecting an exhibit. In recognition of this act, the bureau issued a directive outlining the regulations governing Chinese laborers, who were specifically outlawed from entering the country under the Chinese Exclusion Act of 1882. They were required to provide evidence of official employment, identification, and a $500 bond to immigration officers. Further, they were to return to China thirty days after their employment at the fair ended.[69] Although C. I. Sagara of the Japanese Association of America told Moore that the regulations, which were also extended to the Japanese, were harshly criticized in Japan and "the results w[ould] be decidedly detrimental to the Japanese exhibit at the Exposition," fair officials maintained that both the Japanese and Chinese governments would deem them reasonable once they were fully understood.[70]

After the announcement of these regulations, federal officials, fair officials, and Chinese representatives worked to find a solution that avoided the unpleasant experiences of St. Louis. When a nurse at the Angel Island hospital poorly treated a Chinese laborer brought to work at the fair, the Chinese Commission complained to immigration officials and elicited a rapid response. U.S. Immigration commissioner A. C. Caminetti promised that he intended to make the entry of Asian laborers as easy as possible, so he proposed a scheme to avoid the humiliation that Chinese workers had experienced in St. Louis. Rather than forcing Chinese laborers to line up for periodic inspections on the grounds (to ensure that all were present and accounted for), plainclothes immigration officials would meet with Chinese commissioners weekly to determine whether all workers were present.[71] No existing evidence indicates any conflicts over the entry of the Chinese during the fair, suggesting that these pre-fair discussions successfully resolved the issue.

Chinese officials worried not only about their workers' reception but also about how Chinese tourists would be treated upon arrival in the United States. When eight first-class passengers on a Japanese steamer were taken to Angel Island and held there for a day, a practice usually reserved for those of questionable immigration status, it became clear the officials' concerns were warranted. Inui immediately informed Moore that the situation would "undoubtedly be a source of irritation in Japan."[72] No further documents of this encounter survive, but the incident and the treatment afforded the laborer in the Angel Island hospital reveals that Japanese and Chinese concerns about ill-treatment were well founded. Later that year, immigration officials acquiesced to the requests of the fair officials and the Chinese government and declared that "wealthy and refined Chinese coming first-cabin as visitors to [the] Exposition" would be exempted from the humiliating hookworm examination routine for all Asian arrivals. They would instead be released immediately from the ship upon its arrival in San Francisco.[73] Such assurances were essential for convincing the Chinese government that their citizens would be treated with respect rather than contempt as they arrived in San Francisco.

That Moore and other fair officials engaged in these varied political maneuverings—from opposing the Alien Land Law to lobbying for reduced immigration restrictions—demonstrates the significance they placed on Chinese and Japanese participation in the PPIE. This importance empowered Chinese and Japanese officials and strengthened their advocacy for improved treatment for their citizens in California's traditionally hostile political culture. Although the fight against the Alien Land Law failed, both Chinese and Japanese authorities succeeded in their struggle to gain respectful treatment from exposition officials, as evidenced by the elaborate dinners and receptions held in their honor, as well as by Moore's lobbying for relaxed immigration restrictions. Although California was at the center of anti-Asian agitation, and had been for sixty years, the economic exigencies of the exposition enabled Chinese and Japanese governments to challenge California's anti-Asian policies and culture and to offer alternative visions of their citizens as economic partners rather than as competitors.

The debate over the Alien Land Law revealed that California's anti-Asian sentiment often expressed itself in cultural depictions of Chinese and Japanese as exotic others. Yet during the fair years, significant publicity portrayed both nations in positive ways, smoothing the way for their participation in the fair. Much of this change was owed to the PPIE's publicity bureau, whose press releases became the basis of newspaper articles that described China and Japan as nations progressing toward American definitions of "modernity" and "Western" ways. An article on the Chinese exhibits, for instance, first described the elaborate displays and then praised them as being "characteristic of the new feeling of China, which ... [has] declared for modern ways and put the old behind it."[74] A piece on the Japanese exhibit noted: "Japan will show to the world her culture and her civilization, her natural resources and industrialization, and give a new impetus to her trade and commerce."[75] These descriptions privileged white American culture but allowed for the possibility that Asia could emulate that culture, a distinct difference from the position of the permanent other that the Chinese and Japanese held in the minds of many white Californians. Not all publicity described the two nations in these ways, but these articles offered readers a new framework through which to understand China and Japan.

Other pieces of pre-fair publicity about local Chinese and Japanese residents described them as valuable members of San Francisco's society rather than as unassimilable threats to the American body politic. Raymond Rast argues that post-earthquake publicists began to reimagine Chinatown as a uniquely San Franciscan attraction that was a cultural curiosity instead of a threat.[76] One early article in *International Fair Illustrated*, an exposition-backed publication designed to publicize the fair nationwide, noted that the earthquake had "destroyed old joss-houses, out-worn idols, thieves' quarters, ancient mercantile habits."[77] Publicists depicted San Francisco's Chinatown not as a den of vice and iniquity but as an interesting and safe area of the city's modern skyline.[78] One piece of exposition publicity noted that "the gilded domes of her pagodas add striking features to the beauty of the new city."[79] Chinese residents themselves contributed to this image, as Look Tin Eli's four-page spread on "Our New Oriental City" for a Western Press Association 1910 guidebook revealed. The new Chinatown was "more beautiful, artistic, and so much more emphatically Oriental" than the old one, he asserted.[80] Departing from the separate, racialized neighborhood depicted in nineteenth-century publications, these images and texts presented a Chinatown integrated into greater San Francisco.[81]

Other publicity emphasized the integration of Chinese and Japanese Americans into American political life. This tactic must have pleased the governments of China and Japan and local Chinese and Japanese residents interested in demonstrating their value to the city.[82] The *San Francisco Standard Guide Including the Panama-Pacific Exposition* reassured visitors that "the American spirit has caught the [Chinese American] population," and "a goodly number of American born Chinese men and women . . . are voters." Most important, it noted, "Chinese citizens of San Francisco, who are among the city's most patriotic," actively assisted in bringing Chinese exhibits to the upcoming exposition.[83] Sometimes such praises even extended to the often-reviled Japanese. A *San Francisco Chronicle* report on Japanese farmers in the Central Valley characterized them as responsible for "breathing vitality into sterile soil." The author assured readers that "when admitted to citizenship, the Japanese will certainly vote with as much independence and intelligence as any other race of naturalized citizens."[84] This portrayal of Chinese and Japanese residents as citizens and participants in American political life contrasted starkly with other articles that perpetuated California's long-held anti-Chinese and anti-Japanese sentiment.

As Doris Barr's visit to the Japan section reveals, the governments of China and Japan mounted elaborate displays designed to showcase their strength and progress. As with the ethnic and religious groups that used the fair to construct social and political identities, foreign nations also created identities at the fair. Officials of the youthful Chinese republic were particularly concerned about demonstrating their nation's achievements and recovery from its recent civil war. Although China had participated in previous fairs, the PPIE was the first fair in which the nation would participate as a republic, and officials were particularly interested in demonstrating their internal stability to the skeptical West. Prior to 1912, the subservient nineteenth-century relationship between China and Great Britain meant that the Chinese themselves had not designed the exhibits. Instead, the Chinese Customs Service, under the control of Sir Robert Hart, had determined the nature of the nation's exhibits.[85] The PPIE therefore offered the first chance for the Chinese government to control its own representation and to determine its participation.

Visitors to the official Chinese exhibits encountered a combination of cultural artifacts and items designed to highlight Chinese efforts toward political and economic development and industrial progress. The "small walled city" of the exhibit enclosed a 100,000-square-foot area that included replicas of the Imperial Audience Hall in the Forbidden City; the Tai-Ho-Tien, or "Hall of Eternal Peace, used by the new Government as a Temple of Ceremonies"; and a Chinese home "furnished with tapestries, teak tables, lacquered furniture, intricate carvings and other works of art."[86] The most concerted effort to show off the nations' progress toward modernity was in the enormous school display in the Palace of Education and Social Economy, which featured evidence of the nation's new Westernized school system and the work of "thousands of grammar schools, middle schools, high schools, and colleges."[87] In the Palace of Transportation, the Chinese section featured the glories of modern-day

Fig. 37. Chinese Buildings at the PPIE. (San Francisco
History Center, San Francisco Public Library.)

transportation in China in an attempt to showcase both China's scenery
and its new technologies. The extensive pamphlet handed out to visitors
in this exhibit illustrated China's desires to appear "modern." Echoing
the inclination of American progressives to emphasize government efficiency and organization, the publication included organizational charts,
maps of railway lines, and detailed information about the volume of mail
delivered by the Chinese postal service.[88]

Japanese organizers also seized the opportunity to display both cultural artifacts and technological innovations to millions of potential visitors.[89] They erected teahouses and a reproduction of the Nikko shrines
on its four-acre site and dedicated key resources to exhibits in the Palaces
of Manufactures, Agriculture, Food Products, Mines and Metallurgy,
Liberal Arts, Education and Social Economy, Transportation, and Fine
Arts.[90] Japanese exhibits occupied more than 80,000 square feet of space
in these halls—more territory than any other foreign nation had—plus
an additional 145,500 square feet in its national building. Like China,
Japan devoted space to its education system. Its exhibit in the Palace of
Education and Social Economy featured examples of pupils' work from
the elementary school through college levels, as well as displays of the
Japanese Red Cross Society, Tokyo's public utilities, and photographs of
the "poor houses" and "houses of correction" in the nation.[91]

Fig. 38. Japanese Gardens. (Donald G. Larson Collection, Special
Collections Research Center, California State University, Fresno.)

At the fair the Japanese and Chinese representatives also took the
advantageous opportunity to stage large public celebrations that would
shape a particular image of their respective nations for fair visitors and
readers of the local press. Some viewers even recognized the power of
the fair to shape such images. "In a thousand different ways," noted the
San Francisco Examiner in March, "Japan is using the Exposition to interpret the Oriental mind to the Occidental understanding."[92] Japan hosted
numerous impressive cultural celebrations at the fair, including a celebration of the New Year, a traditional Doll Festival, and the Iris Festival.[93] The
Japanese delegation took a leading role in hosting many social events as
well, bringing together the PPIE Woman's Board and Board of Directors,
representatives from other foreign nations, and other key groups at many
dinners and receptions. Although Chinese officials hosted fewer such
gatherings, the local press regularly noted their activities. These articles
offered remarkably positive coverage that again offered city residents and
fairgoers visions of China and Japan that contradicted old stereotypes.
The *San Francisco Chronicle* reported quite positively on an April dinner
hosted by the Japanese commission, noting that "the toasts of the eve-

Fig. 39. Japanese Red Cross exhibit. (San Francisco
History Center, San Francisco Public Library.)

ning were indicative of the purpose of amity on the part of the Japanese
commissioners." Said toasts included that of Japanese commissioner Jiro
Hirada, who proclaimed that Japan "stands with her arms outstretched
and heart wide open to the friendship of the world."[94]

It is reasonable to assume that foreign officials realized the power of
these spectacles. China's approach particularly suggests that officials carefully orchestrated the content of these events. Although the dedication
of the Chinese Building in March included Chinese music, little other
pageantry occurred during the event. The featured musicians were local
Chinese children who sang both American and Chinese songs in English.[95] Reports mentioned their presence—and the *San Francisco Examiner* even included a picture—suggesting that the Chinese may have
been trying to highlight the presence of a Chinese American population
in the city.[96] At the late September celebration of China Day, a sedate
observation occurred in the Chinese Pavilion and featured an address
by Kai Fuh Shah, Chinese minister to the United States. The *San Francisco Chronicle* noted, "No Orientalism for Chinese Programme," and the
report remarked that Chinese residents of San Francisco would celebrate

Fig. 40. China Day. (#1959.087—ALB, 3:130, Bancroft
Library, University of California, Berkeley.)

the day with a "strictly orthodox Exposition program."[97] Kai's remarks
emphasized China's long friendship with the United States and called for
their continued economic relationship.[98] The event included speeches
by exposition and Chinese officials but none of the spectacle and pageantry that other nations usually featured in their celebrations. Its organizers rejected traditional Chinese costumes and displays in favor of a
focus on the nation's recent political and economic progress. Similarly,
the featured speech at the Chinese Students' Day, given by Y. C. Yang, a
Chinese graduate of the University of Wisconsin, concentrated on China's "new consciousness . . . new civilization and a new understanding."[99]
The decision by organizers and participants to ignore China's past and
emphasize its future as a progressive republic suggests a belief that making connections with the "new" China was more important than reminding listeners of a history associated in the popular white American mind
with imperial decadence and moral decay.

Japanese officials had no such qualms about asserting Japanese culture at the exposition. Fair officials bent over backward to make Japan
Day a success. They issued numerous press releases about the event and
forbade the Exposition Band from playing offensive music (i.e., *The
Mikado*).[100] Japan Day's elaborate festivities included the ritual bless-
ing of the national building by a Shinto priest and a huge parade contain-

Fig. 41. At the Tea Room in the Japanese exhibit, visitors were served by Japanese women dressed in traditional garb. (Donald G. Larson Collection, Special Collections Research Center, California State University, Fresno.)

ing floats designed to represent Japanese history.[101] The active participation of local Japanese children, who were noted as such in newspaper reports, drew attention to the presence of the Japanese in California.[102] The Japanese delegation's choice to celebrate traditional holidays, such as the Doll Festival and the Iris Festival, at the PPIE suggests that they felt none of the qualms that the Chinese had about displaying aspects of their culture that white Americans could perceive as exotic. Such events echo Japan's exhibitionary strategy at the 1910 Japan-British Exhibition in London, at which Lockyer argues Japanese officials sought to emphasize the value of their "civilization of an old and high order . . . into which modern civilization had been grafted."[103] It is likely that organizers of the Japanese exhibit in San Francisco had similar goals for the PPIE. They sought to highlight both their nation's history and its future, taking a path unlike that of Chinese officials, who sought simply to focus on the future. These tactics reflect the fact that among white Americans, Japanese officials did not face the same stereotypes associating its ancient society with decay or decadence that China did. White Americans perceived the Japanese as primarily a military, economic, and demographic threat and not a moral one. Japanese officials may have believed they could safely celebrate their culture without fear of playing into white American stereotypes.

Another way to understand the power of these events rests in the interactions between people at the fair that contributed to the exposition's social and cultural messages. These elaborate Japanese celebrations often facilitated exchanges between Japanese and Japanese Americans and fair visitors. Rather than static exhibits upon which fair visitors could gaze with interest, the Japanese hosted social events during which Japanese men, women, and children displayed their culture for fair visitors. The May 6, 1915, issue of the *San Francisco Examiner* featured an example of this interaction by running a photograph of a Japanese woman and a white woman, both dressed in Japanese garb, at the traditional Japanese Boy's Festival celebrated at the fairgrounds. The two women posed for the camera, but they were also involved in the celebration and, presumably, in communicating with each other.[104] Although a report on the Japanese New Year's celebration summed up the participation of Japanese women with the note that visitors "mingled gaily with ... the pretty little Oriental maids who grace the Japanese tea gardens," the very act of mixing American visitors and Japanese workers (whether foreign or American residents) threw an element of uncertainty into the association that makes it impossible to characterize.[105] Living exhibits, such as those on the Zone, are inherently unpredictable, and an understanding of that unpredictability must be included in analyses of these events.[106] The conversations between these fairgoers had the potential to disrupt their expectations of each other and to introduce a human element not present in a static exhibit of Japanese culture or a staged performance.

Visions of both Chinese and Japanese as exotic and bizarre others persisted at the fair despite the attempts of the Chinese and Japanese delegations to use the fair to assert their nations' equality on the world stage. Pre-fair publicity promised curious tourists that California's proximity to the Orient would add an exotic touch to the exposition, one that would only be possible at a San Francisco event. "The displays from the Orient will be particularly lavish," claimed one pamphlet. "The nations of the Orient, stirring from the sleep of centuries to the call of progress, will startle the Occidental mind with the most bizarre and novel effects ever witnessed."[107] Clearly, publicists hoped to lure potential visitors by drawing on Orientalist tropes of essentialism, passivity (only to be awakened by the West), and otherness. These "bizarre and novel" effects were unlikely to complement the developing political and industrial powers that the Chinese and Japanese governments sought to emphasize in their exhibits.

This vision of Asia replaced the stereotypical threats of gambling, opium smoking, prostitution, military invasion, and miscegenation with another equally racialized vision of Asia. In response to the "call of progress," issued presumably by the United States, the Orient would display "bizarre" effects that would validate China's and Japan's status as others in relation to the United States. Such a vision emphasized the region's inability to move forward on its own. It undermined the Asian nations' attempts to display themselves as strong, modern states by crediting their development solely to their relationship to the West.

Publicists attempted to lure visitors to the city with depictions of its Asian American population as attractions that were to be viewed and consumed as the other exhibits at the fair were. This rhetoric stood in direct contrast to other images of the Chinese and Japanese as active participants in the state's political life. To counteract potential visitors' voiced fears of "the large number of Orientals in the city," publicists promised visitors that San Francisco's immigrant population was a harmless source of entertainment rather than an alien threat.[108] Instead of de-emphasizing the Chinese presence in San Francisco in response to the public's fears of an Asian invasion, publicists chose to turn Chinatown into an attraction to be viewed and again consumed during one's visit to the city. A 1913 guide promised that "this quaint Oriental community" was the "most fascinating" of San Francisco's attractions.[109] Another praised the city for having "the most cosmopolitan population of any city in the world" and suggested that "a visit to these colonies is interesting and instructive."[110] In this context, immigrant communities became other educational (and exotic) exhibits to visit alongside the official exhibits presented at the exposition.

The Lure of San Francisco: A Romance amid Old Landmarks, a novel published in San Francisco in July 1915, encapsulated this consumerist attitude toward the Chinese in particular. The book's heroine, a white native San Franciscan, attempts to convince her Boston beau of San

Francisco's charms, and during their tour of the city, they dine at both "Spanish" (Mexican) and Chinese restaurants. The authors described their Chinese meal in great detail:

> [W]e seated ourselves in the big carved armchairs. Sipping the delicious beverage, we glanced toward the other tables, where groups of Chinamen were talking in a curious jargon and dexterously handling the thin ebony chopsticks. On the wide matting-covered couches extending along the sidewalls, lounged sallow-faced Orientals.... Snowy rice cakes, shreds of candied cocoanut, preserved ginger and brown paper-shell nuts with the usual Chinese eating utensils were placed before us. We tried the slender chopsticks with laughable failure.... We took a farewell look at the gilt carved screens and long banners, which in quaint Chinese characters wished us health and happiness.[111]

The novel implies that a visitor to Chinatown could expect to encounter novel foods, odd utensils, and exotic people. Each of these elements authenticated the experience. Although a novel, this book also served as a tour guide to San Francisco, as implied by its publisher, the Paul Elder Company, which also produced a good bit of fair publicity.[112] Its appearance in July, halfway through the fair, also suggests it was intended in part to guide visitors through the city during their exposition visit. Its vision of San Francisco as a site for the consumption and viewing of foreign cultures fits very neatly with the image offered by fair publicity. Tourists were urged to view the Chinese residents of San Francisco as commodities who were available to entertain, supply, and feed them rather than as equal participants in American or international society.

This dual depiction of Chinese San Franciscans as both loyal American citizens and exotic others demonstrates the uneven nature of the racialization of the Chinese in early twentieth-century California. Although much publicity presented a safely tamed Chinatown, many white visitors still viewed the neighborhood as exotic and bizarre, subject to commodification and consumption, and not as the home of American citizens. This image had the potential to draw fascinated tourists to the fair and the city. Moreover, because popular stereotypes that associated the

Chinese with gambling, opium, and prostitution still circulated in popular culture, this publicity constructed an impression of the Chinese as permanent others, incapable of integration into American society.

Neither San Francisco residents nor tourists had to look far to encounter persistent cultural stereotypes of both the Chinese and Japanese as threats to American society. Throughout the years leading up to the fair and during it, local newspapers published anti-Japanese and anti-Chinese articles alongside articles lauding China's and Japan's participation in the fair. Three days before the *San Francisco Examiner* published an editorial welcoming the members of the Chinese Industrial Commission to the fair, the paper had reported on the newest installment of a popular film serial with the headline "Elaine Is Liberated by Her Chinese Captors." In that episode, Elaine "rejoins her family and in the resulting great joy the threat of the Chinese is forgotten."[113] With this and other such reminders in the press, however, it was doubtful that many white San Franciscans could forget the Chinese "threat." Throughout the fair, papers published articles on the violence in Chinatown with titles such as "Chinese Tong War Is Brought to an End" and "Tongs' Peace May Be Only Short Lived" alongside positive reports describing the activities of Chinese representatives on the ground.[114] We cannot know what readers made of these articles, but certainly such sensationalism frustrated local Chinese residents. It reinforced decades of white Americans' perceptions of the Chinese as dangerous, violent people who posed a menace to white society and particularly to white women.[115] Papers published fewer such articles on the Japanese, but a pair of October 1915 articles published in the *San Francisco Examiner* detailing supposed Japanese plans for an invasion of the California coast reminded readers of the potential dangers that Japanese immigrants posed to the nation and to white women, in particular, who, the article promised, preferred to marry Japanese men.[116]

Exposition press releases echoed these assumptions that Asians were permanently outside of white American society when they foregrounded "exotic" Asia over the more "modern" image. One description of Japan's displays at the fair brushed off Japan's exhibits showcasing technological progress with the line, "What Japan has done to absorb western ideas is not as interesting to us of the occident as it is to that wonderful nation itself." The author of the piece focused on describing scenes that fit the stereotypical Japan of the American imagination: geishas, tea ceremonies, exotic silks, and Sumo wrestlers.[117] The author suggested these elements, rather than the artists and exhibitors who displayed the nation's political, social, and technological changes, constituted the authentic Japan. While an appreciation of Japan's heritage may be lauded, it is important to note that these images perpetuated Western fantasies of Japan, rather than reality, since they failed to include the nation's emphatic moves toward modernization.[118]

The conflict over Underground Chinatown demonstrates the most extreme example of this tension between modern and exotic visions of Asia. As noted previously, this amusement concession drew on popular negative stereotypes of the Chinese to create an attraction that purportedly revealed the reality of Chinese American life to curious visitors. No vision of Chinese Americans as citizens appeared there; instead, visitors saw Chinese residents as drug addicts, gamblers, and prostitutes. Although the local Chinese community and its white supporters loudly protested the concession, it took the intervention of an official Chinese government representative, Chen Chi, to convince President Moore to step in and close the concession. Even after the concession reopened as Underground Slumming, the connections to stereotypes of the Chinese remained, making the change appear as less than sincere.

Underground Chinatown's presence at the fair demonstrates how the fair became a source of debate over the relationship between California and China. That fair officials approved all of the Zone's concessions, including Underground Chinatown, which started up not long after opening day and despite the concerns of the Chinese Committee of the PPIE, suggested that they took no sustained effort to keep the Zone free of images that might offend the local Chinese population. Yet how could Underground Chinatown and then Underground Slumming coexist with the fair's other sponsored images of a developing China? If fair officials believed that China was essential to the fair's success, why did they work so hard in the years before the fair to ease Chinese participation but then fail to rid the fair of the offensive underground attractions? Quite simply, the underground attractions existed because they reinforced racial stereotypes and were thus strong moneymakers. Moreover, they were located on the Zone, a space dedicated to amusement and immediate

Fig. 42. Japan Beautiful exhibit in the Zone at the PPIE. (San Francisco History Center, San Francisco Public Library.)

profit rather than to education and a space where critics and fair officials debated the line between the entertaining and the prurient. Many Zone attractions failed to make money, and fair officials were barraged with requests to bail out struggling concessions. Both underground concessions consistently made a profit, and fair officials seemed unwilling to jeopardize a moneymaking scheme. Most important, these attractions did not pose nearly the same kind of threat to the fair that pre-fair events had. China had already invested a great deal in its exhibits at the fair, and it was highly unlikely that the nation would withdraw partway through the event. Moreover, the persistence of these attractions demonstrates that fair officials, as a body, saw no need to fight these anti-Chinese images. Profit motivated their pre-fair politicking, their defense of Underground Chinatown, and their approval of Underground Slumming.

The Japanese equivalent to Underground Chinatown was considerably more benign and raised no complaints from the Japanese community. Japan Beautiful featured an enormous Buddha guarding the gates to a complex that featured geisha girls serving tea, replicas of streets of Tokyo and Kyoto, sumo wrestling, and numerous opportunities for visitors to buy cheap replicas of Japanese goods. Robert Rydell notes that this "trivialization of Japanese culture" offset the image of progress that the official Japanese exhibits conveyed.[119] No record exists of any objections voiced by the Japanese delegation to this attraction, and the only conflict that emerged around it involved the manager's complaint that his workers were harassed at the gates of the fair. A local Japanese businessman ran the concession and hired local residents, and these factors may have helped insulate it from criticism. It may have played down advancements in Japanese culture, but it also made money for local Japanese residents. Its trivialization of Japanese culture more closely resembled that of concessions that featured European cultures than it did the powerful racial messages of Underground Chinatown, so no movement arose to shut it down.

Both Japan Beautiful and the underground concessions reveal the challenges facing Japan and China as they approached the PPIE and other expositions. No matter how hard Chinese and Japanese representatives worked to construct positive images of their nations, they were continually faced with Western perceptions of, and appropriations of, their cultures as exotic and different.[120] They had to combat both negative stereotypes of their cultures and the expectations of visitors such as Doris Barr who came to the fair to see "traditional" culture instead of evidence of industrial progress. These visitors eagerly spent their dollars on Japan Beautiful or Underground Chinatown. This demand meant that PPIE officials gladly perpetuated these exotic images of China and Japan, further complicating Chinese and Japanese efforts to control their representations at the fair and contributing to an event full of competing agendas and images.

Asian exhibits drew visitors by offering a taste of the exotic and, in the case of the underground concessions, the morally titillating. The debates over these depictions, as with the discussions about the city's development before the fair, demonstrate how deeply enmeshed the PPIE became in contemporary political discussions. Visitors also flocked to the Zone to watch scantily clad women perform in various concessions, launching yet another controversy at the fair. The Woman's Board worked hard to make the fair a place where they would not be subject to sexual exploitation or to sexually suggestive shows. But the male fair directors demonstrated little commitment to this effort or much interest in ridding the grounds of such potentially profitable Zone attractions. The fair directors' desire for profit again came into conflict with the agendas of other interest groups, this time making the fair into a battleground over gender and female sexuality and the place of vice in public life.

5 ❧ Sex and Other Vices at the Fair

After spending a day at the fair, San Francisco resident Harry Thieder-man complained to President Charles Moore about his visit to the Joy Zone. He voiced his frustration about the presence of attractions that showcased female sexuality, telling Moore, "Cairo dances and women shows are relegated to the lowest sections of border cities and should have no place at this otherwise beautiful exposition."[1] He believed that such performances belonged only in poor towns along the U.S.-Mexican border. Middle-class men might visit these places alone but never with their wives and daughters. The exposition should uplift visitors, he reasoned, rather than expose them to the salacious side of life in the American West. But as a fair is supposed to be fun, too, many visitors to the Panama-Pacific International Exposition eagerly spent their money on alcohol, gambling, and dancing.

Thiederman's letter encapsulated a persistent complaint about the fair. City residents, fair directors, and members of reform organizations weighed in on the moral content of the exposition from the moment the city won the fair. They debated whether alcohol, gambling, and risqué dances belonged on the grounds, with local residents again expressing a deep interest in the content of the fair. Resolution came only after public complaints reached the ears of state politicians. The sometimes troubled relationship between the PPIE Woman's Board and the PPIE Board of Directors exacerbated this issue. The coming of the fair offered reform-ers a compelling reason to clean up San Francisco's vice district in order to ensure the respectability of the fair. And many tried. Unfortunately for them, San Francisco's long history of tolerance of alcohol, gambling, and prostitution, combined with the fair directors' interest in profits, meant that reformers had limited success in ridding the city or the fair of vice.

Fair directors hoped the moral protective work that the PPIE Woman's Board and its associated women's organizations undertook would alleviate concerns about the fair's and the city's morality. Although contemporary histories of the fair recall the success of this union, close examination of the relationship suggests a rather different story, one that reveals another instance of the breakdown of "civic unity" in the city. These conflicts expose the male organizers' opposition to moral reform and to assertions of female power. The Board of Directors and the Woman's Board had rather different ideas about the place of female sexuality in society. Their debates ignored both the female Zone performers, whose voices were conspicuously absent from public discussions, and those fairgoers of all races and classes who wished to enjoy attractions on the Zone that featured alcohol, gambling, and sexually suggestive dances.

San Francisco's reputation as a "wide-open town," where vice ran rampant, posed a publicity problem for the PPIE in the reform-minded Progressive Era.[2] Moral reform movements gained strength during this time, as middle-class men and women united to rid society of various social evils: gambling, drinking, and prostitution. These movements originated in the antebellum Northeast and regained momentum in response to the excesses of the late nineteenth century's Gilded Age. The immigrants who flooded into the cities during the late nineteenth and early twentieth centuries heightened middle-class anxieties about morality and respectability. The increasing number of young women entering the workforce also worried reformers, who believed the women's morality and chastity were at risk. In some cities elite male urban leaders entered into coalitions with female reformers in the hopes of maintaining middle-class social values and control over working-class immigrants and people of color.[3] They used reforms to try to hold sway over the increasingly unruly and diverse urban population.

Concerns about the safety and morality of the city and the fair began to surface almost as soon as San Francisco won the right to host the fair. One concerned potential fairgoer wrote to Moore, "Glimpses of the ornate and beautiful architecture of its wonderful buildings and objects of attractions, . . . have aroused visions of the grandeur and glory of the [fair]. . . . But with that vision, there comes another of the Red-Light way and the notorious Barbary Coast, where the lowest forms of vice and sin, show themselves, in all their hideousness and deformity."[4] Such fears were driven by a preoccupation with the possible exploitation of young white women. A railway poster displayed in North Dakota high-lighted one of the main accusations that the fair would become a center of prostitution and the downfall of innocent young women:

> Warning! The women of San Francisco are determined to prevent the letting of a portion of the fair grounds for the purpose of establishing houses of prostitution and are doing all in their power to stay the evil. . . . Let it be remembered that the country will be scoured for girls to supply the demand of this nefarious business, and every means that is possible for man to conceive will be used to snare and mislead these girls in order to secure them. Every girl should be warned against advertisements of positions in San Francisco . . . the door that will be open for the strange girl will be the door that leads to perdition.[5]

Rumors had long circulated about the thousands of young women who had gone missing after the 1893 Columbian Exposition in Chicago and the 1904 Louisiana Purchase Exposition in St. Louis. Oft-repeated stories told of innocent farm girls who left home for the city and never returned.[6] Those same stories emerged in 1915, as the apparent warning from the "women of San Francisco" demonstrated. The fair's Board of Directors and Woman's Board worked hard to combat this type of bad publicity.

These rumors had substance. San Francisco's vice district, the Barbary Coast, had evolved along with the city, serving the desires of Gold Rush miners, sailors, and the thousands of local residents who frequented the area's saloons, dance halls, and brothels.[7] By the 1880s, approximately two thousand saloons and brothels flourished in the city. The center of this activity was the Barbary Coast, a neighborhood known across the nation as an "assemblage of dance halls, drinking places, lodging houses and dives, first known to deep sea sailors and later exploited in many a novel."[8] Appalled visitors often commented on the Barbary Coast's immorality. Only three years before the fair, a Chicago police captain returned home from a visit to report that San Francisco was "the worst vice-ridden city in the country."[9]

San Franciscans, however, did not always oppose the activities in the Barbary Coast.[10] As a *San Francisco Bulletin* columnist argued in 1912, San

Franciscans "like to think about it [the Barbary Coast] and to talk about it and to look at its displays and even take part . . . [often one sees] groups of handsomely dressed people . . . among the night revelers on the Barbary Coast. . . . They seem to think they are having a great lark."[11] This laissez-faire attitude, the result of the city's diverse and cosmopolitan population, helps to explain many San Franciscans' tolerant attitude toward an active vice district during a time when such venues were frequently under siege by Progressive reformers. After the earthquake the quick erection of a huge brothel—citizens called it "the municipal brothel" since a good portion of the profits went to city hall—and the official creation of the Municipal Clinic, where prostitutes could get free medical care, demonstrated the generally tolerant atmosphere in the city toward the "social evil."[12] San Francisco basically segregated prostitution to the vice districts—the Barbary Coast, the uptown Tenderloin, and, to some extent, Chinatown—allowing most city residents to ignore its presence.

The city's large Chinese immigrant population, often connected in the popular mind with gambling, opium use, and prostitution, contributed a racial aspect to the city's reputation for vice. As in other parts of the country, popular culture linked nonwhite men to hypersexuality and vice. In San Francisco, Chinese men were predominantly presented in this symbolic role, with the media often depicting them as a threat to white women. The uneven male–female ratio in the Chinese community and the real history of Chinese prostitution in California meant that whites often viewed all Chinese women as prostitutes.[13] In San Francisco, as elsewhere, vice had an explicitly racial component that contributed to the construction of the city's social hierarchy and moral order. The association of Chinese men and women with vice—as male slavers and female prostitutes, respectively—bolstered the city's racial hierarchy and the dominance of white men and women over Asians. These links masked the reality that many more whites than Asians participated in the vice trade, as well as helped shift the blame for social disorder onto the perceived Asian menace. For white Americans who were familiar only with these negative images of the Chinese and Chinatown, this association exacerbated their fears about visiting San Francisco.

But fairs also attracted visitors by featuring morally questionable attractions. In 1893 the success of Chicago's "Midway Plaisance," which had

Aeroplane View Main Group of Exhibit Palaces Panama-Pacific International Exposition

Plate 1. Aeroplane view, main group of exhibit. (Library of Congress.)

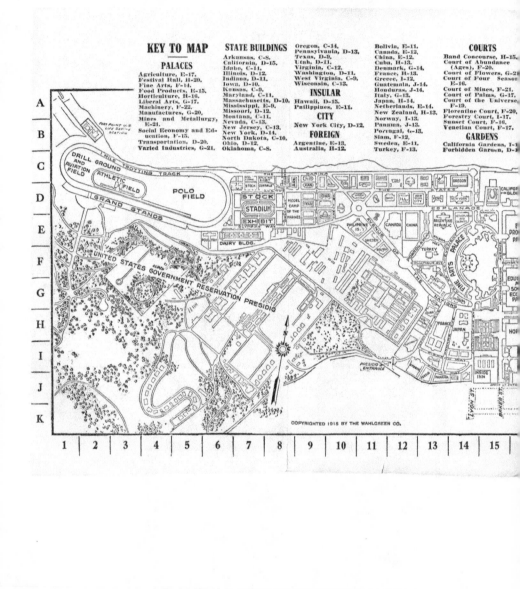

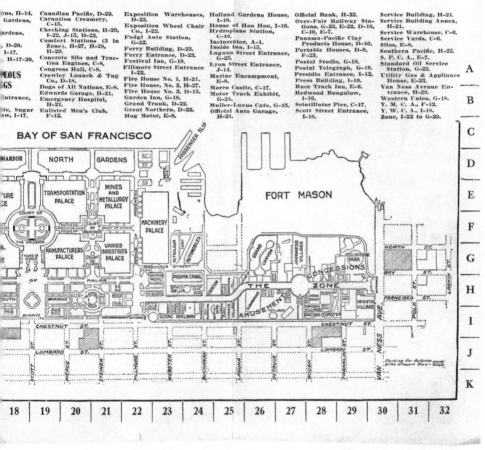

ens, H-14,
Gardens,

ardens,

D-20,
I-17,
H-17-20,

EOUS
GS

Entrance,

te, Sugar
w, I-17,

Canadian Pacific, D-22.
Carnation Creamery,
  C-15.
Checking Stations, H-29,
  I-22, J-15, D-23.
Comfort Stations (3 in
  Zone), H-27, H-28,
  H-22.
Concrete Silo and Trac-
  tion Engines, C-8.
Congress Hall, C-8.
Crowley Launch & Tug
  Co., D-18.
Dogs of All Nations, E-8.
Edwards Garage, H-21.
Emergency Hospital,
  H-21.
Enlisted Men's Club,
  F-12.

Exposition Warehouses,
  D-23.
Exposition Wheel Chair
  Co., I-22.
Fadgl Auto Station,
  G-22.
Ferry Building, D-23.
Ferry Entrance, D-23.
Festival Inn, G-19.
Fillmore Street Entrance
  I-22.
Fire House No. 1, H-21.
Fire House, No. 2, H-27.
Fire House No. 3, D-15.
Garden Inn, G-18.
Grand Trunk, D-22.
Great Northern, D-22.
Hog Motor, E-8.

Holland Gardens House,
  I-16.
House of Hoo Hoo, I-16.
Hydroplane Station,
  C-16.
Incinerator, A-4.
Inside Inn, I-15.
Laguna Street Entrance,
  G-25.
Lyon Street Entrance,
  J-14.
Marine Encampment,
  E-8.
Morro Castle, C-17.
Motor Truck Exhibit,
  G-24.
Muller-Luxus Cafe, G-15.
Official Auto Garage,
  H-21.

Official Bank, H-22.
Over-Fair Railway Sta-
  tions, G-23, E-22, D-16,
  C-10, E-7.
Panama-Pacific Clay
  Products House, D-10.
Portable Houses, D-9,
  F-23.
Postal Studio, G-18.
Postal Telegraph, G-19.
Presidio Entrance, I-12.
Press Building, I-19.
Race Track Inn, E-6.
Redwood Bungalow,
  I-16.
Scintillator Pier, C-17.
Scott Street Entrance,
  I-18.

Service Building, H-21.
Service Building Annex,
  H-21.
Service Warehouse, C-6.
Service Yards, C-6.
Silos, E-8.
Southern Pacific, H-22.
S. P. C. A., E-7.
Standard Oil Service
  Station, G-23.
Utility Gas & Appliance
  House, E-23.
Van Ness Avenue En-
  trance, H-29.
Western Union, G-18.
Y. M. C. A., F-12.
Y. W. C. A., I-18.
Zone, I-22 to G-29.

Plate 2. Map of the fairgrounds. (*Official Guide.*)

Plate 3. "Get Your Congressman to Vote." (Donald G. Larson Collection, Special Collections Research Center, California State University, Fresno.)

Plate 4. "California Welcomes the World." (Donald G. Larson Collection, Special Collections Research Center, California State University, Fresno.)

Plate 5. Another variation on "California Welcomes the
World," this postcard emphasized the marriage of progress and
commerce at the fair. (Personal collection of author.)

Plate 6. At the PPIE the grizzly bear image signified the city's recovery
from the 1906 earthquake and fire. (Library of Congress.)

Plate 7. "The Greatest, Most Beautiful and Most Important in History . . ." The official fair poster designed by Perham Nahl. (Donald G. Larson Collection, Special Collections Research Center, California State University, Fresno.)

Plate 8. The South Gardens, opening day. (#1959.087—ALB, 2:23, Bancroft Library, University of California, Berkeley.)

Plate 9. PPIE participant badge. (Collection of the Oakland
Museum, gift of Mr. Guy M. Walden.)

Plate 10. Autochrome of *Fountain of Energy*, PPIE. (PG #3565.14, National Museum of American History, Smithsonian Institution.)

Plate 11. Autochrome of flower beds and Arch of the West, PPIE. (PG #3565.11, National Museum of American History, Smithsonian Institution.)

Plate 12. Exposition grounds, three months before
opening day. (Library of Congress.)

Plate 13. Festival Hall. (*Souvenir Views of the Panama-Pacific
International Exposition*, San Francisco, 1915.)

Plate 14. Autochrome of Siam Pavilion. (PG #3565.02, National
Museum of American History, Smithsonian Institution.)

Plate 15. PPIE, San Francisco Day ticket, 1915. (Gift of Mrs. Charles H. Jurgens, Collection of the Oakland Museum of California.)

Plate 16. The Scintillator. Electric lighting made nights at the exposition particularly impressive. (Donald G. Larson Collection, Special Collections Research Center, California State University, Fresno.)

Plate 17. The Palace of
Fine Arts illuminated.
(*Souvenir Views
of the Panama-
Pacific International
Exposition*, San
Francisco, 1915.)

Plate 18. The Tower of Jewels and exhibit palaces illuminated. (*Souvenir Views of the Panama-Pacific International Exposition*, San Francisco, 1915.)

Plate 19. Palace of Liberal Arts and the *Fountain of Energy*. (*Souvenir Views of the Panama-Pacific International Exposition*, San Francisco, 1915.)

Plate 20. Advancement of health exhibit at the PPIE. The Race Betterment Booth introduced visitors to the "science" of eugenics. (San Francisco History Center, San Francisco Public Library.)

Plate 21. The $100,000 typewriter, found in the Palace of Liberal Arts, impressed many guests with its enormous size. Postcards such as this one helped to advertise the fair's wares across the nation. (Donald G. Larson Collection, Special Collections Research Center, California State University, Fresno.)

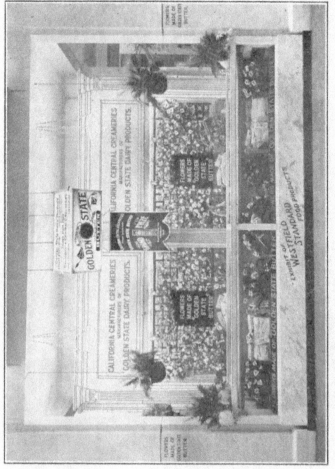

EXHIBIT OF

Golden State Butter

—AT—

PANAMA PACIFIC INTERNATIONAL EXPOSITION

San Francisco
1915

VIEWED BY MILLIONS

Plate 22. Exhibit of Golden State Butter, one of many California agricultural industries advertised at the fair. (Donald G. Larson Collection, Special Collections Research Center, California State University, Fresno.)

Plate 23. Palace of Horticulture and the South Gardens. (*Souvenir Views of the Panama-Pacific International Exposition, San Francisco, 1915.*)

Plate 24. The South Gardens and the Tower of Jewels. (*Souvenir Views of the Panama-Pacific International Exposition, San Francisco*, 1915.)

Plate 25. The great South Gardens. (*Souvenir Views of the Panama-Pacific International Exposition.* San Francisco, 1915.)

Plate 26. Autochrome of the Tower of Jewels. (PG #3565.06, National Museum of American History, Smithsonian Institution.)

Plate 27. Autochrome of the Tower of Jewels' interior. (PG #3565.02, National Museum of American History, Smithsonian Institution.)

Plate 28. View of the Zone at the PPIE showing the Chinese Village and the Battle of Gettysburg, Alt Nurnberg, and Tehuantepec Buildings. (San Francisco History Center, San Francisco Public Library.)

Plate 29. Samoan dancers and the golden Buddha of Japan Beautiful in the Zone at the PPIE. (San Francisco History Center, San Francisco Public Library.)

Plate 30. Chinese restaurant inside the Palace of Food Products, PPIE. (San Francisco History Center, San Francisco Public Library.)

Plate 31. The Inside Inn. (San Francisco History Center, San Francisco Public Library.)

Plate 32. Autochrome of the Colonnades, Palace of Fine Arts. (PG #3565.03, National Museum of American History, Smithsonian Institution.)

featured the *dance du ventre* (belly dance) of "Little Egypt," convinced later fair organizers that an amusement section was necessary for a successful fair. Likewise, that success drew fire from those who objected to such displays of female sexuality.[14] PPIE publicists emphasized the fair's educational nature while actively promoting the Joy Zone. There, they promised, visitors would find a set of attractions that "in novelty, interest and 'thrill' surpass[ed] any similar gathering of amusement enterprises ever seen in this country or Europe."[15] Many visitors eagerly anticipated going to the Zone, with its roller-coaster rides, talking horse, dance halls, and scale model of the Panama Canal.

The Zone, and the fair itself, offered countless spots for young men and women to socialize unchaperoned. Reformers consequently worried that young people would use the space of the fair for both licit and illicit activities. Movie theaters, amusement parks, and dance halls throughout the nation drew young men and women to their doors, reflecting a new style of socializing that worried the older generation. Young women, many of them employed and with their own spending money, formed relationships with their male peers that often turned sexual.[16] Scholars have documented the evolution of working-class attitudes toward sexuality that differed from those of the middle-class.[17] In turn, the explosion of these working-class amusements in cities across America during the late nineteenth and early twentieth centuries brought working-class and nonwhite sexual standards into view, and they came under fire from Progressive reformers who associated them with prostitution and white slavery.[18] These changes, along with the rise of film and the media culture, contributed to rapid changes in public sexuality and an accompanying set of concerns about vice.[19]

World's fairs also troubled some because the events featured a wide diversity of people and chances for interaction not only between men and women but also between people of different races, ethnicities, and classes. The Zone offered opportunities for heterosexual socializing in an environment that featured people of color and blatant displays of female sexuality. This combination frightened those who feared for their own virtue and that of their families. The myth of the male black rapist, used to justify lynching and terrorism of the black community in the South, held power nationwide in the Progressive Era and added to concerns about protecting white female sexuality. The nonwhite men present on the Zone performed as examples of primitive cultures, but their very presence threatened the racial and gender order of the fair. The freedom of the Zone meant that they could interact with white women in ways that risked overturning the carefully constructed social hierarchy of the fair and, by extension, of white America.[20] These concerns reflected nationwide panic about prostitution and white slavery. Apprehensive reformers believed that rings of white slavers—often stereotyped as nonwhite immigrants—plotted to kidnap and sexually enslave unsuspecting young white women. The prevalence of these alien or dark white-slave traders in the white-slave literary narratives heightened public anxieties about the peril and convinced many white Americans that their daughters were at risk.[21]

Real concerns about the effect of vice on men, women, and the family contributed to the growth of female moral reform organizations such as the Young Woman's Christian Association (YWCA), the Woman's Christian Temperance Union (WCTU), and scores of other local groups across the country.[22] They wanted to abolish the sexual double standard and protect working women from the dangers of the city, so they tried to provide healthy alternative entertainments for young city dwellers.[23] San Francisco, like all Progressive Era cities, had its share of female reform organizations.[24] By 1915, the YWCA had a wide array of services and programs aimed at the young, single, working women of the city, as did other groups including the Catholic-sponsored Society for Befriending Girls and the Traveler's Aid Society, a group that focused specifically on aiding new arrivals to the city.[25]

These simmering conflicts about society's moral standards converged on the PPIE, making it a focus for Progressive Era debates about the intersection of gender, race, sexuality, and class. Critics questioned whether the fair would be a safe place for white women and children. They worried it might expose them to unseemly practices of working-class and nonwhite culture. Simultaneously, organized groups of local white women hoped they could use the fair as a place from which to work on improving moral conditions in the city. Although the Board of Directors appeared not to possess much intrinsic interest in moral reforms, these pressing issues forced the men to take a stand in order to protect their profits;

so they took steps to reassure potential visitors that the event would be one worth traveling across the country to visit.

Exposition directors understood the need to downplay San Francisco's reputation for debauchery. They relied on the PPIE Woman's Board to accomplish this goal. Integrating an active Woman's Board into the fair bureaucracy allowed publicists to reassure visitors that these women would ensure the moral health and stable gendered order of the exposition and in the city. As President Moore noted in a letter to a concerned religious leader, the "high quality of women on the Woman's Board" would uphold morality at the exposition.[26] Fair directors hoped that the activities of these prominent women and their assurances of the safety of the fair and city would reassure nervous midwesterners and easterners that they would be safe venturing to the wicked city of San Francisco.

The Woman's Board deliberately integrated the YWCA and similar organizations into the fair. After the San Francisco YWCA found itself unable to expand its travelers' aid work, the board organized a California auxiliary to the New York–based Traveler's Aid Society. This group focused particularly on assisting female travelers who needed help finding lodgings in a new city.[27] Traveler's Aid workers promised that they would help all visitors find safe, affordable lodgings and avoid the racketeers who took advantage of naive visitors to the big city. Even more important, Traveler's Aid workers were on the lookout for traffickers in women. Reformers worried that the opening of the Panama Canal would cause such an increase in immigration that more immigrants would fall in with the wrong influences once they arrived in the city.[28] The exposition offered the organization the chance to expand its outreach work and to publicize the dangers inherent in travel. After the fair, the Woman's Board turned over all of its remaining funds to the Traveler's Aid Society.

Phoebe Hearst's position as honorary head of the Woman's Board facilitated the strong relationship that emerged between the board and the National Board of the YWCA. The YWCA constructed a large, centrally located building on the fairgrounds from which the organization served both men and women. There, fairgoers could purchase cheap meals at the cafeteria, find safe and affordable lodging in the city, enjoy a cup of coffee, or sit and recuperate from the rigors of enjoying the fair. As we shall see, YWCA workers also reached out to the young female workers

Fig. 43. California Building. (Donald G. Larson Collection, Special Collections Research Center, California State University, Fresno.)

on the Zone. The YWCA was the visible manifestation of the fair directors' promise to keep the fair clean and safe for women and families.[29]

Fair publicity painted the relationship between the Woman's Board and the fair in glowing terms. Propaganda promised concerned visitors that "any woman of any country may come to San Francisco during the Exposition and rest assured of protection."[30] Closer examination of the relationship between the Woman's Board, its sister organizations, and the male exposition directors reveals a much rockier relationship. It calls into question the fair directors' dedication to reform and suggests the obstacles that female reformers faced in such cities as San Francisco, where the entrenched establishment had little interest in reform. Philip Ethington argues that San Francisco's elite men were not friendly to female power in the city, and the fair's relationship with the Woman's Board bears out this observation.[31]

Elite Bay Area women founded the Woman's Board independently of the fair's administrative structure. The negotiation over the relationship between the PPIE Board of Directors and the Woman's Board vexed members of both entities. One male official urged women to take on solely social responsibilities, "not because its members are capable of social affairs only, but because the character of the other work to be discharged is of a nature that women could only with difficulty, embarrassment and great discomfort perform." Yet, the same writer almost immediately noted that the women's political influence in California meant that the Woman's Board could be very helpful regarding California political affairs.[32] His contradictory approach helps explain the tension that emerged between the Woman's Board and the fair directors. By 1911, women had earned the vote in California, granting them real political power. Yet some male leaders remained disconcerted with that fact and did not favor involving women in the fair as anything other than hostesses.

Some male officials were frustrated because they had no control over determining who sat on the Woman's Board. When Gavin McNab, an exposition lawyer, reported on the proposed contract between the two bodies, he vociferously criticized the composition of the Woman's Board and its claim to represent the women of California. He argued that placing all of women's affairs under the board's jurisdiction granted the members too much power and denied the points of view of other interested women. Probably more significant, he objected to the policy of allowing a board not formed under the direction of the exposition Board of Directors to "control the participation of women in the state of California . . . without their consent."[33] Curtis Lindley, another of the fair's counsels, dismissed McNab's concerns, suggesting "there is involved something more" in the conflict and reminding him that appointing another Woman's Board would only cause more problems for the fair.[34] McNab's reluctance to recognize the Woman's Board implies that he felt threatened by its potential power and points to a conflict over territory between the two bodies.[35] Probably displeased at having no input over choosing members of the exceptionally well-organized and well-funded Woman's Board, some of the men on the Board of Directors might have feared that the women would use their advantages to further their own agenda.

The struggle continued over the wording of the agreement, suggesting that McNab was not the only male board member to harbor distrust of the Woman's Board. In mid-November 1911, Woman's Board president Helen Sanborn complained that the new proposed contract would require the Woman's Board to fund all activities related to women at the fair, including "such activities as may be from time to time assigned to it by your board." This stipulation, she pointed out, violated the Woman's Board's own bylaws, for to require one corporation to fund undertakings determined by another corporation was both legally and morally questionable. Sanborn suggested alternate phrasing to clarify that such activities required mutual agreement.[36] Evidently, she and her peers were equally uneasy with their relationship with the male board. The final contract removed the offending phrase and simply stated that the Woman's Board would "provide for sufficient funds to effectively organize and conduct all such activities as may properly fall within the Department of Women's Affairs." Despite this concession, the agreement still required the Woman's Board to submit an outline of all activities to the Committee on Woman's Affairs and described the Woman's Board as "an auxiliary agency of this Board . . . subject to the supervisory control of the Board of Directors."[37] Although an independently funded corporation, members of the Woman's Board had to answer to the men in charge, establishing a relationship potentially fraught with conflict.

Not surprising, conflicts arose out of this relationship. Some dealt simply with practical issues, such as repairs and improvements required in the California Building that the Woman's Board were not authorized to order.[38] Other, more serious conflicts emerged over the city's moral issues. Pressure from nationally based moral reform organizations to clean up San Francisco mounted during 1914, forcing the Woman's Board and fair management to respond. In September, President Sanborn asked Director Hale to prepare a statement about moral reform efforts, reminding him "our board was busy long before the formation of a Traveler's Aid, defending the reputation of the Exposition, especially its Concessions department."[39] After Hale failed to respond, she reminded him that the real problem was not the morality of the exposition but of the city: "If this be a wide open town—drinking, dancing, and gambling everywhere—the very atmosphere inviting the unprincipled and lewd to us—we may labor earnestly in a Traveler's Aid or in any protective field and accomplish mighty little."[40]

Sanborn and others wanted fair directors to cooperate more fully with attempts to tackle vice issues in the city, but they recognized the challenge that such a job posed and did not want to be blamed for any failure to regulate conditions in the city and at the fair. As Sanborn wrote Hearst,

Fig. 44. Woman's Board of the Panama-Pacific International Exposition Day, October 29, 1915. (#1959.087—ALB, 3:70, Bancroft Library, University of California, Berkeley.)

"I think . . . Mr. Moore & Mr. Burt & all of them had better understand it. A nice time we should have trying to regulate moral conditions. We are willing to help in all ways possible, but the <u>responsibility is not ours.</u> Am I right?"[41] Here, Sanborn seemed acutely wary of the fair directors' hope that the Woman's Board could serve as a shield against criticisms of moral disorder, even while they failed to support such efforts fully. Later events would validate her concerns, as angry fair visitors blamed the Women's Board for failing to maintain a morally clean fair.

The strained relationship between these two bodies extended to include the groups affiliated with the Woman's Board. Traveler's Aid workers complained in late 1914 that exposition officials, rather than responding themselves, sent all queries about moral concerns at the fair to them. Cassie Hitchcock of Traveler's Aid reminded Executive Secretary Joseph Cumming that "we will always be glad to answer any communications distinctly covered by our work, but the Traveler's Aid Society in no way is caring for or guaranteeing the morale of the Exposition or of the City."[42] Like Sanborn, Hitchcock was frustrated that the male directors appeared to be shifting all responsibility for the city's and the fair's moral conditions to the Woman's Board and its associated groups.

The Board of Directors' relationship with the YWCA seemed to be no better. Exposition officials denied YWCA organizers the location they desired for their building on the grounds. The YWCA had chosen a centrally located site near the South Garden and adjacent to Festival Hall. Fair officials attempted to force the organization into an ungraded site located on the northern edge of the grounds that would have been even more expensive for the already financially strapped YWCA. In their protest, YWCA officials reminded the fair board, "Mrs. Hearst wishes me to say to you that in the placing of our building, you are doubtless remembering the purpose of our being on the Exposition grounds.... You will be interested to know that we are being flooded with inquiries from all over the country as to what provision is being made for the protection and welfare of young women at the Exposition."[43] Hearst's name pointedly reminded the board of the influence behind the YWCA, of the alliance between the YWCA and the Woman's Board, and of the responsibility of fair directors to work with those groups. The women of the YWCA sought to draw upon their one advantage, the threat of negative publicity for the fair, to convince officials to support their work. The final site of the YWCA building was located directly to the left of the Scott Street entrance, not far from Festival Hall but not adjacent to it.

Fair directors also resisted upholding their commitment to the Traveler's Aid Society. Officials denied free passes to Traveler's Aid workers in the spring of 1915. The enraged parent society threatened to withdraw all workers from the grounds immediately unless the exposition relented. Simultaneously, Orin Baker, a representative of the society's New York office who was brought in to help implement the San Francisco program, planned to inform the New York office of the exposition's lack of support of the group's work. This notice would almost certainly bring on a spate of bad publicity.[44] When Hale questioned Anna Pratt Simpson, who sat on both the Traveler's Aid Board of Directors and the Woman's Board, about what she thought the fair should do, she reminded him of the exposition's commitment to welfare work at the fair. She admitted, "I can advance nothing but my conviction at this time" as to its effectiveness.[45] Hale seemed skeptical at best, but the board relented and issued the requested six passes.

Although fair directors publicly proclaimed support for the Woman's Board, YWCA, and Traveler's Aid, their actual interactions with these groups were more fraught. Much evidence, however, suggests that fair officials understood the problem that San Francisco's moral reputation posed for the fair. President Moore and other officials repeatedly attempted to convince potential visitors that the fair and the city would be safe places to bring their families. When Professor Shailer Matthews, president of the Federated Churches of Christ, visited the city in March 1913, the Board of Directors hosted an elaborate dinner in his honor at the Palace Hotel. Moore informed the directors, "The organization of which Professor Matthews is the head represents a membership of about 17,000,000 and it is very important that he be given a proper impression of San Francisco both for its influence in inducing the Federated Churches of Christ to hold its 1915 Congress here and to offset the circulation of stories in the East about the vice condition in San Francisco."[46] The previously mentioned conflicts, though, suggest that despite Moore's desire to dispel "stories of vice" in the East, he and the rest of the board resisted committing to cooperate fully with the organizations they had delegated to handle the problem. The root of this conflict bears investigation. Two legal issues that arose during the planning years of the fair suggest why exposition directors actively resisted moral reforms.

After women earned the vote in 1911 in California, they immediately began to find sponsors to introduce legislative reform measures to improve the lives of the state's women and children. These proposals included a bill to mandate a minimum wage for women, a state training school for girls, and a "bastardy" law that required fathers to support illegitimate children.[47] Two of the issues debated during this legislative session regarded the regulation of vice in San Francisco—the Kehoe Bill, a temperance act aimed at the exposition, and the "Red-Light Abatement Act," which was an antiprostitution bill designed to flush brothels from the city. Although state Progressive Party supporters and many female activists supported these bills, the PPIE directors opposed them both, again involving themselves in state politics to further the interests of the fair.

Local and national temperance leaders seized upon the fair to further their campaign against alcohol. They warned potential visitors that free-flowing alcohol available at the fair and in the city would corrupt impressionable young people. The Kehoe Bill deliberately targeted the exposition by banning "the serving of alcoholic liquors in any building or upon the grounds, or within 150 yards of the exterior boundaries of any such building or grounds used for the purpose of an exposition aided by funds furnished by the State."[48] Concerned citizens from across the country wrote to the exposition to voice their support for the bill and their opinion that liquor must be controlled at the fair and in the city. As one man warned Moore, "We will never attend a World's Fair where liquor and the social evil are not barred out. Better support the bills in your legislature to accomplish this."[49]

Despite pleas from temperance leaders across the nation, exposition officials firmly opposed the bill, realizing that prohibiting alcohol on or near the fairgrounds would threaten their profits and offend the sensibilities of many San Franciscans. It also could discourage those who might come to San Francisco expressly for its illicit pleasures. Few San Franciscans, moreover, supported temperance. Even though the fair forcibly relocated local saloons, it did so not out of any support for temperance but out of a desire to keep fairgoers, and their funds, on the fairgrounds. Many saloon owners and anti-temperance organizations financially backed the exposition, making it unadvisable for the exposition to oppose their interests. Fair officials had no reason to risk displeasing the many San Franciscans who supported the fair and disapproved of temperance.

Fair officials publicly opposed the bill. Frank Brittain, the exposition's general attorney, testified against the bill during a joint meeting of the California Senate and Assembly Committee on Public Morals. Progressive newspaper columnist Franklin Hichborn reported that Brittain's appearance was most notable because he stated that the PPIE Woman's Board—which the fair had used to assure everyone of the city's morality—had adopted resolutions opposing the measure. Presumably this statement was intended to sway those who believed that the exposition was caving into the demands of the city's liquor trade. No evidence exists, however, to support Brittain's claim. At least one Woman's Board member denied that the board opposed the measure and insisted she had no knowledge of the supposed resolutions. Regardless, clearly fair officials attempted to fight the bill with whatever power they had.[50] Fair officials eventually succeeded in swaying enough legislators to defeat the bill, twenty-three votes to fourteen.[51]

The debate over the Kehoe Bill revealed that fair directors were far more interested in preserving their relationship with the city's liquor industries, saloon owners, and immigrant communities than in supporting any kind of social reform agenda. It was one thing to delegate the safety of women to the Woman's Board and to involve such organizations as the YWCA in the fair, but they balked at making the fair dry. Saloon owners' financial support for the fair, San Franciscans' general enthusiasm for alcohol consumption, and the possibility that selling alcohol on the grounds would make a profit, in the minds of the fair board, trumped the vehement opposition expressed by potential tourists from other, drier parts of the nation. Financial gain was again at the root of the fair directors' politicking.

California's women fought harder to change the state's antiprostitution laws. Legislators introduced antiprostitution bills in the 1911 legislative session, but it was not until 1913, when women had gained concrete political power, that public concerns about white slavery brought the bills to fruition. National and statewide publicity about the Red-Light Abatement Act, as it came be called, forced legislators to take action to control prostitution in the state. Much of the publicity focused on San Francisco and the Barbary Coast. The fair became a part of this anti-vice campaign, although the fair directors, along with many San Franciscans, had no desire to become involved in this particular piece of legislation.

The WCTU of California spearheaded the campaign for the act. Its members drew on the support of prominent Progressives in the state, of the states' most important women's organizations, and of concerned citizens around the nation who pressured exposition officials to support the bill.[52] The State Federation of Women's Clubs proved particularly important in coordinating efforts to pressure legislators and to draw public attention to the cause.[53] Motivated in part by the successful suffrage campaign, the WCTU hoped particularly to prove that women would indeed "purify" politics. The union's members sought to use their new political power to rid society of the sexual double standard and the flagrant sexuality of working-class and nonwhite communities. Their well-organized campaign drew support from sister organizations around the country. The Grant-Bohnett Bill was modeled on a similar red-light abatement act that had passed in Iowa in 1909. It represented a move away from the older, geographically segregated method of regulating prostitution in red-light districts. Many citizens had resigned themselves to the existence of prostitution, as long as it was contained to these areas. Middle- and upper-class men and women often believed prostitution was necessary to meet the sexual needs of lower-class immigrant men, and thus they tolerated these districts' operations as a way to control the perceived immigrant masses.[54]

The new red-light abatement bills implemented a system that cracked down on all selling of sex. The Grant-Bohnett Bill targeted property owners, however, rather than individual prostitutes or madams. It declared houses of prostitution or assignation to be public nuisances and allowed any citizen to bring a suit against an owner or proprietor for maintaining a nuisance. If proven to be a nuisance, the building's contents would be sold, with the plaintiff's costs paid out of the proceeds and the rest turned over to the defendant. The property would be closed for one year unless the owner furnished a bond for the value of the property guaranteeing that the nuisance would not continue.[55] The theory behind this approach was that property owners would become more careful about those to whom they leased their buildings, making it harder for those interested in selling sex to find places to run their operations.[56] Holding owners responsible for the activities carried out in their properties and assessing a significant financial penalty if a site was found to be a nuisance would in theory appeal to the economic interests of property owners who might not be swayed by moral arguments.

Letters supporting the measure and threatening a boycott of the fair if the bill did not pass poured into the exposition headquarters. One Rhode Island minister told PPIE president Moore, "We have a church convention there at the time of the Exposition. I want many of our young people to attend, but I can urge no one to attend if these evils are to flaunt themselves and offer their enticements wherever people may go in the neighborhood of the Exposition."[57] Many letter writers threatened Moore that if the bill failed to pass, they would not support the exposition's efforts to draw state exhibits or tourists. Others, who realized that the exposition was intended to boost California, argued that they would not form a favorable impression of a state and city with such rampant vice. "I feel certain that we may enjoy the Exposition more fully and form a better impression and one more likely to be of more value to California if these Bills become laws and the laws shall be enforced," wrote one potential visitor.[58]

Despite intense pressure from women's organizations and from Christian groups, San Francisco business interests and state politicians opposed the bill. They resisted arguments that it was necessary to abolish the sexual double standard; instead, they relied on old arguments in favor of the segregated system that assumed prostitution was an inevitable fact of life and that it was better to regulate it than to drive it underground. If the system of segregation was ended, they argued, prostitutes would simply spread out across the city, threatening the virtue of all the women of the city. If it were no longer contained to the Barbary Coast, the women of San Francisco would not be safe on the streets, the bill's opponents warned. One member even predicted that the governor would be forced to call out the militia to protect them. San Francisco–based legislators, moreover, argued that female visitors to the fair also would not be safe on the streets of the city if the bill passed.[59] The San Francisco legislative delegation therefore voted against the measure. Perhaps the most succinct statement against the bill came from President Pro Tem of the State Senate Boynton, who stated that "San Francisco is a clean city. It has its vices and hell-holes. But you know where the rotten part of the apple is and you can avoid it."[60] The bill passed despite the city's opposition.

Exposition officials did not directly involve themselves in the public debate over the Grant-Bohnett Bill, but when San Francisco politicians voiced their opposition, they drew the ire of reformers and did little to reassure concerned potential visitors that the city and fair would be safe for middle-class women. While these bills' debates revealed the power of these moral issues to polarize the public, both locally and nationally, they also demonstrated that the city of San Francisco remained opposed to such reforms. The fair directors' attitudes toward these particular issues reflected those held by many city residents, who did not see temperance or the suppression of prostitution as issues of pressing importance.

The reasons behind the male fair directors' opposition to the Grant-Bohnett Bill are less clear than those that motivated their opposition to the Kehoe Bill. Some conclusions can be drawn, however. First, the fair board deliberately excluded San Francisco's crusading reformers who had led the graft trials. Board members were not Progressive Party members; instead, they were generally conservative businessmen who demonstrated little interest in social reforms. They had likely not voted for women's suffrage in 1911 and probably had little desire to empower moral reformers or to share power with newly enfranchised female voters. As a group, they opposed temperance and saw no need to reform prostitution laws. To question the sexual double standard and the status of prostitution would directly attack their white male privilege.

Fair directors' solutions to the problem of the city's reputation proved halfhearted precisely because they opposed the tenets of moral reform. Handing off the work to the Woman's Board, the YWCA, and the Traveler's Aid Society was a convenient way for fair officials to temporarily stave off challenges from local women who wanted to participate in the fair and from reformers concerned about San Francisco's morality. The directors undoubtedly realized that San Francisco's illicit reputation was as much of a draw for some visitors as it was a problem for others. They hoped that walking the line between supporting and opposing moral reform would allow them to please all parties and make the fair as financially successful as possible. But the conflicts that emerged between these women's groups and fair officials in 1915 revealed the weakness of that strategy.

Concerns about gender, race, class, and female sexuality at the fair converged on the Joy Zone. There white and nonwhite young working-class women performed sexually suggestive dances for curious visitors. Men and women interacted unchaperoned in the public dance halls where young working-class women served free-flowing alcohol. Appearing as objects for the tourists' gaze, people of color often performed in minimal clothing, drawing attention to their bodies and implying the presence of the unbridled sexuality that many whites believed ran rampant in their communities. Concerns about the moral effects of amusement sections had accompanied world's fairs since the emergence of midway attractions at the 1893 Columbian Exposition, but San Francisco's moral reputation made people's concerns about the Panama-Pacific International Exposition even more pointed.[61] The PPIE Woman's Board and female reformers, meanwhile, used their privileged social position to attack the exploitation of young women's sexuality for profit in what became a direct critique of the race and gender system from which they themselves had benefited.

Fair directors took some steps to make the Zone and the fair appear "clean." Publicists issued guides that emphasized the wholesome and educational nature of the Zone.[62] Moore offered private assurances to concerned citizens and reformers that nothing immoral would occur there.[63] And the members of the fair's Committee on Concessions and Admissions made decisions about attractions that suggested that they understood the importance of maintaining moral standards.[64] But the committee failed to consistently oppose shows that featured female sexuality so visitor complaints persisted throughout the fair.

National social reform journals published pieces that drew attention to San Francisco's moral conditions. *Survey*, for instance, printed an article titled "Warnings to Girls from San Francisco" in April, followed by a report on the YWCA's work on the Joy Zone in July, and "Facts on Vice in San Francisco" in September. The April piece warned young women they should not come to San Francisco and search for work during the exposition because of the city's high unemployment rate. It emphasized the YWCA's reform work on the Zone while drawing attention to the problem of the fair's moral standards. The September article censured the fair and the mayor for failing to keep their pre-fair promises to clean up the city. Although these reports were read mainly by those already interested in moral reform, they both reinforced the perception that the fair and the city exploited female sexuality and motivated those who desired to reshape San Francisco.[65]

Reformers veiled their attacks as critiques of the city's moral conditions, but when they focused on the presence of alcohol and saloons, they also attacked the city's immigrant and working-class culture. In March John B. Hammond, ex-mayor of Des Moines and author of Iowa's Red-Light Injunction and Abatement Bill, resigned in protest from his position as chairman of the PPIE's Vice Commission. He declared that the exposition "planned an entertainment for the world on the immorality of San Francisco as a basis . . . with a white-slave market unapproached by any competitor in the world, with more saloons in proportion to population than any other city on the continent, with a total repudiation of the American Sabbath."[66] Such publicity perpetuated the idea that San

Francisco remained a wide-open town where fair directors reneged on their promises to make the fair a space friendly to white, middle-class values and families.

Critics differed regarding whom they blamed for these conditions. Female reformers often portrayed the female performers on the Zone as misguided victims of male exploitation, but some male reformers blamed unbridled female sexuality as the problem. Bascom Johnson, a representative of the American Social Hygiene Association (a group that worked for moral purity), condemned the "obscene" dances that women on the Zone performed and the coarse and suggestive language of the spielers who tried to lure unsuspecting visitors into the shows. He blamed the "low" women who danced and solicited men to buy drinks and perhaps sex for the situation as much as he held the men themselves accountable. He showed no concern for the welfare of the women who danced and supposedly prostituted themselves. In his opinion they caused the exposition's (and society's) moral decline. Only in the Cairo Café, where a "roistering, rough class of men ... frequent the place," did he deem the women at all "respectable."[67] Both he and Hammond blamed the PPIE directors and Woman's Board for failing to honor their promises to keep the fair morally clean. But they really attacked the behavior of the men and women who acted in ways that did not fit their white, middle-class expectations of appropriate conduct.

Some local residents defended the city just as loudly and publicly as reformers criticized it, demonstrating the real difference of opinion about the place of gender and sexuality on the Zone. *San Francisco Chronicle* feature columnist Helen Dare repeatedly wrote on this issue. In one column, she dismissed the efforts of those reformers who worked to protect young women by warning them to avoid San Francisco during the fair. "Our fervid and philanthropic protectors of innocence and conservators of virtue are so ingeniously desirous," she wrote, "so naively ambitious to make business for themselves, to justify their being, to offer results to the contributors of funds . . . that they have not the patience to wait in the ambush of their own doorway, but have dashed out into the open shouting: 'Wolf!' 'Wolf!'"[68] In fact, she argued, San Francisco was "safer than any tradition-saturated city of the Old World, safer than many a convention-bound city of the East, safer than the cities of the

South with the terrors of the race problem."[69] A few months later, she responded to criticisms of the Zone by commenting on "September Morn," a show in which a woman wearing very little clothing appeared in suggestive poses. She noted that it was "a sort of adventure into the unconventional, to be sneaked upon and giggled at; not in the least to be taken seriously."[70] Dare failed to buy arguments that the display of female sexuality threatened society. Yet the title she chose for the second article, "Strained Relations between the Clubman and the Lady," light-hearted though it might have been, both pointed to the conflict between female reformers and elite men and acknowledged the struggle in the city over the place of female sexuality in public life.[71]

Meanwhile, the city's female reform groups had been attacking the Barbary Coast for years, and their campaign picked up momentum after women won the vote.[72] They backed a 1913 campaign against the Barbary Coast that drew on the cooperation of local improvement organizations and churches to pass a law banning the serving of alcohol in the area's dance halls.[73] That campaign resulted in the closure of many such establishments, the loss of work for many women, and a widely publicized claim that the Barbary Coast was now "clean." The Downtown Association and other local improvement organizations launched another campaign against the area in the spring of 1915, hoping to close all establishments that allowed both dancing and the sale of liquor. An April editorial in the *San Francisco Examiner* accused the mayor and the police commissioner of allowing vice to persist. Neither had any interest in closing down the Barbary Coast, the writer alleged, and did so in 1913 only to mollify an outraged public.[74] Ten days later, a prominent front-page article charged that rather than serving the "near beer" currently allowed, numerous dance halls were selling real beer and whiskey in their establishments in flagrant disregard for current law.[75] The North Beach Promotion Association, one group that had attacked the dance halls in 1913, soon adopted a set of resolutions condemning conditions on the Barbary Coast.[76]

The association's report concluded that despite the presence of illegally run dance halls, "San Francisco is morally cleaner than any other city of its size in the United States."[77] But many in the city continued to fight against the presence of vice. After the ensuing publicity and investigation, the Board of Supervisors turned over responsibility for the dance halls to the Police Commission and granted it the license to issue all permits for such businesses.[78] The *San Francisco Examiner*'s editor noted in response, "There are a number of good things an energetic Police Commission can do to profit San Francisco. Let us hope that they can."[79] At the same time, the Recreation League, another reform group, began a series of "penny dances" to keep young women away from the city's dance halls.[80] The issues at the fair, therefore, reflected the situation in the city at large, as San Franciscans debated just how much vice they were willing to tolerate.

Some fair visitors likewise had no problems with the alcohol, dancing, and gambling found on the Zone. One local resident defended the gambling at the '49 Camp, telling Moore, "It is a matter of congratulations that the persons who have the 49 concessions have been able to provide a game furnishing so much harmless diversion together with so small an expenditure."[81] Local papers often failed to take attacks on the Joy Zone seriously.[82] Boosters of California and San Francisco continued to argue that the fair was in fact quite moral and clean. *Sunset*, the popular western monthly published in San Francisco, countered negative reports of the city's morals in a May 1915 piece. In response to the resolutions passed by the Church Federation Council and Illinois Vigilance Association condemning the exposition and urging a boycott by all American Christians, *Sunset* replied that San Francisco had no more of a vice district than did any other city. Young Christians "of either sex are in no more danger in San Francisco than they are in Chicago." Moreover, the editor insisted, the Zone was "absolutely clean and inoffensive," unlike the Midway Plaisance of Chicago.[83] Even the editor of the Catholic diocese paper, the *Monitor*, chimed in when he launched a similar campaign in his paper to repudiate charges that San Francisco was "wild" and "wide open."[84]

Yet the complaints of unhappy visitors persisted. They objected to the Zone attractions that featured "muscle dances," which they found "vulgar and immoral," and they complained as much about the barkers, or spielers, who stood outside the attraction and called to customers as they did about the performances themselves. The presence of these displays of working-class sexual mores offended many white middle-class visitors. Visitors also reported that spielers used extremely suggestive language. "Living Venes [sic] is very vulgar and the man on the outside makes it even more so when he tells the public that the girls on the inside have no clothes on, also tells the people that a man with crutches went in and was a new man when he came out," wrote one unhappy customer.[85] Such remarks upset visitors who found themselves unable to avoid eager barkers on their foray through the Zone. Their presence in the area's main thoroughfare made their risqué spiel available to all fairgoers. These episodes confirmed the reformers' fears that the rampant sexuality of these attractions might spill outside the doors of the dance halls and theaters to reach all visitors.

Other fairgoers complained about the suggestive nature of the dances that women performed inside the performance halls, criticizing them as exploitative of the young female dancers. As the local Women's Christian Temperance Union secretary informed Moore, "These dances . . . are so vile and sensual that the effect of witnessing them must be disastrous to the moral nature of our young people."[86] Half-clothed women in gauzy material moved in ways that suggested sex and repulsed moral reformers. Audiences less concerned about middle-class notions of propriety, however, no doubt enjoyed the acts.[87] The performances of spielers and dancers brought issues of voyeurism and sexuality to the fore; however, no one insinuated that sex itself actually took place in the dance theaters.

Reformers alleged that men and women engaged in far more dangerous behavior in the Zone's cafés and dance halls. Men and women mixed freely without chaperones and amid freely flowing alcohol. These places evoked the spirit of frontier days and drew upon the city's reputation as a wide-open town. One local minister called the 101 Ranch Café "a regular Barbary Coast Dance Hall, a market place of prostitution, transferred to the protection of the Exposition. Only this is worse . . . [for] your '101 Ranch Café' provides the means of getting women drunk."[88] Critics alleged that the management paid women to flirt with customers and coerce them into spending their hard-earned money on alcohol. Women flaunted their sexuality in far more public and dangerous ways than the performers of the dance halls did. One anonymous undercover investigator at the '49 Camp reported: "The waiter sent us two girls at our request, who danced and drank with us between dances. One who was an entertainer on small salary stated that she would not 'do business' with men, but that one other girl . . . and herself were the only 'straight' girls there. . . ." In addition, the report charged, one of the women admitted to

Fig. 45. Entrance to 101 Ranch in the Zone at the PPIE. The 101 Ranch
Café came under fire from protesters for alleged lewd behavior therein.
(San Francisco History Center, San Francisco Public Library.)

having been "immoral" in San Francisco since she had arrived there two
weeks before.[89] The accuracy of this report is impossible to determine,
but it demonstrates the real conflict between the lives of working-class
women and the ideals of middle-class reformers. The trading of sexual
favors for money or other commodities was not uncommon for young
working-class women, but they did not then view themselves as prostitutes. These activities allowed them to survive an often-hostile working
world and did not indicate a descent into moral turpitude, as reformers believed.[90]

Fair officials struggled amid this criticism to reconcile their desire for
profit with accusations of immorality and corrupt behavior. Allegations
of illegal gambling forced fair management to close the '49 Camp within
the first week of the fair. The accusations directed toward the camp concession concerned gambling and alcohol rather than immoral sexual
behavior. But reformers saw liquor, loose sexuality, and the exploitation
of women as intimately linked. Reports of prostitution at the '49 Camp
continued throughout the fair. The camp re-opened quickly—in March,

with assurances that it was cleaned up—but the allegations continued, and in mid-April, the attraction was shut down again for gambling.[91]

Letters from frustrated visitors flooded the offices of the Woman's Board and the YWCA. Representatives of both bodies pressured fair officials to fulfill their pre-fair promises and to rid the Zone of influences cited in the criticisms levied against San Francisco. They envisioned a fair in which female sexuality was not for sale and its workers met middle-class standards of respectability. Local religious leaders allied with the Woman's Board to oppose what they saw as the exploitation of women for the fair's profit. Oakland minister Albert Palmer accused the exposition of sharing the "blood money" that these immoral concessions earned "by exploiting womanhood" and in turn of "lowering the tone of dramatic performance throughout the country." He objected to a lengthy list of attractions, including the hula dancing on the Streets of Cairo, the "apache dance, the snake dance, and the muscle dance in 'The Model's Dream,' the muscle dancing on The Streets of All Nations, and the second show of 'The Girl in Blue.'"[92] Only in early August, after unrelenting pressure from these groups, did the fair board finally respond to allegations of immoral activity and close both the Streets of Cairo and the Cairo Café.[93]

Fair officials continued to approve new concessions that relied heavily on female sexuality, demonstrating their lack of commitment to the tenets of moral reform. The Committee on Concessions and Admissions approved applications in June for Buddha's Paradise, an "Oriental" dancing act that included an illusion of a living model, and the Mona Lisa Smile, a mechanical device that showed the face and bust of a nude woman and featured "an infinite number of expressions."[94] These attractions also used female sexuality and innuendo to attract viewers and soon came under fire from reformers. By August, Buddha's Paradise was one of a number of concessions about which the YWCA raised severe objections.[95] When the exposition's legal counsel recommended closing the Cairo Café and then reopening it under strict behavioral guidelines, the committee did so only to avoid legal problems and not out of any real concerns about morality.[96] Clearly the committee was more interested in keeping the Zone full of profitable concessions than in avoiding the ire of moral reformers. Only the possibility of legal action and bad press convinced it to clean up the Zone.[97]

Fig. 46. The Diving Girls exhibit in the Zone at the PPIE. Although
not targeted by protesters, it was one of many Zone attractions that
featured scantily clad women both outside and inside the concession.
(San Francisco History Center, San Francisco Public Library.)

The restrictions on the Cairo Café remind us that these attacks on concessions primarily affected the working-class women who worked there as
waitresses, dancers, and performers. They bore the brunt of the practical
effects of these restrictions as their working environments were altered
and their behavior critiqued. Many of them lost their jobs when their
concessions folded, a fact that reformers never addressed in debates over

Fig. 47. The September Morn featured scantily clad
women, as this image reveals. (*The Blue Book.*)

the Zone's activities. They failed to consider either the economic consequences of their actions or that these young performers might enjoy their
jobs. Instead they assumed that given proper guidance, the performers
would realize that they could, and should, support themselves in other
ways.[98] While it may have been true for some women, other Zone performers likely enjoyed their jobs and preferred dancing for appreciative
audiences to their only alternatives—domestic or factory work.[99]

The white middle- and upper-class female reformers had a complicated relationship with the fair's directors and the narrative about race

and gender created on the fairgrounds. They used their class and race status to claim control over the behavior of the working-class women employed on the Zone, but they did so in part because they felt that the female workers of the Zone were victims of male exploitation. The reformers saw only the dangers that the Zone posed to fairgoers and not the opportunities. They believed that unbridled female sexuality was a threat to all women and men. They advocated abolishing the sexual double standard, arguing that it contributed to the exploitation of women in society. Furthermore, they believed in the dominance of white, middle-class conventions of female sexual purity, and they knew that their claim to power rested on upholding those conventions.[100] But that attack on the sexualized attractions of the Zone in fact subverted the very hierarchy from which they benefited. Paradoxically, removing the sexualized images of women from the Zone meant removing the foils against which pure white women were defined.

White male fair officials shared their female peers' assumptions about race and class, but the men had different conceptions about the place of female sexuality in public life. Unlike the female reformers, fair officials did not believe that that the presence of overt public sexuality threatened society. As products of a white male elite society that generally accepted a sexual double standard and turned a blind eye to male infidelity but condemned displays of sexuality by white middle-class females, they had no incentive to clamp down on the sexual activities on the Zone.[101] They were leaders of a city renowned for its disreputable pleasures, a reputation that brought its own income to the city. They wanted the Zone to make money and made decisions in keeping with this goal. This narrative also suggests that elite male San Franciscans had little interest in sharing power with enfranchised women. Blocking female reformers' efforts to affect conditions at the fair may have been an attempt to stymie women's political power in the city.[102]

It took the intervention of the California State PPIE Commission to resolve the struggle over moral conditions at the fair. Progressive Party governor Hiram Johnson had appointed the commission to oversee the PPIE's spending of the $5 million that the state bond issue had raised.[103] Earlier in the year, the commission had objected to some concessions. In late September it renewed its campaign on the alleged gambling at the '49

Fig. 48. Hon. Hiram Johnson, governor of California and
State Exposition Commission. (#1959.087—ALB, 1:7, Bancroft
Library, University of California, Berkeley.)

Camp. "Lately . . . with your knowledge and consent," it charged the Board
of Directors, "gambling in a more flagrant form has been resumed. . . .
These games are conducted with a view of enriching a few professional
gamblers and of making some money for the Exposition at the expense
of gullible visitors." More important, it maintained, this activity occurred
"at the sacrifice of the good name of the City of San Francisco and the
State of California."[104]

The exposition responded by closing the '49 Camp's casino, pending
an investigation of the commission's allegations. Chester Rowell, a leading Progressive Party supporter and member of the commission, publicly expressed his skepticism, telling the *San Francisco Examiner*, "The
statement that the gambling is stopped pending investigation is made
to save the faces of the Concessions Committee."[105] Frank Burt, chief
of the Department of Concessions and Admissions, revealed in a statement to the press that the exposition was more concerned about profits
than purity: "The lights will burn just as brightly there, and there will be

dancing and other entertainments. The demonstration of gambling will be temporarily discontinued."[106] Despite Burt's assertion, by early October, the entire camp folded, unable to sustain itself without the attraction of the casino. Fair officials were right to assume that the fair's illicit pleasures made them a profit.[107]

In October, bolstered presumably by its success in closing the '49 Camp, the state commission decided to rid the Zone of the "girl shows" once and for all and issued a formal protest to the board about them. Rowell told the *Examiner*, "We have been deluged with protests against these shows, and I am told the Woman's Board has received an avalanche of letters."[108] The next day, the fair board finally ordered the permanent closure of a number of shows, including the notorious Streets of Cairo, the 101 Ranch Café, the muscle dance on the Street of All Nations, and the second show of the Girl in Blue and the Model's Dream.[109] They also warned all spielers to stop mentioning anything objectionable. Rowell explained, "It is not the desire of the commission to act as police officers of the Zone, but it seems that function has been relegated to us." He was also careful to emphasize that the commission only acted on submitted complaints. The commissioners did not go out of their way to "police the Zone."[110] And with that, barely two months before the end of the exposition and more than seven months after its opening day, the debate about moral standards on the Zone was put to rest and not at the behest of the elite, San Franciscan male Board of Directors but on the direct order of the Progressive-dominated California State PPIE Commission. San Francisco's bastion of male power fought its battle to the bitter end. Female reformers won a victory as well, demonstrating that with the right allies, they could defeat vice and insist that local men respect their burgeoning political power.

The conflict between male fair directors and female reformers came to a head as simmering social conflicts about temperance, gambling, and female sexuality converged on the Zone. The performers remained caught in the middle, unable to respond to the public censure about their acts or the threat these attacks posed to their livelihoods. Nor did those involved consider the wishes of audiences who might enjoy salacious and suggestive shows. The debate generally ignored the actions of individual employees and focused instead on their employers, or the concessions themselves. Other issues emerged, both on the Zone and in other locales around the fair, when fair employees behaved in ways that did not fit with the expectations of fair officials or visitors. These conflicts over race, class, and, again, gender offer us another snapshot of the ways in which contemporary social conflicts intruded into the fair makers' ideal city and offered an alternative vision of society for visitors and employees alike.

6 &/ Performing Work

When Joy Zone employee Princess Wenona adopted a white baby from a local San Francisco woman in June, a "storm of protest" erupted among San Francisco residents. The local branch of the Society for the Prevention of Cruelty to Children informed Wenona that she must return the child.[1] Wenona was an employee of the 101 Ranch, the internationally renowned Wild West Show performing at the fair, and she gave "some crack rifle shooting demonstrations" in her performance as a "Sioux Indian princess."[2] Determining Wenona's exact racial background is difficult, but she performed and was perceived by audiences as an Indian woman.[3] Two weeks later, a picture appeared in papers around the nation of Wenona and the babe, likely a publicity photograph from the 101 Ranch itself, with details that suggested Wenona was adopting the baby as a favor for an old friend, a Mrs. Lillian Clayton.[4] Whether this was a staged publicity tactic or a favor for an old friend, or even a true adoption, remains a mystery. But her experience points to the intense scrutiny under which fair employees worked. As with celebrities today, the dancers and performers of the Zone were fodder for newspaper articles and public interest. When performers acted in a way that violated mainstream white society's expectations, they were vulnerable to criticism and attack. Wenona might have been nationally celebrated for her abilities with a rifle, but as an Indian woman, she could not adopt the role of white motherhood without repercussions. Fair officials, visitors, and local residents scrutinized the activities of employees on the fairgrounds because their work was both ideological and physical. When their behavior crossed the lines of race, class, or gender, they subverted the fair's imagined social hierarchy and raised the ire of observers in the process.

Thousands of people labored at the fair to maintain the "twenty-five-million-dollar mirage" that the fair officials had created.[5] Only recently have scholars begun to explore the role of employees in making an exposition and acknowledged that their work was a part of the spectacle of the fair.[6] Officials of the Panama-Pacific International Exposition expected this work to maintain the fair's messages about the dominance of the white, middle class over the working class and people of color. Princess Wenona's story demonstrates that the workers' priorities were not always in line with the exposition's ideological goals. As fair officials and their employees came into conflict over standards of behavior, the carefully constructed spectacle of an ideal city crumbled and larger social frictions intruded on the fair. Disputes between workers also challenged that spectacle. Labor elites ignored the needs of unskilled workers in order to protect their relationship with fair officials, and black and white workers clashed over space and behavior. All of these disagreements reveal the ways that larger social tensions affected the day-to-day work of the fair. The work of theorists who argue that everyday conflicts may be understood as nascent political acts with the power to undermine social hierarchies helps to place these debates in a larger context.[7] Workers at the fair used everyday transgressions and acts of resistance to challenge the restrictions fair officials, labor leaders, visitors, and other workers placed on them, and in so doing the employees constructed their own understandings of class, gender, and race.

Labor histories traditionally begin with unions, and we can also begin examining the experience of fair employees from that perspective. Scholarly interpretations of the exposition concluded that the informal accord reached between fair directors and local union leaders created a "Pax Panama-Pacifica" that kept the grounds of the fair free of labor disputes.[8] But, barely a month after the exposition opened, Dan P. Regan of the Local Joint Executive Board of Allied Culinary Workers and Bartenders of San Francisco complained that "we have been noting with interest how the papers have been lauding to the skies that the Fair was built under union conditions, but it does not state the rotten conditions under which the members of the culinary crafts have to work."[9] He reported that employers were failing to pay workers and resisting hiring union labor at the fair. The story of waiters and waitresses at the fair reveals quite a different version of the Pax Panama-Pacifica from what existed between skilled labor unions and fair directors.

Labor unions and the political struggle between labor and capital dominated San Francisco by the early twentieth century. Close to fifty thousand organized workers labored in San Francisco in 1903. One hundred and thirty unions belonged to the San Francisco Labor Council, which counted approximately thirty thousand individual members, many of whom were unskilled. The Building Trades Council claimed thirty-five member unions and more than fifteen thousand members.[10] Although Asians and African Americans were sometimes excluded from these unions, the city also had unions representing many less frequently organized occupations, including "dishwashers and kitchen helpers, gasworkers, milkers, laundry workers, miscellaneous women factory workers, poultry dressers, and gravediggers," as well as the more traditional male trade unions.[11] Unskilled and skilled trades unionized in San Francisco. The city's waitresses, for instance, formed their first local in May 1886 with the assistance of the Federated Trades Council and the International Workingmen's Association.[12] The creation of the Union Labor Party in 1902 and Eugene Schmitz's subsequent election as mayor solidified labor's political power in the city and ushered in a period of conflict between labor and business that contributed to San Francisco's reputation in the national press as a place where "unionism holds undisputed sway."[13]

PPIE officials realized the need to reach an agreement with labor leaders both to ensure smooth construction of the site and to keep labor upheavals from scaring away potential exhibitors or visitors. National manufacturers dedicated to antiunion, open-shop conditions feared coming to a city with the potential for labor unrest, high wages, and the closed shop. Local union leaders, meanwhile, were haunted by the vision of hordes of low-paid laborers working on the fairgrounds and undercutting local labor. To alleviate such concerns and to demonstrate their support for a venture that would bring businesses and jobs to the city, the BTC and the SFLC entered into an informal accord with the fair directors. The councils outlined their agreement in a 1912 joint letter to President Moore. According to the agreement, no union would demand shorter hours or higher wages for workers employed on the fairgrounds; union workers would use all building materials, whether produced under "fair" or "unfair" conditions; the building trades' unions would include all men at work on the grounds; no rules "limiting output" would be enforced; no objections would be made to exhibitors bringing their own employees to set up exhibits; and no protest would be voiced about hiring nonunion-ized men if insufficient union men could be found.[14] Despite reports to the contrary, the agreement remained informal, and the exposition never entered any formal contractual agreement with either labor body.[15] Nonetheless, this accord was widely publicized and soothed the nerves of both manufacturers and labor unions concerned about labor unrest at the exposition.

Some national manufacturers still responded to news of this labor agreement with horror, believing that the exposition had entered into an unholy alliance with San Francisco labor unions. The National Asso-ciation of Manufacturers flooded the exposition with queries about the relationship between the exposition and organized labor. Association member C. W. Post reminded fellow members of their experience in St. Louis at the Louisiana Purchase Exhibition in 1904: "Their tyrannies took form in multiplying the ordinary wage charged and in delaying the work by factional disputes and interfering in all sorts of ways with the employees of the exhibitors. We decided at that time never to exhibit at an Exposition controlled by union leaders."[16] Facing these objections, Moore worked hard to mollify manufacturers and employers. He met with representatives of the Federated Employers Association of the Pacific Coast in October 1912. He assured them that "any contractor, no matter what his affiliations may be as to closed or open-shop operation may obtain plans and be permitted to bid on any structure." If they were the lowest bidder and could give assurances that they could finish the work on time, they would "be awarded the contract, whether such contrac-tor shall be a resident of San Francisco or of any other city." Materials would not require a union label. Exhibitors were free to use any labor they wished, "be that labor native, foreign, white or colored," to erect and install their displays.[17] These assurances undermined many of the gains that organized labor had made in the city, and labor's failure to pro-test them indicated the power of the Pax Panama-Pacifica. The fair also issued extensive publicity that depicted the city as unmarred by orga-nized labor and emphasized the city's status as the commercial center of the Pacific coast.[18]

Moore's attempts to play down the strength of labor unions in San Francisco must be understood on a number of levels. First it was a concerted publicity campaign aimed at changing the image of San Francisco. Moore and other city leaders understood the city's vulnerabilities and did what they could to paint the city in a more positive light, whether regarding racism, vice, or, in this case, labor unions. His maneuverings must also be understood as financially motivated. Without manufacturers and other businesses displaying their newest inventions, the fair could not claim to be showcasing the newest technologies and products for the world. The fair had to have exhibitors to succeed, and if doing so meant minimizing the place of labor unions in the city, then it would have to happen.

Publicly, the agreement did maintain the labor peace; however, internal labor disputes arose during the building of the fair. In late 1913, members of the plasterer's union struck to protest the hiring of more carpenters than plasterers to affix "staff" (plaster and fiber mixture) to the buildings. They demanded that the unions share the work equally. Patrick McCarthy—the head of the BTC, the city's former mayor, a fair director, and a former carpenter himself—accused the plasterers of not understanding "the principle of Unity." He promptly advertised for replacement workers and dispatched a telegram to the central office of the American Federation of Labor (AFL), requesting a decision on the dispute. AFL president Samuel Gompers supported McCarthy, awarding the majority of the staff work to the carpenters, who coincidentally comprised the largest union in the AFL.[19] This dispute reveals not only the BTC's power in controlling labor relations in the city but also McCarthy's firm adherence to maintaining peace on the grounds, no matter the potential cost to local unions. In 1914, a conflict emerged between two factions of the Painters' Union Local No. 19, when one faction accused McCarthy of excluding its members from working on the fairgrounds by denying them the ability to gain a BTC work card. These men took their complaints to Director of Works Harris Connick, but no record exists of the resolution of this issue.[20] Both disputes, however, point to resentment from some union members about McCarthy's methods of dealing with the fair and with union members.

Contemporary reporting and subsequent histories have taken this narrative and argued that fair officials made the fairgrounds a world apart from the heated labor conflicts that had shaped San Francisco politics.

Although thousands of unemployed men flooded the city in the winter of 1913–14 hoping to work on the grounds, their presence merely annoyed fair organizers rather than stimulated any kind of widespread labor revolt. The national recessions of both 1911 and 1913–14 affected the Bay Area and "prevented a degree of tightness in the local labor market which would have strengthened the bargaining position of workers and encouraged them to make demands." Those who were lucky enough to have work on the fairgrounds knew not to risk their jobs by breaking the agreements the SFLC leaders had set with the fair directors.[21] Despite labor upheavals around the state in 1913 and 1914, the situation in San Francisco remained stable.

Outside of San Francisco, however, the years before the fair witnessed violent labor conflicts across California that undermined the fair boosters' vision of a bountiful, benign countryside. The 1913 Wheatland Hop Riot, a result of unfair wages and inadequate living conditions for fieldworkers in the Central Valley, culminated in a violent confrontation between sheriff's deputies and workers led by the Industrial Workers of the World. It brought both labor radicalism and the appalling conditions of farm workers to the state's attention. The Stockton "Open-Shop War" of 1914 continued for six months until its final conclusion in December 1914, only two months before the exposition. The truce was reached with the help of San Francisco labor leaders, who no doubt feared that the Stockton conflict could in fact threaten San Francisco's fragile labor peace and the exposition.[22] In the city, however, fair directors united with elite labor leaders to regulate the behavior of unionized employees on the fairgrounds and kept them from disrupting the exposition. Labor papers printed positive articles about the fair, and the daily papers carried no reports of labor conflict on the grounds. But then how do we explain Regan's accusation in March 1915 that the situation on the fairgrounds for some workers was "rotten"?

When labor leaders and exposition officials discussed the question of labor unions, both sides focused on unions and workers involved in physically constructing the fair. They did not consider those unskilled workers who took jobs on the fairgrounds during the event. Exposition officials never guaranteed that concessionaires would refrain from discriminating on the basis of union membership. Nonetheless, most union members assumed that the fair would be unionized and that they would have no problems dealing with employers on the grounds. SFLC president Andrew Gallagher confidently stated in January 1915 that there would be "no difficulty in having only union men and women employed on the grounds," and the Labor Clarion reported that Gallagher would meet with Moore shortly to settle the question.[23] Whatever the content of that meeting, however, it did not guarantee that the fair would remain a closed shop.

As Regan's letter revealed, members of the culinary unions in the city soon learned how difficult it would be to make the fair friendly to unskilled labor. By mid-March, he reported, "very few of the men are being paid on the grounds," and one local had gone so far as to "levy attachments" to force the payment of wages to members. Moreover, employers actively refused to allow their workers to unionize. In one case, a concessionaire refused to allow union representatives even to pay to enter the concession. Regan pleaded with SFLC secretary John O'Connell for aid in publicizing the problem. "It is all very well," Regan argued, "for the men … that helped to build the fair [to] crow about how thankful Labor should be … but how about the unskilled man that has to work under the rotten conditions imposed upon them by the concessionaries [sic]."[24]

Employee complaints about working conditions focused on the Zone because most of the restaurants on the grounds were located there. Regan accused the Vienna Café of the most egregious violations, asserting that owners had not paid some employees since the beginning of the fair. By late March, thirty-one waitresses, fifty-two waiters, ten cooks, and eleven assistant cooks were owed wages.[25] O'Connell claimed that seven restaurants on the grounds had no union men and had "practically ejected the business representatives of the Cooks' Union from their establishments."[26] Some restaurants failed to pay other employees as well. In late March, the Young Restaurant Company owed back wages both to members of Musicians Union Local No. 6 and to waiters.[27]

A week after employees filed official complaints with the fair, Connick arranged for the payment of wages that totaled less than $100. But the problems continued.[28] In mid-April the SFLC referred to the Executive Committee of the fair's Board of Directors a request from the Cooks'

Fig. 49. The Old Faithful Inn was the site of many social events throughout the fair, but labor unions deemed its restaurant as "unfair." (Donald G. Larson Collection, Special Collections Research Center, California State University, Fresno.)

Union to declare Muller's Luxus Café, Old Faithful Inn, and Alt Nurnberg Café "unfair."[29] The next week, the joint board of culinary workers requested a boycott of several cafés on the grounds.[30] By late April, union organizers were becoming frustrated. Union leader Laura Molleda informed O'Connell that the Waitresses Local was lodging a complaint against the Waffle Kitchen. The establishment's manager had been fair to the local at first, but he had eventually let "all the union help go and gives our Business Agent no encouragement in regard to straightening out the house and enforcing Union conditions."[31]

In early May, McCarthy finally stepped in to address the issue. He reminded Connick that many labor conventions, including the AFL, were coming to San Francisco for the exposition. The SFLC did not want to have to warn union stalwarts away from certain concessions.[32] Connick's response to McCarthy's pressure did not survive, but one piece of evidence suggests that Connick must have taken some action to improve matters. The *Labor Clarion* soon reported that the Waiters' Union gained an increase in wages for banquet workers at the Old Faithful Inn and that the restaurant was employing union members only. In addition, the union was working to win the same conditions at the Inside Inn.[33] Moreover, no further complaints or notes appeared in either the *Labor Clarion* or in the SFLC's papers about the situation for culinary workers on the grounds, suggesting that the situation improved.

The story of the Pax Panama-Pacifica does not account for this conflict. It can only be understood by placing these culinary workers in the larger political and social context. The agreement between the fair and the SFLC and BTC, informal as it was, applied to the powerful building trades' unions and not to the unskilled workers on the grounds. Labor leaders may have neglected the culinary workers in part because their unions were heavily influenced by socialists, whose presence angered the labor council's traditional trade unionists.[34] Moreover, lower-wage cooks, waiters, and waitresses were simply not as powerful in the city's labor community.[35] The influx of workers to the city, drawn by the promise of fair jobs, limited the bargaining power of unskilled workers. The *Labor Clarion* dutifully reported on the dispute, but its articles were brief and the dominant reportage on the fair was incredibly positive, indicating the relatively good relationship between labor's elite and the exposition. The editors neither indicted the fair management for failing to keeping the grounds friendly to organized labor nor called for action in support of the culinary workers.

This conflict reflected the nationwide debate over the open versus closed shop. A burgeoning antiunion movement existed in San Francisco, sparked by the founding in 1914 of the Merchants' and Manufacturers' Association of San Francisco, which soon incorporated the Citizens' Alliance, an earlier open-shop organization, and the East Bay Merchant's and Manufacturer's Association. Although small, the membership included men who represented some of San Francisco's most important businesses: Southern Pacific Company, Santa Fe Railroad, Owl Drug, Pacific Gas and Electric Company, and Emporium department stores.[36] Although Frederick Koster, a prominent San Francisco businessman and supporter of the open-shop campaign, remembered that the fair "forced upon many of the conflicting elements the obligation of laying aside their differences" during 1915, this episode suggests that these conflicts continued to simmer beneath the surface of the fair

Fig. 50. Two Exposition Guards on a truck at the PPIE. (San
Francisco History Center, San Francisco Public Library.)

and the city.[37] The attempts by Zone restaurateurs to stifle union activity
brought these conflicts to the fairgrounds, as unskilled workers sought
to assert themselves as employees who deserved both respect from their
employers and the right to unionize. Conditions improved only after
labor leader McCarthy threatened the fair directors with bad publicity, demonstrating again that for the PPIE board, profit was the bottom
line. Directors proved willing to consider mollifying their employees
only when the alternative threatened the public image of the fair and
the company's profits. Let us then turn to closely examine the relationship between the fair and its nonunionized employees, whose behavior
was strictly regulated by fair management.

The structure of employment at the PPIE reflected and supported
the fair's gender and racial hierarchy. White men regulated behavior,
white women upheld moral order, and people of color performed menial
jobs—as janitors, washroom attendants, and drivers—or performed
as racialized and sexualized others on the Zone. The culinary workers
labored mainly on the Zone in jobs that were easily recognizable to visitors. The threat they posed to the fair was simply bad publicity if they

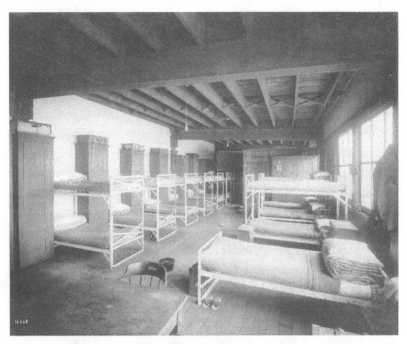

Fig. 51. Interior of the guards' living quarters at the PPIE. (San
Francisco History Center, San Francisco Public Library.)

exposed the fair's antiunion stance. Thousands of other people worked
in other parts of the fair where their behavior either supported the social
hierarchy created in this ideal city or threatened to upend it. Fair officials
therefore closely scrutinized their behavior. The disruptions they caused
generated controversy both on and off the grounds, again bringing local
and national political debates onto the fairgrounds.

The Exposition Guards were the most visible workers on the grounds.
Composed of honorably discharged military men, the highly organized
cadre of white male guards reassured visitors that the exposition was a
"safe" space, with a clear and familiar racial hierarchy. Fair officials laid
out rules that regulated all aspects of life for the guards while under the
fair's employ. The PPIE housed them on the grounds. They received one
day of leave per month, with an unexcused absence of more than three
days constituting desertion and loss of their position. The guards were
held to a high standard of personal conduct both on and off duty that
required them to keep their hair trimmed, their whiskers shaved, and

their comportment respectably quiet and orderly. Bringing any alcohol onto the grounds or drinking alcohol or smoking while on duty would result in immediate dismissal.[38]

Fair officials recognized that a surface appearance of order and respectability reassured visitors of the city's and the fair's moral order. Employing former soldiers in a highly regulated group of guards helped to maintain order on the grounds. Their refusal to create a unit of black guards only reemphasized the guards' symbolic significance.[39] Creating an integrated or, what would have been more likely, separate unit of black guards would have diluted the racial power vested in the guards, whose position as the fair's internal police force reinforced the symbolic power vested in white men at the fair.

The hundreds of young, white female cashiers who labored at the fair also reassured visitors about the stability of the fair's moral and racial order. In all, 965 cashiers reported for work on the first day of the fair, ready to greet the crowds that thronged toward Harbor View and the exposition site. These women likely came from a broad region, both within and outside the Bay Area. Letters submitted to exposition officials requesting jobs at the fair poured in from around the nation. Although the bulk of women employed probably came from the Bay Area, others may have come to the city seeking employment, as did Rose Boyd, a young southern woman who sought employment with the fair to "further her interests."[40] Without these women, no money changed hands at the fair. They sold tickets to concessions, postcards and silver spoons, and food products, and they admitted visitors to dance halls and amusement rides. Their work was essential to the monetary success of the fair, for the PPIE took a percentage of every sale conducted on its grounds. The women were required to wear a "simple [blue] serge suit" furnished by the exposition for $3.00 each (regular cost, $5.85). Concession stands hawking souvenir goods were located in every corner of the fairgrounds and "in all sorts of little nooks and crannies."[41] Chaos reigned for the first few days as cashiers mastered the details and procedures of their work and as officials and cashiers alike learned the location of all of the fair's hundreds of stations. Any problems soon ironed themselves out, and hundreds of young women settled in for nine months of work in a place that carried a unique set of challenges and concerns.[42]

The visibility of these young women meant that their behavior was subject to strict scrutiny. Although the exposition presumably outlined expectations for the women when they were hired, less than a month after opening day the Department of Concessions and Admissions found it necessary to remind female cashiers of the expected standards of behavior. Supervisors would not tolerate cashiers holding "animated or extended conversations" with either employees or guests in front of their booths. Most important, they were not to "be seen arm in arm with Male [sic] employees" or to frequent any of the numerous dance halls of the fair. Instead, they were to spend their break times (lunch and dinner hours) "eating their meals and attending to their personal comfort." They were absolutely forbidden from associating with other fair employees or visiting other concessions either while on duty or during their lunch and supper hours. Officially issued almost a month after the fair began, this memo suggests that male and female employees on the Zone had been consorting and perhaps even visiting dance halls together. The Exposition Guards also received a copy, along with a note reminding them that these rules would "save these young ladies some embarrassment," since "cooperation upon the part of male employees would perhaps save these young ladies their jobs."[43]

Fair officials restricted the behavior of the female cashiers (and, by extension male guards) on the Zone and around the fair, because their misbehavior threatened the racial and gender order upon which the fair was built. If these young women wandered the fair dressed in their work uniforms, perhaps dancing and drinking or even flirting with the male guards, they would be reaffirming the concerns of those who feared a fair in San Francisco would be debauched and immoral. Visiting the Zone did offer tourists a taste of San Francisco's famously libertine pleasures. As noted previously reformers fought the presence of sexually suggestive shows on the Zone while fair officials tolerated (and even promoted) their presence because they were profitable. These shows, however, were performances, and the associated women displayed as sexual objects did not interact with customers. They could thus be viewed safely at a distance.

The young white cashiers acted as a visual foil for the sexualized female performers. Since the former constantly interacted with customers, fair directors found it necessary to ensure that their behavior was above reproach. Such assurances helped to maintain a boundary between the sexually explicit shows of the Zone and the rest of the fair and the city. If young white cashiers could work in proximity to such shows but still continue to act as morally upright, innocent young women, then the racial and gender lines of the fair remained in place. If they did not, then the fair director's carefully constructed image of a respectable fair might begin to crumble.

Young women did not always accept these restrictions on their behavior. As we have seen, as more young men and women entered the urban labor force, new sexual mores emerged that challenged old ideas about female chastity and public sexuality.[44] Away from their homes and families, many young working-class women spent their hard-earned money on dance halls, movies, and fashionable attire, to the horror of middle-class reformers.[45] Although little evidence exists about the specific backgrounds of the fair's cashiers, it is reasonable to assume that many of them hoped to take advantage of the fun that the fair offered.

Clothing presented a place to start. In June, cashiers tired of their plain blue serge uniforms and petitioned fair officials for a change. A committee of cashiers met with Department of Concessions and Admissions head Frank Burt to protest their restrictive dress code. A tongue-in-cheek article in the *San Francisco Examiner* reported that the meeting was the culmination of months of complaints about the uniforms, which were just too simple for the working women's taste. "It's just impossible to look like anything in those blue uniforms," stated one of the women, "we want to wear white." Apparently flummoxed by the women's desire to wear something that he believed would only get soiled on the fairgrounds, Burt threw up his hands and gave in to their request. The workers voted on the choice the next day, and according to the report, it was sure to be unanimous.[46] Given the article's flippant tone, it is difficult to ascertain the true nature of the meeting between Burt and the cashiers, but surely the report contains some grain of truth. In this case, the cashiers successfully lobbied the exposition to make a fairly significant change in their work environment.

As workers in an environment that privileged appearance and spectacle above all else, some cashiers felt frustrated by their dowdy attire. The utilitarian blue serge suits met standards of middle-class respectability but not the fashion desires of young women. Historians have begun to recognize the importance of dress to working women, who used clothing as a way to claim identity and power on and off the job.[47] This episode at the PPIE may thus be seen as a victory for working women to assert their identity and to fight against the regulations placed on their behavior and bodies at the fair. Choosing to wear white—a color they deemed more appealing than blue—also allowed these women to insert themselves into the spectacle as attractive young women rather than simply as service workers in plain blue uniforms. Cashiers claimed their status as privileged workers by wearing white uniforms, thus bolstering their status in the fair's hierarchy.

Scattered evidence suggests that some young, white female fair employees attempted to use the fairgrounds to their own social and recreational ends, engaging in behaviors that would have shocked reformers and that flouted the rules set out by fair officials. Certainly the chastising memo regarding cashier behavior implies that some women flirted with male guards and took advantage of the fair's amusements. The cashiers asserted their right to public sexuality and entertainment, rejecting white middle-class gender ideals that required white women to be pure and chaste. In a more flagrant example, Exposition Guards twice discovered Dixie Burg, a young female employee of the concession September Morn, occupying a back room at the '49 Camp. Burg claimed to have permission to sleep there. When a guard later discovered a man occupying the adjoining room, he escorted Burg to the chief of concessions, who ordered her to leave the grounds immediately.[48] She lost her job because she failed to live up to expectations of female moral behavior at the fair. The incident revealed both the high degree of surveillance under which Zone employees lived and worked and the ways that some women attempted to circumvent the expectations of fair directors and female reformers.

These conflicts over the appropriate behavior of young white women reflected the same larger struggles over gender, race, and female sexuality of the Progressive Era that emerged in debates over the "girl shows" of the Zone. Not only did reformers target brothels, prostitutes, and dance shows in their attempt to control public displays of sexuality, but they also rushed to regulate the behavior of unchaperoned young people in cities across the nation. Reformers viewed department-store saleswomen as potential victims of male sexual exploitation, for instance, because "the public nature of the store, its sumptuous atmosphere, and its low wages combined, ... [could] make the transition from the counter to the bordello all too easy."[49] Fair cashiers were equally at risk. Numerous groups organized to protect young female workers in the city and at the fair. The 1913 and 1915 campaigns against the Barbary Coast and the Recreation League's efforts to keep young women away from public dance halls in the city reflected these same impulses.[50]

Exposition officials delegated the work of policing the behavior of these young women to the female reform organizations active on the grounds: the YWCA, the Society for Befriending Girls, and the Traveler's Aid Society.[51] An official exposition press release explained the YWCA's role at the fair: "To the welfare of the three thousand women and girls employed ... throughout the Exposition, the committees have devoted exhaustive attention, recognizing ... the majority of them are young girls, some of whom have their homes in San Francisco, but very many of whom are strangers from the East come here to 'better themselves,' and that such are exposed to the numerous dangers with which a big city teems for the unprotected girl."[52] YWCA workers focused their attention on the Zone, offering "a helping hand to any who may need advice or help of any sort," and staying there until the last cashier packed up her till and was ready to leave.[53] Although according to a YWCA report, the spirit of friendliness such work fostered was "heartily appreciated both by the employer and the employee," reformers continued to worry about the lure of the Zone.[54]

No record exists of the young women's response to these opportunities, but the reaction of one young Kansas City waitress to news of the YWCA's work among her peers suggests the possible sentiments of these young women. She commented: "The working woman ... doesn't have to be told where she ought not go in the evenings. ... Neither does she want to be coddled, or sung to, or preached to, or patronized, or taught pleasant indoor games by a lot of other young women who are paid to make her contented."[55] Similarly, after San Francisco women helped force the dance halls on the Barbary Coast to close in 1913, many of the dance hall girls who lost their jobs rejected assistance from female reformers, for they had no desire to undertake the more respectable employment that the middle-class women offered.[56] Some of the young women who worked at the fair also likely viewed the "help" that reformers extended them with comparable skepticism.

Reformers harbored an even darker fear—that of interracial sex.[57] The myth of the black male rapist, an idea used to justify lynching and white terrorism of black communities, persisted across the nation.[58] In California, where race relations could not be reduced to a simple black-white binary, concerns proliferated about sexual relationships between white women and nonwhite men. Anti-Asian sentiment also focused on the perceived danger that Chinese and Japanese men posed to white women and to the future of the white race.[59] Public concerns about white slavery that identified the white slaver as an immigrant or person of color also projected social concerns onto white-nonwhite relationships.

These anxieties about race and sex permeated the fair as well. When a black employee made "insulting remarks" to a white female worker, he was sent to the Exposition Guards for disciplinary action.[60] Another young man who worked for the Hawaiian Village was accused of paying excessive attention to and making "insulting remarks" to white women. His behavior, combined with his parents' tendency to refuse to perform when asked, resulted in their dismissal from their positions.[61] Although his race was not stated, the report implies he was nonwhite—perhaps native Hawaiian or Asian. Whatever his race, he was not deemed a suitable partner for the white women who visited the Hawaiian Village, and his behavior disrupted the fair's carefully regulated race and gender norms. Fair officials concerned about financial profit could not tolerate racial transgressions by nonwhite men, because as with sexual transgressions by white women, their behavior threatened the public image of the fair.

A series of conflicts between African American workers and white fair visitors reveal persistent tensions between whites and blacks on the grounds. Local blacks hoped to use the fair to demonstrate their status as U.S. citizens and to establish pride in their race. But these conflicts suggest that the fair did little to further black interests, although some black workers actively attempted to assert a measure of control over their work environment.

In late July, an Exposition Guard brought Helen Castro, a black matron in the women's lavatory in the Palace of Horticulture, and Lovinia Johnson, a white woman who worked at the Pine Apple Concession in the building, into the guard headquarters.[62] The two women had been involved in a dispute over Johnson's refusal to pay the five-cent fee for using the rest room.[63] According to Johnson, after paying the fee, Castro demanded another payment, and when she refused, Castro "caught her arm and hurt same and that she [Johnson] then struck the maid in the face." Castro maintained that Johnson had refused to pay the fee at all and that she did not touch Johnson until the other woman had already hit Castro in the face. In response, Castro's employer, the Western Sanitary Company, promised to fire Castro.[64]

This conflict between two working-class women was not an aberration but one of a number of similar incidents between black washroom attendants and white visitors and employees that point to racial tensions on the grounds.[65] Only a week before this incident, Castro had been reported for overcharging and insulting the wife of an army captain. Although the Western Sanitary Company had determined then that "she was evidently unfitted for this type of work" and had resolved to terminate her employment, she continued to work a week later.[66] During the nine months of the fair, white patrons accused black lavatory attendants of hitting them, grabbing them, accusing them of not paying, or insulting them in toilet facilities in the Fine Arts Palace, Education and Social Economy Palace, Horticulture Palace, Palace of Mines and Metallurgy, and Liberal Arts Building and in locations near Van Ness Avenue and the Tower of Jewels and on the Zone.[67] Both male and female visitors reported similar conflicts, demonstrating the prevalence of these reports. No other conflict between employees and visitors was reported to the guards with such regularity.

Displeased visitor Bill Smith wrote a lengthy letter to Moore about his experience that suggests some of the reasons for these conflicts. "Why have a band of free colored HIGHWAYMEN in each one [restroom] to rush at a man with a whisk broom and then demand 'largesse'–money, coin of the relm [sic], simply because a man goes in to use the urinal?" he queried. "Why they even grab you by the arm and demand the money. It is a shame and a lasting disgrace to your Fair that such things should be done."[68] Smith's account suggests that white visitors and black workers approached their interactions with different expectations. When white visitors wanted to use a free restroom, which, according to Smith, were few and far between, those people who finally found one were probably in no mood to then offer a tip.[69] The black attendants, however, assumed that white visitors would tip them for their service and attempted to provide the kind of assistance that would earn a tip, such as cleaning a man's suit. These conflicts demonstrate a contrast of worldviews. Some visitors to the fair might have been used to tipping black workers, such as train porters, but others viewed the offending restroom attendants as overstepping their supposed place by demanding a tip. The existence of both pay and free facilities at the fair may have confused other visitors who had no idea whether they needed to tip an attendant.

These conflicts suggest black workers attempted to demand the meager benefits their demeaning positions offered and reveal the power of everyday interactions to turn into acts of resistance.[70] For black workers, the profits gained from their jobs were the only benefit they gained from the fair, and they guarded those profits carefully. They likely resented patrons' attempts to ignore their presence since they mirrored the larger dismissal of their presence on the part of fair officials. The fair offered no advantages for working-class blacks: the fees were high, jobs were few, and no collection of exhibits honored their heritage or place in California. African Americans were relegated to the position of primitive other at the fair either in sideshows or as menial laborers. Moreover, the Progressive Era—and the year 1915–saw heightened anxiety about race relations across the country, with the release of the film *Birth of a Nation* and the rebirth of the Ku Klux Klan. Certainly many white and black fair visitors and employees were aware of the film's release and its blatant messages about the dangers of interracial sex.

These encounters between black and whites at the fair must be understood in the context of these racial tensions and as attempts by white visitors, employees, employers, and exposition officials to reinforce white supremacy through their daily interactions. Regulating the behavior of black men in relation to white women and the behavior of washroom attendants who might be claiming too much authority were ways for whites to assert social dominance over nonwhites. For blacks, defending their work space and demanding the respect of patrons were ways to define themselves as individuals deserving respect. The relatively large number of these encounters suggests that they should not be dismissed as simple misunderstandings and that they were symptomatic of a racial system in flux.

The criticism levied against Princess Wenona demonstrated the visibility afforded to the laborers of the Zone. Although fair visitors might have viewed them as performers, they were workers who were subject to the same kinds of regulations under which the Exposition Guards, cashiers, and washroom attendants labored. The Zone featured hundreds of people who to most visitors appeared to be living exhibits rather than workers: the Hopi Indians of the Grand Canyon concession, the Somalis of Somaliland, and the Samoans of the Samoan Village, among others. But these people were workers, similar to the cashiers and washroom attendants, although the performers' work might have been disguised as demonstrating traditional dances or traditional ways of living. And as Princess Wenona's attempt at interracial adoption revealed, in many cases, these workers faced more intense restrictions on their behavior than did those employees whose work was more recognizable to their contemporaries as labor.

The most provocative conflict between Zone performers and exposition officials involved what should be identified as a labor stoppage. The race and immigrant status of participants meant that contemporaries failed to see their actions as a labor action. During the spring of 1915, the Somali men and women of the Somaliland concession stopped working when their employer failed to pay their wages. Then they refused to vacate their houses until the exposition evicted them. The concession featured thirty-one Somali villagers who had been brought to the exposition under the charge of Vahan Cardashian, Turkish commissioner to the exposition. The villagers were hired to perform dances and the rituals of daily life for visitors. By late March, a mere month after opening day, however, the concession was not making money, so Cardashian canceled his $750 per week contract with the villagers, who were represented by a man named Ahaoun. The exposition took over and ran the show, but the Somali workers refused to perform, staging a labor stoppage. They maintained that they had not received their full wages from either Cardashian or the exposition. When the exposition disbanded the show, the Somalis had no resources to fund their departure from San Francisco, so they insisted on remaining in their space on the fairgrounds. In mid-May, the *San Francisco Examiner* reported that fair officials had ordered them to vacate the premises. As Ahaoun told the paper, "I sent word to Mr. Bryan that if we were removed they would have to call upon the Exposition guard to do it. They haven't put us out yet, but of course they will tear our houses down."[71]

As Ahaoun predicted, the exposition did force the Somali workers out with the assistance of immigration officials. According to fair historian Frank Morton Todd, "Bryan laid the matter before Immigration authorities, took a platoon of Guards to the compound, loaded the dark strangers on a Fadgl train, and escorted them to the Yacht Harbor, where a Government tug awaited them for Angel Island, whence they were . . . deported."[72] Unfortunately, details do not remain regarding what happened to the workers after they arrived at Angel Island. Todd reports that they were deported, but according to a *San Francisco Examiner* article, to what nation they would return was unclear. They had come to California from New York and had traveled to New York from France. At that point, they could have been returned to either Africa or Europe. The other option was that they could continue the entertainment circuit, for the newspaper reported that they had tentative offers to appear both in Chicago and in Venice, California.[73]

The Somali labor conflict demonstrates the difficulties that faced the employees of many Zone concessions. Immigrant workers—and colonial subjects—brought to the United States solely as performers depended on their employer for everything from wages to housing. If their act was unpopular, they had no choice but to follow the concessionaire when he closed up shop. As low-paid immigrant members of a despised minority group in the United States, the Somalis had little to no bargaining power. Despite their attempt to stage a strike—refusing both to dance and to vacate their dwellings on the grounds—they proved no match for the power of the exposition and the U.S. government. The exposition controlled the land on which their houses were located and had the authority to tear their houses down once their presence became an obstacle to the spectacle of the exposition.

Moreover, a troop of African immigrants camped out on the Zone, but not participating in its spectacle, called into question basic assumptions about the exposition itself as a space. As long as the Somali men and women lived on the Zone and curious visitors could watch them perform, they were a moneymaking curiosity that supported the fair's racial hierarchy. Once the Somali workers ceased to engage in the spectacle and demanded fair treatment from the exposition, they challenged the fair's racial hierarchy and colonial message. As colonial subjects, the Somalis' appearance at the fair justified the imperial system by juxtaposing their "primitive" ways of life with those of white Americans and Europeans displayed in the fair's exhibit palaces. Such colonial subjects, however, by definition could not stage a strike, so their actions threatened the fair both financially and ideologically. Although the Somalis' actions probably went unnoticed by most fair visitors, the episode served as a potent critique of the race and class system that governed employment on the Zone. White waiters and waitresses and cashiers might have their own frustrations with their working conditions, but their racial status, nationality, and terms of employment gave them a degree of power not granted to the black Somalis. Once the Somalis ceased to generate income, fair officials viewed them simply as obstacles to more profitable ventures on the Zone.[74]

Exposition officials scrutinized the behavior of all workers—white male guards, white female cashiers, menial nonwhite workers, and Zone performers—to ensure that their actions reinforced the fair's social hierarchy. But the fair did not always work in the way that officials expected, and the system of employment was no different. Unskilled workers fought to organize, while their employers fought for an open shop. Young men and women, as did their contemporaries across the nation, flirted and danced and acted in ways that threatened the fair's image as a morally "safe" and "clean" place to visit. African American workers found themselves at odds with fellow workers and visitors over their behavior. Other threats to the fair's race and gender hierarchy came from within. Officials invited hundreds of groups to hold their meetings and congresses at the fair. We have seen how racial and ethnic groups took advantage of this fact to meet on the grounds and to claim a place in the body politic. So, too, did women's groups. More than a hundred different groups of women met on the grounds during 1915. Many were nonpolitical, but others forwarded radical political agendas and made the fair into a stage for global discussions of women and their role in society.

7 ❦ Women Take the Political Stage

Thousands of visitors gathered to watch five hundred progressive women stage the Pageant of Peace in the fair's Court of Abundance on June 5. The performance's "seven scenes and fourteen tableaux" included angels of peace, Campfire Girls, and local college students embodying various nations of the world.[1] Earlier that afternoon, fifty-six speakers addressed the question of peace in meetings in thirty-three different buildings across the fairgrounds.[2] Following the conclusion of the meetings, a procession of participants singing Charlotte Perkins Gilman's "Hymn of Peace," marched across the grounds to the Inside Inn.[3] Speakers at the ensuing dinner included Madame Chen Chi, wife of the Chinese commissioner-general, and Madame Abiko, wife of the managerial head of the Japanese Newspaper Association of the United States.[4] The International Conference of Women Workers to Promote Permanent Peace (ICWWPPP) and the Women's Congress of Missions (WCM), two conventions being held simultaneously at the Panama-Pacific International Exposition, cosponsored these events and designed them as enormous spectacles with serious moral and political meanings. Fueled by a devotion to Christian principles, the female organizers of both groups perceived the exposition as a place where women from around the world could work together to further the causes of peace and women's well-being.

Visitors to the fair encountered an even larger event two months later. Women suffragists staged a spectacular pageant in the Court of the Universe to celebrate the conclusion of the first-ever national convention of women voters. Ten thousand people packed the venue to watch a carefully scripted pageant that included local Chinese schoolgirls dressed in traditional Chinese costume and young women garbed to represent the women of other enfranchised nations. The event culminated in a grand send-off of the two women chosen to escort a three-mile-long right-to-vote petition on its cross-country automobile trip to Congress. City residents opened up their newspapers the next morning to find accounts of the event, and two days later subscribers to the *San Francisco Bulletin* read an entire edition dedicated to suffrage and women's issues.

Women's groups of all kinds took advantage of the fair to meet, discuss, and publicize their work and ideas. Women's organizations sponsored 114 of the 928 congresses and conventions that met in conjunction with the PPIE, a significantly larger number than at any previous exposition. College alumnae groups met and reminisced. Teachers discussed how to improve their working conditions. Nurses shared the newest techniques and professional opportunities. Missionaries addressed the challenges they faced both at home and abroad. And, as the earlier examples suggest, groups with more explicit political motives, and a sometimes global view of female internationalism, seized the opportunity to display their vision of the world to fairgoers.[5] As with other groups that met at the fair, these women staged parades, pageants, and speeches for all fairgoers, as well as for the attendees of their meetings. Local newspapers disseminated their ideas by reporting on their events. In this way suffragists, peace activists, temperance crusaders, and Christian proselytizers took the opportunity to make the fair into an enormous public political stage.

Given the Progressive Era's political context, it is not surprising that organized womanhood seized this opportunity. Women's organizations flourished in the late nineteenth century, and by 1915 women had solidly claimed the authority to speak on issues regarding women, children, and urban life. By the teens, suffragists used public spaces of all kinds to rally for their cause. They held huge parades, created advertisements, designed pageants, and otherwise inserted themselves into public spaces to gain supporters and force unwilling male politicians to pay attention to their demands. Fairs offered women excellent venues for organizing. Few scholars, however, have considered how women's use of fairs changed between the 1890s, when the impressive Woman's Building at the Columbian Exposition defined women's participation in public life and fairs, and 1915, when the PPIE, despite its location in a suffrage state, did not include a Woman's Building.[6] Only recently have scholars begun to seriously consider the activities of women beyond these buildings.[7] The plethora of women's organizations during the 1910s and the active political role of California women meant that women's activities at the fair were so varied that it is impossible to consider them all. A closer look at the activities of some of the most visible groups of organized women reveals the multiple strategies that women used to make the fair into a political space. In addition, the fair's close links to Asia and the Pacific created an unparalleled opportunity for organized women to facilitate public conversations about the global role of women.

San Francisco's women had long been involved in political causes. Women were the driving force behind the city's social welfare programs from the 1850s through the 1880s. They reshaped the city's policies and its social landscape.[8] In the later nineteenth and early twentieth centuries, middle- and lower-class women became more actively involved in social and political causes, working for child labor laws and campaigning on both sides of the temperance issue.[9] San Francisco Waitresses Local 48 successfully campaigned against a 1906 law that would have banned them from working in businesses that served liquor.[10] During the 1907 streetcar strike, working-class suffragists came into conflict with their middle-class sisters, as union women supported the strike and most mainstream suffragists opposed it.[11] This division continued throughout the decade, as middle- and upper-class female reformers united with male reformers to urge reform of the city's apparently corrupt municipal government. During the graft trials, organized middle-class women actively supported the prosecution, while working-class women generally opposed it.[12]

This local history of female political involvement facilitated the activities of organized women at the fair. The 1911 suffrage victory politicized many women. During the campaign itself supporters used city streets, ferries, hotels, department store windows, and theaters, as well as more traditional political venues, to publicize their message. They worked to make suffragists and the suffrage message common sights around the state and in the press.[13] Members of Bay Area women's clubs, such as Berkeley's Twentieth-Century Club, hoped to use the fair as a place to meet, campaign, and raise awareness of political issues.[14] This population offered a ready audience for social events, conventions, parades, and pageants. The financial backing of Phoebe Hearst, the head of the exposition's Woman's Board, and of other prominent Bay Area women and the support of the Woman's Board itself eased the integration of

Fig. 52. Woman's Party Congressional Union booth at the San Francisco exposition, spring 1915. *L–R, front*: Mrs. May Wright Sewall, Mrs. Kate Waller Barrett (Alexandria, Virginia); *rear*: Miss Anita Whitney (California), Mrs. Mary Beard, Miss Vivian Pierce, Miss Margaret Whittemore. (Library of Congress.)

suffragists on the fairgrounds and allowed them to stage a significant presence at the fair.[15]

Like ethnic and racial groups, groups of women seized upon the visual and performative nature of the fair to construct social and political identities. Members of the newly formed Congressional Union (CU) for Woman Suffrage, under the national radical leadership of Alice Paul and Lucy Burns, erected and manned a booth, held meetings and conventions, and staged pageants and parades. Their events had one goal—to convince male and female voters to support a federal amendment for women's suffrage. Although the male fair organizers demonstrated no evidence of support for women's suffrage, the success of California's 1911 suffrage referendum forced male fair directors into tolerating the activities of politically organized women on the fairgrounds.

Suffragists operated out of the official CU booth, which stood alongside similar exhibits of reform and educational groups in the Palace of Education and Social Economy. The CU was not the only exhibit of organized women in the building. Visitors would also have encountered displays and representatives from such groups as the Woman's Christian Temperance

Union, the Girls' Friendly Society of America, and the National Council of Jewish Women.[16] The booth composed part of the fair's extensive exhibit on "social economy" and served as a paean to the accomplishments of the white woman suffragists of the nineteenth century. Banners greeted all who entered the comfortably furnished booth: "The world has progressed in most ways, but not yet in its recognition of women," and "We demand an amendment to the United States Constitution enfranchising women."[17] A petition demanding the passage of the "Susan B. Anthony Amendment" to the U.S. Constitution that would allow women the right to vote formed the centerpiece of the exhibit. Suffrage workers urged all passers-by to sign the ever-lengthening petition. The booth included portraits of Anthony and other prominent suffragists, as well as a reading area with extensive literature on voting for those interested in the history of the movement.

Suffragists used other venues around the grounds to stage speeches, meetings, and conventions that combined spectacular displays with political messages. They used the YWCA auditorium, the Inside Inn, and the very boulevards of the fair to hold these events. According to organizer Sara Bard Field, "The booth had of course to be publicized and to that effect we had many prominent people . . . (who cared about woman suffrage) speak for us at the booth. . . . It became one of the well-known and publicized portions of the . . . Exposition."[18] In April, Crystal Eastman Benedict, Mary Beard, Kate Waller Barrett, and May Wright Sewall spoke at the YWCA, with a reception following at the suffrage booth.[19] Less than two weeks later, Alice Park, a prominent California suffragist, rallied for the cause at the booth.[20] These events continued throughout the fair, ensuring that suffrage remained in the news both on and off the fairgrounds.

Bay Area women provided an audience for events both on and off the grounds. In the spring of 1915, wealthy San Francisco women, some of whom were also involved with the PPIE's Woman's Board, brought the topic of suffrage to their local clubs. In March San Francisco Chronicle society columnist Anne Wilde noted that "suffrage is becoming suddenly popular and respectable." She observed that the outbreak of war in Europe had convinced many women of the need to vote, but the presence of the CU booth at the exposition and its dedication two days before certainly

Fig. 53. Sara Bard Field, suffrage activist. (Library of Congress.)

helped as well. She claimed that within the previous week, many in San
Francisco who had previously believed suffrage to be "not entirely ladylike" had changed their opinion. Three months later, during the June suffrage conference, she again reported that "an orgy of suffrage and peace
has marked the record of activities in local club circles during the past
week."[21] The interest in suffrage also extended across the bay. The *Oakland
Sunshine* reported that the Civic Center, a black women's club, hosted a

speech by prominent white California suffragist Charlotte Anita Whitney on the topic of securing a national suffrage amendment.[22] Whether or not suffragists were "ladylike," they definitely made suffrage a topic of discussion both on and off the fairgrounds.

Suffragists gained extensive publicity in September when Fremont Older, editor of the *San Francisco Bulletin* and husband of a local suffragist, turned the editorship of the paper over to Alva Belmont, Sara Bard Field, and Alice Paul for a day. The women produced an entire edition of the *Bulletin* dedicated to the political life and progress of women in conjunction with the Woman's Voter Convention. With articles about the exposition, as well as covering national politics and the suffrage movement, the paper reinforced the connection between suffrage, the fair, and women's political possibilities. Devoting an issue entirely to women's matters introduced some male and female readers to a new perspective on the topic, even though the *Bulletin* was already the city's most reform-minded paper.[23]

Suffragists used these articles, speeches, and performances to depict a world peopled by politically active women who confidently acted in the public sphere. An editorial in the suffrage edition of the *San Francisco Bulletin* expressed their vision with great clarity: "Voting doesn't take women out of the home, because to a certain extent they are already out of the home. Because they are in the world, working in shirtwaist factories, and preaching, and doctoring, and lawyering, and raising children, and being exploited, they have the right to have a say in the political management of the world. Otherwise democracy is a joke. You can't be for democracy without being for equal—or, it would be better to say, honest—suffrage."[24] Other articles reflected the CU's campaign for equal rights, as well as the vote.[25] Articles titled "Woman's Place in Industry," "Women and the Art of Today," and "Woman—Her Part Today and Tomorrow" presented their vision to readers of the *Bulletin*.[26] They insisted upon women's place in public life, arguing that women should be preachers, doctors, lawyers, and shirtwaist workers, and that this participation meant women should have equal rights with men. This perspective radically challenged the limited vision of women's roles sanctioned by, and offered by, the fair's Board of Directors. The articles offered a vision of a world in which all women—from shirtwaist workers to lawyers to housewives—had the potential to participate in the political process.

This view of the world relied on racial and class assumptions that meshed with the fair's dominant racial narrative. Just as the fair celebrated the ascendance of the white male "pioneer" in California, the white women who dominated the suffrage movement also focused their efforts on enfranchising white women. They often deliberately ignored the situation of nonwhite women and working-class women in the United States. They were not afraid to use arguments that played on fears of immigrant threats to white dominance.[27] During one set of PPIE suffrage meetings, well-known reformer Florence Kelley made her case for a national amendment in part by blaming the "the steerage vote" (meaning working-class male immigrants) for having obstructed the cause thus far. She argued, "There is nothing the matter with our men in the State of New York. Our trouble is with the steerage. . . . They inundate our shores year after year. . . . Each year there is the same battle with ignorance and foreign ideas of freedom and the 'place of women.'"[28] Other speeches and articles in the CU's official publication, The Suffragist, echoed these sentiments and demonstrated the frequency with which white middle- and upper-class suffragists used race- and class-based rhetoric in their campaigns.[29] The history of class-based antagonism between the working-class suffragists of San Francisco and their middle- and upper-class peers reminds us of these divisions in the suffrage movement.

The CU's display at the fair articulated these assumptions as well. One exhibit case in the booth held a collection of cartoons reflecting the history of suffrage and included one cartoon that depicted "President Wilson as a two-headed orator raised upon a monument of his own historic literature which is crowned by his work on the New Freedom. One of Mr. Wilson's heads, wreathed in smiles, is turned toward a little Filipino man; the other head, directed toward a disfranchised American woman, wears an extremely nipped and frosty expression."[30] This image played on popular perceptions of Filipinos as "little brown men" who were not equal to whites.[31] The Filipino man depicted was heavily racialized—showing him as child size, bowing toward President Wilson, and wearing a vacant smile on his face—while the respectable white woman was drawn as an adult, with the word "womanhood" on her dress.[32] The U.S.

government had recently enfranchised Filipino men in their native territory. How, wondered suffragists, could Wilson justify extending the vote to Filipino men but not to white women? Similarly, the *Suffragist* published a number of articles during 1915 that reflected related concerns about maintaining the racial hierarchy at home, citing statistics that implied that the enfranchisement of female voters would assist in maintaining white supremacy.[33]

These racialized images and rhetoric did not represent all of the work that suffragists at the PPIE undertook. Just as their wider campaign contained contradictory messages about gender and race, so too did their fair campaign. Suffragists used the fair to draw attention to the fact that women in some western states and territories, as well as in some foreign nations, could vote. They juxtaposed the enfranchised women of foreign nations against the disenfranchised white women of the United States. In June, the California branch of the CU sponsored a session on the status of women's suffrage around the world. Organizers designed this "International Suffrage" meeting to draw attention to the inadequacies of the United States. The meeting included speeches from representatives from all of the nations and states in which women had been granted the vote. Madame Chen Chi, wife of the commissioner-general to the exposition from China, described her experience with suffrage, as did Rouva Mayi Maya from Finland; Coodalook Eide, an Alaskan Inuit; and Neah Tagook, an Alaskan Indian. Dorothy Morrell, a Zone worker who performed as a cowgirl with the 101 Ranch, spoke for her home state of Wyoming. These five women were featured in an article and displayed in a photo in the *San Francisco Chronicle* in which they wore their "native" costumes— including a full fur hood for Eide, a blanket for Tagook, and Morrell's cowgirl outfit, hat and all—on a June day in California.[34]

That these women appeared in their native costumes suggests that organizers hoped to play on the tropes of an exposition and the displays of "exotically" dressed women to make a political statement. It is difficult to deduce exactly the content of that statement. White women's claim to social power in the late nineteenth century rested in part on their role as participants in what Louise Newman has called "civilization-work," which included all activities designed at uplifting a race. Bringing Christianity and the ideals of white, middle-class society to native peoples and

African Americans at home and to primitive nations abroad was all a part of that work.[35] Of the meeting's participants, Coodalook Eide and Neah Tagook qualified as representatives of peoples most white reformers would identify as "primitive." As a Chinese woman, Madame Chen Chi was a member of a group that in the United States was not perceived as primitive but was stereotyped as either prostitutes or silent victims of foot binding. Given the prevalence of anti-Chinese racism in the United States, her appearance at the meeting as a political actor contradicted the dominant U.S. racial hierarchy. Presenting these three women as female voters created a curious paradox. Their clothing drew attention to their racial otherness and their difference from white American society, but the Congressional Union had invited these women to speak as voters and to discuss their experiences with voting and participating in the political process.[36] The resulting publicity portrayed them as voters, therefore subverting the fair's racial hierarchy.

Chen played a significant role at the fair. She spoke at the CU meeting, at the September convention of women voters, and at the meetings held by the ICWWPPP. She also represented China at events across the fairgrounds. Local papers frequently noted her presence and participation, revealing to local readers that this Chinese woman, at least, possessed a political voice and set of opinions. Such a fact was ironic, given that were she a resident of the United States, as a female Asian immigrant she would be doubly disenfranchised in most parts of the country. Her participation, and that of other Asian women at the fair, reveals that the PPIE's strong ties to Asia offered an unusual visibility for both Asian and Asian American women in the United States during the Progressive Era. Little scholarship exists on the public role of Asian American women in the early twentieth-century United States, so this glimpse into an event that allowed Asian and Asian American women a public stage suggests the need to explore further the attention paid to women like Chen. Local politics—in this case San Francisco's desire to serve as an entrée to the Pacific—again created opportunities for disenfranchised groups to assert themselves at the fair.

Suffragists used visual strategies to draw attention to their cause as well.[37] The *San Francisco Chronicle* in August featured a photograph of a woman dressed in "fantastic garb"; however, she was not a woman in

Fig. 54. Mrs. Chen Chi. (Buchanan, *History of the Panama-Pacific International Exposition.*)

native dress but a suffragist, adorned in purple and yellow dominoes and a sandwich board advertising a mass meeting of the Congressional Union at the YWCA auditorium. Jessie D. Hampton of New York, Mrs. M. B. Stone of Boston, and Miss Ruth Miller of Berkeley all wore the costumes and paraded the grounds, waving flags and exhorting onlookers to listen to their message. According to the report, this effort was but one of a series of such attempts to publicize the upcoming CU convention in September.[38] It was a clever turning of the tables on both the press and the exposition. When suffragists took advantage of the attention that the fair paid to women to forward their own political message, they turned the objectification and commodification of women to their own advantage.

Suffragists appropriated the grounds most spectacularly on the evening of September 16, when ten thousand men and women packed into the Court of the Universe to view a suffrage pageant marking the conclusion of the CU-sponsored Woman Voter's Convention. The display again juxtaposed enfranchised against disenfranchised women. Hundreds of women in colorful costumes from nations in which women were enfranchised filled the stage. The young Chinese female students of San Francisco's Oriental School in "quaintly colorful native costumes" occupied one end of the stage, again offering a visual counter to the fair's racial hierarchy. The CU members, dressed in the organization's colors of purple, white, and gold, occupied center stage. Behind them hung both the American flag and the suffrage banner, which read "We demand an amendment to the Constitution of the United States, enfranchising women." The ceremony opened with a rousing rendition of a new suffrage anthem set to the "Marseillaise." Then, Sara Bard Field and Frances Joliffe, the two women chosen to escort the suffrage petition to Washington, and actress Margaret Anglin each addressed the crowd. The spectacle culminated in a grand send-off for Field and Joliffe, as the other women on the stage escorted them to the gates of the exposition grounds while accompanied by audience members. There, Field and Joliffe met the car that would take them across the country to Washington, where they would deliver their message to Congress. With great ceremony, the gates opened, the crowd cheered, and the car drove solemnly away, marking the end of what the *San Francisco Bulletin* described as "the most dramatic and significant suffrage convention that has probably ever been held in the history of the world."[39] The carefully staged pageant made all of the local papers and again focused attention on the campaign for women's suffrage.

The elaborate September pageant marked the beginning of Field and Joliffe's cross-country trek and the conclusion of the politically revolution-

Fig. 55. Suffrage envoy Sara Bard Field (*left*), driver Maria Kindberg (*center*), and machinist Ingeborg Kinstedt (*right*) during their cross-country journey to present suffrage petitions to Congress, September–December 1915. (Library of Congress.)

ary first-ever national convention of women voters. Organizers designed the pageant and convention to showcase women's political power. Opening speaker and New York philanthropist Alva Belmont urged attendees to "forego alliances with any existing man's political party, and to work for a new, woman-made civilization."[40] Organizers hoped to show women voters in the western United States their political possibilities and to inspire women in the East, who were tired of fighting what often appeared to be a losing battle, that success was indeed possible. The fair offered space for a potent combination of politics and performance that sparked the political imagination of suffragists nationwide.[41]

Suffragists displayed their vision of womanhood to fair visitors in multiple ways. They offered women the opportunity to take a concrete, if small, step toward national suffrage by signing their petition for a national amendment. By the time they sent it to Washington in September, it had grown to three miles in length and included the signatures of more than 500,000 women. The appearance of well-known suffragists at the fair also ensured that visitors had ample occasions to hear women experienced in the fight make their case for the cause. Field argued that it fostered incredible unity among women. "I can hardly speak of it without possible exaggeration," she remembered. "They heard the women from all the other states who didn't know about the Congressional Union, who cared or didn't care perhaps until they heard some of the wonderful and beautiful speeches made about the Eastern women. I think they got a new vision of something they could do with their vote outside of their own immediate state. . . . They signed readily, there was no urging or begging. They just came up and wanted to sign."[42] The mere presence of the suffrage booth in the Palace of Education and Social Economy validated the organization's existence and provided a headquarters for these activities. Even if only a few visitors stopped each day, that number was more than organizers could hope for by setting up shop in any other venue.

Women's activism at the PPIE encompassed more than political campaigns. Suffragists frequently cooperated with the YWCA, another group of active, organized women that appropriated space at the fair to exhibit themselves, their work, and their worldview to fairgoers. As we have seen the YWCA was involved in the debates about the Zone, cooperating with the Woman's Board to clamp down on the "girl shows" and gambling contained therein. Their other activities at the fair demonstrated another set of strategies used to stimulate public awareness and discussion of women's role in society. As a religious organization, the YWCA had a multifaceted mission at the fair. Organizers sought both to proselytize and to meet the practical needs of visitors and employees. Through their example of Christian service, they hoped to improve the lot of others while inspiring them to a life of faith.[43] Although these goals differed from those of the women suffragists, they shared common concerns about the need for white women to actively participate in the political world and an ambiguous attitude at times toward the needs and position of nonwhite women. Both goals occasionally challenged the male fair officials' worldview.

The YWCA Building combined utility with display and performance in an extraordinarily effective way. According to one description, "Here during every open hour of the Exposition the Young Women's Christian Association will render to the women visitors the special aid and service that the Exposition demands, and here, in one form and another, many

Fig. 56. YWCA Building. (San Francisco History
Center, San Francisco Public Library.)

of the characteristic activities of the association will be displayed." The
building offered an attractive combination of services: good cheap food,
friendly advice about the city to women (and men), and plentiful sitting
areas along with movies depicting the YWCA's work across the nation and a
series of speakers on "home economics, hygiene, physical training, recreation, questions of thrift and efficiency, and kindred subjects."[44] Although
the YWCA focused on serving female visitors, particularly those attending
the many conventions that women's groups held during the fair, its members welcomed and served any visitors who entered. The YWCA developed
a working relationship with women's clubs in the city and with those organizations holding conventions during the fair in an effort to coordinate
activities and to advertise its facilities for women visitors. The decision
to combine service with exhibits showed a canny understanding of how
best to appropriate the space of the fair to the organization's advantage.

YWCA leaders hoped that displaying their work for all to see would
inspire others to follow suit and strive to ensure the safety of young work-

ing women. Films featuring the work of YWCA branches nationwide ran daily in the second-floor assembly room, which was also the site of "lectures, and debates on different subjects of interest to women."[45] Glass cases exhibiting the results of a series of national contests that reflected the YWCA's values and goals lined the building's halls. One such series of competitions determined the most skilled in a variety of fields: dressmaking, wardrobe design, writing, and art.[46] Another display featured the winning model wardrobes designed for the "college girl" and the "business girl."[47] These contests and the resulting displays created national publicity for the fair and the Y. At the fair, they showcased the values and benefits of the organization for visitors. This combination of action and exhibits did not escape those interested in the YWCA's work. Local newspaper columnist Helen Dare remarked, "They [the YWCA] are not only going to show what they do for their members, but they are going to show, especially, why they do what they do—and in an extraordinarily convincing way."[48]

Visitors to the YWCA Building entered a world organized, administered, and run by and for women. It offered a version of a "Woman's Building" at the PPIE, despite the exposition's lacking such an official venue. The white female organizers of the YWCA envisioned a world in which some women worked outside the home and, in some cases, attended college. Like the suffragists, they believed that women belonged in public, and they often cooperated with the Congressional Union by hosting speakers and meetings in the YWCA Building. Yet their assumptions about womanhood also relied on beliefs about race, class, and female sexuality that privileged the ideals of white, middle-class womanhood.[49] As with many social reformers of the Progressive Era, they believed that the city teemed with dangers for the unaccompanied young woman, and they made it their mission to "protect" young women from sexual exploitation.[50] As the debates concerning the Zone and the behavior of its female cashiers revealed, this so-called protection rejected new, freer, working-class understandings of sexuality and the many modern amusements that young men and women came to the city to enjoy.[51]

The work of the YWCA demonstrates the need to reconsider the line between formal exhibits and informal encounters on the fairgrounds. Just as the presence of local Asian and black residents at the fair offered alternative visions of their communities to fair visitors, so too did the rhetorical work of the Y extend beyond the exhibits and events staged within the walls of the Y Building. YWCA officials believed that the real value of their presence came from their interactions with visitors and workers at the fair. The organization's national monthly journal described their work as "not a moving picture film, nor a stand of statistical charts, but a throng of living people—this is the exhibit of the National Board of the Young Women's Christian Association at the Panama-Pacific International Exposition in 1915."[52] The Y's welfare work constituted a key part of the organization's presence, and exhibits, at the fair. By providing friendly and helpful services—meals, a place to rest, referrals to safe lodgings, a children's day nursery, and Sunday church services—YWCA workers hoped to serve the needs of visitors and in so doing convince them of the value of the world the workers created in the YWCA Building.

Many visitors certainly remained unaware of much of the work YWCA representatives did to promote "the economic, physical, social, intellectual and spiritual interests" of the women who worked on the grounds. Y employees provided classes, dinners, parties, and individual counseling to the thousands of women employed at the fair. They wanted to protect them from the dangers of the city, and the fair, and to help them "lead . . . straightforward, normal, Christian, li[ves]." Through their Zone club house they provided women workers, from the cashiers to the dancing girls and other women of the native villages, with cheap hot meals, hot water, a sewing machine, footbaths, books, and comfortable chairs. There, YWCA workers hoped, women might gain courage "for another day of this life which she believes she is forced to lead; or the greater courage necessary to make a fresh start in a more normal and less perilous career."[53]

Through this "personal work" YWCA workers hoped to convey the value of their vision of womanhood to young women and to provide them with necessary services.[54] They envisioned a world in which women's sexuality was not for sale and in which young women could safely appear in public without fear of sexual exploitation. Their view was based on a set of class-based assumptions. As the previous quote indicates, many Y workers believed that the female performers of the Zone, and other women who seemed to have "fallen," were misguided and lost. They assumed that these young women did not know what was best for their lives and needed the example of white, middle-class Christian women to set them on the right path. Despite these patronizing assumptions, YWCA workers did offer physical benefits to young women at the fair.

The YWCA generally subscribed to the same racial assumptions that undergirded the fair itself. An exposition press release about the YWCA, for instance, reported that its building "is a striking monument . . . of the progress in the race in general in those ethics of civilized societies which impel us to care, not alone of self or friends, but also of the 'Stranger within our Gates.'"[55] As this quote suggests, the women of the YWCA were active proponents of "civilization-work." In their case, it meant welfare work among working-class white women. These efforts, as Newman notes, "helped consolidate an imperialist rhetoric that delegitimized dissent from nonwhite and non-Christian women."[56] The YWCA Building showcased the progress of the white race in implicit contrast to that of the nonwhite people displayed in other parts of the fair. It was the very "civilized nature" of white society that compelled and emboldened white women YWCA workers to reach out to nonwhite, non-Christian women. The work these white women did actively reaffirmed their position in the racial and social hierarchy.

Yet at moments the Y's efforts proved more ideologically complex and contradictory. The workers provided for the needs of many nonwhite women whom society, and the fair, willfully disregarded. One YWCA worker's account about her forays on the Zone illuminates the complicated relationships of race, class, and gender at work. She reported that "one thing that seems quite evident is that we do not regard the show girl and the foreigner as womankind, but rather as belonging to some strange species entirely outside of any need for friendly interest."[57] If we assume her turn of phrase to be a critique of society—"we" being society rather than the YWCA—we see that she challenged society's, and the fair's, disregard for the welfare of these young women. Her description of Hawaiians, "colored young women," cowgirls, and Japanese women who attended the YWCA's getting-to-know-you dinner at the fairgrounds supports that assumption.[58] Its club house on the Zone certainly served the "dancing girls," with one report noting that they particularly appreciated the footbaths.[59] The women of the YWCA provided for the physical needs of all women on the grounds without regard for their racial or ethnic background. Bringing them together and serving their needs during a time when many such facilities were segregated potentially undermined assumptions about racial hierarchy for the young women involved, if not also for interested visitors who might encounter the YWCA's work on the Zone.[60]

These displays of the YWCA's welfare work—and the efforts themselves—served a variety of purposes at the fair. They publicized the work of the YWCA and public awareness of the dangers facing young women in the city. In so doing, these activities bolstered the organization's basic philosophy that young working women should be able to live and support themselves in the city without risking the fall to prostitution. This vision challenged the fair directors' use of sexualized images of women to advertise the fair. Although these displays affirmed the dominance of white, middle-class Christian social values and the role of white, middle-class women as bearers of civilization, the activities undertaken by YWCA workers proved more ambiguous. By serving the needs of white and nonwhite women equally and by serving them together rather than in segregated facilities, YWCA workers also emphasized the commonalities between these young working-class women, opening a space for them to form relationships and friendships that could undermine the fair's strict emphasis on the differences between whites and nonwhites.

Other groups of women (and some men) met at the fair to discuss women's global, rather than domestic, role. The International Conference for Women Workers to Promote Permanent Peace and the Women's Congress of Missions each drew attendees from around the world, and they came together on the evening of June 5, as the chapter's opening anecdote indicated, to create a vision of permanent peace. Hundreds of local residents attended the conventions, demonstrating sizable support for the projects in the Bay Area. The WCM took advantage of the city's cosmopolitan nature to reach out to immigrant communities and to include women of many nationalities in the group's discussions. Meanwhile, the ICWWPPP's events offered women a platform from which to create a vision of international cooperation that subverted both the war raging in Europe and colonial relationships worldwide.

The WCM meetings, although infused with a deep sense of Christian evangelism, forwarded a vision of international peace and cooperation that existed uneasily alongside the fair's glorification of conquest and imperialism. The more than two thousand women who attended the WCM advanced a vision of international cooperation that depended on both Christian principles and a deep devotion to worldwide evangelism. Their meetings brought together female missionaries who worked both at home and abroad and who told the audiences about their efforts to bring Christianity to Native Americans in the United States and to spread the gospel to Asia. The congress was officially a joint meeting of the Federation of Foreign Boards and the Council of Women for Home Missions. Women from twenty-two Protestant denominations attended, demonstrating the breadth of interest in these topics.[61] The eight-day-long congress, held primarily at San Francisco's First Congregational Church, included workshops, lectures, and discussions of literature on a variety of issues. Many sessions focused specifically on women. African American leader Mary Church Terrell, for instance, spoke to the assembly on "The Progress and the Problem of the Colored Women," in one of the few examples of an African American woman addressing an integrated audience at the PPIE.[62]

The WCM meetings privileged a vision of womanhood grounded in Christianity that insisted on women's potential to be international actors. Their message was that female missionaries could and should actively work to bring the Christian faith to foreign peoples. Moreover, at least one speaker called for the breaking down of barriers between nations, as well as the acknowledgement of "the suspicion, hatred, and prejudice, which we have for many years regarded the non-Christian peoples," calling instead for missionaries to "protect the alien races."[63] Although such rhetoric continued to assume the superiority of Christianity, it called for a respect and cooperation between nations that echoed the messages of the more secular women's peace movement.

The WCM, like the suffragists, blurred the line between the city and the fair by taking their activities outside the grounds. Their week of events included meetings with the Chinese women at the Presbyterian mission home, a reception with Japanese residents of the city, a rally at a Russian church, and a service for local Persians. According to Frank Morton Todd, these events "added to the interest of the congress, but they did much more than that, for they enlisted the interest of women outside mission work, who were brought, through such events, into touch with those leading in the movement."[64] Organizers were certainly aware of this likelihood when they planned their events. According to one report, the congress was designed in part to "deepen the conviction of individual responsibility in the hearts of the women of the churches."[65] Participants in this and other congresses thus gained a captive audience at the fair, and in the city, by choosing to host their meetings at the PPIE.

Both the WCM and the ICWWPPP sought to involve women in the movement for international cooperation and permanent peace. May Wright Sewall, veteran exposition participant and proponent for peace, designed and organized the ICWWPPP. Her credentials included chairing the World's Congress of Representative Women at the 1893 Columbian Exposition and actively participating in the International Council of Women. After the PPIE, in December 1915, she was slated to accompany Henry Ford on his European peace expedition to Europe. Planning for the PPIE began in the spring of 1914, when President Moore appointed Sewall as chairman of an organizing committee for an "International Conference of the Woman Worker." Sewall originally wanted to focus on "cooperative internationalism" and to include participants drawn from leading officials of all international societies of women who would come together to share ideas about advancing "the various social, moral and civic reforms that are involved in present international efforts."[66] This discussion, like that of the suffragists and the YWCA, fit easily within the fair's theme of "service" that linked together its hundreds of congresses and conventions.

The war forced Sewall to change her strategy. She recognized that women of the belligerent nations would likely be unable to travel internationally; moreover, they might be unable to escape wartime nationalist feelings enough to discuss a future of internationalism. The topic of the meeting therefore became "permanent peace," a more well-defined goal than the "cooperative internationalism" originally proposed. Recognizing the difficulties in asking international bodies headquartered in European capitals to send delegates in a time of war, Sewall called on women to attend the conference as individual supporters of peace.[67]

Speakers at the conference addressed a variety of perspectives and experiences. They ranged from Madame Chen Chi to William Jennings

Fig. 57. Attendees at the International Conference of Women Workers to Promote Permanent Peace. (#19xx.485 G:13, Bancroft Library, University of California Berkeley.)

Bryan. All drew on the assumption that women possessed maternal qualities that made them more inclined toward peace. As Chen noted in her speech, "It has been conceded the world over that women are instinctively more gentle than men."[68] Many speakers echoed these assumptions, reflecting contemporary beliefs that women were inherently maternal, peaceful, and self-sacrificing. Female activists used these ideas to justify their political involvement in causes from municipal reform to peace activism. Yet, although this message was the subtext of the conference, and indeed of the women's peace movement in general, many women delivered speeches in which they claimed a key role for women in global affairs. The fair's location in San Francisco and its emphasis on Latin America, Asia, and the Pacific meant that the ICWWPPP included diverse perspectives that had rarely been voiced in pre–World War I international gatherings of women.

Although "permanent peace" remained the underlying philosophy of the conference, the participants' speeches revealed persisting nationalist tensions. When California suffragist Alice Park rose to speak for the women of Ireland, she began by reminding the audience, "Ireland,

although many people seem not to recognize the fact, is a separate country." As with the men who spoke at the fair's St. Patrick's Day celebration, she used the fair as a space from which to assert Ireland's independence from its colonial master. She further outlined the ways in which the Irish Women's Franchise League had "stood against the influence of the mass psychology of the other people in Great Britain and Ireland and in some other countries" by its refusal to engage in relief work and its persistent opposition to war recruitment.[69] Such comments reflected the ongoing struggle for independence in Ireland and the persistent antiwar (and at times pro-German) sentiment among the Irish both at home and in the United States.

Señora Isabel S. Shepard, an American woman born in Colombia who spoke for Latin American women at the conference, offered the most pointed critique of U.S. foreign policy.[70] She began, like most speakers, by calling on Christian principles to guide the work of the peace effort, even indicting Islam with the comment that "we may not, as Mahomet preached, spread religion by means of the sword." She praised the United States for its recent positive relations with both Spain and China. Then, she turned to the intense anti-American sentiment of many Colombians. "No one can realize," she warned the audience, "how intense is the feeling of hatred towards the United States in Colombia," after the 1903

U.S.-supported revolution that resulted in carving the new nation of Panama out of Colombian territory. "She feels herself despoiled and cheated and robbed," she said, providing both an intriguing counter to the fair's celebration of the Panama Canal and a critique of U.S. actions in Latin America. Shepard went on to indict U.S. colonial attitudes toward Latin America. "Do not make fruitless efforts to force your own language, your own ways, and your own customs upon an unwilling people," she warned. Instead, she asked the audience to learn Spanish, to learn about the cultures of Latin America, and to remember that "each Republic is a separate entity," as different from each other as were Mexico and the United States. To become better acquainted with the women of Latin America, she suggested that women of the United States travel to South America, where they could visit natural wonders on par with those found in Europe and Asia and where their money would "pour so much needed gold into the empty pockets" that residents would bless the "Yankees."[71]

Shepard's speech upended the fair's celebration of the Panama Canal and explicitly called for a Pan-Americanism facilitated by women. Although some American female internationalists critiqued U.S. economic and military tactics in Latin America, Shepard's pointed attack on American attitudes stood out among the other attitudes that were expressed during the rest of the conference and the fair. Historian Leila Rupp has noted that for the most part, early twentieth-century internationalist female organizations were platforms for the women of Europe and the United States. There was very little room for the voices of women from other parts of the world.[72] The PPIE's emphasis on Latin America and the Pacific, combined with the war in Europe, meant that Sewall and other organizers worked hard to bring women from those areas to the conference. They created a space for a public dialogue that countered the fair's larger celebration of U.S. economic and cultural imperialism.

Although Shepard's critique of American attitudes toward Latin America gestured at an acknowledgment of U.S. racial stereotypes of Latin America, her own perspective also reflected early twentieth-century Latin American perceptions of race and class. She made no mention of indigenous or poor women. Instead she called for Pan-American unity of middle- and upper-class women who were more alike than not. Her description of South American women reflects this claim: "Her dress is Parisian and her social etiquette. Most frequently her education is obtained in a French convent."[73] Although such characteristics were true of a handful of women from Colombia and other South American nations, the vast majority of South American women at the time lived lives far removed from Paris or its convents. Shepard's statements echoed the desires of elite early twentieth-century South American men and women who looked to Europe for models of culture and civilization in an attempt to demonstrate their nations' progress and culture. Such biases were hardly uncommon among the women involved in international organizing. They were generally well-educated, wealthy women whose worldviews were shaped by their own experiences.

Shepard's call for a female Pan-American movement reminds us that women's activism at the fair dovetailed with the goals of other international organizations. Supporters of Pan-Americanism, many of whom also supported the PPIE, sought to bring the women of the Americas closer together in an acknowledgment of women's growing political influence across the region. A group of women from Latin America and the United States held a Woman's Auxiliary Conference in conjunction with the late December 1915 Pan-American Scientific Congress held in Washington DC. Organized in part by Ellen Foster Lansing, wife of Vice President Robert Lansing, the meetings included the numerous women who came to the congress as wives and family members of the delegates. The General Federation of Women's Clubs sent a message of friendship to the women of Latin America, and the group heard a number of talks about women in Latin America. The most significant achievement of the meeting was the unanimous passage of a resolution calling for the foundation of a Pan-American women's organization.[74] In 1922, the U.S. League of Women Voters sponsored the creation of such an organization at a Pan-American Conference of Women in Baltimore. The Pan-American Association for the Advancement of Women took on the cause of suffrage, among other issues, and marked the beginning of a Pan-American women's movement.[75] Whether links existed between the ICWWPPP and these later meetings of Pan-American women is unclear, but these developments indicate an emerging awareness of a female Pan-American internationalism.

The fair's focus on Asia and the strength of the local Chinese and Japanese communities meant that Chinese and Japanese women also actively participated in the ICWWPPP meetings. Eleven women, the largest delegation from any foreign nation, represented Japan. Two Japanese women, Madame Abiko and Madame Inui, addressed the conference and emphasized the growing movement for peace in Japan while avoiding any discussion of Japan's belligerent actions toward China. They drew on the idea of "the sisterhood of all women of the world," offering the vision of a world in which all women could work together for peace without regard for national borders or racial animosity.[76]

Inui offered a rather unexpected critique of American racial prejudice in her speech. She told the story of

> a little Japanese girl reared by a loving American mother who did not realize she was different from her little playmates. One day, rather unkindly some one said to her, "You are a little Japanese," and the little girl ran to her mother and said, "Mother, I am not a Japanese, I am an American, am I not?" But today she is glad to be a Japanese, to be with Japanese people, whom in her childhood she did not wish to accept as her own. She with her countrywomen is glad to join in this happy union of the nations in striving to realize a common ideal of peace.[77]

Although she chose not to expound further on the moral lessons of this anecdote, Inui's choice to present this story suggests her desire to critique anti-Japanese racism in the United States. Having grown up in California and graduated from Stanford University, she was certainly aware of the depth of the state's anti-Japanese movement. Her comments suggest that she found affirmation of her Japanese heritage at the fair and a place to be proud of her identity. The chance to speak at the ICWWPPP allowed her to voice those sentiments to a larger audience, as well as to find common ground with other Japanese and Japanese American women.

China, too, captured the attention of conference attendees. Conference organizer Sewall echoed the sentiments voiced by many participants when she praised China's inherently peaceful culture. "The doctrine of peace has been incorporated in the very nature of the Chinese people for centuries," she noted, in a comment that might have been intended as a contrast to the perceived militarism of the Japanese.[78]

Madame Chen spoke for China. She did not draw on Christian principles in her talk; instead, she referred to the legacy of Confucian teachings for the Chinese devotion to peace. Although a plea for peace, her speech contained veiled references to China's relationship with Japan, as well as with European imperial powers, when she noted that "in the past China's peaceful intentions have been totally ignored." Yet, she hastened to praise the United States for its role in assisting China in recent years.[79] Given that her audience was one of women concerned with international relations and peace, likely many would have understood her oblique references to the contemporary tensions with Japan. This conference offered Chen an opportunity to represent her home nation to an international audience and to offer comments, however veiled, on China's desire for peace with Japan, as well as in Europe. She also referred to China's years of subservience to foreign powers and its renewed attempts—as a newly constituted republic—to assert its independence from old pseudo-colonial relationships.

The varied activities of women on the fairgrounds offer us our last insight into the forces that shaped the PPIE. Visitors found no designated Woman's Building at the Panama-Pacific International Exposition, but they did encounter visions of society that politically minded women carefully crafted. Despite fair officials' attempts to confine women to the role of hostess, women boldly asserted their newfound political power and agitated for social and political reforms both at home and abroad. As they did so, they revealed the extent to which current political issues bled onto the fairgrounds. No matter what their intent, fair officials could not keep progressive ideas about city development, race relations, social reform, international affairs, or women's rights from repeatedly intruding onto the grounds. The result was a spectacularly diverse vision of California, the United States, and the Pacific, one that greeted all who entered the gates of the fair.

Epilogue

When the Panama-Pacific International Exposition closed its gates on December 4, 1915, San Francisco residents mourned the passing of the spectacular event. The Catholic diocesan newspaper, the *Monitor*, remarked, "This has been an 'annus mirabilis,' a wonderful year."[1] Mary Eugenia Pierce noted in her diary, "Everybody tired to death today! and yet all lamenting the Fair!"[2] Walter De Vecchi remembered, "Thousands of people were reluctant to leave. . . . I saw many ladies and men too . . . with tears in their eyes, knowing that this grand party was over for all time."[3] To all of these San Franciscans, the PPIE was a significant event, a part of which they each claimed as their own. But after nine months, the lights went out, the celebration ended, and the exposition became a part of San Francisco's history.

Many San Franciscans believed 1915 was an annus mirabilis. Together, fair officials and city residents made the PPIE into a financial success—recouping expenditures and ending with a profit—and an event that celebrated San Francisco's dominance of Pacific trade. Foreign nations such as China and Japan invested huge sums in elaborate buildings and displays, and the city hosted hundreds of foreign dignitaries during the fair. Millions of visitors poured into the city and spent funds both on and off the fairgrounds. Residents who held a season pass enjoyed world-class concerts, theater performances, and appearances by world-renowned figures ranging from Helen Keller to Theodore Roosevelt. San Francisco proved it was no longer a frontier town perched on the edge of the Pacific Ocean but a cosmopolitan, twentieth-century American city.

During the following years, the city and state would feel the legacy of the fair as city leaders continued to sing the fair's praises. "It was our exposition," noted one 1916 *San Francisco Chronicle* column, and "we rejoice to tell the world" about its successes. The early months of 1916 witnessed an economic upsurge in all key indicators in the city, and pundits gave

Fig. 58. Destruction of the Court of the Universe. (San Francisco History Center, San Francisco Public Library.)

credit to the fair.[4] As the city continued to prosper economically, migrants poured into the state over the next decades. California's tourist board reported that almost 700,000 people visited the PPIE from out of state, creating unmatched publicity for the city and state.[5] Just as fair boosters had wished in 1910, the fair advertised the bounty and opportunities of California to the rest of the nation and world. The displays of California counties alone offered impressive snapshots of the state's natural bounty. Early reports indicated that many counties felt the effects of the fair. "So it is that the Exposition did much for us in Central California," reported a Napa County representative. "We are discovered now. And with the close of the Exposition has come the awakening to the fact that tourist travel means dollars raining down on every line of business."[6]

The fair generated immediate benefits for the city of San Francisco. It sped up the city's post-earthquake reconstruction and created new streetcar lines, allowing the eventual development of the fair site into the Marina neighborhood. But it also revealed simmering urban social and political conflicts. The civic unity sought by fair builders was an illusion in 1915; it would fracture completely over the next few years. The coalition of the business community around the PPIE helped it shift the balance between labor and capital in the years after the fair. The Chamber of Commerce, for instance, used tactics adopted by PPIE management to resolve a June 1916 waterfront strike.[7] A far more serious conflict erupted in July, with the bombing of a Preparedness Day parade. The same businessmen who had created the PPIE sponsored the parade, and more than twenty thousand of the city's professional class and their wives participated in it. The July 22 bombing killed nine and injured forty others. Allegations of perjury during the trials of five suspects and the subsequent conviction and sentencing of two of them—Warren Billings and Thomas Mooney—to life in prison and execution, respectively, polarized the city and drew national attention to the city's radical politics.[8]

The next decades witnessed continued citywide debates over city development, public ownership, and the expansion of the municipal railways. The construction of the Stockton Street Tunnel in 1914, as part of the expansion of the railways for the PPIE, provided the model for the 1918 Twin Peaks Tunnel. These rail lines, and later expansion, fostered a postwar construction boom in western regions of the city.[9] The eventual development of the exposition's site into the Marina, a wealthy neighborhood, fulfilled the fears of the opponents of Harbor View: the long-term benefits of the work done on the site benefited property owners rather than the city at large. By 1924, a local real estate corporation had acquired the property, built streets, installed utilities, and subdivided it into parcels for housing.[10] Of all the exposition's many buildings, only the Palace of Fine Arts remained.

The ethnic, racial, and gender conflicts that the fair brought to light persisted long past 1915. The California legislature passed a strengthened Alien Land Law in 1920, and the 1924 Immigration Restriction Act—based on national quotas—codified Asian exclusion. The internment of Japanese Americans in California in the 1940s represented the culmination of the anti-Japanese racism visible in the 1913 debates on the Alien Land Law. Although San Francisco Catholics were fully accepted members of society, as their extensive participation in the fair demonstrates, the 1920s saw extensive anti-Catholic activity in other parts of the nation. The debates over female sexuality at the fair, particularly in the exposi-

Fig. 59. Palace of Fine Arts. (Donald G. Larson Collection, Special
Collections Research Center, California State University Fresno.)

tion's Joy Zone, reflected the much larger discussions in U.S. society about
female sexuality. By the 1920s, developments resulted in the new "flap-
per" image for women, in which their bodies and sexuality were far less
disguised than they had been in previous decades. Although suffragists
emerged victorious in 1920 with the passage of the Nineteenth Amendment, the drive further splintered the women's movement as women
worked for a variety of different goals rather than focusing on the single
goal of suffrage. The diversity of female voices present at the PPIE had
offered a glimpse of the future of women's organizing, as suffrage was only
one of many causes forwarded by politically minded women after 1920.

Although the PPIE is often perceived as the last world's fair of the
Victorian Era and a marker of the Progressive Era's decline, it should be
equally understood as a harbinger of things to come. San Francisco's cosmopolitan population, its status as a suffrage state, its relatively large Asian
population, its businessmen shifting their focus to the Pacific rather than
to Europe for economic expansion, and its history of tolerance toward
vice and sexuality—all of these elements reflected growing trends in U.S.
society. These issues influenced the fair in ways that offered glimpses not
only of the past but also of the future. In this way, this particular world's
fair stands out for two reasons: it celebrated a contemporary event—

the completion of the Panama Canal—and it offered insights into the social and political conflicts of the coming decades.

The fair left concrete legacies for the city. Many PPIE activities occurred at the Civic Center Auditorium, a downtown building constructed by the PPIE. As part of the $5 million bond issue raised by the city, city supervisors required that the PPIE use part of the money to construct a building that would be of permanent use for the city. The city and the fair both contributed to the auditorium's construction, and the complex included a new city hall and public library. After the fair ended, the PPIE donated the organ it had purchased for the Festival Hall to the center.[11] The Civic Center Auditorium remains an important San Francisco landmark.

Most of the fair's buildings were razed in 1916. A few were put to other uses. The Ohio Building was sailed down the bay to serve a variety of recreational uses until it was torched in the 1950s.[12] The California State Building and the *Column of Progress* remained standing along the Marina Green since the fair owned the land under the column and part of the California Building. Plans proceeded for the California Building to be converted to a State Normal School until its location was deemed too close to the Presidio and its military men. Both the California Building and the column were eventually destroyed.[13]

As many San Franciscans know, the only building from the PPIE still standing today is the Palace of Fine Arts. The home of the Exploratorium Museum until 2013, the current structure is a reconstruction of the original. As the PPIE drew to a close, supporters organized to save the palace, arguing it was a fitting tribute to the fair. Over the ensuing decades the space was put to many uses. During the New Deal, Works Progress Administration artists repaired the peeling artwork and crumbling statuary. In 1934, the palace found a new function when it became the site of eighteen tennis courts. During World War II the U.S. Army requisitioned it as storage for army jeeps, resulting in additional damage to the already fragile structure. When the army relinquished the palace to the city after the war and the building was determined to be unsafe for public use, a debate erupted about the structure's future. Would it house tennis courts? A National Guard armory? Or something else entirely?[14]

The debate continued at the local and state level for the next decade, until in 1957 Assemblyman Caspar Weinberger finally convinced legislators to approve a grant of $2 million toward rebuilding the structure if matching funds could be found. Local businessman Walter Johnson, a "struggling young lawyer" at the time of the PPIE and head of the Palace of Fine Arts League, agreed two years later to donate the matching gift.[15] City residents passed a $1.8 million bond issue the next year, and soon the city had sufficient funds to begin the restoration. Supporters failed to raise enough money to fully restore the building, but architects met the challenge of modifying the plans and began the project. The original building was gutted, leaving only the shell. Artists rebuilt the statues and gardeners replanted the grounds, re-creating a structure that echoed with its past majesty. It is now a significant part of the San Francisco skyline and a treasured San Francisco landmark.

The PPIE demonstrated to the world that the city of San Francisco was reborn. It sped up urban development and solidified the city's claim as empress of the Pacific. The fair also highlighted contemporary social and political issues that would persist for decades to come. Although the city would not remain the largest city on the West Coast for long, today it is still a significant economic center of the West Coast and of the Pacific Rim, goals it sought to solidify through the PPIE. City residents cherished their memories of 1915, and even after the city hosted another fair, the Golden Gate International Exposition of 1939, the PPIE occupied a fond place in many residents' hearts. For many, 1915 marked a truly annus mirabilis, one that they remembered when they gazed on the Palace of Fine Arts or the Marina Green.

Notes

The Bancroft Library reorganized the Panama-Pacific International Exposition Company papers since I began the research for this project. Therefore, my references reflect both organizational systems. Those with a folder name (not number) and carton number are from the old system, while those with a folder number and carton number are from the current system.

INTRODUCTION

1. Untitled memo begins "Participants are requested to read," n.d., folder 20M, Rolph Papers.
2. "People Open the Greatest of Expositions," *San Francisco Chronicle*, February 21, 1915.
3. The grounds opened at 7 a.m., with the exhibit palaces opening at 9 a.m., and closed at 11 p.m. Todd, *The Story of the Exposition*, 3:7.
4. Only one scholarly monograph has been published on the PPIE, and it focuses on the fair from an art history perspective. See Moore, *Empire on Display*.
5. The foremost proponent of this perspective is Robert Rydell, whose synthesis of Victorian Era fairs is the classic in the field. See his *All the World's a Fair*. Other scholars who have followed Rydell's lead include Mona Domosh and Meg Armstrong. Domosh analyzes "how the discourse of civilization was deployed in the promotion of American cultural empire" at the 1893 Columbian Exposition. See Domosh, "A 'Civilized' Commerce," 181. Meg Armstrong focuses on the meanings of the midway or amusement sections at fairs, arguing that "whereas the ethnological exhibits 'order' the chaos of the foreign, the midways exhibit the other in a state *prior to* the ordering processes of European powers." See Armstrong, "'A Jumble of Foreignness,'" 201.
6. Benedict, *Anthropology of World's Fairs*, 6.
7. Eleven fairs were held: Chicago (1893), Atlanta (1895), Nashville (1897), Omaha (1898), Buffalo (1901), St. Louis (1904), Portland (1905), Jamestown (1907), Seattle (1909), San Francisco (1915), and San Diego (1915–16). See Rydell, Findling, and Pelle, *Fair America*, 8–9.
8. For works on other fairs, see Greenhalgh, *Ephemeral Vistas*. See Rydell, Findling, and Pelle, *Fair America*, for an excellent short introduction to the his-

toriography of American fairs. See also the bibliographic essay in Rydell and Kroes, *Buffalo Bill in Bologna*. Other historians have included considerations of such fairs as the 1893 Chicago Columbian Exposition in larger works. William Cronon and Allen Trachtenberg, for instance, have both pointed to Chicago's White City of 1893 as an expression of the triumph of the city and of the incorporation of late nineteenth-century America: Cronon, *Nature's Metropolis*; and Trachtenberg, *The Incorporation of America*. Scholars of art and architectural history have focused on the sculpture, architecture, and art of the events. See the following collections for examples of such work: Harris et al., *Grand Illusions*; and Benedict, *Anthropology of World's Fairs*. Other works celebrate fairs without scholarly analysis. See Ewald and Clute, *San Francisco Invites the World*; and McCullough, *World's Fairs Midways*.

9. Numerous works have demonstrated that both the production and use of popular culture are sites of struggle. One of the key originators of these ideas is Stuart Hall in his "Notes on Deconstructing 'The Popular,'" in Samuel, *People's History and Socialist Theory*, 239. See also Bederman, *Manliness and Civilization*; Enstad, *Ladies of Labor*; Davis, *The Circus Age*; and Collins and Lutz, *Reading "National Geographic."*

10. My understanding of fairs and the various uses to which competing groups put them is informed in part by the works of Hoffenberg, *An Empire on Display*, 29; Walden, *Becoming Modern in Toronto*; Gleach, "Pocahontas at the Fair," 420; Bank, "Telling a Spatial History," 349–66; Rambon, "Theatres of Contact," 157–90; Kramer, "Making Concessions," 77; and Lockyer, "Japan at the Exhibition, 1867–1877," in Umesao, Lockyer, and Yoshida, *Collection and Representations*, 17:74.

11. Gilbert, *Whose Fair?*

12. Alexander Geppert, *Fleeting Cities: Imperial Expositions in Fin-de-Siècle Europe* (London: Palgrave Macmillan, 2010), 241; and Pieter van Wesemael, *Architecture of Instruction and Delight: A Socio-historical Analysis of World Exhibitions as a Didactic Phenomenon, 1798–1851–1970* (Rotterdam: Uitgeverij 010 Publishers, 2001).

13. See Moore, *Empire on Display*, for an interpretation that foregrounds the masculine aspects of the fair.

14. Berglund, *Making San Francisco American*, 216.

15. Todd, *Story of the Exposition*, 1:35–37.

16. "World's Fair for This City," *San Francisco Chronicle*, November 25, 1906.

17. Davies, *Saving San Francisco*, 2.

18. Davies, *Saving San Francisco*, 2.

19. Todd, *Story of the Exposition*, 1:41.

20. "Programme of Festival Decided," *San Francisco Chronicle*, October 1, 1909.

21. "Programme of Festival Decided"; and "Portola Colors Seen on Streets," *San Francisco Chronicle*, October 6, 1909.

22. "Red Men Will Hold a Pow-Wow and Dance," *San Francisco Chronicle*, October 3, 1909; and "Sorosis Club Gives Portola Programme," *San Francisco Chronicle*, October 5, 1909.

23. "Makes Low Rates for Portola Week," *San Francisco Chronicle*, October 7, 1909.

24. "Our Hotel Accommodations," *San Francisco Chronicle*, October 14, 1909; "Finds Many Rooms for Portola Week," *San Francisco Chronicle*, October 14, 1909; and "City's Reputation for Hospitality," *San Francisco Chronicle*, October 17, 1909.

25. "Portola Attracting Universal Attention," *San Francisco Chronicle*, October 12, 1909.

26. "The Portola Atmosphere," *San Francisco Chronicle*, October 21, 1909.

27. "Portola Colors Seen on Streets"; "Chinatown: The Home of the Festivals," *San Francisco Chronicle*, October 17, 1909; and "Parade Was Colorful with California Life," *San Francisco Chronicle*, October 22, 1909.

28. Todd, *Story of the Exposition*, 1:42.

29. Buchanan, *History of the Panama-Pacific*, 30; and Todd, *Story of the Exposition*, 1:47.

30. Todd, *Story of the Exposition*, 1:48.

31. Todd, *Story of the Exposition*, 1:49.

32. Todd, *Story of the Exposition*, 1:56–57. For a list of the members of the Ways and Means Committee, see Todd, *Story of the Exposition*, 1:57–59.

33. Buchanan, *History of the Panama-Pacific*, 30.

34. See discussion of the campaign in Todd, *Story of the Exposition*, 1:38–99.

35. Todd, *Story of the Exposition*, 1:63–66. For a recent history of the San Diego exposition, see Bokovoy, *San Diego World's Fairs*.

36. For the campaign from New Orleans's point of view, see *The Logical Point*, 1 (1910). For the arguments used by San Francisco boosters, see "A Few Arguments for Holding the Pacific Ocean Exposition in 1913," folder 74, box 8, Hale Papers.

37. Todd, *Story of the Exposition*, 1:90.

38. Todd, *Story of the Exposition*, 1:94–95.

39. Todd, *Story of the Exposition*, 1:96.

40. After San Francisco's victory became clear, New Orleans withdrew its campaign, and the actual measure in favor of San Francisco passed instead by 259 to 43. Todd, *Story of the Exposition*, 1:98.

41. On Panama Canal Exposition, House, vol. 46, part 2, 61st Cong., *Congressional Record*, January 18–February 6, 1911, 1741.

42. On Panama Canal Exposition, Senate Congressional Committee on Industrial Expositions, vol. 46, part 3, 61st Cong., *Congressional Record*, February 7–20, 1911, 2328.

43. House, *Congressional Record*, 1739–40.

44. The fair occupied an odd space between the public and private spheres. Officially recognized by the federal government as a federally supported "international exposition," the event was run by a private company, the Panama-Pacific International Exposition Company, yet funded by both private subscriptions and public bond money. This contradiction would raise a number of issues for the project that will be further explored.

45. Gavin McNab, quoted in Todd, *Story of the Exposition*, 1:54.

46. Risse, *Plague, Fear, and Politics*.

47. On the transformation of San Francisco, see Barth, *Instant Cities*. On the impact of the Gold Rush, see Johnson, *Roaring Camp*; and Rorbaugh, *Days of Gold*.

48. For a history of the Barbary Coast, see Asbury, *The Barbary Coast*. San Francisco had long had a skewed male–female ratio. In 1910, the city had 236,901 men and 180,011 women, demonstrating that although the gap had lessened since the Gold Rush days, a still significant difference contributed to the sense of the city as male territory. U.S. Department of Commerce, Bureau of the Census, *Thirteenth Census*, 2:174–75.

49. In 1851 and 1856, groups of citizens formed a "Committee of Vigilance" to deal with crime and corruption in the city. Glen Gendzel argues the committee contributed to a political culture of vigilantism in San Francisco. See Gendzel, "Vigilantes and Boosters," 462. See also Jolly, "Inventing the City."

50. Christopher Lee Yip argues that outside discrimination forced the Chinese community to build strong internal institutions, which in turn formed "a complex social hierarchy that functioned as a quasi-government for the community." Yip, "San Francisco's Chinatown."

51. For discussions of Chinese immigration and anti-Chinese sentiment in California, see Takaki, *Iron Cages*; Takaki, *Strangers from a Different Shore*; Saxton, *Indispensable Enemy*; Daniels, *Asian America*; and Chinn, *Bridging the Pacific*. For a contemporary report on the issue, see McKenzie, *Oriental Exclusion*.

52. The act was broadened in 1888 to include "all persons of the Chinese race," with exceptions for Chinese officials, teachers, students, tourists, and merchants. The act was renewed in 1892 and extended indefinitely in 1902. Yet Chinese communities persisted in the West, despite facing extreme prejudice that sometimes erupted into outright violence.

53. For histories of early Japanese immigration and the anti-Japanese movement, see Daniels, *The Politics of Prejudice*; Ichioka, *The Issei*; Chuman, *The Bamboo*

People; Ichihashi, *Japanese in the United States*; Takaki, *Iron Cages*; Takaki, *Strangers from a Different Shore*; Daniels and Olin, *Racism in California*; and Daniels, *Asian America*.

54. Fradkin, *Great Earthquake*; Pan, *Impact of the 1906 Earthquake*; and Yip, "San Francisco's Chinatown."

55. Ichihashi, *Japanese in the United States*, 234–36.

56. See Takaki, *Strangers from a Different Shore*, chapter 5, for a discussion of the Japanese experience. Also see Ichioka, *The Issei*, for a nuanced interpretation of the Japanese immigrant experience.

57. Whether Abe Ruef was a "boss" is subject to scholarly debate. Regardless of whether he fit the definition of a boss, he was an opportunist who took advantage of political circumstances to enrich himself and his colleagues. For contrasting interpretations of Ruef, see Bean, *Boss Ruef's San Francisco*; James P. Walsh, "Abe Ruef Was No Boss: Machine Politics, Reform and San Francisco," *California Historical Quarterly* 51 (1972): 3–16; Fradkin, *Great Earthquake*; and Gendzel, "Vigilantes and Boosters."

58. Gendzel, "Vigilantes and Boosters," 479–80.

59. Issel and Cherny, *San Francisco*, 58. For a contemporary report on the graft trials, see Hichborn, *"The System."*

60. Issel and Cherny, *San Francisco*, 58.

61. "F. J. Heney Shot in Courtroom," *New York Times*, November 14, 1908.

62. Buchanan, *History of the Panama-Pacific*, 57.

63. Dobkin, "A Twenty-Five-Million-Dollar Mirage," in Benedict, *Anthropology of World's Fairs*, 73–74.

64. For a list and description of the directors and their occupations, see Todd, *Story of the Exposition*, 1:110–18.

65. Dobkin, "A Twenty-Five-Million-Dollar Mirage," in Benedict, *Anthropology of World's Fairs*, 75.

66. Cordato, "Representing the Expansion."

67. "List of Women Appointed as Assistants to the Various Departments," carton 11, file 4, Panama-Pacific International Exposition Company Papers, Bancroft Library (hereafter PPIE-BL)

1. THE SPECTACLE OF THE FAIR

1. "Charm of Hawaii Will Pervade Exposition," *San Francisco Chronicle*, June 11, 1915.

2. I use the preferred Hawaiian spelling of Hawai'i in the text to refer to the territory and the accompanying generally accepted adjectival form of "Hawaiian." I maintain the original spelling in direct quotations or references to events named in 1915.

3. "Hawaiian Day Observed at Exposition," *San Francisco Chronicle*, June 12, 1915.

4. See Rydell, *All the World's a Fair*, for the clearest statement of this perspective.

5. Rydell, *All the World's a Fair*; Stern, *Eugenic Nation*; and Kline, *Building a Better Race*.

6. Post, *By Motor to the Golden Gate*, 229–30.

7. The acreage of other fairs was Philadelphia, 285; Chicago, 686; Buffalo, 350; St. Louis, 1,240; Jamestown, 350; and Seattle, 255. Todd, *Story of the Exposition*, 1:164.

8. Panama-Pacific International Exposition Company, *Condensed Facts*, copy in Pamphlets, Panama-Pacific International Exposition, vertical files (hereafter PPIE-SFPL).

9. Boas, *Society of Six*, 55.

10. Neuhaus, *Art of the Exposition*, 51.

11. Mary Austin, "Art Influence in the West," *The Century Magazine*, April 1915, 830, quoted in Gray Brechin, "Sailing to Byzantium: The Architecture of the Fair," in Benedict, *Anthropology of World's Fairs*, 100.

12. Lee, *Victorious Spirit*, 141.

13. Lee, *Victorious Spirit*, 214.

14. Brinton, *Impressions of Art*, 43.

15. Brinton, *Impressions of Art*.

16. Adams, *Ansel Adams*, 19.

17. Doris Barr Stanislawski, Diary, vol. 6, Barr Stanislawski Papers.

18. Doris Barr Stanislawski, Diary, vol. 6, Barr Stanislawski Papers.

19. Annie Fader Haskell, Diary for 1915, May 21, 1915, vol. 40, box 8, Haskell Family Papers.

20. "Official Daily Program, Panama-Pacific International Exposition" (San Francisco: Wahlgreen, 1915), copies in Mechanics' Institute Library.

21. A. Sterling Calder, "Sculpture," *California's Magazine*, Cornerstone Number (1915): 321.

22. "San Francisco Proves Her Splendid Confidence," *San Francisco Chronicle*, February 21, 1915.

23. Homer S. King, "California's Exposition Ambitions," *Sunset* 25 (1910): 624.

24. King, "California's Exposition Ambitions," 624.

25. Calder, "Sculpture," 321.

26. Todd, *Story of the Exposition*, 2:296.

27. Todd, *Story of the Exposition*, 2:296.

28. Neuhaus, *Art of the Exposition*, 43.

29. Barry, *City of Domes*, 15.

30. Calder, "Sculpture," 321.

31. Neuhaus, *Art of the Exposition*, 29.

32. Calder, "Sculpture," 323.

33. *The End of the Trail* has become a ubiquitous image in American popular culture, appearing on buttons, sweatshirts, china patterns, key chains, the tattoos of baseball players, and motel signs in locations as unlikely as Madison, Wisconsin. For a discussion of the later history of the statue and uses of the image, see McGrath, "The Endless Trail," 8–15.

34. *The Blue Book*, 50.

35. *The Blue Book*, 51.

36. Gordon, *What We Saw*, 44.

37. Gendzel, "Pioneers and Padres," 55–79.

38. Barry, *City of Domes*, 45.

39. Booth, "Sculpture," 487.

40. Elizabeth Armstrong, "Hercules and the Muses: Public Art at the Fair," in Benedict, *Anthropology of World's Fairs*, 123.

41. Panama-Pacific International Exposition Company, *Official Guide*, 52.

42. Murray, *Emancipation and the Freed*, 175–78.

43. Frink, "San Francisco's Pioneer Mother," 87.

44. Simpson, *Problems Women Solved*, 146.

45. "Motherhood Monument to Be Dedicated to Pioneer Mothers," folder 11, box 52, San Francisco Misc/Ephemera Oversize Pamphlets Relating to the Panama-Pacific International Exposition, PPIE-CHS.

46. Editorial, *The Northern Crown*, July 1913, quoted in Keller, *Anna Morrison Reed*, 162.

47. The groups involved included the Association of Pioneer Women, the Women's Auxiliary of the Society of California Pioneers, the Daughters of California Pioneers, Sons and Daughters of the Santa Clara County Pioneer Society, Native Sons of the Golden West, and Native Daughters of the Golden West. For a list of prominent individual contributors, see Simpson, *Problems Women Solved*, 151–53.

48. Simpson, *Problems Women Solved*, 156.

49. "The Pioneer Mother's Monument—What It Should Be," *San Francisco Call*, June 26, 1914.

50. Frink, "San Francisco's Pioneer Mother," 103–4.

51. Simpson, *Problems Women Solved*, 150.

52. Frink, "San Francisco's Pioneer Mother," 106.

53. Wilder, *West from Home*, 37.

54. The original Forbidden Garden was an area reserved for the Franciscan fathers at the mission and forbidden to women. Simpson, *Problems Women Solved*, 85.

55. Panama-Pacific International Exposition Company, *The Panama-Pacific International Exposition*.

56. Simpson, *Problems Women Solved*, 30–31, 64.

57. "Outline for County Auxiliaries: Woman's Board Panama-Pacific International Exposition," San Francisco–PPIE 1915, carton 10, Hearst Papers.

58. *Hercules Pamphlet*, copy in Pamphlets: Hercules Pamphlet, PPIE-SFPL.

59. See Jacobson, *Whiteness of a Different Color*.

60. Although the use of Italy in this context seems contradictory, since Italians were not often considered "white" in the early twentieth century, the emphasis on the Italian Riviera implies that it is likening California to the tourist district, presumably one populated by many Europeans who are not Italian. Moreover, it was most often southern Italians who were constructed as "not white," while northern Italians were more often perceived as assimilable and white. Thus, I believe it is still possible to see this tactic as one that echoed with racial meaning for potential tourists. See Jacobson, *Whiteness of a Different Color*, on the construction of "whiteness" in the United States. Moreover, in California, Italians did not face the same kinds of discrimination that they did in other parts of the country owing to the timing of their entry into the labor market and the presence of Chinese and Japanese immigrants who bore the brunt of anti-immigrant sentiment in the state. See di Leonardo, *Varieties of Ethnic Experience*, chapter 2.

61. "Orange County Holds Notable Celebration," *San Francisco Chronicle*, April 20, 1915.

62. "Knox Warm in Praise of Site Chosen for Exposition," *San Francisco Call*, May 8, 1912.

63. "Knox Warm in Praise."

64. "Report of the South American Commission by D.O. Lively," folder 10, carton 140, PPIE-BL.

65. John Barrett, "Pan-American Commerce and the Panama Canal—What They Mean to San Francisco," *The Star*, April 10, 1915, Magazine Articles, PPIE-SFPL.

66. "Salutory," *Las Americas*, July 1, 1914.

67. Gonzalez, *Designing Pan-America*, 64.

68. John Barrett to Theodore Hardee, June 2, 1913, folder 11, carton 88, PPIE-BL.

69. Dominican Site Dedication, folder 30, carton 50, PPIE-BL. The Dominican Republic did not end up coming to the fair, but as a number of other nations did, it dedicated a site in 1913.

70. Prisco, *John Barrett*, 66–90.

71. "Warm Welcome Given to Republic of Honduras," *San Francisco Chronicle*, March 21, 1915.

72. Todd, *Story of the Exposition*, 3:203.

73. Barrett, "Pan-American Commerce."

74. Todd, *Story of the Exposition*, 3:230–34.

75. Todd, *Story of the Exposition*, 3:285.

76. Bruml, *Electric Lights Dazzling*.

77. The Argentine Commission, *Argentine Republic*, 11.

78. The Argentine Commission, *Argentine Republic*, 16.

79. See Todd, *Story of the Exposition*, 3:286; and Buchanan, *History of the Panama-Pacific*, 93.

80. Buchanan, *History of the Panama-Pacific*, 28.

81. Buchanan, *History of the Panama-Pacific*, 68.

82. Bruml, *Electric Lights Dazzling*.

83. Panama-Pacific International Exposition Company, *The Panama-Pacific International Exposition Illustrated*.

84. Doris Barr Stanislawski, Diary, vol. 6, Barr Stanislawski Papers.

85. Bruml, *Electric Lights Dazzling*, July 19 entry.

86. Bruml, *Electric Lights Dazzling*, July 23 entry.

87. Wilder, *West from Home*, 105.

88. "Daily Official Program, Panama-Pacific International Exposition, Feb. 20–23" (San Francisco: Wahlgreen, 1915), 16, Mechanics Institute Library.

89. "Daily Official Program," 28.

90. Wilder, *West from Home*, 39–40.

91. Jane C. Desmond, *Staging Tourism: Bodies on Display from Waikiki to Sea World* (Chicago: University of Chicago Press, 1999), 251.

92. "The Fascinating South Seas Villages at the Great San Francisco Fair," *San Francisco Examiner*, American Magazine Section, June 13, 1915.

93. "Japan at the Big San Francisco Exposition," *Los Angeles Examiner*, American Magazine Section, reprinted in *San Francisco Examiner*, June 20, 1915.

94. Helen Dare, "Feminine Fashions Seen on (and off) the Zone," *San Francisco Chronicle*, April 24, 1915.

95. "Dusky Damsels to Seek Queenly Honors," *San Francisco Chronicle*, March 13, 1915.

96. Quoted in Todd, *Story of the Exposition*, 4:40.

97. Todd, *Story of the Exposition*, 4:39. In his book, Todd included a photograph of the booth with the caption, "Improving the Human Breed," in a clear comment on the booth's eugenic intentions. See page 4 and the plate between pages 46 and 47.

98. Todd, *Story of the Exposition*, 4:40.

99. For the best contemporary statement of these theories, see Grant, *Passing of the Great Race*. For historical interpretations of social Darwinism, see Hawkins, *Social Darwinism*; and Hofstadter, *Social Darwinism*.

100. On the participation of Hawai'i in other fairs, see Imada, *Aloha America*.

101. A. P. Taylor, Hawaii Promotion Committee, to C. C. Moore, August 5, 1915, Complaints—Hawaiian Village, carton 9, PPIE-BL.

102. A. P. Taylor, Hawaii Promotion Committee, to C. C. Moore, August 5, 1915, Complaints—Hawaiian Village, carton 9, PPIE-BL.

103. "Dedication of Hawaiian Building," Historical Photographs Collection, AAE-0530, San Francisco Public Library.

104. A. P. Taylor, Hawaii Promotion Committee, to C. C. Moore, August 5, 1915, Complaints—Hawaiian Village, carton 9, PPIE-BL.

105. Imada, *Aloha America*.

106. "Wedding Today in Fair Palace," *San Francisco Examiner*, March 1, 1915; "Cupid Invades Big Exposition," *San Francisco Chronicle*, March 1, 1915; "Law Stops Wedding of Hawaiian Singer," *San Francisco Examiner*, March 2, 1915; and "Exposition Romance Is Shattered by Law," *San Francisco Chronicle*, March 2, 1915. No further reports exist, so I do not know if they eventually married.

2. UNITING SAN FRANCISCO

1. Todd, *Story of the Exposition*, 1:98.

2. Todd, *Story of the Exposition*, 1:129.

3. Those sites that appeared to merit serious consideration were the following: Newlands's waterfront plan, the Bay View site, the Islais Creek site, the Sutro Forest site, the Lake Merced site, the Golden Gate Park site, and Harbor View. "Many Claims Are Made for Sites," *San Francisco Chronicle*, April 3, 1911.

4. "Report on Sites for the Exposition," May 18, 1911, folder 1, box 1, PPIE-CHS.

5. For an example of the publicity issued in favor of the park, see "Seven Reasons Why the PPIE Should Be Placed in Golden Gate Park," folder 70, box 7, Hale Papers.

6. "Britton Tells Why Parks Site Plan Appeals to Him," *San Francisco Chronicle*, July 1, 1911.

7. William Hammond Hall to PPIE, May 1, 1911, folder 70, box 7, Hale Papers.

8. Terence Young provides a history of the city's park during this period but does not discuss the PPIE debate. Young, *Building San Francisco's Parks*, 5.

9. Young, *Building San Francisco's Parks*, 6.

10. "Works Board Angry at New Injunction," *San Francisco Chronicle*, October 5, 1909.

11. For a pictorial history of the neighborhood (now known as the "Marina"), see Lipsky, *San Francisco's Marina District*.

12. Walter De Vecchi, "The Panama-Pacific International Exposition," *North Mission News* (1984), folder 16, box 52, San Francisco Misc/Ephemera Oversize Pamphlets Relating to the Panama-Pacific International Exposition, PPIE-CHS.

13. "Must Raze Huts at Harbor View," *San Francisco Chronicle*, November 29, 1911.

14. "Must Raze Huts at Harbor View."

15. "Report on Sites for the Exposition," May 18, 1911, folder 1, box 1, PPIE-CHS.

16. "Report on Sites for the Exposition," May 18, 1911, folder 1, box 1, PPIE-CHS.

17. North Beach Promotion Association to PPIE, April 11, 1911, folder 70, box 7, Hale Papers.

18. Park Richmond Improvement Club to R. B. Hale, May 5, 1911, folder 70, box 7, Hale Papers.

19. "Uncertainty Stops Activity in Realty," *San Francisco Chronicle*, April 22, 1911; "View Is Optimistic on Immediate Future," *San Francisco Chronicle*, April 29, 1911; "Signs of Progress Seen on All Sides," *San Francisco Chronicle*, May 27, 1911; and "Various Causes Contributed to Affect City's Real Estate Market," *San Francisco Chronicle*, June 3, 1911.

20. W. S. Oliver to R. B. Hale, April 10, 1911, folder 70, box 7, Hale Papers.

21. A. C. Sylvester to Reuben Brooks Hale, July 19, 1911, folder 70, box 7, Hale Papers.

22. "South of Army Street Improvement Association, in Regular Meeting Assembled, Columbus Hall, July 13, 1911," folder 70, box 7, Hale Papers.

23. Unsigned letter to the Committee of the World's Fair Panama Exposition, April 20, 1911, folder 70, box 7, Hale Papers.

24. Scott, *The San Francisco Bay Area*, 137.

25. E. B. Norton (commissioner of public supplies, city of Berkeley) to Moore, May 31, 1911, folder 18, carton 32, PPIE-BL.

26. "We the Undersigned," folder 26, carton 32, PPIE-BL; San Francisco Hotel Men's Association to the PPIE Board of Directors, folder 17, carton 32, PPIE-BL; and Chinese Chamber of Commerce to Executive Committee, PPIE, folder 18, carton 32, PPIE-BL.

27. "To Executive Committee," April 13, 1911, folder 16, carton 32, PPIE-BL.

28. "To Executive Committee," April 13, 1911, folder 16, carton 32, PPIE-BL.

29. Virginia Vanderbilt owned fifty-five acres, Theresa Oelrichs eighteen, and Dr. Law thirty-one. A. W. Markwart to Frank Morton Todd, September 4, 1914, folder 6, carton 140, PPIE-BL.

30. William Wadron and Winchester Halet to R. B. Hale, June 26, 1911, folder 70, box 7, Hale Papers.

31. "High Bids Sought for Useless Work," *San Francisco Chronicle*, April 25, 1911.

32. "Seek Governor's Aid for Golden Gate Park," *San Francisco Chronicle*, April 27, 1911.

33. "Northern Ideas on Expositions," *San Francisco Chronicle*, May 5, 1911.

34. "Cleverest Operators Engage in Big Deals," *San Francisco Chronicle*, May 13, 1911.

35. "The Question of the Site," *San Francisco Chronicle*, June 30, 1911.

36. "Suggested Design for the Exposition: Offered as an Exhibit in Connection with the Formal Presentation of the Parks Site Made by M. H. de Young," *San Francisco Chronicle*, July 23, 1911.

37. "Property Owners Offering Lands between Two Parks for Exposition," *San Francisco Chronicle*, July 2, 1911.

38. The proposed plan called for the construction of a large boulevard originating at Telegraph Hill, extending along the waterfront to the Harbor View site, and running along the bay to the Presidio, through the Presidio to Lincoln Park, and on to Golden Gate Park. This permanent boulevard would, they hoped, be a permanent benefit to the city and would assist in locating the fair in two sites. I. W. Hellman, John Barneson, and Andrew M. Davis to the President and Board of Directors of the Panama-Pacific International Exposition, July 25, 1911, folder 71, box 7, Hale Papers. For a discussion of the Burnham plan for San Francisco, see Starr, *Americans and the California Dream*, 240–45.

39. Starr, *Americans and the California Dream*, 240–45.

40. "Location Assures Permanent Improvements in Both Parks," *San Francisco Chronicle*, July 26, 1911.

41. "Directors Voice Their Approval," *San Francisco Chronicle*, July 26, 1911.

42. Executive Architectural Council to Board of Directors, December 6, 1911, folder 3, carton 66, PPIE-BL.

43. Todd, *Story of the Exposition*, 1:167.

44. "Want Exposition in City's Park," *San Francisco Chronicle*, January 26, 1912.

45. "The Proposed Exposition at Harbor View," n.d., folder 20, carton 32, PPIE-BL.

46. "The Proposed Exposition at Harbor View," n.d., folder 20, carton 32, PPIE-BL.

47. Land Department, folder 35, carton 66, PPIE-BL.

48. A. H. Markwart to Todd, September 4, 1914, folder 6, carton 140, PPIE-BL.

49. A. H. Markwart to Todd, September 4, 1914, folder 6, carton 140, PPIE-BL.

50. No title, n.d., list of names, folder 6, carton 156, PPIE-BL.

51. G. H. Umbsen & Co. to PPIE, April 11, 1912, folder 6, carton 156, PPIE-BL.

52. Ida West Hale to Rolph, February 16, 1912, folder 33, carton 61, PPIE-BL.

53. Mary Suters to PPIE Board of Directors, April 17, 1912; and Director of Works to Mary Suters, April 20, 1912—both in folder 32, carton 61, PPIE-BL.

54. Frank Fassio to Moore, March 19, 1912, folder 33, carton 51, PPIE-BL; and Secretary to the President to Fassio, March 21, 1912, folder 33, carton 61, PPIE-BL.

55. R. C. MacLachlan to Frank Brittain, June 30, 1915, folder 15, carton 156, PPIE-BL.

56. R. C. MacLachlan to Todd, November 9, 1914, folder 6, carton 140, PPIE-BL.

57. Ben Macomber, no title, *San Francisco Chronicle*, March 21, 1915.

58. Macomber, no title.

59. "City Engineer Gives the Lie to Enemies of Street Car Bonds," *San Francisco Examiner*, June 1, 1913.

60. Issel and Cherny, *San Francisco*, 172.

61. Voters had rejected bond issues to fund municipal ownership in 1902, 1903, and earlier in 1909. Issel and Cherny, *San Francisco*, 173.

62. "Traction Downs Fair Board and Supervisors," *San Francisco Examiner*, February 6, 1913.

63. The four lines ran the following routes: one from Stockton and Market, out Stockton, along Columbus to Bay, and along Bay to the exposition grounds; a line along Van Ness to Market and then down Eleventh Street into the Potrero and perhaps the Mission; a line along the Embarcadero; and a spur from the Union Street line. "How to Provide Street Cars for the World's Fair Crowds," *San Francisco Examiner*, February 8, 1913.

64. "Let the City Solve Its Own World's Fair Transportation," *San Francisco Examiner*, February 8, 1913.

65. The following articles ran in the *Examiner*, February 9, 1913: "S.F. in Great Chorus OK's World Fair Car Plans"; "Dr. A.S. Musante Indorses 'Quick, Safe, Convenient'"; "Promotion Leader Says Car Problem Is Solved"; and "Supervisors' Stand Solidly for Big Car Project."

66. "S.F. in Great Chorus OK's World Fair Car Plans," *San Francisco Examiner*, February 9, 1913.

67. "Must Have System Say Fair Directors," *San Francisco Examiner*, February 9, 1913.

68. For more details on the plan, see San Francisco City Engineer, "Report on Extensions of Municipal Railways to Provide Transportation for the Panama-Pacific Exposition, April 5, 1913," copy in Bancroft Library.

69. "Fair Directors Are Neutral on Street Bonds," *San Francisco Examiner*, May 29, 1913.

70. "Stenographic Report of Meeting of the Board of Directors of Panama-Pacific International Exposition," May 28, 1913, folder 36, box 4, Hale Papers.

71. "Stenographic Report of Meeting of the Board of Directors of Panama-Pacific International Exposition," May 28, 1913, folder 36, box 4, Hale Papers.

72. "Fair Directors' Stand on Bonds Is Deprecated," *San Francisco Examiner*, June 3, 1913.

73. "Fair Directors' Stand."

74. Thornwell Mullally was a local attorney and assistant to the president of the United Railroads. Todd, *Story of the Exposition*, 1:116.

75. Ciabattari, "Urban Liberals, Politics," 522.

76. Ostrander, *Prohibition Movement*.

77. See Boyer, *Urban Masses*.

78. Executive Secretary to Police Commissioner, n.d., Complaints, carton 9, PPIE-BL.

79. A. D. Cutler to C. C. Moore, March 26, 1912, correspondence with city clubs, agencies, organizations, carton 21, PPIE-BL. Emphasis in the original.

80. President Moore to Police Commissioner, March 28, 1912, correspondence with city clubs, agencies, organizations, carton 21, PPIE-BL.

81. C. C. Moore to Honorable Board of Police Commissioners, April 4, 1912, correspondence with city clubs, agencies, organizations, carton 21, PPIE-BL.

82. For more examples, see letters contained in correspondence with city clubs, agencies, organizations, carton 21, PPIE-BL.

83. Executive Secretary to Police Commissioner, n.d., Complaints, carton 9, PPIE-BL.

84. Minutes of the Executive Committee, March 3, 1914, vol. 125, PPIE-BL; and F. Brittain to H. D. H. Connick, March 7, 1914, Liquor Licenses, carton 93, PPIE-BL.

85. "The Hotel City," Hotels, PPIE-SFPL.

86. Report of Director Frank L. Brown to the President, folder 13M, box 31, Rolph Papers.

87. Untitled letter from George Hough Perry, January 30, 1915, Hotel Bureau, carton 15, PPIE-BL.

88. Charles Moore to "Gentlemen," February 20, 1914, Hotel Situation, carton 23, PPIE-BL.

89. Charles Moore to "Gentlemen," February 20, 1914, Hotel Situation, carton 23, PPIE-BL.

90. "Association Business Meeting Crowded," *San Francisco Hotel Journal*, September 1914, Executive Sub-Committee Inside Inn Files, carton 29, PPIE-BL.

91. Charles Moore to "Gentlemen," February 20, 1914, Hotel Situation, carton 23, PPIE-BL.

92. George Hough Perry to the president, February 2, 1915, Hotel Bureau, carton 15, PPIE-BL.

93. Untitled letter from George Hough Perry, January 30, 1915, Hotel Bureau, carton 15, PPIE-BL.

94. "Official Exposition Hotel Guide," Hotels, PPIE-SFPL.

95. Director of Concessions (Frank Burt) to Curtis H. Lindley, June 17, 1915, Executive Sub-Committee Inside Inn Files, carton 29, PPIE-BL.

96. "Final Report of the Advisory Board of the Official Hotel Bureau to the Panama-Pacific International Exposition," Hotels, PPIE-SFPL.

97. Minutes of Executive Committee, November 24, 1914, Executive Sub Committee Inside Inn Files, carton 29, PPIE-BL.

98. Mrs. C. H. McKenney to James Rolph, folder 20M, box 32, Rolph Papers.

99. Helen Dare, "Beating—and NOT Beating—the Gate at the Exposition," *San Francisco Chronicle*, April 4, 1915.

100. An adult admission cost $0.50, and children paid $0.25, except when they came in school groups. As an example of working people's salaries in San Francisco at the time, the PPIE paid male laborers on the grounds a daily rate of approximately $2.50, carpenters $5.00, and plumbers $6.00; and female stenographers earned $17.30 a week. "Payroll," folder 10, box 2, PPIE-CHS. According to various calculators, $1.50 in 1915 is comparable to approximately $34.00 in 2012 dollars. See US Inflation Calculator, Coinnews Media Group, http://www.usinflationcalculator.com/.
101. Annie Fader Haskell, Diary for 1915, March 1, 1915, vol. 40, box 8, Haskell Family Papers.
102. Annie Fader Haskell, Diary for 1915, May 9, 1915, vol. 40, box 8, Haskell Family Papers.
103. Annie Fader Haskell, Diary for 1915, May 21, 1915, vol. 40, box 8, Haskell Family Papers.
104. Mary Eugenia Pierce, Diary for 1915–17, March 20, 1915, Pierce Family Papers.
105. Todd, *Story of the Exposition*, 2:381.
106. Mary Eugenia Pierce, Diary for 1915–17, March 25, 1915, Pierce Family Papers.
107. Charles L. Huyck, "Ten Years Later: A Retrospect of the 1915 Exposition," Huyck Papers, 2.
108. Clemens Max Richter, "Autobiography and Reminiscences," Bancroft Library.
109. See letters in Miscellaneous Suggestions and Proposals Regarding Admission Prices, etc., carton 21, PPIE-BL.
110. Minutes of the Executive Committee, Sept. 28, 1915, vol. 126, PPIE-BL.
111. Mrs. C. H. McKenney to Mayor Rolph, March 2, 1915, folder 20M, box 32, series 5M, Rolph Papers.

3. CLAIMING THEIR PLACE

1. Alameda County is located in the East Bay and contains the cities of Oakland and Berkeley, among others.
2. "Chinese Students Day at the Panama-Pacific International Exposition," Cardinell-Vincent Co., reproduced on the cover of Chinn's *Bridging the Pacific*.
3. For this interpretation of fairs see Rydell, *All the World's a Fair*. See Holt's "Marking," 16, for his argument about minstrel shows for an interpretation of how these shows answered the question of who was an American.
4. "Information for the Exposition History," to Frank Morton Todd, November 3, 1915; and List of State and Foreign Organizations of the Panama-Pacific International Exposition—both in folder 11, carton 140, PPIE-BL.

5. "Information for the Exposition History," to Frank Morton Todd, November 3, 1915, folder 11, carton 140, PPIE-BL.

6. F. L. Halse to Frank Morton Todd, November 11, 1915, folder 3, carton 145, PPIE-BL; and James Kaplan, "For the Future: The Swedish Pavilion at the Panama-Pacific International Exposition of 1915," *The Swedish-American Historical Quarterly* 57 (2006): 101.

7. Kaplan, "For the Future," 101.

8. "A Called Meeting of the Welsh Residents," September 7, 1912, folder 3, carton 18, PPIE-BL.

9. Kaplan, "For the Future," 107.

10. Edward Delger to Moore, November 18, 1913, folder 1, carton 18, PPIE-BL.

11. F. W. Dohrmann to Moore, November 13, 1912, folder 1, carton 18, PPIE-BL.

12. Edward Delger to Moore, July 6, 1914, folder 1, carton 18, PPIE-BL.

13. "Final Report to Members of the German-American Auxiliary to the Panama-Pacific International Exposition," folder 3, carton 145, PPIE-BL.

14. "Final Report to Members of the German-American Auxiliary to the Panama-Pacific International Exposition," folder 3, carton 145, PPIE-BL.

15. "Germans to Hold Big Celebration," *San Francisco Chronicle*, July 18, 1915.

16. "Fatherland Cheered by Army of Sturdy Sons: Exposition Is Captured by German-Americans," *San Francisco Chronicle*, August 6, 1915.

17. "Germans at Fair in Demonstration," *Decatur (Illinois) Review*, August 6, 1915; and "German Day at Exposition," *Los Angeles Times*, August 6, 1915.

18. "Fatherland Cheered."

19. "Hot Letter to Wilson Modified: Local Meeting of German National Alliance in Clash over Message," *San Francisco Chronicle*, August 5, 1915.

20. "German-Americans Appeal for Liberal Legislation," *San Francisco Chronicle*, August 4, 1915.

21. Walsh, *San Francisco Irish*, 21.

22. See Burns, "The Immigrant Church," in Burns, *Catholic San Francisco*, 189–97, for a brief description of the immigrant origins of the San Francisco Catholic community. For anti-Catholicism, see Massa, *Anti-Catholicism in America*; and Wallace, *Rhetoric of Anti-Catholicism*.

23. Sarbaugh, "Exiles of Confidence," in Meagher, *From Paddy to Studs*, 165–66.

24. On Italian-Irish relations see Rubin, *Signs of Change*, 125; and Gumina, *The Italians of San Francisco*, 52.

25. On nineteenth-century American views of the Chinese, see Choy, Dong, and Hong, *Coming Man*. Other discussions of the racialization of the Chinese include Shah, *Contagious Divides*, especially chapter 2; and Moy, *Marginal Sights*. See Nee and Nee, *Longtime Californ'*, for evocative firsthand accounts of the treatment that the Chinese experienced in twentieth-century San Francisco.

26. See Ngai, *Lucky Ones*, for an interesting perspective on the development of the Chinese immigrant community in San Francisco.

27. For the story of this transformation, see Lee, *Picturing Chinatown*.

28. In 1910, there were approximately 1,642 blacks in San Francisco per the U.S. Department of Commerce, Bureau of Census, *Thirteenth Census of the United States*, 174–75.

29. In 1910, 70 percent of black women held jobs as domestics and 10 percent worked in manufacturing, while 47.5 percent of men held domestic jobs, 10.9 percent held jobs in manufacturing, and 10.8 percent in transportation. See Broussard, *Black San Francisco*, 39–41; and Daniels, *Pioneer Urbanites*, 31.

30. Broussard, *Black San Francisco*, 58; and Dellums, *C.L. Dellums*.

31. W. E. B. Du Bois, "Colored California," *The Crisis* 6 (1913): 194–95.

32. "The Fifth Annual Report of the NAACP," reprinted in *The Crisis* 9 (1915): 301.

33. "'Clansman' Is Welcomed by Big Audience," *San Francisco Examiner*, April 20, 1915.

34. Daniels notes the presence of racist cartoons in local newspapers in the early twentieth century, such as one found in the *San Francisco Chronicle*, August 5, 1914, and reproduced in Daniels, *Pioneer Urbanites*, 84.

35. "Our Responsibility to the Panama Exposition," *Young China*, August 1, 1912, with translation by Winifred Chang.

36. "The Panama International Exposition and Entrepreneurs," *Chung Sai Yat Po*, February 27, 1915, with translation by Winifred Chang.

37. "Information Regarding the Panama International Fair for My Chinese Countrymen," *Chung Sai Yat Po*, January 23, 1915, with translation by Winifred Chang.

38. Minutes of the Executive Committee, January 20, 1914, vol. 124, PPIE-BL.

39. Chinese Consolidated Benevolent Association to Charles Moore, February 18, 1914, Underground Chinatown—protests against Concession, carton 23, PPIE-BL.

40. M. J. Brandenstein to Charles Moore, February 14, 1914, Underground Chinatown—protests against Concession, carton 23, PPIE-BL.

41. "Ireland to Have a Big Exhibit in 1915," *Leader*, June 7, 1913.

42. This goal is in keeping with Timothy Sarbaugh's argument that Irish republican nationalism was a powerfully unifying force among the San Francisco Irish that only grew in strength in the post-fair years. See Sarbaugh, "Exiles of Confidence," in Meagher, *From Paddy to Studs*, 167–74.

43. "No Travesties Wanted at the 1915 Exhibit," *Leader*, May 17, 1913.

44. For a laudatory description of the African American presence at the exposition, see Beasley, *The Negro Trail Blazers*, 301–4.

45. "Negro Day at PPIE," *Western Outlook* (Oakland CA), April 3, 1915.

46. W. E. B. Du Bois to Stewart; and Stewart to Du Bois—both in folder 33, carton 38, PPIE-BL. My thanks to Amanda Cannata for locating these undated letters.

47. S. L. Mash to C. C. Moore, January 14, 1915, Racial Discrimination, Charges of, carton 23, PPIE-BL.

48. Taussig to Mash, February 6, 1915, Racial Discrimination, Charges of, carton 23, PPIE-BL.

49. J. S. Tobin to Moore, January 25, 1915, Racial Discrimination, Charges of, carton 23, PPIE-BL.

50. Untitled editorial, *Oakland Sunshine*, December 11, 1915.

51. "The Exposition," *Western Outlook* (Oakland CA), January 30, 1915.

52. "Mass Meeting, Fifteenth Street Church," *Western Outlook* (Oakland CA), February 13, 1915.

53. "Central Bureau of Information for Colored People," *Western Outlook* (Oakland CA), March 13, 1915.

54. "Fair Visitors Attention!," *Western Outlook* (Oakland CA), March 6, 1915.

55. Chen, *Chinese San Francisco*, 206–10.

56. *Chung Sai Yat Po*, February 22, 1915, quoted and translated by Chen in *Chinese San Francisco*, 206.

57. Chen Chi to Charles C. Moore, March 19, 1915, Underground Chinatown, carton 23, PPIE-BL.

58. On Chinese female prostitutes in the city, see Tong, *Unsubmissive Women*.

59. On contemporary fears of white slavery and its links to Asians, see Rosen, *The Lost Sisterhood*, 119–23.

60. Chinese Six Companies to C. C. Moore, March 19, 1915, Underground Chinatown, carton 23, PPIE-BL.

61. Chinese Six Companies to C. C. Moore, March 19, 1915, Underground Chinatown, carton 23, PPIE-BL.

62. Chinese Six Companies to C. C. Moore, March 19, 1915, Underground Chinatown, carton 23, PPIE-BL.

63. J. H. Laughlin et al. to C. C. Moore, March 20, 1915, Underground Chinatown, carton 23, PPIE-BL.

64. Chan Sing Kai et al. to C. C. Moore, March 20, 1915, Underground Chinatown, carton 23, PPIE-BL.

65. Ng Poon Chew et al. to C. C. Moore, n.d., Underground Chinatown, carton 23, PPIE-BL.

66. Chen Chi to C. C. Moore, March 19, 1915, Underground Chinatown, carton 23, PPIE-BL.

67. Minutes of the Committee on Concessions and Admissions, March 26, 1915, vol. 123, PPIE-BL.

68. "New Concession Shows Evils of Drug Habit," *San Francisco Chronicle*, June 9, 1915, 145.

69. "On the Zone," advertisement, *San Francisco Call*, June 19, 1915.

70. Mumford, *Interzones*.

71. Minutes of the Committee on Concessions and Admissions, June 24, 1913, vol. 122, PPIE-BL.

72. "The Irish Village," *Leader*, September 27, 1913; and "That Irish Exhibit," *Leader*, November 1, 1913.

73. "Ireland at the 1915 World's Fair," *Monitor*, March 14, 1914.

74. "The 'Shamrock Isle' Starts Caricaturing in Advance," *Leader*, April 4, 1914; and "Irish Village at the World's Fair," *Leader*, March 6, 1915.

75. Todd, *Story of the Exposition*, 2:359.

76. "Nations of the West," *Monitor*, July 3, 1915.

77. "The Nations of the West," *Monitor*, August 7, 1915.

78. Archbishop Patrick Riordan passed away in 1914, and the reins of power in the San Francisco Catholic community passed to then bishop Hanna.

79. Nordstrom, "Danger on the Doorstep." The publication of the anti-Catholic, Chicago-based Masonic group Guardians of Liberty supports this argument. See "To Promote Patriotism," "Are Civil Liberties Endangered," and "Political Medicine in the Public School"—all in the first volume of *The Guardian of Liberty*, 1913.

80. H. W. Moore to Charles Moore, September 19, 1913, Complaints, carton 9, PPIE-BL.

81. "The Protest against Nathan," *America*, June 20, 1914, quoted in D'Agostino, *Rome in America*, 84.

82. See D'Agostino, *Rome in America*, 84–93, for a description of the protests that occurred prior to Nathan's appointment as commissioner general to the PPIE.

83. In addition, D'Agostino argues, the protest revealed the dormant anti-Semitism among some American Catholics. D'Agostino, *Rome in America*, 3, 85.

84. "We Will Not Have Him," *Monitor*, February 28, 1914.

85. John Brasser to Charles Moore, March 30, 1914, Complaints, carton 9, PPIE-BL.

86. "Specific Bigoted Acts of Nathan, Cockney Jew," *Leader, June 27, 1914*; and "Which Shall It Be? Nathan's Recall or Dead Exposition?," *Western Catholic* (Springfield IL), May 1, 1914, quoted in D'Agostino, *Rome in America*, 95.

87. The only mention of the controversy over Nathan's appointment that appeared in *Emanu-El*, the journal of the San Francisco Temple Emanu-El, was a reprint of a letter from the Anti-Defamation League of Chicago written in response to the anti-Semitic attack by the *Western Catholic*. "Catholic Paper Attacks Ernesto Nathan," *Emanu-El*, June 12, 1914. Other articles

on Nathan included "Distinguished Jewish Representative of Italy Arrives," *Emanu-El*, June 5, 1914; and "Ex-Mayor of Rome Visits the Golden Gate," *Emanu-El*, June 5, 1915. For a discussion of Jews in San Francisco and a brief mention of their role in shaping the PPIE, see Rosenbaum, *Visions of Reform*.

88. Rosenbaum, *Cosmopolitans*; and Cherny, "Patterns of Toleration," 130–41.

89. W. P. Oliver to Moore, n.d., Complaints, carton 9, PPIE-BL.

90. Lincoln Court, No. 5, Guardians of Liberty, Chicago IL, July 16, 1914, Complaints, carton 9, PPIE-BL.

91. "Refuse to Take Nathan's Hand," *Monitor*, June 6, 1914.

92. "Discredited," *Monitor*, June 20, 1914. Also see articles in *The Guardian of Liberty*, 1 (1914), celebrating Nathan's arrival.

93. Untitled editorial, *Monitor*, August 1, 1914.

94. See issues of *San Francisco Chronicle* and *Monitor* from February 20, 1915.

95. D'Agostino, *Rome in America*, 99.

96. Rubin, *Signs of Change*; and Cinel, *From Italy to San Francisco*.

97. Minutes of the Executive Committee, August 4, 1914, vol. 125, PPIE-BL.

98. Minutes of the Executive Committee, October 13, 1914, vol. 125, PPIE-BL.

99. Minutes of the Executive Committee, October 20,1914, vol. 125, PPIE-BL.

100. Minutes of the Executive Committee, January 5, 1915, vol. 125, PPIE-BL.

101. "A Catholic Victory," *Monitor*, May 29, 1915. It is not clear why the fair officially canceled the convention in January but did not announce the news until May.

102. Whether the exposition officials played any role in this debate is unclear. The evidence is unfortunately spotty. In late 1914, some discussed creating a separate African American exhibit at the fair, but those involved concluded that since the opportunity was coming so late, any such exhibit would "be indicative of self-desired race segregation, which is not to be encouraged by California Negroes." "Do We Want a Negro Day at the Exposition?," *Oakland Sunshine*, May 27, 1915; and "The 1915 Exposition Committee," *Western Outlook* (Oakland CA), December 26, 1914.

103. "No Negro Day for Us," *Western Outlook* (Oakland CA), April 3, 1915.

104. "Do We Want a Negro Day?"

105. Daniels notes that similar objections were raised to Colored American Day at the 1894 Midwinter International Exposition because some perceived it as "a needless drawing of the color line." Yet he argues that the day in fact "allowed them to demonstrate appreciation of their historical and cultural tradition through speeches, songs and a dance in the evening." Daniels, *Pioneer Urbanites*, 120.

106. "No Negro Day for Us"; and "Do We Want a Negro Day?"

107. "Negro Day at PPIE," *Western Outlook* (Oakland CA), April 3, 1915.

108. Wilson, *Negro Building.*

109. "Jim Crow Day at PPIE," *Western Outlook* (Oakland CA), May 15, 1915.

110. "Resolutions that Ring True," *Western Outlook* (Oakland CA), April 24, 1915.

111. "Resolution," *Western Outlook* (Oakland CA), May 1, 1915.

112. "From Rev. Newman," *Western Outlook* (Oakland CA), May 1, 1915.

113. "The Following from . . . ," *Western Outlook* (Oakland CA), May 1, 1915.

114. Wilson, *Negro Building*, 147.

115. Hudson, "'This Is Our Fair,'" 26–45.

116. See Broussard, *Black San Francisco*, 76–79, for a description of the community's successful mobilization against *Birth of a Nation.*

117. "Prayer Opens World Fair," *Monitor*, February 27, 1915.

118. "Padres' Days Live Again," *Monitor*, July 24, 1915.

119. "Mass at Exposition," *Monitor*, August 28, 1915.

120. Gendzel, "Pioneers and Padres."

121. "Notes on the conference had by Dr. Skiff with Dr. H.H. Bell, secretary of the Committee of One Hundred for Religious Work," July 17, 1914, "Religion," carton 16, PPIE-BL; Executive Secretary to T. Hardee, July 5, 1915, "Religion," carton 16, PPIE-BL; Hardee to Moore, June 18, 1915, Executive Sub-Committee, June 3, 1915–June 24, 1915, carton 29, PPIE-BL; and Executive Sub-Committee to Hardee, June 18, 1915, Executive Sub-Committee, June 3, 1915–June 24, 1915, carton 29, PPIE-BL.

122. "Calendar of Special Days and Special Events Scheduled from July 1st to December 4th," Days: Calendar, PPIE-SFPL.

123. "Chinese Students Day at the Panama-Pacific International Exposition," Cardinell-Vincent Co., reproduced on the cover of Chinn's *Bridging the Pacific.*

124. "Far East Students at Exposition," *San Francisco Chronicle*, August 5, 1915.

125. "March 17th to Be Fair's Great Event," *Leader*, March 6, 1915.

126. "Wearers of the Green Loyally Celebrate Saint's Day," *San Francisco Chronicle*, March 18, 1915.

127. "The 17th Was a Big Day," *Leader*, March 20, 1915.

128. "Mass Meeting," *Western Outlook* (Oakland CA), May 29, 1915; and "Alameda County Day Committee," *Oakland Sunshine*, June 5, 1915.

129. "Mass Meeting"; and "Should We Take Part in Alameda County Day at the Exposition," *Oakland Sunshine*, May 29, 1915.

130. Editorial, *Oakland Sunshine*, June 12, 1915.

131. Editorial, *Western Outlook* (Oakland CA), December 6, 1915.

132. Hudson, "'This Is Our Fair,'" 41.

133. Todd, *Story of the Exposition*, 5:100–121.

134. On Chinese women in San Francisco see Yung, *Unbound Feet.*

135. Marvin Nathan, "Visiting the World's Columbian Exposition at Chicago in July 1893: A Personal View," *Journal of American Culture* 19 (1996): 79–102.

136. Yung, *Unbound Voices*, 271.

137. Yung, *Unbound Voices*, 270.

138. Yung, *Unbound Voices*, 287.

139. T. Tatsumi to Moore, February 25, 1915, Correspondence Re. Complaints, carton 8, PPIE-BL.

140. T. Tatsumi to Moore, July 16, 1915, Correspondence Re. Complaints, carton 8, PPIE-BL.

141. "Refused by Our Own," *Western Outlook* (Oakland CA), March 6, 1915. See also "Extracts from the Daily Reports of the Guards, August 1915," August 19, 1915, carton 83, PPIE-BL.

142. Taussig to Burt, February 25, 1915, Correspondence Re. Complaints, carton 8, PPIE-BL.

143. Photograph captioned "Fair's Latest Love," *San Francisco Call and Post*, September 23, 1915, section 2, 1.

144. For a discussion of the way in which photographs of the San Francisco Chinese were manipulated to construct a sense of "foreignness," see Moy, *Marginal Sights*.

4. ECONOMIC PARTNER, EXOTIC OTHER

1. Doris Barr Stanislawski, Diary, vol. 6, Barr Stanislawski Papers.

2. Report of the speech made by Dr. Frederick James V. Skiff before the Assembly Judiciary Committee, April 2, 1913, Correspondence—Alien Land Law, carton 61, PPIE-BL.

3. "Panama-Pacific International Exposition, San Francisco 1915," Exhibits-Info., Advance, PPIE-SFPL.

4. Hunt, *Making of a Special Relationship*.

5. "Report to accompany HJ Res. 213, Calendar No. 1063, Senate, 'Panama-Pacific International Exposition,' Feb. 9, 1911," submitted by Mr. Jones, copy in Mechanics' Institute Library.

6. "Will Keep Up Bar against Japanese; Taft Assures Pacific Senators that Treaty Change Will Not Harm Exclusion Policy," *New York Times*, January 28, 1911. On the treaty, see Ichihashi, *Japanese in the United States*, 253–60. Many were concerned that the treaty threatened the exclusionary practices set up in the Gentlemen's Agreement. See also "Treaty with Japan Angers California; Resolution against It Passed by State Senate Unanimously and without Discussion," *New York Times*, February 23, 1911; and "California Not Yet Reassured by Taft; Two Messages Regarding New Japanese Treaty Fail to Prevent Attack in Legislature," *New York Times*, February 24, 1911.

7. Lee, "The Contradictions of Cosmopolitanism," 279.

8. On anti-Asian sentiment see Takaki, *Iron Cages*; Takaki, *Strangers from a Different Shore*; Saxton, *Indispensable Enemy*; Daniels, *Asian America*; and Chinn, *Bridging the Pacific*.

9. Ichihashi, *Japanese in the United States*, 230. On the relationship between racial formation, health, and the Chinese in San Francisco, see Shah, *Contagious Divides*; and Risse, *Plague, Fear, and Politics*.

10. Speakers at the meeting included Mayor James Phelan and Professor Edward Alsworth Ross of Stanford. Report of mass meeting in San Francisco, California, May 8, 1900, quoted in I.C. Reports, 23:167, in Ichihashi, *Japanese in the United States*, 231.

11. Fradkin, *Great Earthquake*; and Pan, *Impact of the 1906 Earthquake*.

12. Ichihashi, *Japanese in the United States*, 234–36.

13. For the participation of these nations at earlier fairs, see: Christ, "Sole Guardians," 675–709; Christ, "Japan's Seven Acres," 2–15; Vennman, "Dragons, Dummies, and Royals," 16–31; Edwards, "Imperial East," 32–41; Clevenger, "Through Western Eyes," 42–45; Harris, "All the World a Melting Pot?," in *Cultural Excursions*, 29–55; and Lockyer, "Japan at the Exhibition," in Umesao, Lockyer, and Yoshida, *Collection and Representation*, 17:67–76.

14. "Relations with Orient Helped by Exposition," *San Francisco Chronicle*, January 15, 1915.

15. Kyokwai, *Japan and Her Exhibits*, 3.

16. Lockyer, "Japan at the Exhibition," 209.

17. Matsuzo Nagai to Charles C. Moore, August 8, 1911, Japan 1911–1913, carton 63, PPIE-BL.

18. "De Young Finds Interest," *International Fair Illustrated* 1, no. 4 (1912): 21, copy in Mechanics' Institute Library.

19. Levy, *Chronological History*.

20. C. S. Chan to C. C. Moore, January 27, 1912, China, May 1910–October 1913, carton 61, PPIE-BL. See also "An Account of the Work Accomplished by the Chinese Government Commission to the Panama-Pacific International Exposition," China, May–December 1914, carton 61, PPIE-BL.

21. Robert E. Connolly to C. C. Moore, September 10, 1912, China, May 1910–October 1913, carton 61, PPIE-BL. This series of correspondence includes a series of clippings from two Southern California papers that reported that the Chinese government was considering switching its exhibit from San Francisco to San Diego because of the anti-Chinese activities in San Francisco. "Chinese Plan to Switch Exhibit," *San Diego Union*, September 5, 1912; and "May Lose Its Glory," *Pasadena News*, September 5, 1912.

22. "Advocating the Pro-Japanese Sentiment," *Japanese American News*, September 22, 1912, with translation by Ben Rosenberg.

23. Moore to Secretary of State Philander Knox, October 3, 1912, U.S. Agencies (primarily State Dept.), carton 39, PPIE-BL. I was unable to determine the content of the offensive billboards.

24. Nagai to Moore, September 25, 1912, folder 30, carton 2, PPIE-BL. The sequence of this letter and the one to Knox suggests that they were related, although there is no mention of the billboards in Nagai's letter.

25. Nagai to Moore, September 25, 1912, folder 30, carton 2, PPIE-BL.

26. Shima to Moore, December 23, 1912, folder 1, carton 139, PPIE-BL.

27. To Shima, n.d., folder 1, carton 139, PPIE-BL.

28. David Starr Jordan to President William H. Taft, January 26, 1912, folder 2, carton 139, PPIE-BL.

29. Ichihashi, *Japanese in the United States*, 261–82.

30. Olin, *California's Prodigal Sons*, 83. The Democratic, Republican, and Socialist Parties all included anti-Asian language in their platforms. Ichihashi, *Japanese in the United States*, 252.

31. Olin, *California's Prodigal Sons*, 84–85.

32. Daniels, "The Progressives Draw the Color Line," in Daniels and Olin, *Racism in California*, 120–27.

33. Moore to J. B. Boynton, January 6, 1913, folder 3, carton 139, PPIE-BL.

34. F. C. Tognazzini to C. J. Rector, January 6, 1913, folder 2, carton 139, PPIE-BL.

35. Daniels, "The Progressives Draw the Color Line," in Daniels and Olin, *Racism in California*, 127.

36. "Report of the Proceedings of the Deputation from the Panama-Pacific International Exposition which proceeded to Sacramento, 2 April 1913," California Alien Land Law, carton 61, PPIE-BL.

37. Hichborn, *Story of the Session*, 227.

38. Hiram Johnson, quoted in Daniels, "Progressives Draw the Color Line," 129.

39. Ralph Newman, quoted in Daniels, "Progressives Draw the Color Line," 129.

40. Hichborn, *Story of the Session*, 229.

41. Hichborn, *Story of the Session*, 234.

42. Hichborn, *Story of the Session*, 233.

43. "Exposition Trouble," *Leader*, February 8. 1913.

44. Knight, *Industrial Relations*, 239. Factions within the San Francisco labor community, however, voiced their unhappiness about the fair's relationship with Asia. See H. F. McMahon to SFLC [San Francisco Labor Council], Anti-Jap Laundry League, carton 2, San Francisco Labor Council Papers.

45. "Save the Tea-Garden!," *Sacramento Union*, January 8, 1913, copy in Japan-California Papers, carton 63, PPIE-BL.

46. B. P. Schmidt to C. C. Moore, April 28, 1913, PPIE Papers, Complaints, carton 9, PPIE-BL.

47. Japanese Association of America to Moore, December 19, 1912, folder 1, carton 139, PPIE-BL.

48. Moore to George Shima, January 14, 1913, folder 1, carton 139, PPIE-BL.

49. For the Japanese diplomatic response to the laws, see Ichihashi, *Japanese in the United States*, 271–76.

50. Ira Bennett to Charles Moore, February 12, 1915, folder 2, carton 139, PPIE-BL.

51. Memo, heading reads "Vancouver BC, March 19, 1913," California Alien Land Law, carton 61, PPIE-BL.

52. Charles C. Moore to Chester H. Rowell, April 12, 1913, California Alien Land Law, carton 61, PPIE-BL.

53. "California Scheme Angers Japanese," *New York Herald*, April 9, 1913; and "Irritation in Japan," *New York Herald*, April 10, 1913—both found in California Alien Land Law, carton 61, PPIE-BL.

54. Olin, *California's Prodigal Sons*, 85.

55. Y. Numano to Moore, September 10, 1913, Moore Personal Correspondence N-R, carton 11, PPIE-BL.

56. Charles Moore to Ira E. Bennett, May 7, 1913, Correspondence, May 1913—Alien Land Law, carton 61, PPIE-BL.

57. Ira E. Bennet to Charles Moore, May 9, 1913, Correspondence, May 1913—Alien Land Law, carton 61, PPIE-BL.

58. Moore to K. S. Inui, May 13, 1913, folder 4, carton 139, PPIE-BL.

59. "Urge Japanese to Send Exhibit," Japan 1911–13, carton 63, PPIE-BL.

60. George W. Guthrie to Secretary of State, December 10, 1913, Japan 1914, carton 63, PPIE-BL.

61. Moore to Shima, January 26, 1914, folder 3, carton 139, PPIE-BL.

62. President's Daily Letter, January 3, 1914, folder 27, carton 17, PPIE-BL.

63. Minutes of the Executive Committee, June 16, 1914, vol. 125, PPIE-BL.

64. Sue Bradford Edwards argues that such events for visiting Chinese delegations affected the way that the Chinese were perceived in St. Louis in 1902. Edwards, "Imperial East," 37–41.

65. Paul S. Reinsch to William Jennings Bryan, December 15, 1913, China, November 1913–April 1914, carton 61, PPIE-BL. See also Chen, *Chinese San Francisco*, 152; and Edwards, "Imperial East," 39.

66. Edwards, "Imperial East," 39.

67. Edwards, "Imperial East," 39; and Ngai, *Lucky Ones*.

68. Paul S. Reinsch to William Jennings Bryan, December 2, 1913, China, May 1910–October 1913, carton 51, PPIE-BL.

69. "Regulation Governing the Admission and Return of Chinese Participating in the Panama-Pacific International Exposition," Hale, Reuben B., carton 16,

PPIE-BL; and General Attorney to Director-in-Chief, July 16, 1914, folder 13, carton 169, PPIE-BL.

70. C. I. Sagara to C. C. Moore, May 20, 1914, Foreign Immigration, carton 39, PPIE-BL.

71. To F. Skiff, July 6, 1914, folder 24, carton 169, PPIE-BL.

72. Executive Secretary to Vice President Hale, February 16, 1914, Japan 1914, carton 63, PPIE-BL.

73. Samuel W. Backus to T. G. Smallsmith, June 27, 1914, China, May–December 1914, PPIE-BL.

74. "The Forbidden City at the Exposition," *San Francisco Chronicle*, May 2, 1915, Sunday Magazine.

75. "Japan's Exhibit Is True to Life," *San Francisco Chronicle*, February 21, 1915. See also Jiro Harada, "Japan at the Panama-Pacific International Exposition," *San Francisco Chronicle*, February 21,1915.

76. Rast, "Cultural Politics of Tourism," 29–60.

77. Elbert Hubbard, "The Cheerful Loser Is a Winner," *International Fair Illustrated* 1 (December 1911): 14.

78. See Lee, *Picturing Chinatown*, 149–200, for a discussion of the changing nature of Chinatown and its relationship to tourists and the city.

79. *San Francisco Standard Guide*.

80. Look Tin Eli, "Our New Oriental City—Veritable Fairy Palaces Filled with the Choicest Treasures of the Orient," in *San Francisco: The Metropolis of the West* (San Francisco: Western Press Association, 1910), n.p.

81. On images of Chinatown, see Lee, *Picturing Chinatown*; and Rast, "Cultural Politics of Tourism."

82. This approach stands in direct contrast to the situation Lee identifies in Seattle. She argues that the rhetoric surrounding the fair deliberately denied any chance that the Japanese could become citizens. Lee, "Contradictions of Cosmopolitanism," 290.

83. *San Francisco Standard Guide*.

84. "Breathing Vitality into Sterile Soil," *San Francisco Chronicle*, January 16, 1915.

85. Vennman, "Dragons, Dummies, and Royals," 18.

86. Todd, *Story of the Exposition*, 3:291–92, 289–90.

87. Todd, *Story of the Exposition*, 3:291–92.

88. "Modern Transportation and Communications in the Republic of China," Report presented by Mr. C. T. Hsia, special commissioner to the Ministry of Communications of Peking, China, to the Panama-Pacific International Exposition, Palace of Transportation, n.d. Copy in Mechanics' Institute Library.

89. For discussions of Japanese participation at earlier fairs, see Christ, "Sole Guardians"; Christ, "Japan's Seven Acres"; Clevenger, "Through Western Eyes"; and Harris, "All the World a Melting Pot?"

90. Panama-Pacific International Exposition Company, *Official Guide*, 85. Like China, Japan also showcased its modern forms of transportation at the exposition, as a pamphlet on its railways reveals. See "Japan: Imperial Government Railways," Japan, PPIE-SFPL.

91. Kyokwai, *Japan and Her Exhibits*, 161–67.

92. "Oriental Has Parable for Occidentals," *San Francisco Examiner*, March 7, 1915.

93. "Japanese Celebrate on Their New Year's Day," *San Francisco Chronicle*, February 12, 1915; "To Observe Old Japanese Holiday," *San Francisco Chronicle*, March 2, 1915; and "Japan to Celebrate Festival of Iris," *San Francisco Chronicle*, May 2, 1915.

94. "Japan's Ideal as Seen at Exposition," *San Francisco Chronicle*, April 9, 1915.

95. "Republic's Hymn Rings over Fair," *San Francisco Examiner*, March 10, 1915.

96. "Republic's Hymn"; and "Chinese Dedicate Building Today: Boys and Girls of Flowery Kingdom Will Sing in English," *San Francisco Chronicle*, March 9, 1915.

97. "No Orientalism for Chinese Programme," *San Francisco Chronicle*, September 23, 1915.

98. "Friendship of China for U.S. Is Emphasized," *San Francisco Chronicle*, September 24, 1915.

99. "Far East Students at the Exposition," *San Francisco Chronicle*, August 5, 1915.

100. Special Events to L. Cassassa, September 25, 1915, folder 20, carton 143, PPIE-BL; and Mr. Levy to Mr. Kingsley, August 28, 1915, folder 20, carton 143, PPIE-BL.

101. "Exposition Honors Japan: Great Celebration Planned," *San Francisco Chronicle*, February 12, 1915.

102. "Unique Features for Japan's Day," *San Francisco Chronicle*, February 23, 1915.

103. Ambassador Kato, quoted in Lockyer, "Japan at the Exhibition," 137–38.

104. Photograph, no title, *San Francisco Examiner*, May 6, 1915.

105. "Japanese Celebrate on Their New Year's Day," *San Francisco Chronicle*, February 12, 1915. See also "Society Women Guests at Japanese Doll Fete," *San Francisco Examiner*, March 4, 1915.

106. Cherubim A. Quizon and Patricia O. Afable, "Rethinking Display of Filipinos at St. Louis: Embracing Heartbreak and Irony," *Philippine Studies* 52 (2004): 439–44.

107. "Panama-Pacific International Exposition 1915," Exhibits: Info, Advance, PPIE-SFPL.

108. Herbert P. Woodin to Moore, February 17, 1913, Liquor and Red-Light Abatement, carton 23, PPIE-BL.

109. *San Francisco Standard Guide*.

110. Panama-Pacific International Exposition, *Facts for Boosters*, "Population" section, Bancroft Library.

111. Potter and Gray, *Lure of San Francisco*, 62.

112. That the book had an ulterior motive is made clear in the preface, which reads in part: "May this little book aid in the general awakening of the dormant love of every Californian for his possessions and be a suggestion to the casual visitor that we are entitled to the dignity of age." Potter and Gray, *Lure of San Francisco*, n.p.

113. "Greetings to Our Chinese Guests," *San Francisco Examiner*, May 6, 1915, editorial page; and "Elaine Is Liberated by Her Chinese Captors," *San Francisco Examiner*, May 3, 1915.

114. "Chinese Tong War Brought to an End," *San Francisco Chronicle*, April 27, 1915; and "Tongs Peace May Be Only Short-Lived," *San Francisco Chronicle*, April 28, 1915.

115. See Lee, *Orientals*, 83–105, for a discussion of the ways in which white Americans perceived Asians as a sexual threat.

116. "Japan's Plans to Invade and Conquer the United States Revealed by Its Own 'Bernhardi,'" *San Francisco Examiner*, American Magazine section, October 3 and October 10, 1915. My thanks to Robert Chase for pointing me to these articles.

117. "Japan Artistic and Japan Beautiful at the Panama-Pacific Int. Exp," Japan, PPIE-SFPL.

118. My thanks to Constance Chen for this formulation of Western images of a "Japan that did not exist."

119. Rydell, *All the World's a Fair*, 228.

120. See Lockyer, "Japan at the Exhibition," in Umesao, Lockyer, and Yoshida, *Collection and Representations*, for a clear articulation of this dilemma for Japan.

5. SEX AND OTHER VICES AT THE FAIR

1. Harry Thiederman to Moore, n.d., Protests against Certain Concessions, carton 23, PPIE-BL.

2. On concerns about morality and the city during the Progressive Era, see Boyer, *Urban Masses*.

3. Boyer, *Urban Masses*. On female moral reformers see Pascoe, *Relations of Rescue*; Scott, *Natural Allies*; and Frankel and Dye, *Gender, Class*.

4. Frederick P. Church to Moore, February 18, 1913, Liquor and Red-Light Abatement, carton 23, PPIE-BL.

5. "Warning, the Women of San Francisco," Panama-Pacific International Exposition Pamphlets, Bancroft Library.

6. See Simpson, *Problems Women Solved*, for the discussion of this issue and the story of one of these "lost" women, 62–66.

7. See Boyd, *Wide-Open Town*, for an excellent overview of the evolution of San Francisco's vice district and the city's reputation as a "wide-open town."

8. "'Barbary Coast' Menaced," *New York Times*, September 15, 1913.

9. Captain Meagher quoted in *San Francisco Argonaut* 71 (December 14, 1912): 389.

10. Gendzel, "Vigilantes and Boosters," 282.

11. John D. Barry column, *San Francisco Bulletin*, March 22, 1912.

12. Woods, "A Penchant for Probity," in Deverell and Sitton, *California Progressivism Revisited*, 102.

13. For the history of Chinese prostitutes in San Francisco, see Tong, *Unsubmissive Women*.

14. For a brief discussion of the Woman's Christian Temperance Union's crusade against midway shows, see Parker, *Purifying America*, 129–32.

15. Panama-Pacific International Exposition Company, *California Invites the World*.

16. For a discussion of this phenomenon in the Bay Area (Oakland) in the 1910s and 1920s, see Odem, *Delinquent Daughters*, especially chapter 2.

17. Sharon Ullman demonstrates that young working-class women did engage in sex for pay in Northern California in ways that challenged middle-class norms and the traditional images of "the prostitute." Ullman, *Sex Seen*, 103–36. For discussions of working-class attitudes toward sexuality in a broader context, see Meyerowitz, *Women Adrift*; Stansell, *City of Women*; Peiss, *Cheap Amusements*; and Hunter, *To 'Joy My Freedom*. Mary Odem, however, reminds us not to overemphasize the difference between working- and middle-class sexual mores. Many working-class parents, for instance, valued female chastity just as highly as did middle-class parents. Moreover, such attitudes were contingent on religious and ethnic background. Odem, *Delinquent Daughters*, 38–47.

18. D'Emilio and Freedman, *Intimate Matters*, 196–97. See also Mumford, *Interzones*.

19. Ullman, *Sex Seen*, 136.

20. At least one nonwhite male worker did behave in a way that was deemed inappropriate toward white women, and he was fired. See Frank Burt to Cumming, September 3, 1915, Correspondence Re. Complaints, carton 8, PPIE-BL.

21. Rosen, *Lost Sisterhood*, 113; and Connolly, *Response to Prostitution*, 118.

22. For discussions of women's organizations during the Progressive Era, see Scott, *Natural Allies*. For an excellent discussion of "female moral authority" in the American West, including San Francisco, see Pascoe, *Relations of Rescue*.

23. Luker, "Sex, Social Hygiene," 611. For more on female reformers' work with young women in particular, see Odem, *Delinquent Daughters*.

24. See Gullett, "City Mothers," in Harris and McNamara, *Women and the Structure of Society*, for a discussion of women's political organizations in the city immediately following suffrage.

25. *The Record of the Young Women's Christian Association of San Francisco* 2 (1913): 2, copy in San Francisco and Marin YWCA Archives. See also "Befriending Young Girls," *Monitor*, March 20, 1915; "The Society for Befriending Girls," *Monitor*, November 6, 1915; "Society for Befriending Girls Really Does That," *San Francisco Chronicle*, April 6, 1915; and "Society for Befriending Girls," Working Girls—Restrooms and Quarters, carton 23, PPIE-BL.

26. Moore to Rev. Charles N. Lathrop, January 15, 1915, Complaints—immorality, moral standards, carton 9, PPIE-BL.

27. See *History of the San Francisco Young Women's Christian Association*, San Francisco and Marin YWCA Archives, for more information on earlier Traveler's Aid work.

28. "Survey of Traveler's Aid Work," Traveler's Aid Society of California, carton 10, Hearst Papers.

29. The Catholic Society for Befriending Girls also established a presence on the fairgrounds, staffing a rest room in the Palace of Horticulture in an attempt to provide amusement and resources for working women and for visitors.

30. Panama-Pacific International Exposition Company, *Condensed Facts*, copy in Pamphlets, PPIE-SFPL.

31. Phoebe Hearst biographer Alexandra Nickliss paints the relationship in glowing terms, glossing over the conflicts that erupted between the two groups. One reason may be that she ignores the conflicts that arose over the Joy Zone, and they were the clearest indication that the PPIE board was not interested in supporting the social goals of the Woman's Board. See Nickliss, "Phoebe Apperson Hearst." See also Ethington, *The Public City*, 368.

32. "The Board of Lady Managers may be made . . . ," folder 48, box 5, Hale Papers.

33. Gavin McNab to PPIE Board of Directors, October 24, 1911, "Women's Affairs," carton 71, PPIE-BL.

34. Curtis H. Lindley to John A. Britton, October 27, 1911, "Women's Affairs," carton 71, PPIE-BL.

35. Executive Secretary Cummings reported to Moore in relation to the episode: "Mrs. Lewandowski submitted an agreement to us in connection with the 'Woman's Affairs,' and it was submitted to Mr. McNab and Mr. Metson. Both of them, without the knowledge of the other, fell on the agreement and smote it, hip and thigh. Then for good measure, jumped on it some more. They are both opposed to the whole proposition and claim it is very dangerous to delegate any powers to any outside corporation." J. M. Cumming to Moore, October 27, 1911, J. M. Cumming correspondence with Charles C. Moore, carton 39, PPIE-BL.

36. Helen P. Sanborn to Committee on Women's Affairs, November 15, 1911, folder 48, box 5, Hale Papers.

37. Chairman, Committee on Women's Affairs, to Board of Directors, December 12, 1911, San Francisco—PPIE 1915, carton 10, Hearst Papers.

38. Helen P. Sanborn to Hale, March 6, 1915, folder 48, box 5, Hale Papers.

39. Helen P. Sanborn to R. B. Hale, September 27, 1914, Women's Affairs, carton 71, PPIE-BL.

40. Helen P. Sanborn to R. B. Hale, October 4, 1914, Women's Affairs, carton 71, PPIE-BL.

41. Helen P. Sanborn to My dear Muttchen [Phoebe Hearst], undated, box 46, Hearst Papers, cited in Nickliss, "Phoebe Apperson Hearst," 335. Emphasis in the original.

42. Cassie Hitchcock to Cumming, December 29, 1914, Correspondence with City Clubs and Organizations, carton 22, PPIE-BL.

43. Executive Secretary, Exposition Committee of YWCA, to H. D. H. Connick, December 19, 1913, YWCA (#4), carton 10, Hearst Papers.

44. Minutes of Director's Meeting of the Traveler's Aid Society of California, March 26, 1915, Traveler's Aid Society of California, carton 10, Hearst Papers.

45. Anna Pratt Simpson to Rueben Brooks Hale, March 29, 1915, Women's Affairs, carton 71, PPIE-BL.

46. President's Weekly Letter to Directors, March 28, 1913, folder 11M, box 30, Rolph Papers.

47. Helen Bary, "Bills before California's Legislature," *Woman's Bulletin*, April 1913; and "Items of California's Legislative Session, 1912–13," *Woman's Bulletin*, June 1913.

48. Hichborn, *Story of the Session*, 290.

49. B. H. Winsland to Moore, February 17, 1913, Liquor and Red-Light Abatement, carton 23, PPIE-BL.

50. According to Franklin Hichborn, Progressive press correspondent, one of the names of the Woman's Board members that he read as an example of support of the measure was that of Annie Bidwell, who later informed the Senate that she had no knowledge of the resolutions and would not have supported them had she known of them. See Hichborn, *Story of the Session*, 290–91n280.

51. Hichborn, *Story of the Session*, 292. By February 1913, Moore's office had received ninety-one letters from eighteen states, as well as a few from Canada. President's Weekly Letter to Directors, February 25, 1913, folder 11M, box 30, Rolph Papers.

52. The groups included the California Federation of Women's Clubs, the California Civic League, the California Mother's Congress, the Women's Parliament, the Alameda County Welfare League, the Social Workers of Central California, the Juvenile Protective Association of San Francisco, and the Council of Women, as well as numerous churches. "Objections Answered, Leaflet No. 8," Red-Light Injunction, carton 9, Hearst Papers.

53. Teresa Hurley and Jarrod Harrison, "Awed by the Women's Clubs: Women Voters and Moral Reform, 1913–1914," in Cherny, Irwin, and Wilson, *California Women and Politics*, 242.

54. Shumsky, "Tacit Acceptance," 665–79.

55. Hichborn, *Story of the Session*, 322.

56. "The Red Light Injunction and Abatement Law, Leaflet No. 5," Red-Light Abatement, carton 9, Hearst Papers.

57. George S. Wheeler to Moore, February 17, 1913, Liquor and Red-Light Abatement, carton 23, PPIE-BL.

58. Edward S. Lee to Moore, February 15, 1913, Liquor and Red-Light Abatement, carton 23, PPIE-BL. See other letters in this folder for other examples from across the nation.

59. Hichborn, *Story of the Session*, 338.

60. "Redlight Is Given Curb by Senate," *San Francisco Examiner*, March 29, 1913.

61. See Rydell and Kroes, *Buffalo Bill in Bologna*, 68.

62. Panama-Pacific International Exposition Company, *California Invites the World*.

63. See Moore to Rev. Charles N. Lathrop, January 25, 1915, Complaints—immorality, moral standards, carton 9, PPIE-BL.

64. The committee rejected the first proposal for the '49 Camp because of "objectionable features" and only approved the project after they were removed. The members also approved a public dance hall pending a guarantee of "absolutely genteel" conduct. Minutes of Committee on Concessions and Admissions, December 2, 1912, and March 23, 1914, vol. 122, PPIE-BL.

65. "Warnings to Girls from San Francisco," *Survey* 34 (1915): 39; "The Y.W.C.A. at Work in the Joy Zone," *Survey* 34 (1915): 389; and "Facts on Vice in San Francisco," *Survey* 34 (1915).

66. "Immorality at Panama Exposition," *Manitoba Free Press*, March 25, 1915, copy in Protests against Certain Concessions, carton 23, PPIE-BL.

67. Johnson, "Moral Conditions," 589–609.

68. Helen Dare, "Misrepresenting San Francisco," *San Francisco Chronicle*, April 11, 1915.

69. Dare, "Misrepresenting San Francisco."

70. Helen Dare, "Strained Relations between the Clubman and the Lady," *San Francisco Chronicle*, September 8, 1915.

71. Dare, "Strained Relations."

72. See Gullett, "City Mothers," in Harris and McNamara, *Women and the Structure of Society*, 150–51, for a discussion of women's political organizations in the city immediately following suffrage.

73. Gullett, "City Mothers," in Harris and McNamara, *Women and the Structure of Society*.

74. "Fair Question Fairly Answered," *San Francisco Examiner*, April 1, 1915.

75. "Coast Lid Floats on Heavy Sea of Liquor," *San Francisco Examiner*, April 11, 1915.

76. "Demand Is Made that Low Dives Be Closed," *San Francisco Examiner*, April 10, 1915.

77. "Barbary Coast under Scrutiny," *San Francisco Chronicle*, June 12, 1915; and "Coast Dives Condemned in Report," *San Francisco Examiner*, June 9, 1915.

78. "Divekeepers Defeated in Evading Law," *San Francisco Examiner*, June 15, 1915.

79. "Now It's Up to the Police Board," *San Francisco Examiner*, June 13, 1915.

80. "Says Dance Halls Need Regulation," *San Francisco Chronicle*, March 20, 1915; and "Penny Dance Will Be Opened Next Month," *San Francisco Chronicle*, March 29, 1915.

81. "A Stockholder" to C. C. Moore, September 22, 1915, Complaints, carton 9, PPIE-BL.

82. "Girl Shows Closed by the Purity Censors," *San Francisco Chronicle*, October 8, 1915.

83. "The Morals of San Francisco," *Sunset* 34 (1915): 853–56.

84. Editorial, *Monitor*, March 20, 1915; and "Talking over San Francisco," *Monitor*, May 22, 1915.

85. "A friend of long standing" to Moore, June 16, 1915, Protests against Certain Concessions, carton 23, PPIE-BL.

86. Frances G. Gilmore to Moore, July 18, 1915, Protests against Certain Concessions, carton 23, PPIE-BL.

87. See Julia George to Moore, July 16, 1915, Protests against Certain Concessions, carton 23, PPIE-BL, for report on the situation at Streets of Cairo specifically.

88. Albert W. Palmer to C. C. Moore, October 6, 1915, Protests against Certain Concessions, carton 23, PPIE-BL.

89. Untitled report, begins "After this talk the crowd," Protests against Certain Concessions, carton 23, PPIE-BL.

90. See Ullman, *Sex Seen*, for a discussion of this conflict.

91. "'49 Camp's Sad, Lid on Gambling," *San Francisco Examiner*, April 13, 1915.

92. Albert W. Palmer to C. C. Moore, October 6, 1915, Protests against Certain Concessions, carton 23, PPIE-BL.

93. "Cairo Streets Closed by Woman's Board," *San Francisco Examiner*, August 1, 1915; and "Biff! Goes the Lid on this Oriental Joy Zone Concession," *San Francisco Chronicle*, August 20, 1915.

94. Minutes of Committee on Concessions and Admissions, June 14, 1915, and June 21, 1915, vol. 123, PPIE-BL.

95. Mary S. Merrill to Moore, July 23, 1915, Protests against Certain Concessions, carton 23, PPIE-BL.

96. Waitresses were forbidden from soliciting customers in front of the cafe, drinking with customers, or smoking in public. They also were forbidden from conversing with customers, except to take orders and deliver food, and the café was to close at midnight exactly. Minutes of the Committee on Concessions and Admissions, August 9, 1915, and August 30, 1915, vol. 123, PPIE-BL.

97. Minutes of the Committee on Concessions and Admissions, August 9, 1915, and August 30, 1915, vol. 123, PPIE-BL.

98. Elizabeth Wilson, "By the Fountain of Energy," *Association Monthly* 9 (1915): 428.

99. Gullett argues that after San Francisco women forced the closure of city dance halls in 1913, one report indicated that "dance hall girls rejected the offers of assistance because they valued the independence of their work." Their stance put them in opposition to female reformers, who viewed their activities as dangerous and immoral. Gullett, "City Mothers," in Harris and McNamara, *Women and the Structure of Society*, 158.

100. See Pascoe, *Relations of Rescue*, for a discussion of the invention of "female moral authority."

101. Although in many urban centers elite men united to oppose obscenity, this phenomenon did not occur in San Francisco. Nicola Beisel explores a similar phenomenon in Philadelphia in her "Class, Culture, and Campaigns," 44–62. Gerald Woods argues that it was San Francisco's immigrant, working-class culture that in fact kept alive a tolerance for vice. Woods, "A Penchant for Probity," in Deverell and Sitton, *California Progressivism Revisited*, 96–116.

102. Leigh Ann Wheeler examines debates over vice in Minneapolis in the 1920s after the enfranchisement of women and argues that male opposition to female anti-obscenity reform was motivated by the desire to defeat female political power. Wheeler, "Battling over Burlesque," 149.

103. The commission comprised Matt I. Sullivan, Marshall Stimson, Chester H. Rowell, and Arthur Arlett, all Progressive Party members appointed by Governor Johnson. See *California Blue Book, 1913–1915* (Sacramento: California State Printing Office, 1915), 486–87, for biographical sketches of each man. The State Commission was the body appointed to oversee the spending of the funds raised through the state bond issue, which passed in November of 1910, for an amount that totaled $5 million. The commission was charged with ensuring that the money was expended to "establish, maintain, operate and support the Exposition." The Exposition Company thus applied to the commission for funds, and the commission had to approve all expenditures of the money. Todd notes that the relationship between the two bodies was harmonious, but this particular episode suggests otherwise. Todd, *Story of the Exposition*, 1:119–21.

104. Matt Sullivan to Board of Directors, September 21, 1915, Protests against Certain Concessions, carton 23, PPIE-BL.

105. "Says that '49 Camp Lid Will Stay Down," *San Francisco Examiner*, September 25, 1915.

106. "State's Protest Ends '49 Gaming," *San Francisco Examiner*, September 24, 1915; and "Committee Rules Gaming Tables out of '49 Camp," *San Francisco Chronicle*, September 24, 1915.

107. "Gaming Ended, Fair '49 Camp Shuts Its Gates," *San Francisco Examiner*, October 3, 1915.

108. "Fair Curtain to Drop on 'Girl Shows,'" *San Francisco Examiner*, October 7, 1915.

109. "Girl Shows Closed by the Purity Censors," *San Francisco Chronicle*, October 8, 1915.

110. Rowell continued, "We are told there is gambling in the Japan Beautiful, but do not know for certain. I believe it is alleged that theer [*sic*] is a gambling club of Zone employees. We will take any necessary steps to close any infringements of the law of which we are told if we find upon investigation that we are correctly informed." "Zone Is Minus Its Girl Shows," *San Francisco Examiner*, October 8, 1915.

6. PERFORMING WORK

1. "Adoption of White Babe Is Questioned," *San Francisco Chronicle*, April 14, 1915.

2. "Adoption of White Babe."

3. Princess Wenona's given name was Lillian Frances Smith, and she was a world-famous performer who had performed for Queen Victoria in 1887. Born in 1871, she was a bitter rival of Annie Oakley's and was touted as a Sioux Indian princess, but the reality of her heritage is unknown. Historian Michael Wallis asserts that she was Indian, since in the 1880 census she was labeled with an *I* for Indian. Record of her tribal affiliation, however, has not survived. It is unlikely that she was in fact Sioux, given that she was born in California. For more information on Smith, see Wallis, *The Real Wild West*, 309–16. See also WGBH, "Biography: Lillian Smith," *American Experience*, 2006, http://www.pbs.org/wgbh/americanexperience/features/biography/oakley-smith/.

4. "Fulfilling an Old Friendship Vow, Squaw Adopts Child of White Girl," April 29, 1915, *The Rockford Register Gazette*. Thank you to Julia Bricklin for pointing me to this article.

5. Dobkin, "A Twenty-Five-Million-Dollar Mirage," in Benedict, *Anthropology of World's Fairs*.

6. See Quizon and Afable, "Rethinking Display of Filipinos"; Parezo and Fowler, *Anthropology Goes to the Fair*; and Gilbert, *Whose Fair?*

7. The work of James Scott, Robin D. G. Kelly, Mona Domosh, and Tim Cresswell all inform my thinking here. Each offers ways to analyze an individual's behavior as a political act. See Kelley, "We Are Not What We Seem," 75–112; Domosh, "Those 'Gorgeous Incongruities,'" 209–26; and Cresswell, *In Place/Out of Place*, 9.

8. Kazin, *Barons of Labor*; and Issel and Cherny, *San Francisco*.

9. Dan P. Regan to John O'Connell, March 19, 1915, Labor Organizations and Trade Associations, carton 93, PPIE-BL.

10. Knight, *Industrial Relations*, 98–99. Philip Foner notes that "unskilled workers [in San Francisco] gained improvements in working conditions ordinarily enjoyed only by skilled craftsmen." See his *History of the Labor Movement*, 3:293.

11. Knight, *Industrial Relations*, 97.

12. Cobble, *Dishing It Out*, 61.

13. Baker, "A Corner in Labor."

14. Todd, *Story of the Exposition*, 1:325–30.

15. Moore responded to the agreement with the following statement: "Of course, you realized fully that being a public institution, we cannot, any more than can a Department of the Government, a State of the Union, or a municipality, make any agreements involving restrictive conditions, but your earnest and conscientious efforts to aid a work that is designed to be an expression of national sentiment and for public welfare, is most pleasing and causes us to feel encouraged in the belief that the difficulties encountered in previous Expositions will be eliminated and that the work can proceed along the lines of national credit and local pride and offer a guarantee of industrial satisfaction." Moore to Labor Council and Building Trades Council, September 7, 1912, Labor Conditions—Correspondence Re., carton 36, PPIE-BL.

16. C. W. Post to member of National Association of Manufacturers, September 30, 1912, Labor Conditions—Correspondence Re., carton 36, PPIE-BL.

17. Memorandum, undated attached to W. Francis to Moore, October 14, 1912, Correspondence with Clubs, Agencies, and Organizations, carton 22, PPIE-BL.

18. Panama-Pacific International Exposition Company, *Good Business Judgment*, copy in Bancroft Library.

19. Kazin, *Barons of Labor*, 229–30.

20. W. A. Jenkins to Connick, October 16, 1914, folder 20, carton 61, PPIE-BL.

21. Knight, *Industrial Relations*, 237.

22. See Miller, "Stockton Open Shop War"; Vaught, *Cultivating California*; and Daniel, *Bitter Harvest*.

23. *Labor Clarion*, January 15, 1915.

24. Dan P. Regan to John O'Connell, March 19, 1915, Labor Organizations and Trade Associations, carton 93, PPIE-BL.

25. Dan P. Regan to John O'Connell, March 19, 1915, Labor Organizations and Trade Associations, carton 93, PPIE-BL. See also "List of Steady Waitresses Who Were Employed at Vienna Café as Steady Waitresses," March 23, 1915; SFLC to H. D. H. Connick, March 14, 1915; and SFLC to Connick, March 26, 1915—all in San Francisco-PPIE, carton 16, San Francisco Labor Council Papers.

26. John A. O'Connell to H. D. H. Connick, March 31, 1915, Labor Organizations and Trade Associations, carton 93, PPIE-BL. The establishments he listed were Old Faithful Inn, Why Café, Waffle Kitchen, Marine Café, Nurenberg Café, Muller's Luxus Café, and the Inside Inn.

27. San Francisco Labor Council to H. D. H. Connick, March 29, 1915, San Francisco-PPIE, carton 16, San Francisco Labor Council Papers.

28. H. D. H. Connick to John O'Connell, March 31, 1915, San Francisco-PPIE, carton 16, San Francisco Labor Council Papers.

29. "Synopsis of Minutes of Regular Meeting Held April 9, 1915, SFLC," *Labor Clarion*, April 16, 1915.

30. "Synopsis of Minutes of Regular Meeting," *Labor Clarion*, April 23, 1915.

31. Laura Molleda to John O'Connell, April 29, 1915, Labor Organizations and Trade Associations, carton 93, PPIE-BL.

32. P. H. McCarthy to H. D. H. Connick, May 3, 1915, Labor Associations and Trade Associations, carton 93, PPIE-BL.

33. "Minutes of SFLC," *Labor Clarion*, May 21, 1915.

34. Knight, *Industrial Relations*, 270–71.

35. Little has been written about culinary workers in the city. The exception is Dorothy Sue Cobble's excellent work on waitresses, *Dishing It Out*, but she does not discuss relations between waitress locals and male trade union locals in the 1910s.

36. Knight, *Industrial Relations*, 291.

37. Koster, *Law and Order*, 5. See Gutman, *Work, Culture, and Society*; and Montgomery, *Fall of the House of Labor*, for introductions to this conflict between skilled and unskilled workers.

38. "Regulations for the Guidance of the Exposition Guards of the Panama-Pacific International Exposition," PPIE-CHS.

39. S. L. Mash to C. C. Moore, January 14, 1915, Racial Discrimination, Charges of, carton 23, PPIE-BL; and J. S. Tobin to Moore, January 25, 1915, Racial Discrimination, Charges of, carton 23, PPIE-BL.

40. Eugene Shelby to Hardee, January 6, 1915, folder 22, carton 89, PPIE-BL.

41. Todd, *Story of the Exposition*, 2:279.

42. Todd, *Story of the Exposition*, 2:279.

43. Bulletin to cashiers, March 14, 1915, in Extracts of Daily Reports of the Guards, March–April 1915, carton 83, PPIE-BL.

44. On changing public sexuality, see D'Emilio and Freedman, *Intimate Matters;* and Ullman, *Sex Seen.*

45. Meyerowitz, *Women Adrift;* Peiss, *Cheap Amusements;* and Hunter, *To 'Joy My Freedom.*

46. "'Let Us Look Pretty!' Cry Girls at Fair," *San Francisco Examiner,* June 12, 1915.

47. See Enstad, *Ladies of Labor;* Clark-Lewis, "'This Work Had a End,'" in Groneman and Norton, *"To Toil the Livelong Day,"* 202–3; Hunter, *To 'Joy My Freedom;* and Green, *Canal Builders.*

48. "Extracts from Daily Reports of the Guards for August 4, 1915," and "Extracts from Daily Reports of the Guards for August 20, 1915," in Extracts from Daily Reports of the Guards, August 1915, carton 83, PPIE-BL.

49. Benson, *Counter Cultures,* 135.

50. "Says Dance Halls Need Regulation," *San Francisco Chronicle,* March 20, 1915.

51. For a history of the work of working-girls' clubs such as that done by YWCA-sponsored one at the fair, see Murolo, *Common Ground.*

52. "Welfare Work at the Panama-Pacific International Exposition," Social Service, PPIE-SFPL.

53. "Report of Work: YWCA Building, Exposition Grounds, March 8, 1915," YWCA (#2), carton 10, Hearst Papers.

54. "Report of Work: YWCA Building, Exposition Grounds, March 8, 1915," YWCA (#2), carton 10, Hearst Papers.

55. *Mix and Server,* February 1920, 30, quoted in Cobble, *Dishing It Out,* 76.

56. Gullett, "City Mothers," in Harris and McNamara, *Women and the Structure of Society,* 158.

57. See Mumford, *Interzones,* for an excellent discussion of how anxieties about interracial sex permeated the Progressive Era (and after).

58. Bederman, *Manliness and Civilization,* 4. See pages 1–5 for a discussion of the ways in which prizefighter Jack Johnson's relationships with white women and his defeat of white fighter Jack Jeffries polarized the nation. The Johnson-Jeffries fight had been scheduled for San Francisco, but Governor Gillett refused to authorize it out of fear that it might jeopardize the chance to gain the PPIE. See Farr, *Black Champion,* 69–71.

59. See Lee, *Orientals.*

60. The report read, "Cpl. Stewart reports that he was informed by Mr. Wales that a colored janitor employed in the International Harvester Co. booth, made insulting remarks to Miss Andrews, Telephone Operator. After being identified by Miss Andrews, man was sent to Desk Sergeant." "Extracts of Daily Reports of the Guards, March 31, 1915," Extracts of Daily Reports of the Guards, March–April 1915, carton 83, PPIE-BL.

61. Frank Burt to Cumming, September 3, 1915, Correspondence Re. Complaints, carton 8, PPIE-BL.

62. The report describes Castro as "colored," a term that could mean African American. Given that her surname was a Spanish one, it is also possible that she was of Hispanic descent. Nonetheless, it remains clear that she was perceived as "colored," and thus "nonwhite," as were the other attendants whose actions are described in this section. Extracts from Daily Reports of the Guards, July 25, 1915, Extracts from Daily Reports of the Guards, July 1915, carton 83, PPIE-BL.

63. A system of free and pay restrooms existed on the grounds, with quite a few more pay than free toilets available, causing confusion for visitors as to whether they should pay for using the facilities.

64. Extracts from Daily Reports of the Guards, July 25, 1915, Extracts from Daily Reports of the Guards, July 1915, carton 83, PPIE-BL.

65. It is worth noting that the position of washroom attendant was one of the few jobs available to blacks on the grounds, and these reports suggest that a large number of these attendants were African American. The same was true at the 1893 Columbian Exposition. See Reed, *"All the World Is Here!,"* 76.

66. Extracts from Daily Reports of the Guards, July 18, 1915, Extracts from Daily Reports of the Guards, July 1915, carton 83, PPIE-BL.

67. See Extracts from Daily Reports of the Guards, carton 83, PPIE-BL.

68. Bill Smith to C. C. Moore, 5 October 1915, Correspondence Re. Complaints, carton 9, PPIE-BL.

69. Bill Smith to C. C. Moore, 5 October 1915, Correspondence Re. Complaints, carton 9, PPIE-BL.

70. See Kelley, "We Are Not What We Seem," for a discussion of the ways in which African Americans in the Jim Crow South asserted their identities through these kinds of interactions.

71. "Somali Natives at Fair 'Broke,'" *San Francisco Examiner*, May 14, 1915. My thanks to Jamaica Hutchins for reminding me of this incident at a crucial juncture in my writing.

72. Todd, *Story of the Exposition*, 2:375.

73. "Somali Natives in U.S. Charge," *San Francisco Examiner*, May 15, 1915.

74. Todd, *Story of the Exposition*, 2:375.

7. WOMEN TAKE THE POLITICAL STAGE

1. "'Pageant of Peace' at Exposition Today," *San Francisco Chronicle*, June 5, 1915.

2. "Programme Special Day, I.C.W.W.P.P.P., Friday, June 4, 1915," Women Workers to Promote Permanent Peace, PPIE-SFPL.

3. Attendees at the International Conference of Women Workers to Promote Permanent Peace sang a hymn that Gilman composed titled "Peace to the World," which I assume is the same song that this reporter titled the "Hymn of Peace." Sewall, *Women and Permanent Peace*, 78.

4. "1915 Panama-Pacific International Exposition Bulletin of Information Concerning the International Conference of Women Workers to Promote Permanent Peace," Women Workers to Promote Permanent Peace, PPIE-SFPL.

5. For a complete list of congresses and conventions held at the fair, see Todd, *Story of the Exposition*, 5:100–121.

6. Although the United States hosted dozens of world's fairs after 1893, scholars of women and world's fairs continue to return to Chicago's 1893 Columbian Exposition, with its active Board of Lady Managers, impressive Woman's Building, and Congress of Representative Women, as the highlight of women's organizing. After Chicago, most scholars argue that women's exhibits became integrated into the larger fair, and the activities of organized women ceased to be politically motivated. For examples of this argument, see Cordato, "Representing the Expansion"; Darney, "Women and World's Fairs"; Gullett, "'Our Great Opportunity'"; and Scott, *Natural Allies*, 128–34. Despite repeated attempts to participate in the Chicago fair, African American women's organizations were repeatedly excluded. See F. L. Barnett, "The Reason Why," in Ida B. Wells, *The Reason Why: The Colored American Is Not in the World's Columbian Exposition* (Chicago: author, 1893), 79, quoted in Carby, *Reconstructing Womanhood*, 5; Bederman, *Manliness and Civilization*; and Boisseau, "White Queens," 33–81.

7. See the essays in Boisseau and Markwyn, *Gendering the Fair*.

8. Mary Ann Irwin, "Going About and Doing Good: The Lady Managers of San Francisco, 1850–1880," in Cherny, Irwin, and Wilson, *California Women and Politics*, 27–57.

9. See Ann Marie Wilson, "Neutral Territory: The Politics of Settlement Work in San Francisco, 1894–1920," 97–122; Joshua Paddison, "'Woman Is Everywhere the Purifier': The Politics of Temperance, 1878–1919," 59–76; and Susan Englander, "We Want the Ballot for Very Different Reasons: Clubwomen, Union Women, and the Internal Politics of the Suffrage Movement, 1896–1913," 209–36—all in Cherny, Irwin, and Wilson, *California Women and Politics*.

10. Englander, "We Want the Ballot," 215.

11. Englander, "We Want the Ballot," 217–19.

12. Gullett, *Becoming Citizens*; and Gullett, "City Mothers," in Harris and McNamara, *Women and the Structure of Society*, 149–59.

13. Sewall, *Women and the Everyday City*; Gullett, *Becoming Citizens*; Finnegan, *Selling Suffrage*; and Mead, *How the Vote Was Won*.

14. For an excellent discussion of the Twentieth-Century Club, see Sandra L. Henderson, "The Civitas of Women's Political Culture: The Twentieth Century Club of Berkeley, 1904–1929," in Cherny, Irwin, and Wilson, *California Women and Politics*, 175–208.

15. During the fair *The Suffragist* faithfully reported on activities at the suffrage booth and included the names of women who joined the Congressional Union for Woman Suffrage during the fair. It included many prominent women, including members of the Woman's Board and wives of the Board of Directors. See the *Suffragist* issues from March to December 1915.

16. Panama-Pacific International Exposition Company, *Education and Social Economy*, 18–20.

17. Field, *Sara Bard Field*, 294; and Ewald and Clute, *San Francisco Invites the World*, 72.

18. Field, *Sara Bard Field*, 294.

19. "Four Notable Women at Suffrage Meeting," *San Francisco Chronicle*, April 4, 1915.

20. "Mrs. Alice Park to Speak at Woman Suffrage Booth," *San Francisco Chronicle*, April 17, 1915.

21. Anne Wilde, "Clubs Are Working for Suffrage," *San Francisco Chronicle*, June 6, 1915. These women included Mrs. Michael H. De Young, Mrs. William Kent, Mrs. Helen Sanborn, and Mrs. Phoebe Hearst.

22. "Civic Center," *Oakland Sunshine*, June 5, 1915.

23. See the September 18, 1915, issue of the *San Francisco Bulletin*.

24. "'Women Don't Vote,' the Old Cry," *San Francisco Bulletin*, September 18, 1915.

25. See "Mrs. Belmont Urges Activism," *San Francisco Bulletin*, September 18, 1915.

26. See *San Francisco Bulletin*, September 18, 1915.

27. For discussions of racial formation during the Progressive Era, see Bederman, *Manliness and Civilization*; and Jacobson, *Barbarian Virtues*. Aileen Kraditor argues that woman suffragists drew on race-based arguments to build national support for the movement in *Ideas of the Woman Suffrage Movement*. See also Newman, *White Women's Rights*.

28. "California Convention of the Congressional Union," *Suffragist*, June 12, 1915.

29. "California Convention of the Congressional Union."

30. "Suffrage at the Panama-Pacific Exposition," *Suffragist*, April 10, 1915. The cartoon appeared on the cover of the *Suffragist* on September 15, 1914, in an issue that contained a number of articles deriding the U.S. government's decision to enfranchise Filipino men (in the Philippines) but not white women at home, a situation to which white suffragists vehemently objected.

31. For a discussion of the national anxieties attached to the relationship of the United States to the Philippines, see Jacobson, *Barbarian Virtues*.

32. The cover of the *Suffragist*, September 15, 1914.

33. "The Federal Amendment and the Race Problem," *Suffragist*, February 6, 1915.

34. "Women Gaining from Iceland to China," *San Francisco Chronicle*, June 3, 1915.

35. Newman, *White Women's Rights*, 8.

36. Hazel Carby argues that the presence of six black women at the World's Congress of Representative Women during the 1893 Chicago Fair was not a sign of racial solidarity or of concern for African Americans. Rather, it was "part of a discourse of exoticism that pervaded the fair." Carby, *Reconstructing Womanhood*, 5.

37. See "Pageants as a Means of Suffrage Propaganda," *Suffragist*, November 28, 1914, for an indication of this very calculated approach to publicity.

38. "Fair Boosters in Fantastic Garb," *San Francisco Chronicle*, August 20, 1915.

39. "Messengers Speed on to Washington," *San Francisco Bulletin*, September 18, 1915.

40. Belmont's comment echoed the Congressional Union's controversial political strategy of actively campaigning against the party in power (in this case the Democrats) for refusing to support women's suffrage. "First Ever Political Campaign of Women Opened at Exposition," *San Francisco Bulletin*, September 14, 1915.

41. See McGerr, "Political Style and Woman's Power," 864–85, for a discussion of the evolution of women's political style in the early twentieth century. He argues that rituals and pageants, such as the suffragists staged, "gave participants a sense of pride, solidarity, and power."

42. Field, *Sara Bard Field*, 300.

43. Wilson, "By the Fountain of Energy," 424–29.

44. "Women's Club Interests Center on the Exposition Activities [sic] Young Women's Christian Association Commands Attention," *San Francisco Chronicle*, February 14, 1915.

45. "Welfare Work at the Panama-Pacific International Exposition," Social Service, PPIE-SFPL.

46. "Y.W.C.A. Will Exhibit Results at Exposition," *San Francisco Chronicle*, January 15, 1915.

47. The Detroit and Akron YWCAs won the respective titles for these contests. "Social Service at the Panama-Pacific International Exposition," Social Service, PPIE-SFPL.

48. "Y.W.C.A. Will Exhibit Results."

49. Adrienne Lash Jones notes that although the YWCA served black women, for instance, they were in separate branches, and the National Board had no black representation. She argues that despite the organizations' multiracial membership, its practices perpetuated segregation. Adrienne Lash Jones, "Struggle

among Saints: African American Women and the YWCA, 1870–1920," in Mjagkij and Spratt, *Men and Women Adrift*, 160–87. In San Francisco, separate branches served both the Chinese and Japanese populations of the city. In Oakland, the YWCA served Native American women but only through separate clubs.

50. See "Little Stories from the Exposition," *Association Monthly* 9 (1915): 465, for an expression of this attitude.

51. On the YWCA's work with working women during this era, see Sarah Heath, "Negotiating White Womanhood: The Cincinnati YWCA and White Wage-Earning Women, 1918–1929," in Mjagkij and Spratt, *Men and Women Adrift*, 86–110.

52. Wilson, "By the Fountain of Energy," 424.

53. Wilson, "By the Fountain of Energy," 425, 429, 428.

54. Wilson, "By the Fountain of Energy," 428.

55. "Welfare Work at the Panama-Pacific International Exposition," Social Service, PPIE-SFPL.

56. Newman, *White Women's Rights*, 8.

57. "Report of Work: YWCA Building, Exposition Grounds, March 8, 1915," YWCA (#2), carton 10, Hearst Papers.

58. "Report of Work: YWCA Building, Exposition Grounds, March 8, 1915," YWCA (#2), carton 10, Hearst Papers.

59. "Social Service at the Panama-Pacific International Exposition," Social Service, PPIE-SFPL.

60. For discussions of the YWCA's racial policies, see Jones, "Struggle among Saints," in Mjagkij and Spratt, *Men and Women Adrift*.

61. "Carry Call to Whole World," *Oakland Tribune*, June 7, 1915; and Mrs. George W. Coleman, "The Women's Congress of Missions," *Missionary Review of the World* 28 (1915): 586.

62. "Questions Ability of Lobbying: But Suffrage Blooms Anyway," *Oakland Tribune*, June 6, 1915. I have found no other examples of African American women playing such a prominent role in an integrated congress at the PPIE.

63. "The Woman's Congress of Missions of the Panama-Pacific International Exposition, June 6–14, 1915," folder 1, carton 142, PPIE-BL.

64. Todd, *Story of the Exposition*, 5:12.

65. Coleman, "Women's Congress of Missions," 586.

66. Sewall, *Women, World War*, xi.

67. Sewall, *Women, World War*, 28.

68. Sewall, *Women, World War*, 152.

69. Sewall, *Women, World War*, 38.

70. Shepard's background is not clear from this talk. She speaks of being harassed as an "American" by Colombians, but she also says she was born

in Bogotá. My assumption is that she was born in Colombia as the child of American parents. Further research did not reveal her family background.

71. Sewall, *Women, World War*, 53, 55, 58, 62.

72. Rupp, *Worlds of Women*.

73. Sewall, *Women, World War*, 58.

74. "The Second Pan-American Scientific Congress," *Bulletin of the Pan-American Union*, 41 (1915), 777.

75. Ann Towns, "The Inter-American Commission of Women and Women's Suffrage, 1920–1945," *Journal of Latin American Studies* 42 (2010): 788.

76. Sewall, *Women, World War*, 45.

77. Sewall, *Women, World War*, 46.

78. Sewall, *Women, World War*, 151.

79. Sewall, *Women, World War*, 153, 152.

EPILOGUE

1. "Exit the Fair," *Monitor*, December 11, 1915.

2. Mary Eugenia Pierce, Diary for 1915–1917, December 5, 1915, Pierce Family Papers.

3. De Vecchi, "The Panama-Pacific International Exposition," copy in folder 16, box 52, San Francisco Misc/Ephemera Oversize Pamphlets Relating to the Panama-Pacific International Exposition, PPIE-CHS.

4. "Our Post Exposition Period," *San Francisco Chronicle*, April 12, 1916.

5. William F. Benedict, "Nineteen-Fifteen: A Year of Contrasts," *San Francisco Chronicle*, January 12, 1916.

6. "California Counties' Development during Exposition Year," *San Francisco Chronicle*, January 12, 1916.

7. Issel and Cherny, *San Francisco*, 177.

8. Issel and Cherny, *San Francisco*. 177–79. Although Governor William Stephens eventually reduced Thomas Mooney's sentence to life in prison, the suspects' struggle for freedom stretched into the 1930s.

9. Issel and Cherny, *San Francisco*, 181.

10. See Dobkin, "A Twenty-Five-Million-Dollar Mirage," in Benedict, *Anthropology of World's Fairs*, 93n47.

11. "No Individual Has a Right to Say He Gave Auditorium to City of San Francisco," *San Francisco Chronicle*, August 27, 1922.

12. Ruth Newhall, *San Francisco's Enchanted Palace* (San Francisco: Howell-North Books, 1967), 59.

13. Newhall, *San Francisco's Enchanted Palace*, 60.

14. Newhall, *San Francisco's Enchanted Palace*, 62–76.

15. Newhall, *San Francisco's Enchanted Palace*, 78.

Bibliography

ARCHIVAL SOURCES

The Bancroft Library, University of California, Berkeley

Arlett, Arthur. Papers.

Barr Stanislawski, Doris. Papers.

Haskell Family Papers.

Hearst, Phoebe Apperson. Papers.

Panama-Pacific International Exposition. Miscellany.

Panama-Pacific International Exposition. Pamphlets.

Panama-Pacific International Exposition Company. Papers (PPIE-BL).

Pierce Family Papers.

Richter, Clemens Max. "Autobiography and Reminiscences."

San Francisco City Engineer. "Report on Extensions of Municipal Railways to
Provide Transportation for the Panama-Pacific Exposition, April 5, 1913."

San Francisco Labor Council Papers.

"Warning! The Women of San Francisco . . ."

California Historical Society, Baker Library, San Francisco

Hale, Reuben Brooks. Papers.

Huyck, Charles. Papers.

Panama-Pacific International Exposition Company. Papers (PPIE-CHS).

Rolph, James J., Jr. Papers.

The California State Library, Sacramento

Little, Edna A. "A Trip to San Francisco by Auto, 1915."

Panama Pacific International Exposition in San Francisco, 1915. A Scrapbook of
California Newspaper Clippings, 1912–14.

The Mechanics' Institute Library, San Francisco

"De Young Finds Interest." International Fair Illustrated 1, no. 4 (1912): 21.

"Modern Transportation and Communications in the Republic of China."
Report presented by Mr. C. T. Hsia, special commissioner to the Ministry

of Communications of Peking, China, to the Panama-Pacific International Exposition, Palace of Transportation. N.d.

Panama-Pacific International Exposition. The Official Daily Program.

Panama-Pacific International Exposition. Pamphlets.

"Report to accompany HJ Res. 213, Calendar No. 1063, Senate, 'Panama-Pacific International Exposition,' Feb. 9, 1911," submitted by Mr. Jones.

San Francisco History Center, the San Francisco Public Library

Panama-Pacific International Exposition. Vertical files (PPIE-SFPL).

San Francisco and Marin Young Women's Christian Association (YWCA), San Francisco

History of the San Francisco Young Woman's Christian Association, 1878–1953.

The Record of the Young Women's Christian Association of San Francisco.

PUBLISHED SOURCES

Adams, Ansel. *Ansel Adams: An Autobiography.* With Mary Street Alinder. Boston: Little, Brown, 1985.

Argentine Commission of the Panama-Pacific International Exposition. *The Argentine Republic: Panama-Pacific International Exposition, San Francisco, 1915.* New York: J. J. Little and Ives, 1915.

Armstrong, Meg. "'A Jumble of Foreignness': The Sublime Musayums of Nineteenth-Century Fairs and Expositions." *Cultural Critique* 23 (Winter 1992): 199–250.

Asbury, Herbert. *The Barbary Coast: An Informal History of the San Francisco Underworld.* New York: A. A. Knopf, 1933.

Baker, Ray Stannard. "A Corner in Labor: What Is Happening in San Francisco Where Unionism Holds Undisputed Sway." *McClure's Magazine* 22 (February 1904).

Bank, Rosemarie K. "Telling a Spatial History of the Columbian Exposition of 1893." *Modern Drama* 47 (2004): 349–66.

Barr, James A. *An Announcement: Congresses, Conferences, Conventions; Panama-Pacific International Exposition, San Francisco, 1915.* San Francisco: The Exposition, 1915.

Barrett, John. "Pan-American Commerce and the Panama Canal—What They Mean to San Francisco." *The Star,* April 10, 1915.

Barry, John D. *The City of Domes.* San Francisco: John J. Newbegin, 1915.

Barth, Gunther. *Instant Cities: Urbanization and the Rise of San Francisco and Denver.* Albuquerque: University of New Mexico Press, 1988.

Bean, Walton. *Boss Ruef's San Francisco: The Story of the Union Labor Party, Big Business, and the Graft Prosecution.* Berkeley: University of California Press, 1952.

Beasley, Delilah L. *The Negro Trail Blazers of California.* Los Angeles, 1919.

Bederman, Gail. *Manliness and Civilization: A Cultural History of Gender and Race in the United States, 1880–1917.* Chicago: University of Chicago Press, 1995.

Beisel, Nicola. "Class, Culture, and Campaigns against Vice in Three American Cities, 1872–1892." *American Sociological Review* 55 (1990): 44–62.

Benedict, Burton. *The Anthropology of World's Fairs: San Francisco's Panama-Pacific International Exposition of 1915.* Berkeley: Scholar Press, 1983.

Benson, Susan Porter. *Counter Cultures: Saleswomen, Managers, and Customers in American Department Stores, 1890–1940.* Chicago: University of Illinois Press, 1986.

Berglund, Barbara. *Making San Francisco American: Cultural Frontiers in the Urban West, 1846–1906.* Lawrence: University of Kansas Press, 2007.

The Blue Book: A Comprehensive Official Souvenir View Book of the Panama-Pacific International Exposition at San Francisco, 1915. 2nd ed. San Francisco: Robert A. Reid, 1915.

Boas, Nancy. *Society of Six: The California Colorists.* San Francisco: Bedford Arts, 1988.

Boisseau, T. J. "White Queens at the Chicago World's Fair, 1893: New Womanhood in the Service of Class, Race, and Nation." *Gender & History* 12 (2000): 33–81.

Boisseau, Tracey Jean, and Abigail Markwyn. *Gendering the Fair: Histories of Women and World's Fairs.* Urbana: University of Illinois Press, 2010.

Bokovoy, Matthew F. *The San Diego World's Fairs and Southwestern Memory, 1880–1940.* Albuquerque: University of New Mexico Press, 2005.

Bolton, Marie. "Recovery for Whom? Social Conflict after the San Francisco Earthquake and Fire, 1906–1915." PhD diss., University of California–Davis, 1997.

Booth, Anna L. "Sculpture at the Panama-Pacific International Exposition." *Fine Arts Journal* 29, no. 2 (August 1913).

Boyd, Nan Alamilla. *Wide-Open Town: A History of Queer San Francisco to 1965.* Berkeley: University of California Press, 2003.

Boyer, Paul. *Urban Masses and Moral Order in American, 1820–1920.* Cambridge MA: Harvard University Press, 1978.

Brinton, Christian. *Impressions of Art at the Panama-Pacific Exposition.* New York: John Lane Company, 1916.

Broussard, Albert S. *Black San Francisco: The Struggle for Racial Equality in the West, 1900–1954.* Lawrence: University of Kansas Press, 1993.

Bruml, Laura. *Electric Lights Dazzling: An Account of One Family's Visit to the 1915 Panama-Pacific International Exposition*. Transcription and additional text by Paul J. Hershey. Los Angeles: Info-Miner Research, 1999.

Buchanan, James A. *History of the Panama-Pacific International Exposition: Comprising the History of the Panama Canal and a Full Account of the World's Greatest Exposition, Embracing the Participation of the States and Nations of the World and Other Events at San Francisco, 1915*. San Francisco: Pan-Pacific Press Association, 1915.

Burns, Jeffrey M. "The Immigrant Church." In *Catholic San Francisco: Sesquicentennial Essays*, edited by Jeffrey Burns, 189–97. Menlo Park CA: Archives of the Archdiocese of San Francisco, 2005.

Carby, Hazel. *Reconstructing Womanhood: The Emergence of the African American Woman Novelist*. New York: Oxford University Press, 1987.

Chen, Yong. *Chinese San Francisco, 1850–1943: A Trans-Pacific Community*. Stanford CA: Stanford University Press, 2000.

Cherny, Robert W. "Patterns of Toleration and Discrimination in San Francisco: The Civil War to World War One." *California History* 74, no. 2 (1994): 130–41.

Cherny, Robert W., Mary Ann Irwin, and Ann Marie Wilson, eds. *California Women and Politics: From the Gold Rush to the Great Depression*. Lincoln: University of Nebraska Press, 2011.

Chinn, Thomas W. *Bridging the Pacific: San Francisco Chinatown and Its People*. San Francisco: Chinese Historical Society of America, 1989.

Choy, Philip P., Lorraine Dong, and Marlon K. Hong. *Coming Man: 19th Century American Perceptions of the Chinese*. Seattle: University of Washington Press, 1995.

Christ, Carol Ann. "Japan's Seven Acres: Politics and Aesthetics at the 1904 Louisiana Purchase Exposition." *Gateway Heritage* 17 (Fall 1996): 2–15.

———. "The Sole Guardians of the Art Inheritance of Asia: Japan and China at the 1904 St. Louis World's Fair." *positions: east asia cultures critiques* 8, no. 3 (Winter 2000): 675–709.

Chuman, Frank F. *The Bamboo People: The Law and Japanese-Americans*. Del Mar CA: Publisher's Inc., 1976.

Ciabattari, Mark. "Urban Liberals, Politics, and the Fight for Public Transit, San Francisco, 1897–1915." PhD diss., New York University, 1988.

Cinel, Dino. *From Italy to San Francisco: The Immigrant Experience*. Stanford CA: Stanford University Press, 1982.

Clark-Lewis, Elizabeth. "'This Work Had a End': African American Domestic Workers in Washington, D.C., 1910–1940." In *"To Toil the Livelong Day": America's Women at Work, 1780–1980*, edited by Carol Groneman and Mary Beth Norton. Ithaca NY: Cornell University Press, 1987.

Clevenger, Martha R. "Through Western Eyes: Americans Encounter Asians at the Fair." *Gateway Heritage* 17 (Fall 1996): 42–45.

Cobble, Dorothy Sue. *Dishing It Out: Waitresses and Their Unions in the Twentieth Century.* Urbana: University of Illinois Press, 1991.

Collins, Jane, and Catherine Lutz. *Reading "National Geographic."* Chicago: University of Chicago Press, 1993.

Connolly, Mark Thomas. *The Response to Prostitution in the Progressive Era.* Chapel Hill: University of North Carolina Press, 1980.

Cordato, Mary Frances. "Representing the Expansion of Women's Sphere: Women's Work and Culture at the World's Fairs of 1876, 1893, and 1904." PhD diss., New York University, 1989.

Cresswell, Tim. *In Place/Out of Place: Geography, Ideology, and Transgression.* Minneapolis: University of Minnesota Press, 1996.

Cronon, William. *Nature's Metropolis: Chicago and the Great West.* New York: Norton, 1991.

D'Agostino, Peter. *Rome in America: Transnational Catholic Ideology from the Risorgimento to Fascism.* Chapel Hill: University of North Carolina Press, 2004.

Daniel, Cletus. *Bitter Harvest: A History of California Farmworkers, 1870–1941.* Ithaca NY: Cornell University Press, 1981.

Daniels, Douglas Henry. *Pioneer Urbanites: A Social and Cultural History of Black San Francisco.* Philadelphia: Temple University Press, 1980.

Daniels, Roger. *Asian America: Chinese and Japanese in the United States since 1850.* Seattle: University of Washington, 1988.

———. *The Politics of Prejudice: The Anti-Japanese Movement in California and the Struggle for Japanese Exclusion.* New York: Atheneum, 1972.

———. "The Progressives Draw the Color Line." In Daniels and Olin, *Racism in California,* 116–34.

Daniels, Roger, and Spencer C. Olin, Jr., eds. *Racism in California: A Reader in the History of Oppression.* New York: Macmillan, 1972.

Darney, Virginia Grant. "Women and World's Fairs: American International Expositions, 1876–1904." PhD diss., Emory University, 1982.

Davies, Andrea Rees. *Saving San Francisco: Relief and Recovery after the 1906 Disaster.* Philadelphia: Temple University Press, 2012.

Davis, Janet M. *The Circus Age: Culture and Society under the American Big Top.* Chapel Hill: University of North Carolina Press, 2002.

Dellums, C. L. *C. L. Dellums: International President, Brotherhood of Sleeping Car Porters, and Civil Rights Leader; an Interview.* With Joyce A. Henderson. Berkeley: Regents of the University of California, 1973.

D'Emilio, John, and Estelle Freedman. *Intimate Matters: A History of Sexuality in America.* 2nd ed. Chicago: University of Chicago Press, 1997.

di Leonardo, Micaela. *The Varieties of Ethnic Experience: Kinship, Class, and Gender among California Italian-Americans*. Ithaca NY: Cornell University Press, 1984.

Dobkin, Marjorie. "The Twenty-Five-Million-Dollar Mirage." In Benedict, *The Anthropology of World's Fairs*, 66–93.

Domosh, Mona. "A 'Civilized' Commerce: Gender, 'Race,' and Empire at the 1893 Chicago Exposition." *cultural geographies* 9 (2002): 181–201.

———. "Those 'Gorgeous Incongruities': Polite Politics and Public Space on the Streets of Nineteenth-Century New York City." *Annals of the Association of American Geographers* 88 (1998): 209–26.

Edwards, Sue Bradford. "Imperial East Meets Democratic West: The St. Louis Press and the Fair's Chinese Delegation." *Gateway Heritage* 17 (Fall 1996): 32–41.

Englander, Susan. *Class Coalition and Class Conflict in the California Woman Suffrage Movement, 1907–1912*. San Francisco: Mellen Research University Press, 1992.

Enstad, Nan. *Ladies of Labor, Girls of Adventure: Working Women, Popular Culture, and Labor Politics at the Turn of the Twentieth Century*. New York: Columbia University Press, 1999.

Esmeralda, Aurora [Ella Sterling Mighels]. *Life and Letters of a Forty-Niner's Daughter*. San Francisco: Harr Wagner Publishing, 1929.

Ethington, Philip. *The Public City: The Political Construction of Urban Life in San Francisco, 1850–1900*. Berkeley: University of California Press, 1994.

Ewald, Donna, and Peter Clute. *San Francisco Invites the World: The Panama-Pacific International Exposition of 1915*. San Francisco: Chronicle Books, 1991.

Farr, Finis. *Black Champion: The Explosive Story of Jack Johnson, Who Dared the World to Find the Great White Hope*. Greenwich CT: Fawcett Publications, 1969.

Field, Sara Bard. *Sara Bard Field, Poet and Suffragist*. Berkeley: Regional Oral History Office, the Bancroft Library, University of California–Berkeley, 1979.

Finnegan, Margaret. *Selling Suffrage: Consumer Culture and Votes for Women*. New York: Columbia University Press, 1999.

Foner, Philip. *History of the Labor Movement in the United States*. Vol. 3, *The Policies and Practices of the American Federation of Labor, 1900–1909*. New York: International Publishers, 1964.

Fradkin, Philip L. *The Great Earthquake and Firestorms of 1906: How San Francisco Nearly Destroyed Itself*. Berkeley: University of California Press, 2005.

Frankel, Noralee, and Nancy S. Dye, eds. *Gender, Class, Race, and Reform in the Progressive Era*. Lexington: University Press of Kentucky, 1991.

Frink, Brenda D. "San Francisco's Pioneer Mother Monument: Maternalism, Racial Order and the Politics of Memorialization, 1907–1915." *American Quarterly* 64, no. 1 (March 2012).

Gendzel, Glen. "Pioneers and Padres: Competing Mythologies in Northern and Southern California, 1850–1930." *Western Historical Quarterly* 32 (2001): 55–79.

————. "Vigilantes and Boosters: Social Memory and Progressive Political Cultures in San Francisco and Los Angeles, 1900–1920." PhD diss., University of Wisconsin–Madison, 1998.

Gilbert, James. *Whose Fair? Experience, Memory, and the History of the Great St. Louis Exposition.* Chicago: University of Chicago Press, 2010.

Gleach, Frederic W. "Pocahontas at the Fair: Crafting Identities at the 1907 Jamestown Exposition." *Ethnohistory* 50 (2003): 419–45.

Gonzalez, Robert Alexander. *Designing Pan-America: U.S. Architectural Visions for the Western Hemisphere.* Austin: University of Texas Press, 2011.

Gordon, Elizabeth. *What We Saw at Madame World's Fair: Being a Series of Letters from the Twins at the Panama-Pacific International Exposition to Their Cousins at Home.* San Francisco: Samuel Levinson, 1915.

Grant, Madison. *The Passing of the Great Race or the Racial Basis of European History with a Documentary Supplement.* 4th ed. New York: Charles Scribner's Sons, 1922.

Green, Julie. *The Canal Builders: Making America's Empire at the Panama Canal.* New York: Penguin Press, 2009.

Greenhalgh, Paul. *Ephemeral Vistas: The Expositions Universelles, Great Exhibitions, and World's Fairs, 1851–1939.* Manchester UK: Manchester University Press. 1988.

Gulick, Sidney L. *The American Japanese Problem: A Study of the Race Relations of the East and the West.* New York: Charles Scribner's Sons, 1914.

Gullett, Gayle. *Becoming Citizens: The Emergence and Development of the California Women's Movement, 1880–1911.* Urbana: University of Illinois Press, 2000.

————. "City Mothers, City Daughters, and the Dance Hall Girls: The Limits of Female Political Power in San Francisco, 1913." In *Women and the Structure of Society*, edited by Barbara J. Harris and JoAnn K. McNamara, 149–59. Durham NC: Duke Press Policy Studies, 1984.

————. "'Our Great Opportunity': Organized Women Advance Women's Work at the World's Columbian Exposition of 1893." *Illinois Historical Journal* 87 (1994).

Gumina, Deanna Paoli. *The Italians of San Francisco, 1850–1930.* New York: Center for Migration Studies, 1978.

Gutman, Herbert G. *Work, Culture, and Society in Industrializing America: Essays in American Working-Class and Social History.* New York: Vintage Books, 1977.

Hall, Stuart. "Notes on Deconstructing 'The Popular.'" In *People's History and Socialist Theory*, edited by Raphael Samuel, 442–53. London: Routledge & Kegan Paul, 1981.

Harris, Neil. "All the World a Melting Pot? Japan at American Fairs, 1876–1904." In *Cultural Excursions: Marketing Appetites and Cultural Tastes in Modern America*, 29–55. Chicago: University of Chicago Press, 1990.

Harris, Neil, Wim de Wit, James Gilbert, and Robert W. Rydell. *Grand Illusions: Chicago's World's Fair of 1893*. Chicago: Chicago Historical Society, 1993.

Hawkins, Mike. *Social Darwinism in European and American Thought, 1860–1945: Nature as Model and Nature as Threat*. Cambridge: Cambridge University Press, 1997.

Hichborn, Franklin. *The Story of the Session of the California Legislature of 1913*. San Francisco: Press of James H. Barry Company, 1913.

———. *"The System" as Uncovered by the San Francisco Graft Prosecution*. San Francisco: Press of James H. Barry Company, 1915.

Hoffenberg, Peter H. *An Empire on Display: English, Indian, and Australian Exhibitions from the Crystal Palace to the Great War*. Berkeley: University of California Press, 2001.

Hofstadter, Richard. *Social Darwinism in American Thought*. Boston: Beacon Press, 1955.

Holt, Thomas C. "Marking: Race, Race-Making, and the Writing of History." *The American Historical Review* 100 (February 1995): 1–20.

Hudson, Lynn. "'This Is Our Fair and Our State': African Americans and the Panama-Pacific International Exposition." *California History* 87 (2010): 26–45.

Hunt, Michael H. *The Making of a Special Relationship: The United States and China to 1914*. New York: Columbia University Press, 1983.

Hunter, Tera. *To 'Joy My Freedom: Southern Black Women's Lives and Labors after the Civil War*. Cambridge MA: Harvard University Press, 1997.

Hutchins, Jamaica. "Constructing Womanhood: Women's Work and Participation at the Panama-Pacific International Exposition, San Francisco, 1915." Master's thesis, University of California–Santa Cruz, 2005.

Ichihashi, Yamato. *Japanese in the United States: A Critical Study of the Problems of the Japanese Immigrants and Their Children*. Stanford CA: Stanford University Press, 1932.

Ichioka, Yuji. *The Issei: The World of the First Generation Japanese Immigrants, 1885–1924*. New York: Free Press, 1988.

Ignatiev, Noel. *How the Irish Became White*. New York: Routledge, 1995.

Imada, Adria. *Aloha America: Hula Circuits throughout the U.S. Empire*. Durham NC: Duke University Press, 2012.

Issel, William, and Robert W. Cherny. *San Francisco, 1865–1932: Politics, Power, and Urban Development*. Berkeley: University of California Press, 1986.

Jacobson, Matthew Frye. *Barbarian Virtues: The United States Encounters Foreign Peoples at Home and Abroad*. New York: Hill and Wang, 2000.

———. *Whiteness of a Different Color: European Immigrants and the Alchemy of Race*. Cambridge MA: Harvard University Press, 1998.

Johnson, Bascom. "Moral Conditions in San Francisco and at the Panama-Pacific International Exposition." *Social Hygiene* 1 (September 1915): 589–609.

Johnson, Susan Lee. *Roaring Camp: The Social World of the California Gold Rush.* New York: W. W. Norton: 2000.

Jolly, Michelle. "Inventing the City: Gender and the Politics of Everyday Life in Gold Rush San Francisco, 1848–1869." PhD diss., University of California–San Diego, 1998.

Kazin, Michael. *Barons of Labor: The San Francisco Building Trades and Union Power in the Progressive Era.* Chicago: University of Illinois Press, 1987.

Keller, John E., ed. *Anna Morrison Reed, 1849–1921.* Lafayette CA: John E. Keller, 1978.

Kelley, Robin D. G. "We Are Not What We Seem: Rethinking Black Working Class Opposition in the Jim Crow South." *The Journal of American History* 80 (1993): 75–112.

Kline, Wendy. *Building a Better Race: Gender, Sexuality, and Eugenics from the Turn of the Century to the Baby Boom.* Berkeley: University of California Press, 2001.

Knight, Robert Edward Lee. *Industrial Relations in the San Francisco Bay Area, 1900–1918.* Berkeley: University of California Press, 1960.

Koster, Frederick J. *Law and Order and the San Francisco Chamber of Commerce: An Address.* San Francisco: Board of Directors, San Francisco Chamber of Commerce, 1918.

Kraditor, Aileen. *The Ideas of the Woman Suffrage Movement, 1890–1920.* New York: Columbia University Press, 1965.

Kramer, Paul. "Making Concessions: Race and Empire Revisited at the Philippine Exposition, St. Louis, 1901–1905." *Radical History Review* 73 (1999): 74–114.

Kyokwai, Hakurankwai. *Japan and Her Exhibits at the Panama-Pacific International Exposition 1915.* Tokyo, 1915.

Lee, Anthony. *Picturing Chinatown: Art and Orientalism in San Francisco.* Berkeley: University of California Press, 2001.

Lee, Portia. *Victorious Spirit: Regional Influences in the Architecture, Landscaping, and Murals of the Panama-Pacific International Exposition.* PhD diss., George Washington University, 1984.

Lee, Robert G. *Orientals: Asian Americans in Popular Culture.* Philadelphia: Temple University Press, 1999.

Lee, Shelley S. "The Contradictions of Cosmopolitanism: Consuming the Orient at the Alaska-Yukon-Pacific Exposition and the International Potlatch Festival, 1909–1914." *Western Historical Quarterly* 38 (2007): 279.

Levy, Louis. *Chronological History of the Panama Pacific International Exposition.* San Francisco: G. B. Tuley and the Panama-Pacific International Exposition Company, 1913.

Lipsky, William. *San Francisco's Marina District*. Chicago: Arcadia Publishing, 2004.

Lockyer, Angus. "Japan at the Exhibition, 1867–1970." PhD diss., Stanford University, 2000.

——. "Japan at the Exhibition, 1867–1877." In *Japanese Civilization in the Modern World*. Vol. 17, *Collection and Representations*, edited by Tadao Umesao, Angus Lockyer, and Kenji Yoshida, 67–76. Osaka: National Museum of Ethnology, Japan, 2001.

Luker, Kristin. "Sex, Social Hygiene, and the State: The Double-Edged Sword of Social Reform." *Theory and Society* 27 (1998).

Massa, Mark S. *Anti-Catholicism in America: The Last Acceptable Prejudice*. New York: Crossroads Publishing Company, 2003.

McCullough, Edo. *World's Fairs Midways: An Affectionate Account of American Amusement Areas from the Crystal Palace to the Crystal Ball*. New York: Exposition Press, 1966.

McGerr, Michael. "Political Style and Woman's Power, 1830–1930." *The Journal of American History* 77 (1990): 864–85.

McGrath, Robert L. "The Endless Trail of the End of the Trail." *Journal of the West* 40 (Fall 2000): 8–15.

McKenzie, R. D. *Oriental Exclusion: The Effect of American Immigration Laws, Regulations, and Judicial Decisions upon the Chinese and Japanese on the Pacific Coast*. New York: American Group Institute of Pacific Relations, 1927. Reprint, New York: American Immigration Library, Jerome S. Ozer, 1971.

Mead, Rebecca. *How the Vote Was Won: Woman Suffrage in the Western United States, 1868–1914*. New York: New York University Press, 2004.

Meyerowitz, Joanne. *Women Adrift: Independent Wage Earners in Chicago, 1880–1930*. Chicago: University of Chicago Press, 1988.

Miller, Dave R. "The Stockton Open Shop War of 1914: California Labor's Sacrificial Stand in the Hinterland." Master's thesis, Sonoma State University, 1997.

Mjagkij, Nina, and Margaret Spratt, eds. *Men and Women Adrift: The YMCA and the YWCA in the City*. New York: New York University Press, 1997.

Montgomery, David. *The Fall of the House of Labor: The Workplace, the State, and American Labor Activism, 1865–1925*. New York: Cambridge University Press, 1987.

Moore, Sarah J. *Empire on Display: San Francisco's Panama-Pacific International Exposition of 1914*. Norman: University of Oklahoma Press, 2013.

Moy, James S. *Marginal Sights: Staging the Chinese in America*. Iowa City: University of Iowa Press, 1993.

Mumford, Kevin J. *Interzones: Black/White Sex Districts in Chicago and New York in the Early Twentieth Century*. New York: Columbia University Press, 1997.

Murolo, Priscilla. *The Common Ground of Womanhood: Class, Gender and Working Girls' Clubs, 1884–1928*. Chicago: University of Illinois Press, 1997.

Murray, Freeman Henry Morris. *Emancipation and the Freed in American Sculpture: A Study in Interpretation*. Washington DC: Freeman Henry Morris Murray, 1916.

Nathan, Marvin R. *San Francisco's International Expositions: A Bibliography*. 1990.

Nee, Victor G., and Brett de Bary Nee. *Longtime Californ': A Documentary Study of an American Chinatown*. Stanford CA: Stanford University Press, 1972.

Neuhaus, Eugen. *The Art of the Exposition: Personal Impressions of the Architecture, Sculpture, Mural Decorations, Color Scheme & Other Aesthetic Aspects of the Panama-Pacific International Exposition*. San Francisco: Paul Elder, 1915.

Newman, Louise Michele. *White Women's Rights: The Racial Origins of Feminism in the United States*. New York: Oxford University Press, 1999.

Ngai, Mae. *The Lucky Ones: One Family and the Extraordinary Invention of Chinese America*. New York: Houghton Mifflin, 2010.

Nickliss, Alexandra. "Phoebe Apperson Hearst: The Most Powerful Woman in California." PhD diss., University of California–Davis, 1994.

Nordstrom, Justin. "Danger on the Doorstep: Anti-Catholicism in American Print Culture, 1910–1919." PhD diss., University of Indiana, 2003.

Odem, Mary E. *Delinquent Daughters: Protecting and Policing Adolescent Female Sexuality in the United States, 1885–1920*. Chapel Hill: University of North Carolina Press, 1995.

Olin, Spencer C., Jr. *California's Prodigal Sons: Hiram Johnson and the Progressives, 1911–1917*. Berkeley: University of California Press, 1968.

Ostrander, Gilman M. *The Prohibition Movement in California, 1848–1933*. Berkeley: University of California Press, 1957.

Pan, Erica Y. Z. *The Impact of the 1906 Earthquake on San Francisco's Chinatown*. New York: Peter Lang, 1995.

Panama-Pacific International Exposition Company. *Calendar of Special Days and Special Events Scheduled from July 1st to December 4th, Panama-Pacific International Exposition*. San Francisco: Panama-Pacific International Exposition Company, 1915.

———. *California Invites the World, 1915: Panama-Pacific Universal Exposition*. San Francisco: Panama-Pacific International Exposition Company, 1913.

———. *The Carnival Spirit of San Francisco*. San Francisco: Panama-Pacific International Exposition Company, 1910.

———. *Condensed Facts Concerning the Panama-Pacific International Exposition San Francisco, 1915: Celebrating the Opening of the Panama Canal*. San Francisco: The Exposition, 1915. San Francisco History Center, San Francisco Public Library, n.d..

———. *Education and Social Economy: Official Catalogue of Exhibitors: Panama-Pacific International Exposition, San Francisco, 1915*. Wahlgreen Company, 1915.

———. *The Exposition Fact Book: Panama-Pacific International Exposition at San Francisco.* San Francisco: The Exposition, 1914.

———. *Facts for Boosters.* San Francisco: The Exposition Company, 1915.

———. *Final Financial Report.* San Francisco: 1921.

———. *Good Business Judgment Should and Will Prompt Machinery Manufacturers to Exhibit Their Products at the Panama-Pacific International Exposition, San Francisco, 1915.* San Francisco: Panama-Pacific International Exposition Company, n.d. Bancroft Library.

———. *Official Guide: Panama-Pacific International Exposition.* San Francisco: Wahlgreen Company, 1915.

———. *Panama-Pacific International Exposition.* San Francisco: Panama-Pacific International Exposition Company, 1914.

———. *The Panama-Pacific International Exposition Illustrated.* San Francisco: Panama-Pacific International Exposition Company, 1914.

———. *The Panama-Pacific International Exposition, 1915: Celebrating the Opening of the Panama Canal Bulletin; Business Facts for Business Men.* San Francisco: Frank Printing Company, n.d.

———. *The People's Easy Guide to the Panama-Pacific International Exposition.* San Francisco: International Exhibitions Bureau, 1915.

———. *Plan and Scope of the Panama-Pacific International Exposition, San Francisco, California, 1915.* San Francisco: Phillips & Van Orden Company, 1911.

———. *Why? Where? When? How? The Celebration Is to Take Place: Panama Canal, San Francisco, 1915 Universal Exposition.* San Francisco: Panama-Pacific International Exposition Company, 1913.

Parezo, Nancy, and Don D. Fowler. *Anthropology Goes to the Fair: The 1904 Louisiana Purchase Exposition.* Lincoln: University of Nebraska Press, 2009.

Parker, Alison M. *Purifying America: Women, Cultural Reform, and Pro-Censorship Activism, 1873–1933.* Chicago: University of Illinois Press, 1997.

Pascoe, Peggy. *Relations of Rescue: The Search for Female Moral Authority in the West, 1874–1939.* New York: Oxford University Press, 1990.

Peiss, Kathy. *Cheap Amusements: Working Women and Leisure in Turn-of-the-Century New York.* Philadelphia: Temple University Press, 1986.

Post, Emily. *By Motor to the Golden Gate.* New York: D. Appleton, 1916.

Potter, Elizabeth Gray, and Mabel Thayer Gray. *The Lure of San Francisco: A Romance amid Old Landmarks.* San Francisco: Paul Elder, 1915.

Prisco, Salvatore, III. *John Barrett: Progressive Era Diplomat: A Study of a Commercial Expansionist, 1887–1920.* University: University of Alabama Press, 1973.

Quizon, Cherubim A., and Patricia O. Afable. "Rethinking Display of Filipinos at St. Louis: Embracing Heartbreak and Irony." *Philippine Studies* 52 (2004): 439–44.

Rambon, Paige. "Theatres of Contact: The Kwakwaka-wakw Meet Colonialism in British Columbia at the Chicago World's Fair." *The Canadian Historical Review* 81 (2000): 157–90.

Rast, Raymond W. "The Cultural Politics of Tourism in San Francisco's Chinatown, 1882–1917." *Pacific Historical Review* 76 (2007): 29–60.

Reed, Christopher Robert. *"All the World Is Here!": The Black Presence at White City*. Bloomington: Indiana University Press, 2000.

Risse, Guenter. *Plague, Fear, and Politics in San Francisco's Chinatown*. Baltimore: Johns Hopkins University Press, 2012.

Rohrbough, Malcolm. *Days of Gold: The California Gold Rush and the American Nation*. Berkeley: University of California Press, 1997.

Rosen, Ruth. *The Lost Sisterhood: Prostitution in America, 1900–1918*. Baltimore: The Johns Hopkins University Press, 1983.

Rosenbaum, Fred. *Cosmopolitans: A Social and Cultural History of the Jews of the San Francisco Bay Area*. Berkeley: University of California Press, 2009.

———. *Visions of Reform: Congregation Emanu-El and the Jews of San Francisco, 1849–1999*. Berkeley: Judah L. Magnes Museum, 2000.

Rubens, Lisa. "The 1939 San Francisco World's Fair: The New Deal, the New Frontier, and the Pacific Basin." PhD diss., University of California–Berkeley, 2004.

Rubin, Ron. *Signs of Change: Urban Iconographies in San Francisco, 1880–1915*. New York: Garland Publishing, 1990.

Rupp, Leila. *Worlds of Women: The Making of an International Movement*. Princeton NJ: Princeton University Press, 1997.

Rydell, Robert. *All the World's a Fair: Visions of Empire at American International Expositions, 1876–1916*. Chicago: University of Chicago Press, 1984.

Rydell, Robert, John E. Findling, and Kimberly D. Pelle. *Fair America: World's Fairs in the United States*. Washington DC: Smithsonian Press, 2000.

Rydell, Robert, and Ron Kroes. *Buffalo Bill in Bologna: The Americanization of the World, 1869–1922*. Chicago: University of Chicago Press, 2005.

Sabraw, Liston F. "Mayor James Rolph, Jr., and the End of the Barbary Coast." Master's thesis, San Francisco State College, 1960.

San Francisco. San Francisco: San Francisco Chamber of Commerce, 1915.

San Francisco Standard Guide Including the Panama-Pacific Exposition. San Francisco: North American Press Association, 1913.

Sarbaugh, Timothy. "Exiles of Confidence: The Irish-American Community of San Francisco, 1880–1920." In *From Paddy to Studs: Irish-American Communities in the Turn of the Century Era, 1880 to 1920*, edited by Timothy J. Meagher, 161–79. New York: Greenwood, 1986.

Saxton, Alexander. *The Indispensable Enemy: Labor and the Anti-Chinese Movement in California*. Berkeley: University of California Press, 1971.

Scott, Ann Firor. *Natural Allies: Women's Associations in American History*. Chicago: University of Illinois Press, 1991.

Scott, Mel. *The San Francisco Bay Area: A Metropolis in Perspective*. 2nd ed. Berkeley: University of California Press, 1985.

Segal, Morley. "James Rolph, Jr., and the Municipal Railway: A Study in Political Leadership." Master's thesis, San Francisco State College, 1959.

Sewall, May Wright. *Women, World War, and Permanent Peace*. San Francisco: John J. Newbegin, 1915.

Sewell, Jessica. *Women and the Everyday City: Public Space in San Francisco, 1890–1915*. Minneapolis: University of Minnesota Press, 2011.

Shah, Nayan. *Contagious Divides: Epidemics and Race in San Francisco's Chinatown*. Berkeley: University of California Press, 2001.

Shumsky, Neil Larry. "Tacit Acceptance: Respectable Americans, and Segregated Prostitution, 1870–1910." *Journal of Social History* 19 (1986): 665–79.

Simpson, Anna Pratt. *Problems Women Solved: Being the Story of the Woman's Board of the Panama-Pacific International Exposition; What Vision, Enthusiasm, Work and Co-operation Accomplished*. San Francisco: The Woman's Board, 1915.

Stansell, Christine. *City of Women: Sex and Class in New York, 1789–1860*. Urbana: University of Illinois Press, 1987.

Starr, Kevin. *Americans and the California Dream, 1850–1915*. New York: Oxford University Press, 1973.

Stern, Alexandra Minna. *Eugenic Nation: Faults and Frontiers of Better Breeding in America*. Berkeley: University of California Press, 2005.

Sunset. "The Morals of San Francisco." 34 (1915): 853–56.

Survey. "Facts on Vice in San Francisco." 34 (September 1915).

——— . "Warnings to Girls from San Francisco." 34 (April 1915): 39.

——— . "The Y.W.C.A. at Work in the Joy Zone." 34 (July 1915): 389.

Takaki, Ronald. *Iron Cages: Race and Culture in 19th-Century America*. New York: Oxford University Press, 1990.

——— . *Strangers from a Different Shore: A History of Asian Americans*. Boston: Little, Brown, 1989.

Todd, Frank Morton. *The Story of the Exposition, Being the Official History of the International Celebration Held at San Francisco in 1915 to Commemorate the Discovery of the Pacific Ocean and the Construction of the Panama Canal*. 5 vols. New York: G. P. Putnam's Sons, 1921.

Tong, Benson. *The Unsubmissive Women: Chinese Prostitutes in Nineteenth-Century San Francisco*. Norman: University of Oklahoma Press, 1994.

Trachtenberg, Alan. *The Incorporation of America: Culture and Society in the Gilded Age*. New York: Hill and Wang, 1982.

Ullman, Sharon. *Sex Seen: The Emergence of Modern Sexuality in America*. Berkeley: University of California Press, 1997.

U.S. Department of Commerce, Bureau of the Census. *Thirteenth Census of the United States Taken in the Year 1910*. Vol. 2, *Population, Reports by States, with Statistics for Counties, Cities and Other Civil Divisions, Alabama–Montana*. Washington DC: Government Printing Office, 1913.

Vaught, David. *Cultivating California: Growers, Specialty Crops, and Labor, 1875–1920*. Baltimore: Johns Hopkins University Press, 1999.

Vennman, Barbara. "Dragons, Dummies, and Royals: China at American World's Fairs, 1876–1904." *Gateway Heritage* 17 (Fall 1996): 16–31.

Walden, Keith. *Becoming Modern in Toronto: The Industrial Exhibition and the Shaping of Late Victorian Culture*. Toronto: University of Toronto Press, 1997.

Wallace, Les. *The Rhetoric of Anti-Catholicism: The American Protective Association, 1887–1911*. New York: Garland Publishing, 1990.

Wallis, Michael. *The Real Wild West: The 101 Ranch and the Creation of the American West*. New York: St. Martin's Griffin, 2000.

Walsh, James. *The San Francisco Irish, 1850–1979*. San Francisco: The Irish Literary and Historical Society, 1978.

Wheeler, Leigh Ann. "Battling over Burlesque: Conflicts between Maternalism, Paternalism, and Organized Labor, Minneapolis, Minnesota, 1920–1932." *Frontiers: A Journal of Women Studies* 20 (1999).

Wilder, Laura Ingalls. *West from Home: Letters of Laura Ingalls Wilder to Almanzo Wilder, San Francisco, 1915*. Edited by Roger McBride. New York: Harper and Row, 1974.

Wilson, Elizabeth. *Fifty Years of Association Work among Young Women, 1866–1916*. New York: National Board of the Young Women's Christian Association, 1916.

Wilson, Mabel O. *Negro Building: Black Americans in the World of Fairs and Museums*. Berkeley: University of California Press, 2012.

Woods, Gerald. "A Penchant for Probity: California Progressives and the Disreputable Pleasures." In *California Progressivism Revisited*, edited by William Deverell and Tom Sitton, 99–116. Berkeley: University of California Press, 1994.

Yip, Christopher Lee. "San Francisco's Chinatown: An Architectural and Urban History." PhD diss., University of California–Berkeley, 1985.

Young, Terence. *Building San Francisco's Parks, 1850–1930*. Baltimore: Johns Hopkins University Press, 2004.

Yung, Judy. *Unbound Feet: A Social History of Chinese Women in San Francisco*. Berkeley: University of California Press, 1995.

———. *Unbound Voices: A Documentary History of Chinese Women in San Francisco*. Berkeley: University of California Press, 1999.

Index

Italian Building, 120
Italy, 118–19, 121–22

Japan: convincing PPIE participation
    from, 16, 139–46, 154–56; U.S. legis-
    lation and, 15, 147, 150–54; women's
    conferences and, 252–53
Japan Beautiful, *fig. 29*, 56, 135, *169*, 169–
    70, 295n110
Japan-British Exhibition, 163
Japan Day, 162–63
Japanese American News, 144
Japanese Americans: discrimination
    against, 14, 135, 145, 207, 252, 257;
    immigration of, 14–15, 52, 142, 144,
    157–58. *See also* women
Japanese Association of America, 145–
    46, 150, 152, 155
Japanese Boy's Festival and Japanese
    New Year, 164
Japanese exhibits and events, 139–40,
    149, 156, 158–61, 167–68, 287n90
Japanese Red Cross Society, 159, *161*
Japantown, 14
"Jewel City," 132
Johnson, Bascom, 192
Johnson, Hiram, 19, 41, 140–41, 146–
    47, 150–51, 200, *201*
Johnson, Lovinia, 221–22
Johnson, Walter, 260
Johnson-Jeffries fight, 298n58
Joliffe, Frances, 238
Jordan, David Starr, 146
Joy Zone, the. *See* Zone, the
Junipero Serra Club of Monterey, 127

Kai Fuh Shah, 161–62
Kaplan, James, 99
Kearney, Denis, 14, 141–42
Kehoe Bill, 185–87, 291nn50–51

Kelley, Florence, 234
Kindberg, Maria, 239
King, Homer S., 7
Kinstedt, Ingeborg, 239
Knox, Philander, 48
Koster, Frederick, 213

Labor Clarion, 211, 212–13
labor disputes, 209–10, 211–14, 224–26
labor market, San Francisco, 105, 210
labor stoppage of Somali workers,
    224–26
labor unions: agreement with PPIE
    officials and, 207–210; discrimi-
    nation and, 104, 105; movement
    against, 210, 213; PPIE construc-
    tion workers and, 207–10; PPIE
    unskilled workers and, 206, 210–14;
    in San Francisco, 18, 206–7
"The Landing of Serra," 127–28
Lansing, Ellen Foster, 251
Las Americas, 48
Lash, Mary, 60
Latin America, 47–53, 249–51. *See also*
    specific countries
Leader, 116, 119, 122, 149
Lee, Portia, 26–28
legislation: anti-Asian, 14, 106–7, 141–
    42, 145–54, 156, 257; immigration,
    14, 141–42, 145, 146, 257; on women,
    185
Liberal Arts Palace, *fig. 19*, *fig. 21*, 28, 29,
    53, 139, 159
Lincoln Park, 71, 272n38
Lindley, Curtis, 181
living exhibits, 164
living quarters of Exposition Guards,
    215
Lockyer, Angus, 143, 163
Look Tin Eli, 157

bian Exposition; Louisiana Purchase Exposition; Midwinter International Exposition; Panama-California Exposition

World War I, 1–2, 46, 100–101

Worthington, Marion Dowsett, 23

Yang, Y. C., 162

Yorke, Peter, 116

Young China, 106

Young Restaurant Company, 211

Youth (Burroughs), 34

Yung, Judy, 134

YWCA (Young Woman's Christian Association): building and exhibits of, 240–42, *241, 244*; PPIE mission of, 240; PPIE vices and, 178, 179–80, 183–84, 191, 197; PPIE workers and, 220; suffrage and, 231; welfare work of, 49, 243–45, 302–3

Zone, the: attractions in, 126, *126, 133*, 136–37; Chinese exhibits in, *111*, 111–14, 168–69; description of, *fig. 28, 25*, 31, 32; Irish Village in, 114–17, *115*; Japan Beautiful in, *fig. 29*, 56, 135, *169*, 169–70, 295n110; labor and, 211, 220, 224; vices and, 173, 177–78, 190–202, *196, 198*, 289n20. *See also* ethnic villages; girl shows

CPSIA information can be obtained
at www.ICGtesting.com
Printed in the USA
LVHW031904130421
684383LV00007B/162

9 781496 224903